Financial Markets and the Ethics of Legal Practice

Financial Markets and the Ethics of Legal Practice

TREVOR CLARK

OXFORD
UNIVERSITY PRESS

OXFORD
UNIVERSITY PRESS

Great Clarendon Street, Oxford, OX2 6DP,
United Kingdom

Oxford University Press is a department of the University of Oxford.
It furthers the University's objective of excellence in research, scholarship,
and education by publishing worldwide. Oxford is a registered trade mark of
Oxford University Press in the UK and in certain other countries.

Published in the United States of America by Oxford University Press
198 Madison Avenue, New York, NY 10016, United States of America.

British Library Cataloguing in Publication Data
Data available

Library of Congress Control Number: 2025942406

ISBN 978–0–19–897717–9

DOI: 10.1093/law/9780198977179.001.0001

Printed and bound by
CPI Group (UK) Ltd., Croydon, CR0 4YY

FSC www.fsc.org MIX Paper | Supporting responsible forestry FSC® C013604

The manufacturer's authorised representative in the EU for product safety is
Oxford University Press España S.A. of Parque Empresarial San Fernando de Henares,
Avenida de Castilla, 2 – 28830 Madrid (www.oup.es/en or product.safety@oup.com).
OUP España S.A. also acts as importer into Spain of products made by the manufacturer.

This book is dedicated to Carol Clark (1940–2019)

Preface

As Katherina Pistor has observed, corporate lawyers are not rent seekers 'skimming the cream' off business transactions, rather 'they make the cream'.[1]

Corporate lawyers, by any measure, constitute a significant proportion of the world's legal profession, and are a not insignificant component of the global economy. Major international law firms employ thousands of lawyers and other staff, have branch offices across the globe, and act for some of the world's most powerful corporations and financial institutions. They are not, as they are often depicted, neutral technocrats simply carrying out their clients' instructions. These lawyers and firms wield powerful influence, since they help create and shape global business law, impacting the conditions of the global economy. This influence extends beyond simply the practice and content of the law itself. This book explores how they materially impact the contractual terms of the often multibillion-dollar corporate and financial market transactions that are undertaken in the shadow of the law. It follows that ethical lapses by corporate lawyers have the potential to create negative externalities which could undermine, and potentially destroy, public trust in the legal profession and do significant harm to society. At the same time, these powerful law firms remain somewhat opaque, so that relatively little is understood about their ethics and their effect on markets. This book sets out to explore these elements by seeking to understand what lawyers who work in major international law firms actually do, why they do it, and the broader implications—including for financial markets—of what they do.

The arguments made in this book are illustrated and supported by an empirically based case study which zooms in on a specific field of major international law firm practice—leveraged finance—to understand its internal practices, logics, and ethics. Before commencing the research for this book in late 2018, for a doctoral thesis at University College London on which this book is based, I had a feeling that trends in loan terms in leveraged buyouts in Europe might be closely connected to the activity of lawyers. This hunch—and at this point it was no more than that—was primarily based on what I would describe as market chatter that had come to my attention during my time in legal practice. I had until the previous year been a solicitor specializing in international finance law spanning a twenty-five-year career, the majority spent as an equity partner of a leading international law firm, based in London and in Asia. I had limited direct experience of this specialist

[1] Katharina Pistor, *The Code of Capital: How the Law Creates Wealth and Inequality* (University Press 2019) 166.

area of legal practice, however. Casual conversations with colleagues and my contacts within banks had alerted me to concerns surrounding the independence of lawyers when acting for the banks arranging leveraged finance loans. These concerns were connected to a practice known as 'lawyer designation'—where the lawyer and firm appointed to advise the banks is chosen (that is, designated), and paid for, by the private equity sponsor; effectively, the borrower of the loan chooses the lenders' lawyer and pays that lawyer's fees—which had become the norm in large-scale leveraged finance transactions in Europe.

The power to designate had, in effect, been delegated by the leading private equity sponsors to the law firms they usually engaged and the partners at those firms that were their relationship lawyers. As a result, partners at leading international firms in London who specialized in advising banks were sourcing most, if not all, of their work from referrals from those private equity lawyers. A series of referral relationships had consequently developed between bank-side and private equity lawyers across several leading international law firms in London that appeared to me to exhibit some of the typical characteristics of a lawyer/client relationship. My curiosity about the ethical implications of these relationships led ultimately to the writing of this book.

Concerns about the ethics of leveraged finance lawyers continued to surface during the course of my research. For example, in October 2022, *The Lawyer* reported that lenders on the £3.5bn leveraged financing of The Access Group were dissatisfied with the role played by their lawyers, and with the designation model under which they were appointed.[2] And then, towards the end of 2023, the International Organisation of Securities Commissions (IOSCO)—an umbrella body comprising securities regulators from across the world and a global standard setter for financial markets regulation—reported that through its own consultation with market participants it had concluded that lawyer designation in leveraged finance meant that the advice that arranging banks receive is not independent.[3] It warned that conflicts of interest arise because the lawyers representing the arranging banks can be reluctant to push back against sponsor lawyers due to the risk that they could be excluded from further lender-side work as a consequence. It is striking that IOSCO directly connected financial market conduct risks—specifically, a lack of transparency—to this lack of lawyer independence. In this book, I put the case that the deep immersion of lawyers in financial markets can create pressure on them to cross ethical red lines, and that this activity can in

[2] 'Lenders Aren't Happy - and Lawyers Are in the Ethical Firing Line' (*The Lawyer*, 6 October 2022) <https://www.thelawyer.com/lenders-arent-happy-and-lawyers-are-in-the-ethical-firing-line/> accessed 6 October 2022.

[3] International Organisation of Securities Commissions, 'Leveraged Loans and CLOs, Good Practices for Consideration, Consultation Report CR05/2023' (September 2023) 34 <https://www.iosco.org/library/pubdocs/pdf/IOSCOPD746.pdf>.

turn affect how markets develop, impacting for example the allocation and pricing of risk between market participants.

I would like to thank all the lawyers who were so gracious in giving up their time to be interviewed by me. I hope they feel it was time well spent. I know from my own career in practice that lawyers that work in major international law firms largely seek to act professionally and ethically. Most ethical misconduct is not the result of the presence of rogue lawyers, or 'bad apples', in large law firms. More often it is down to the pressures and incentives of the workplace environment. My aim in this book is to show how a series of contextual workplace conditions can make ethical misconduct by lawyers more likely to occur. My aim is not to call into question the ethicality of Big Law as a whole, but rather to shed light on some of the often practice area-specific ethical challenges lawyers in these firms encounter daily. My hope is that this book will ultimately help inform debates about how the lawyers who work in major international law firms may be better supported in acting ethically in their daily work.

I would also like to express my deep gratitude to the supervisors of my PhD, Professor Richard Moorhead and Professor Steven Vaughan, for their support and expert guidance throughout what turned out to be an almost five-year project. Their endless patience and good humour made my doctoral study an immensely enjoyable and fulfilling experience. Most of all, they constantly challenged me to go further, question my assumptions, deepen the analysis, and never to compromise. I should say that they have not been involved in the conversion of my PhD thesis into this book, which is in many ways quite different, making as it does, broader arguments about the intersection between lawyers, their ethics, and financial markets. They carry no responsibility for its content, and all errors are, of course, entirely my own.

Finally, thanks to Ben, Molly, and Florence for all your support, and willingness to be deputized from time to time as research assistants. And Sandra, thanks for everything. I will now stop going on about 'the book'.

Trevor Clark

Contents

Figures

1
Introduction

1.1 The aims of this book

This book explores the intersection between major international law firms and financial markets. Specifically, it considers how the lawyers who work in these firms can both be corrupted by, and have a corrupting effect on, markets.

Corporate lawyers, by any measure, constitute a significant proportion of the legal profession, and are a not insignificant component of the global economy.[1] Major international law firms are often referred to under the collective term 'Big Law', since they employ thousands of lawyers and other staff, have branch offices across the globe, and act for some of the world's most powerful corporations and financial institutions.[2] These lawyers and firms wield powerful influence, since they help create and shape global business law and the conditions of the global economy.[3] Katharina Pistor offers a historical account of the role lawyers have played and continue to play in facilitating global capitalism, wealth, and inequality, for example.[4] Pistor shows how they exercise discretion and exert real influence over client actions and outcomes; corporate lawyers are not, as they are often depicted, neutral technocrats,[5] or rent-seekers 'skimming the cream' off business transactions, rather 'they make the cream'.[6] The influence of corporate lawyers and firms extends beyond simply the practice and content of the law itself. This book explores how they can also materially impact the contractual terms of, and the allocation and pricing of risk between the parties to, the often multibillion-dollar

[1] In this book, I use the term 'corporate lawyer' and 'corporate law firm', in the sense meant by John Heinz and Edward Laumann in their 'two hemispheres' model, to denote lawyers and firms advising large companies and business organisations, as opposed to individuals and small businesses. John P Heinz and Edward O Laumann, *Chicago Lawyers: The Social Structure of the Bar* (Russell Sage Foundation 1982).

[2] Manuel Gómez and Marc Galanter define Big Law as 'large multi office and full-service law firms whose main clients are multinationals, large domestic corporations, and wealthy individuals.' Dentons, the largest law firm in the world, has over 12,000 lawyers, for example. Manuel A Gomez and Marc Galanter, 'The Many Lives of Big Law: Three Decades in the Evolution of Large Law Firms' in Richard L Abel, Hilary Sommerlad, Ole Hammerslev and Ulrike Schultz (eds), *Lawyers in 21st-Century Societies: Vol. 2: Comparisons and Theories* (Bloomsbury Publishing Plc 2022) 373, 376.

[3] Michael J Powell, 'Professional Innovation: Corporate Lawyers and Private Lawmaking' (1993) 18 Law and Social Inquiry 423. Katharina Pistor, *The Code of Capital: How the Law Creates Wealth and Inequality* (University Press 2019).

[4] Pistor (n 3).

[5] Trevor Clark and others, 'Agency over Technocracy: How Lawyer Archetypes Infect Regulatory Approaches: The FCA Example' [2021] 24(2), 91–110.

[6] Pistor (n 3) 166.

corporate and financial market transactions that are undertaken in the shadow of the law.

It follows that ethical lapses by corporate lawyers have the potential to create material negative externalities which could undermine, and potentially destroy, public trust in the legal profession more broadly and do significant harm to society.[7] This could be through an incident of scale; corporate lawyers advised financial institutions on the design of the structured finance instruments that enabled them to avoid regulation, a contributing factor behind the global financial crisis of 2007–9, for example.[8] Doreen McBarnet and Christopher Whelan refer to this as 'creative compliance', where lawyers and firms assist their clients to exploit grey areas in the law, even where the spirit, if not the letter, is clear.[9] Alternatively, and just as likely, harm can be the result of a series of 'drip, drip' events.[10] Janine Griffiths-Baker, in her study of corporate lawyers in large London firms, found that large corporate law firms routinely ignored professional rules regarding conflicts of interest, for example.[11] And Tanina Rostain and Mitt Regan highlighted the role of corporate lawyers in large US firms in facilitating widespread and systematic tax avoidance by corporate clients.[12] There is the potential for the corporate legal profession to suffer its own 'Arthur Andersen moment', with similar systemic effects and belated regulatory responses.[13] It is possible this might be connected to a future financial crisis founded in the global leveraged finance market; in late December 2024, the *Financial Times* reported that global leveraged loan defaults had reached their highest level in four years.[14]

At the same time, these powerful law firms continue to remain somewhat opaque, so that relatively little is understood about their ethics and their effect on

[7] See for example, Steven L Schwarcz, 'Keynote Address: The Role of Lawyers in the Global Financial Crisis' (Social Science Research Network 2010) SSRN Scholarly Paper ID 1532794 <https://papers.ssrn.com/abstract=1532794> accessed 13 May 2019.

[8] Joan Loughrey, *Corporate Lawyers and Corporate Governance* (Cambridge University Press 2011) 4; DB Wilkins, 'Team of Rivals? Toward a New Model of the Corporate Attorney/Client Relationship' (2009) 62 Current Legal Problems 478.

[9] Doreen McBarnet and Christopher Whelan, 'The Elusive Spirit of the Law: Formalism and the Struggle for Legal Control' (1991) 54 The Modern Law Review 848.

[10] Hugh Gunz, Sally Gunz, and Ronit Dinovitzer, 'Professional Ethics' [2015] The Oxford Handbook of Professional Service Firms 129; Richard Moorhead, 'Should Clifford Chance's Corruption Initiative Be Taken Seriously?' (*Lawyer Watch*, 20 December 2018) <https://lawyerwatch.blog/2018/12/20/should-clifford-chances-corruption-initiative-be-taken-seriously/> accessed 20 December 2018.

[11] Hugh Gunz, Sally Gunz, and Ronit Dinovitzer, 'Professional Ethics' [2015] The Oxford Handbook of Professional Service Firms 129; Moorhead (n 10). Tanina Rostain and Milton C Regan (eds), *Confidence Games: Lawyers, Accountants, and the Tax Shelter Industry* (MIT Press 2014); Janine Griffiths-Baker, *Serving Two Masters: Conflicts of Interest in the Modern Law Firm* (Hart 2002).

[12] Rostain and Regan (n 11).

[13] See for example, Susan Elaine Squires and Susan Squires, *Inside Arthur Andersen: Shifting Values, Unexpected Consequences* (FT Press 2003).

[14] Harriet Clarfelt and Alan Livsey, 'Defaults on Leveraged Loans Soar to Highest Rate in 4 Years' *Financial Times* (24 December 2024) <https://www.ft.com/content/e6ba508c-4612-4b4a-9a6b-ecde6fc91c12> accessed 27 December 2024.

markets.[15] This book sets out to explore these elements by seeking to understand what lawyers who work in Big Law actually do, why they do it, and the broader implications—including for financial markets—of what they do.[16] This book explores the close connections between the type of work a transactional lawyer in a major law firm does, and the type of clients they act for, and their practices and ethical decision-making. It deploys a methodology and theoretical framework which recognizes the critical importance of a corporate lawyer's particular practice area setting as a factor influencing their practices, logics, and—as a result—their ethics. It then explores both the causes and effects of these dynamics and how they tend to intersect with the logics of financial markets. This book hence draws heavily on the institutional logics perspective as an empirical device to, first, identify the central practices and prevailing logics of a Big Law practice area and, then, understand their influence on lawyer action and ethical decision-making.[17] The prevailing logics of a corporate lawyer's practice setting are critical since they shape how lawyers make sense of their day-to-day practice context and then decide what is appropriate and legitimate conduct.[18] These prevailing logics of a practice area are evident in the distinctive practices[19] and shared understandings of the lawyers that operate in it, and for this reason a principal objective of this book is to identify and analyse them in detail.[20] I offer a more detailed explanation of the institutional logics perspective, and the role that this theoretical framing plays in this book, in the next section.

The arguments made in this book are illustrated and supported by an empirically based case study which zooms in on a specific field of major international law firm practice—leveraged finance—to understand it's internal practices, logics, and ethics. In Chapter 2, I describe and analyse the principal characteristics of the leveraged finance market, and the role that major international law firms play in

[15] This book seeks to build on a relatively limited pool of empirical research into what lawyers in Big Law actually do. John Flood, 'Ambiguous Allegiances in the Lawyer-Client Relationship: The Case of Bankers and Lawyers' 4. Richard Moorhead and Victoria Hinchley, 'Professional Minimalism? The Ethical Consciousness of Commercial Lawyers' (2015) 42 Journal of Law and Society 387, 389. John Flood, *What Do Lawyers Do?: An Ethnography of a Corporate Law Firm* (Quid Pro Books 2013) v. John Flood, 'Anatomy of Lawyering: An Ethnography of a Corporate Law Firm' (ProQuest Dissertations Publishing 1987) 26 <http://search.proquest.com/docview/303616292/?pq-origsite=primo> accessed 18 October 2018.

[16] Big Law's influence is also felt in other ways. For example, Joan Loughrey has noted that 'the top corporate law firms train and employ large numbers of corporate lawyers, including in-house lawyers, and so their influence on the values of the profession cannot be underestimated', Loughrey (n 8) 56.

[17] See, for example, Patricia H Thornton, William Ocasio, and Michael Lounsbury, *The Institutional Logics Perspective: A New Approach to Culture, Structure, and Process* (OUP 2012).

[18] Royston Greenwood and CR Hinings, 'Radical Organizational Change', *The SAGE Handbook of Organisation Studies* (Second, SAGE Publications 2013) 819.

[19] For the importance of material practices in understanding the logics of institutional fields, see Roger Friedland and Roger R Alford, 'Bringing Society Back In: Symbols, Practices, and Institutional Contradictions', *The New Institutionalism in Organizational Analysis* (The University of Chicago Press 1991) 254.

[20] Thornton, Ocasio, and Lounsbury (n 17) 59, 74.

it, for readers less familiar with it, before proceeding to introduce and analyse the data I collected in the subsequent chapters. The narrow focus of this case study facilitates a focus on the potential indicators of a series of ethical challenges prevalent in a leading practice setting found in Big Law.[21] The case study deliberately zooms in on the everyday practices of lawyers. This is because ethical lapses by lawyers in large law firms are often embedded in the collective everyday practices of lawyers, taking effect as a continual stream of often mundane events. I collected extensive data as to these elements in 47 semi-structured interviews, the majority with partners and senior associates working in large international law firms in London. I have included a detailed critical examination of my research methodology in Appendix 1.

This book, therefore, contributes a series of empirically supported insights into what drives the conduct and ethical decision-making of lawyers in major international law firms. I show how these drivers are variable across the firm, meaning that a lawyer in one practice area will tend to think and act differently in their daily work to a lawyer in another practice area. This is because the range of logics that influence their behaviour will also include market-based logics which are unique to their specific practice area setting. When exploring motivations for lawyer action and ethical decision-making, the corporate lawyer literature tends to emphasize the importance of the series of law firm logics which emerged in response to the shift by large law firms to financialized law firm governance which occurred in the 1980s and 1990s.[22] This book puts the case that these law firm logics are only part of the story. To fully understand what influences lawyer action, it is necessary to also connect it to specific practice area logics, which are themselves the product of wider macroeconomic processes affecting the relevant practice area.[23]

In other words, a core argument of this book is that the search for contextual factors influencing corporate lawyer conduct and ethics should not be confined to law firm-wide pressures and incentives, such as those which flow from 'eat what you kill' remuneration models, for example. This book integrates an analysis of the effects of these types of *law firm logics* with an analysis of the effects of macro level forces and events affecting a practice area which can lead to that practice area developing a distinct set of internal *practice area logics*.[24] This approach offers a more nuanced understanding of the drivers of corporate lawyer ethics. For example, it is well established in the 'client capture' literature that a corporate lawyer's susceptibility to their powerful clients and third parties creates challenges to their

[21] David Silverman, *Doing Qualitative Research* (SAGE 2017) 47; Richard Moorhead and others, 'Designing Ethics Indicators for Legal Services Provision' [2012] SSRN Electronic Journal 81 <http://www.ssrn.com/abstract=2159296> accessed 18 October 2018.

[22] Janine Griffiths-Baker, *Serving Two Masters: Conflicts of Interest in the Modern Law Firm* (Hart Publishing 2002) 3–8.

[23] Thornton, Ocasio, and Lounsbury (n 17) vii, 80–1.

[24] ibid.

independence.[25] But this literature does not tend to consider whether this susceptibility might be stronger or weaker depending on which practice setting a lawyer works in. To determine whether lawyers are more or less likely to come under ethical pressure due to pressure from their clients or third parties in the capital markets group or the competition group of a firm, for example, it is necessary to explore the distinct logics of each of those practice settings.

The leveraged finance case study on which this book relies reveals, for example, how the global financial crisis, the regulatory change directed at banks and the market supply and demand disconnect that followed it, and the switch by the bank community to an 'originate-to-distribute' underwriting model are all macroeconomic dynamics which, when combined with the prevailing logics of major international law firms, created new power dynamics and logics which were distinctive to the leveraged finance practice areas of large international law firms based in London. These emergent logics created a series of pathways for strategic action by leveraged finance lawyers that, in turn, transformed the conditions of their practice area setting and the financial markets to which it is most closely connected.

A key finding of the case study is the common practice in leveraged finance known as lawyer designation, whereby private equity sponsors' lawyers select, or designate, the lawyers used by banks.[26] Bank lawyers in turn seek to placate the private equity lawyers by deliberately providing a less diligent standard of document evaluation than would otherwise be the case. We see how this bank lawyer stance gave birth to the practice of relentless contractual boundary pushing by the private equity lawyers. This book makes the case that this boundary pushing by private equity lawyers cannot simply be explained away as endemic of the more general structural problem of financialized law firm governance but rather it is a cultural phenomenon inherent in leveraged finance lawyering.

Whilst practice area logics comprise the framework for lawyer ethical decision-making, this book also emphasizes the importance of an individual lawyer's own discretionary behaviour.[27] We see how real change to the conditions and logics of a practice area can be effected when lawyers take advantage of the opportunities afforded by changes in the logics of both large law firms and the financial markets within which they are deeply immersed.[28] The case study demonstrates how this

[25] See for example, Ronit Dinovitzer, Hugh Gunz, and Sally Gunz, 'Unpacking Client Capture: Evidence from Corporate Law Firms' (2014) 1 Journal of Professions and Organization 99; Emma Oakley and Steven Vaughan, 'In Dependence: The Paradox of Professional Independence and Taking Seriously the Vulnerabilities of Lawyers in Large Corporate Law Firms' (2019) 46 Journal of Law and Society 83.

[26] Designation is explained and analysed in detail in Chapter 3.

[27] The former are commonly referred to as realists, the latter as idealists or social constructionists, Frederick Erickson, 'A History of Qualitative Inquiry in Social and Educational Research', *The SAGE Handbook of Qualitative Research* (SAGE Publications 2018) 54. For a fuller typology of ontological approaches, see Yvonna S Lincoln, Susan A Lyneham, and Egon G Guba, 'Paradigmatic Controversies, Contradictions, and Emerging Confluences, Revisited', *The SAGE Handbook of Qualitative Research* (Fifth, SAGE Publications 2018).

[28] Thornton, Ocasio, and Lounsbury (n 17) 177.

lawyer discretionary and transformative behaviour becomes more pronounced at moments of turbulence in the markets in which lawyers work.

This book explores how this type of corporate lawyer activity can have a dramatic impact on the conditions of financial markets, in the form of shifts in the contractual terms of high-value and complex cross border financial transactions which govern the allocation and pricing of risk by market participants. There is limited existing research in this area. Annelise Riles offers an enlightening and comprehensive account of the role of lawyers and other legal professionals in influencing the terms of international derivatives transactions.[29] Riles mainly studied legal professionals who work in the legal and documentation teams at banks and financial intermediaries, as opposed to large law firms, however.[30] And Mitu Gulati and Robert E Scott reviewed thousands of sovereign debt contracts and found that the lawyers in large international law firms, mainly in New York, who drafted and negotiated the contracts, often did not fully understand their terms, and explored the dramatic consequences of this for the holders of these instruments.[31] I show how, in contradistinction to Gulati and Scott's findings, uncertainty in complex contracts may not simply be unexpected and unplanned but can also be the consequence of lawyer strategies which are openly pursued.

The case study in this book shows how, in the leveraged finance sector, transaction documents have become overwhelmingly one-sided, and the meaning of key provisions has become obscured by pervasive uncertainty in the language used, to the extent where market participants are unable to clearly evaluate, and hence accurately price, the risks that they face under them. The contractual boundary-pushing strategies of private equity lawyers, facilitated by the compromised independence of the bank lawyers they effectively appoint to face them across the negotiation table, have played a key role in this evolution of leveraged loan terms. This lawyer activity has contributed to the removal or material dilution of a series of core protections in transaction documents for banks and other lenders.[32]

Detailed examples of this lawyer-driven evolution of leveraged loan terms and structures are explored, which include controversial 'add backs' in financial covenants, and defects in typical intercreditor agreements, including the controversial 'trap door' and similar mechanisms first deployed in the restructuring of the US

[29] Annelise Riles, *Collateral Knowledge: Legal Reasoning in the Global Financial Markets* (University of Chicago Press 2011) 64.

[30] ibid.

[31] Mitu Gulati and Robert E Scott, *The Three and a Half Minute Transaction: Boilerplate and the Limits of Contract Design* (University of Chicago Press 2012).

[32] 'Hot Leveraged Loan Market Puts Ebitda "Add-Backs" under Scrutiny' *Financial Times* (10 February 2017) <https://www.ft.com/content/ce5d0eee-eea0-11e6-930f-061b01e23655> accessed 15 February 2023; 'When The Cycle Turns: The Continued Attack Of The EBITDA Add-Back' <https://www.spglobal.com/ratings/en/research/articles/190919-when-the-cycle-turns-the-continued-attack-of-the-ebitda-add-back-11156255> accessed 2 July 2022.

retailer, J Crew.[33] The adverse consequences of these findings are examined from multiple standpoints: professional ethical standards including independence, integrity, and competence; the implications for the allocation of risk in transaction structures and terms; the reduced range of restructuring options for lenders in the event of borrower financial distress, as well as the potential wider economic effects, including on the transparency of markets and the potential build-up of systemic risk.

This book not only presents a detailed and comprehensive account of the types of pressures and challenges that corporate lawyers face in their daily work but also considers the implications of these findings on their observance of the rules of professional conduct to which they are subject.[34] I examine the extent to which the findings of the case study indicate that a series of ethical duties in the Solicitors Regulatory Authority's (SRA) Standards and Regulations are likely to have been routinely breached by leveraged finance lawyers in their day-to-day practice. Lawyer designation, for example, and the networks of referral relationships between leading lawyers and law firms that flow from it, place bank lawyers under immense ethical pressure, and likely lead them to breach the solicitors' duties to maintain their independence and to avoid 'own interest' conflicts of interest.

I show how a solicitor's duties to avoid conflicts of interest and to maintain client confidentiality are especially engaged by the emergent practice of what is commonly referred to by market participants as 'virtual trees', or 'trees in the head'. This terminology taken in isolation is itself emblematic of the ethical challenges confronting lawyers in this practice setting, since it is at the same time both misleading and verging on the ridiculous. The use of this terminology in and of itself serves to undermine leveraged finance lawyers' collective ethical credibility.

I also examine the opportunistic practices and strategies that private equity lawyers developed in response to the bank lawyers' constrained independence—including relentless contractual boundary pushing—and how these strategies and

[33] I consider the J. Crew restructuring in some detail in Chapter 7. Kenneth Ayotte and Christina Scully, 'J. Crew, Nine West, and the Complexities of Financial Distress Forum Collection: Bankruptcy and Restructuring in Response to Exogenous Shocks' (2021) 131 Yale Law Journal Forum 363; 'The J.Crew "Trap Door" and Its Implications for the Future of Leveraged Finance'Torys LLP (2019) <https://www.torys.com/Our%20Latest%20Thinking/Publications//2019/05/the-j-crew-trap-door-and-its-implications-for-the-future-of-leveraged-finance/> accessed 23 June 2022.

[34] The Standards and Regulations include the Principles and two Codes of Conduct, one for individual solicitors and one for firms. There is significant overlap between the two Codes, and for simplicity, and since the focus of this book is primarily on the logics and ethics of individual lawyers across different firms who happen to work in the same practice area, I have chosen to focus on the Code that applies to individual solicitors, as opposed to firms. Individual solicitors are personally accountable under this Code and are required to justify their decisions and actions. 'SRA Principles' (25 November 2019) <https://www.sra.org.uk/solicitors/standards-regulations/principles/> accessed 6 July 2020; 'SRA Code of Conduct for Solicitors, RELs and RFLs' (25 November 2019) <https://www.sra.org.uk/solicitors/standards-regulations/code-conduct-solicitors/> accessed 15 November 2020; 'SRA Code of Conduct for Firms' (4 June 2023) <https://www.sra.org.uk/solicitors/standards-regulations/code-conduct-firms/> accessed 4 July 2023.

practices also conflict with their duties as solicitors: in this instance, their duties to act with integrity and not to take unfair advantage. The type of empirical data offered in this book are hence critical to a proper assessment of the effectiveness, or otherwise, of professional ethical frameworks and codes of conduct in promoting the ethical conduct of lawyers in large international law firms.[35]

On the other hand, this book does not contribute to philosophical debates about the 'proper role' of corporate lawyers. The legal ethics literature is in large part a philosophical contest between those scholars who promote the standard conception of the lawyers' role,[36] and those that argue that lawyers' conduct should reflect common morality—as in widely understood norms of 'right and wrong'[37]—and/or ideals of justice.[38] As Alice Woolley and Bradley Wendel argue, the difficulty with these theories is that they 'posit a lawyer capable of independence from situational or institutional pressures' and offer up 'idealized portraits of the moral agent'.[39] Andrew Boon observes that, at best, these theories provide 'a useful theoretical framework—a 'strawman'—against which we can explore the scope of a lawyer's ethical duties'.[40] As Richard Moorhead and others have noted: 'What lawyers ought to do must begin with a clear understanding of how lawyers actually behave *in situ*, and how this relates to their specific practice contexts, as well as wider organizational, social, and economic conditions of their work.'[41] John Flood, in his groundbreaking observational study of a US corporate law firm in the late 1980s, shifted the focus from the social structure of the firm to seeking to understanding what it is that lawyers do.[42] This book is founded in this principle, and that it is necessary, as Steven Vaughan and Emma Oakley observe, to study corporate lawyers as they are, not just as they should be.[43]

Although the focus of this book is the influence on corporate lawyer action and decision-making of the particular practice settings in which they work, it is important to acknowledge at the outset, as Moorhead and others rightly argue, that whether lawyers are prone to unethical conduct, or view types of conduct as ethical or not, is not simply a consequence of contextual factors.[44] David Matsumoto, for

[35] Janine Griffiths-Baker (n 22) 12.

[36] The standard conception features three principal components: zealous advocacy (often referred to as the principle of partisanship), neutrality, and non-accountability, Loughrey (n 8) 62.

[37] David Luban, *Lawyers and Justice: An Ethical Study* (Princeton University Press 1988). Cited in Richard Moorhead, Steven Vaughan, and Cristina Godinho, *In-House Lawyers' Ethics, Institutional Logics, Legal Risk and the Tournament of Influence* (Hart 2018) 14.

[38] Moorhead, Vaughan, and Godinho (n 37) 14. Steven Vaughan and Emma Oakley, '"Gorilla Exceptions" and the Ethically Apathetic Corporate Lawyer' (2016) 19 Legal Ethics 50, 51.

[39] Alice Woolley and W Bradley Wendel, 'Legal Ethics and Moral Character' (2010) 23 Georgetown Journal of Legal Ethics 1065, 1065.

[40] Andrew Boon, *The Ethics and Conduct of Lawyers in England and Wales* (Bloomsbury Publishing 2014) 31.

[41] Moorhead, Vaughan, and Godinho (n 37) 15.

[42] Flood, *What Do Lawyers Do?* (n 15).

[43] Vaughan and Oakley (n 38) 51. See also Moorhead, Vaughan, and Godinho (n 37) 14–15.

[44] Moorhead and others (n 21) 5, 39, 40, 41, 58, 92. On the effect of character and cognition, see, for example, Yuval Feldman, *The Law of Good People* (Cambridge University Press 2018); David

example, notes that there are three major influences on behaviour: human nature (universal psychological processes such as human needs, self-interest), culture (social roles in a group context), and individual personality.[45] Lawyers will hence be influenced by a range of factors, in addition to their market, firm, and practice area context, and all of these factors will interact with, and influence, each other.[46] Personal characteristics and cognition are important factors that may lead to an increased risk of unethical conduct by corporate lawyers.[47] There is plenty of insightful work in this area; for example, Donald Langevoort argues that success in highly competitive environments like large law firms:

> is skewed in the direction of rewarding those who are highly focussed at the business of competing, which of necessity means the cognitive ability to block out concerns – like difficult ethical problems – that are likely to be distracting.[48]

And research by Susan Daicoff suggests that those that choose to become lawyers are 'especially prone to be highly self-critical and anxious about performance', and 'driven by a "never satisfied drive for success'.[49]

These are not universal rules, of course, and individual lawyers may react differently to the same types of ethical pressure. Alice Woolley and Bradley Wendel argue that some lawyers will simply have a 'constrained commitment to ordinary moral values'.[50] On the other hand, Moorhead and Rachel Cahill-O'Callaghan point out that 'equally, even where there is strong situational pressure to behave unethically, most experiments show that a proportion of the cohort resist.'[51] Citing Woolley and Wendel, they argue that this may be because an individual lawyer has a stronger commitment to personal values 'such as courage, honesty, justice, respect for dignity, equality of others, fidelity, agreeableness, being reliable, trustworthy, orderly, dependable, organised, and rule-following, for example.'[52]

Matsumoto, 'Culture, Context, and Behavior' (2007) 75 Journal of Personality 1285; Jennifer K Robbennolt, 'Behavioral Ethics Meets Legal Ethics' (2015) 11 Annual Review of Law and Social Science 75.

45 Matsumoto (n 44) 1286.

46 Moorhead and others (n 21) 5, 39, 40, 41, 58, 92. On the effects of character and cognition, see, for example, Feldman (n 44); Matsumoto (n 44); Robbennolt (n 44).

47 See Richard Moorhead and Rachel Cahill-O'Callaghan, 'False Friends? Testing Commercial Lawyers on the Claim That Zealous Advocacy Is Founded in Benevolence towards Clients Rather than Lawyers' Personal Interest' (2016) 19 Legal Ethics 30, 36.

48 Donald C Langevoort, 'The Organizational Psychology of Hyper-Competition: Corporate Irresponsibility and the Lessons of Enron' (2002) 70 George Washington Law Review 968, 970. Quoted in Milton C Regan, *Eat What You Kill: The Fall of a Wall Street Lawyer* (University of Michigan Press 2004) 303.

49 Susan Swaim Daicoff, *Lawyer, Know Thyself: A Psychological Analysis of Personality Strengths and Weaknesses* (American Psychological Association 2004); Regan (n 48) 298.

50 Woolley and Wendel (n 39) 1093. Cited in Moorhead and Cahill-O'Callaghan (n 47) 35.

51 Moorhead and Cahill-O'Callaghan (n 47) 36.

52 ibid 40; Woolley and Wendel (n 39).

There are few examples of research which adopts an integrated approach, exploring how an individual lawyer's personal history and characteristics work in combination with the contextual pressures and incentives to which that lawyer is subject. More of this type of research is needed. One ambitious, and compelling, example of this approach is offered by Mitt Regan in 'Eat What You Kill'.[53] Regan describes a leveraged buyout that went wrong in the 1980s, leading to a US bankruptcy lawyer, and partner of a leading New York law firm, John Gellene, going to prison.[54] Whilst primarily a comprehensive and in-depth investigation of Gellene's practice context as a causal factor in his ethical decision-making, Regan also sought to gain insights on the influence of Gellene's personal history and characteristics. For example, whilst Gellene was described by a colleague as a 'control freak and a loner',[55] Regan concluded that Gellene wasn't a dishonest person, but rather he was both prone to cut corners, which may have 'eroded some of his resistance to dishonesty' and 'adept at rationalising questionable behaviour' when needed to meet his objectives.[56]

Lawyers may also be prone to certain cognitive biases, affecting how most people make decisions in particular situations.[57] Understanding decision-making, and the degree of influence of the individual, on the one hand, and their context, on the other, is hence key to understanding individual behaviour in a social context.[58] For example, Andrew Perlman draws on experiments which show that merely thinking of a legal problem from the perspective of a client leads to an interpretation of a legal rule in a way which is directed at favouring that client.[59] And research by Mariam Kouchaki and others supports the view that where financial incentives are in play, lawyers will take decisions within a business, as opposed to a moral, or ethical, framework.[60]

I have inevitably had to make some choices as to where to direct the focus of this book. I have chosen to centre this book around the influence of the logics of the specialist field in which corporate lawyers practice on their conduct and ethical-decision-making. This is because, as Woolley and Wendel have noted, 'psychological research demonstrates clearly and consistently that acts correlate most strongly to circumstances ... within contexts, individuals will respond to and make

[53] Regan (n 48).
[54] ibid 78.
[55] ibid 10, 53.
[56] ibid 301–303.
[57] Margaret A Neale and others, 'A Decision Perspective on Organizations: Social Cognition, Behavioural Decision Theory and the Psychological Links to Micro-and Macro-Organizational Behaviour', *The Sage Handbook of Organisation Studies* (Second, SAGE Publications 2013) 486.
[58] ibid 487.
[59] Andrew M Perlman, 'Behavioral Theory of Legal Ethics, A' (2015) 90 Indiana Law Journal 1639. Cited in Moorhead and Cahill-O'Callaghan (n 47) 35.
[60] Maryam Kouchaki and others, 'Seeing Green: Mere Exposure to Money Triggers a Business Decision Frame and Unethical Outcomes' (2013) 121 Organizational Behavior and Human Decision Processes 53; Moorhead and Hinchley (n 15) 400–401.

choices about what to do.'[61] In other words, context is not the only factor that influences the action of lawyers, but it is a powerful factor nonetheless, and likely the most powerful. This book hence explores the extent to which practice area logics may create pathways which facilitate unethical behaviour by lawyers, whilst accepting that how they react to these types of situational cues will also be influenced by their own personal characteristics and susceptibility to cognitive bias.

The case study data on which the arguments I make in this book are founded is inevitably a snapshot of the leveraged finance practice areas of large international law firms as it was when the interviews were undertaken.[62] But this does not detract from the principal argument of this book, that as market dynamics change, so do the practices, logics, and ethics of the corporate lawyers who work in them. My interview data identify a series of transformative lawyer practices and behaviours which, in turn, reveal the structural conditions and logics of the leveraged finance practice area of Big Law at a moment in time. This data has, hence, enabled the comprehensive examination of the potential influences on lawyer action and ethical-decision-making that I undertake in this book.[63] The case study allows the drawing of broader conclusions about how the practices, logics, and ethics of lawyers working in large international law firms—which are often distinctive to the specialist practice setting in which they work—are shaped by, and at the same time can play a significant role in shaping, the conditions and logics of the markets to which they are most closely connected. This facilitates an exploration of the important questions the case study raises about the 'value add' that leading international law firms claim to offer clients, and ultimately also the extent to which clients and the wider public can and should place their trust in these firms.

I know from my own career in practice as an international finance lawyer and partner in an international law firm that lawyers that work in Big Law largely seek to act professionally and ethically. Most ethical misconduct is not the result of the presence of rogue lawyers, or 'bad apples', in large law firms. More often it is down to the pressures and incentives of the workplace environment—many of which are peculiar to a particular practice area of Big Law as opposed to being constant across the law firm as a whole—which can create a 'bad barrel' effect. By this, I mean a series of contextual workplace conditions which make ethical misconduct by lawyers more likely to occur.[64] My aim in this book is hence not to call into question the ethicality of Big Law as a whole, but rather to shed light on some of the often practice area-specific ethical challenges lawyers in these firms encounter

[61] Woolley and Wendel (n 39) 1071.

[62] The interviews were conducted in 2019 and 2020. The dynamics of the leveraged finance market have changed since then. It became less 'hot' as interest rates began to rise in 2022, for example, after a prolonged period in which leveraged debt had been relatively cheap.

[63] Margaret S Archer, 'Morphogenesis versus Structuration: On Combining Structure and Action' (1982) 33 The British Journal of Sociology 455, 458, 466.

[64] Leslie C Levin, 'Bad Apples, Bad Lawyers or Bad Decision making: Lessons from Psychology and from Lawyers in the Dock Book Review Essay' (2009) 22 Georgetown Journal of Legal Ethics 1549.

daily. My hope is that this book will ultimately help to inform debates about how the lawyers who work in Big Law may be better supported in acting ethically in their daily work.[65]

1.2 Institutional logics

This book emphasizes how markets shape the logics of the practice areas of major international law firms, and the role of these logics as important factors influencing lawyer ethics. It draws heavily on the institutional logics perspective as an empirical device to, first, identify the central practices and prevailing logics of a Big Law practice area and then understand their influence on lawyer action and ethical decision-making.[66] In this section, I hence explain what I mean when I refer to logics in this book.

In adopting the institutional logics perspective as a conceptual framework, this book occupies a middle ground between two opposing theoretical extremes: at one end is the structural approach, which sees factors such as economics and power as having the most significant influence on institutional fields, and, at the other end, an approach that sees the discretionary action of individuals as paramount in shaping any social situation.[67] I primarily rely on five key concepts: the institutional field; the field's various 'levels'; the influence of institutional logics on individual action in the field; the influence of logics on the field's practices and shared meanings, and the related concept of institutional work; and, the scope for discretionary and strategic behaviour by the field's actors to shape the field's structural conditions. I will now consider each of these concepts in turn.

The institutional logics perspective, along with the new institutionalism of Paul Di Maggio and Walter Powell, draws on Pierre Bourdieu's notion of field.[68] The actors in a practice area—the lawyers—tend to do the same or similar work, share common practices and understandings, and interface with each other frequently.[69] Looked at from the outside, they collectively form a recognizable area of social and/or economic activity which can be empirically studied.[70] The existence of the

[65] Here, and in general, this book is influenced by Joan Loughrey's leading and comprehensive treatment of the ethics of corporate lawyers, Loughrey (n 8) xiv, 308.

[66] See, for example, Thornton, Ocasio, and Lounsbury (n 17).

[67] ibid 134–9. Moorhead, Vaughan, and Godinho (n 37) 207–8.

[68] Albeit often only implicitly; Di Maggio and Powell, for example, include relatively limited references to Bourdieu in the introduction to their book, Paul J DiMaggio and Walter Powell W, 'Introduction', *The New Institutionalism in Organizational Analysis* (The University of Chicago Press 1991); Barbara Townley, 'Bourdieu and Organizational Theory: A Ghostly Apparition?', *The Oxford Handbook of Sociology, Social Theory, & Organization Studies* (OUP 2014) 53.

[69] W Richard Scott, *Institutions and Organizations* (2nd ed, Sage 2001). Paul J DiMaggio and Walter Powell W, 'The Iron Cage Revisited: Institutional Isomorphism and Collective Rationality', *The New Institutionalism in Organizational Analysis* (CUP 1991) 65.

[70] Roger Friedland and Roger R Alford, 'Bringing Society Back In: Symbols, Practices, and Institutional Contradictions', *The New Institutionalism in Organizational Analysis* (The University of

field can be seen in the extent to which the leveraged finance practice areas of large firms consciously develop strategies which emulate each other, for example, a phenomenon explored later in this book.

Thomas Lawrence and Roy Suddaby argue that institutional fields are both semi-autonomous and integrated with each other.[71] This means that, to identify the institutional logics of a particular field, it is necessary to explore the logics of the fields adjacent to it.[72] As an institutional field, a large law firm practice area tends to exist at the level between two major societal institutions—financial markets and large international law firms—which, as I have already noted, have themselves evolved into significant business organizations.[73] Law firms and financial markets hence interact with, and influence the conditions of, the practice area.[74] The practice area is not, then, simply a collection of lawyers doing the same type of work; it is critical that these lawyers are understood as practising within large bureaucratic organizations with their own logics, whilst at the same time being heavily immersed in, and constantly interacting with, the conditions and logics of financial markets. To understand the practice area field's conditions and logics to determine the most significant factors influencing lawyer action and ethical-decision-making then, it is critical to explore all three of these elements: lawyer/firm/markets, as I do in this book.

The institutional logics perspective also facilitates an analysis of a large law firm's practice area's conditions at its various 'levels'. 'Micro' is the individual lawyer level, and 'macro' is the societal, or economic, level.[75] The 'meso'—the level in between macro and micro—is made up of institutional fields.[76] My focus at the meso level is the practice area field, which is influenced by both objective external forces and events at the macro level. The leveraged finance practice area—the site of the case study—has, for example, been significantly influenced by the global financial crisis of 2007–9, the business logics of law firms (also existing at the meso level), the pressures and incentives on law firm partners to maximize income generation, for example, and the discretionary and strategic behaviour of individual lawyers at the field's micro level.[77] In this book, I have thus adopted this levels approach as a

Chicago Press 1991); Barbara Townley, 'Bourdieu and Organizational Theory: A Ghostly Apparition?', *The Oxford Handbook of Sociology, Social Theory, & Organization Studies* (OUP 2014) 52.

[71] Thomas B. Lawrence and Roy Suddaby, 'Institutions and Institutional Work' in Stewart R Clegg, Cynthia Hardy, Thomas B Lawrence, and Walter R Nord (eds), *The SAGE Handbook of Organization Studies* (SAGE 2006) 249.

[72] ibid.

[73] Lucinda Soon and others also refer to practice areas of large firms as sub-fields of the legal profession field, Lucinda Soon, Almuth McDowall, and Kevin RH Teoh, 'Towards a Context-Specific Approach to Understanding Lawyers' Well-Being: A Synbook Review and Future Research Agenda' [2023] Psychiatry, Psychology and Law 1, 9.

[74] Thomas B. Lawrence and Suddaby (n 71) 247.

[75] Townley (n 68) 54–55.

[76] ibid.

[77] There is no clear consensus on the meaning of 'meso' – at least in organizational theory - nor, for that matter in the meaning of macro and meso, D Brent Smith, Benjamin Schneider, and Marcus W

tool to analyse the practice area as a field in order to identify the logics which tend to influence the ethical decision-making of lawyers.

This type of levels approach also facilitates an exploration of how phenomena found in one level can affect another.[78] So, for example, at the meso level, there are the business conditions and logics of the law firm that I have noted already, and which Chapter 8 explores in detail. At the macro level, there are the conditions and logics of financial markets, which may in turn affect the conditions and logics of large law firms, which are also explored in Chapter 8. This book reveals how changes to the conditions and logics of both large law firms and markets have combined to shape the conditions and logics of the leverage finance practice area field. It is these practice area logics which are often the most accessible to individual leveraged finance lawyers when they make sense of and carry out their roles and decide what is and what is not appropriate conduct.

In exploring the practice area as an institutional field, this book identifies what Lawrence and Suddaby refer to as the 'enduring elements ... that have a profound effect on the thoughts, feelings and behaviour of individual and collective actors'.[79] Patricia Thornton and others, in their leading text, define institutional logics as:

> the socially constructed, historical patterns of cultural symbols and material practices, including assumptions, values, and beliefs, by which individuals and organisations provide meaning to their daily activity, organise time and space, and reproduce their lives and experiences.[80]

These field-specific frames of reference influence the behaviour of the actors situated within them.[81] Lawyer activity in any practice area is hence regulated by its institutional logics.[82] Logics shape how lawyers make sense of their day-to-day practice context and then decide what is appropriate and legitimate conduct.[83] As Richard Scott has observed, these logics 'provide stability and meaning to social life' and are transmitted by various mechanisms, including practices, shared understandings, and routines.[84] The prevailing logics of a practice setting are hence evident in the distinctive practices[85] and shared understandings of the lawyers that

Dickson, 'Meso Organisational Behaviour: Comments on the Third Paradigm', *The SAGE Handbook of Organization Studies* (Second, SAGE Publications 2013) 150.

[78] Thornton, Ocasio, and Lounsbury (n 17) 13.
[79] Thomas B Lawrence and Suddaby (n 71) 125.
[80] Thornton, Ocasio, and Lounsbury (n 17) 2, 51.
[81] Bourdieu's notion of a field's habitus and doxa is also seen in the institutional logics literature. Thornton, Ocasio, and Lounsbury (n 17); Townley (n 68) 54. Thornton, Ocasio, and Lounsbury (n 17) 134–9. Moorhead, Vaughan, and Godinho (n 37) 207–8.
[82] Greenwood and Hinings (n 18) 819; Friedland and Alford (n 19).
[83] Greenwood and Hinings (n 18) 819.
[84] W Richard Scott (n 69) 48; Thomas B Lawrence and Suddaby (n 71) 216.
[85] For the importance of material practices in understanding the logics of institutional fields, see Roger Friedland and Roger R Alford, 'Bringing Society Back In: Symbols, Practices, and Institutional

operate in it, and for this reason a principal objective of this book is to identify and analyse them in detail.[86]

Patricia Thornton and others argue that 'constellations of relatively stable material practices provide core manifestations of institutional logics.'[87] They give the example of democracy as an institutional logic which is represented in tangible form by the practice of voting.[88] They distinguish practices ('a set of meaningful activities that are informed by wider cultural beliefs') from activities (mundane, everyday work).[89] Changes in practices are seen as manifestations of shifting institutional logics.[90] I have collected extensive data as to the emergent practices of the practice area field that is the focus of the case study, and it is this data that has enabled me to identify, and consider what might be the causes and effects of, its emergent and prevailing logics. The lawyer designation model—which I explore in detail in Chapter 3—is a critical practice of the leveraged finance practice area field, for example, because leveraged finance lawyers tend to understand and give it meaning in similar ways. It represents in tangible form the survival logic, and a series of other distinctive logics which prevail in this field of lawyer activity.

This book also considers the extent to which lawyer action in a practice area setting is discretionary or a product of their environment. The two possibilities are not, of course, mutually exclusive. As Brent Smith and others argue:

> the environment cannot be understood without first understanding the people who comprise it, nor can people be understood without examination of the environments in which they are embedded.[91]

Forces both within and outside the individual hence determine their behaviour.[92] A practice area's logics should be seen as a constraint on lawyer action, whilst at the same time also constituting the contextual framework within which they make choices; as a result they frequently pursue discretionary behaviour which has the potential to transform the conditions of their practice area.[93] This book hence

Contradictions', *The New Institutionalism in Organizational Analysis* (The University of Chicago Press 1991) 254.

[86] My aim was, not, however, to cluster individual lawyers into categorical types, and to compare them to a 'pure form'. Thornton, Ocasio, and Lounsbury (n 17) 59, 74.

[87] ibid 129.

[88] ibid.

[89] ibid 128.

[90] ibid 129.

[91] Brent Smith, Schneider, and Dickson (n 77) 151.

[92] Kurt Lewin, 'Behavior and Development as a Function of the Total Situation', *Manual of Child Psychology* (John Wiley & Sons, Inc 1946); Brent Smith, Schneider, and Dickson (n 77) 151.

[93] Thornton, Ocasio, and Lounsbury (n 17) 53–54.

seeks to understand how individual lawyers are both affected by, and affect, the practice area contexts they inhabit.[94]

The practice area can therefore be seen as a collection of practices and logics which lawyers both continually reproduce but also sometimes transform, enabling an assessment of what might be the underlying causes of phenomena which emerge in that practice area setting.[95] Sometimes lawyers will consciously deliberate on how the structural conditions of their practice area constrain them, and at other times they will act subconsciously.[96] Adopting this approach, this book explores what it is about the conditions of their practice area field that might tend to influence a lawyer's practices and decision-making.[97] I have not sought to develop a hypothesis as to the causes of phenomena—that cause *a* necessarily results in effect *b*—however.[98] My explanations operate, at best, as a guide to the future, uncovering and seeking to explain mechanisms in order to predict tendencies.[99]

In summary then, this book facilitates the exploration of the structural conditions of the practice area context in which lawyers work and its influence on lawyer ethical decision-making. But it also supplements this analysis with an understanding of the role that a lawyer's own discretionary behaviour plays, accepting that this discretionary behaviour is both embedded in, but at the same time also partly autonomous from, the structural conditions of their practice area and firm.[100]

In drawing out a range of practice area-specific logics within major law firms, this book offers a series of fresh insights to the institutional logics literature, which has tended to adopt a relatively binary approach with respect to the professions, assuming a 'professional logic' to exist in professional settings, which is often

[94] Richard T Mowday and Robert I Sutton, 'Organizational Behavior: Linking Individuals and Groups to Organizational Contexts' (1993) 44 Annual Review of Psychology 195; Brent Smith, Schneider, and Dickson (n 77) 156.

[95] Steve Fleetwood, 'Bhaskar and Critical Realism', *The Oxford Handbook of Sociology, Social Theory, & Organization Studies* (OUP 2014) 206.

[96] ibid 207. My approach most closely aligns with the critical realist perspective, a framework founded in ontology which offers a pathway through otherwise opposed paradigms, or dualisms, such as structure and agency, and objectivity and subjectivity. Broadly, ontology is a set of beliefs about the way the world is. Critical realism, most closely associated with the work of Roy Bhaskar, emerged in the 1970s and 1980s as a reaction to structural functionalist and positivist perspectives that, according to Steve Fleetwood, see actors as 'puppets, acting out a role determined by society's structure', ibid 182, 186. Berth Danermark and others, *Explaining Society: An Introduction to Critical Realism in the Social Sciences* (Routledge 2005) 202; Norman K Denzin, 'Review of Explaining Society: Critical Realism in the Social Sciences' (2004) 33 Contemporary Sociology 249, 250. Roy Bhaskar, *A Realist Theory of Science* (2nd edn, Routledge 1977). Fleetwood (n 95) 184.

[97] Thornton, Ocasio, and Lounsbury (n 17) 8.

[98] This would necessitate the adoption of a quantitative methodology and method, Silverman (n 21) 181.

[99] Saying something has a *tendency* to result in effect 'x', is not the same as saying it will always *cause* 'x'. Fleetwood (n 95) 192; Claire Laurier Decoteau, 'The Reflexive Habitus: Critical Realist and Bourdieusian Social Action' (2016) 19 European Journal of Social Theory 303, 308; Danermark and others (n 96) 163; Denzin (n 96) 250.

[100] Thornton, Ocasio, and Lounsbury (n 17) 10.

presented as being in tension with a 'market logic'.[101] Professions are generally depicted as having certain 'ideal type' characteristics.[102] Technical expertise, quality of craft, status, and reputation are emphasized, in contrast to the characteristics of the market, which emphasizes self-interest and profit.[103] Thornton and Ocasio, for example, in their empirical study of the publishing sector, depict publishing as a professional field which is influenced by market logics which counter these ideal type characteristics of a profession.[104] According to Thornton and others, professions are 'expected to represent a greater emphasis on ethical norms than the institutional order of the market.'[105] They suggest that the professions act as 'moderators of extreme market practices by providing checks and balances ... a constraint on the unbridled practices of capitalism'. They acknowledge, however, that that this claim hasn't been established by empirical research.[106] The empirically based case study in this book supports the reverse conclusion, which Thornton and others suspected might be the case—that professionals may in fact facilitate 'market corruption'.[107]

1.3 The large law firm context

This book emphasizes the importance of the logics of a corporate lawyer's specific practice area context in shaping how lawyers make sense of their day-to-day practice context and then decide what is appropriate and legitimate conduct. However, there is of course a broader context in which corporate lawyers work, which, together with a lawyer's own discretionary behaviour, shape these practice area logics. This is the organizational context of the large international law firm, which I explore in this section.

There is a significant body of literature on corporate lawyers and the large law firm which offers important background and context to the themes explored in this book. Much of it tends to emphasize rapid law firm growth and increased bureaucracy, whilst at the same time exploring how the social relationships and collegial networks between law firm partners have been impacted by these dynamics.[108]

[101] Patricia H Thornton and William Ocasio, 'Institutional Logics and the Historical Contingency of Power in Organizations: Executive Succession in the Higher Education Publishing Industry, 1958-1990' (1999) 105 American Journal of Sociology 801, 149.

[102] Thornton, Ocasio, and Lounsbury (n 17) 255.

[103] ibid.

[104] Thornton and Ocasio (n 101) 105; Thornton, Ocasio, and Lounsbury (n 17) 64.

[105] Thornton and Ocasio (n 101) 119.

[106] ibid 119–120.

[107] ibid 119.

[108] See eg Erwin O Smigel, *The Wall Street Lawyer* (The Free Press of Glencoe 1964); Heinz and Laumann (n 1); Robert L Nelson, *Partners with Power: The Social Transformation of the Large Law Firm* (University of California Press 1988); Emmanuel Lazega, *The Collegial Phenomenon: The Social Mechanisms of Cooperation Among Peers in a Corporate Law Partnership* (OUP 2001).

For Erwin Smigel, in his empirical study of Wall Street lawyers in the 1950s, corporate law firms had by this time become bureaucratic 'law factories', where lawyers had lost their independence, and become conformist and lacking in creativity.[109] Against this backdrop of bureaucratization, collegial ties were found to continue to exist between partners, however.[110] Emmanuel Lazega, in his study of how collegial networks form in large firms, found that collegial ties were strongest in smaller groups, not just practice-based organizational sub-units of the firm but also multi-discipline, ad hoc 'task forces' brought together to advise a client on a large, complex, and often cross-border transaction.[111]

Significant structural changes occurred in the 1980s and 1990s which had a dramatic effect on the business logics of large law firms.[112] For example, this period saw the emergence of incentives and pressures on law firm partners created under 'eat what you kill' remuneration structures.[113] Firms also grew significantly in size, with many becoming global business organizations.[114] Since the 1990s, large corporate law firms have experienced accelerated growth and globalization,[115] and increasingly adopted corporate-style management strategies.[116] Manuel Gomez and Marc Galanter attribute this expansion to the growth in scale and complexity of global trade during this period.[117]

James Faulconbridge and Daniel Muzio, in their study of the largest firms in England, emphasize how firm growth and globalization was accompanied by the 'financialization' of large law firms and a new found 'obsession' with driving increased profit per equity partner (PEP) —the profits of the firm divided by the number of equity partners—in the period leading up to the global financial crisis.[118] They argue that large English law firms underwent an organizational transformation due to these financial logics in the period between 1993 and 2008, with an emphasis on increasing PEP.[119] Mitt Regan and Lisa Rohrer argue

[109] Smigel (n 108).
[110] Lazega (n 108).
[111] ibid.
[112] See eg Janine Griffiths-Baker (n 22) 3; Regan (n 48).
[113] Mitt Regan and Lisa H Rohrer, *BigLaw: Money and Meaning in the Modern Law Firm* (The University of Chicago Press 2020) 1, 77–95.
[114] Janine Griffiths-Baker (n 22) 3–8.
[115] Carole Silver, 'Globalization and the U.S. Market in Legal Services - Shifting Identities' (1999) 31 Law and Policy in International Business 1093; JR Faulconbridge and D Muzio, 'The Financialization of Large Law Firms: Situated Discourses and Practices of Reorganization' (2009) 9 Journal of Economic Geography 641, 651.
[116] Eg, see Heinz and Laumann (n 1); Nelson (n 108); Gerard Hanlon, 'A Profession in Transition - Lawyers, the Market and Significant Others' (1997) 60 Modern Law Review 798; James Faulconbridge and Daniel Muzio, 'Organizational Professionalism in Globalizing Law Firms' (2008) 22 Work, Employment and Society 7; Christopher J Whelan and Neta Ziv, 'Privatizing Professionalism: Client Control of Lawyers' Ethics Colloquium: Globalization and the Legal Profession' (2011) 80 Fordham Law Review 2577.
[117] Gomez and Galanter (n 2).
[118] Faulconbridge and Muzio (n 115) 642, 659.
[119] ibid 649–55.

that until the late twentieth century, large law firms largely operated in a seller's market.[120] They describe how the global financial crisis of 2007–9 accelerated a shift to a buyer's market, as the 'pie' of corporate legal work reduced dramatically and competition between law firms intensified. The commercial pressures on partners consequently became elevated, as firms laid off significant numbers of partners who were considered unproductive, and increasingly moved to remuneration systems that rewarded productivity over seniority.[121]

Empirical work with respect to large corporate law firms has, at the same time, consistently emphasized the powerful influence of major corporate clients. John Heinz and Edward Laumann, in their large-scale study of lawyers working in Chicago in the 1970s, were primarily concerned with highlighting the distinctions between corporate lawyers and other lawyers; at the same time, they emphasized client type as the most important contextual factor influencing the behaviour of lawyers.[122] Robert Nelson's work builds upon Heinz and Laumann's finding that major clients have a significant influence on large law firms.[123] He shows how lawyers in large law firms have bounded autonomy, since they tend to be subordinate to the influence of a small number of 'partners with power'; these partners absorb the norms of, and are subordinate to, the interests of their major corporate clients.[124] This subordination limits their ability to 'say no' to clients, including when faced with an ethical choice.[125] Gerard Hanlon found that lawyers working in large corporate law firms in the UK were similarly vulnerable to pressure from powerful clients.[126]

This view of corporate lawyers in large firms as vulnerable and subordinate to their large corporate clients has been developed in research into the independence of corporate lawyers in London firms by Claire Coe and Steven Vaughan.[127] They found that there had been a 'shift in the balance of power from law firms to clients' because of the way in which major companies and financial institutions impose their own terms of engagement on firms through a law firm panel process; firms are under pressure to deliver 'value for money' in an increasingly competitive environment; through the procurement and engagement process, firms were losing

120 Regan and Rohrer (n 113) 25.
121 See ibid 16–22.
122 David B Wilkins, 'Some Realism about Legal Realism for Lawyers: Assessing the Role of Context in Legal Ethics' in Leslie C Levin and Lynn M Mather (eds), *Lawyers in Practice: Ethical Decision Making in Context* (University of Chicago Press 2012).
123 Nelson (n 108).
124 Heinz and Laumann (n 1); Nelson (n 108).
125 Nelson (n 108) 5.
126 Hanlon (n 116).
127 Heinz and Laumann (n 1) 167; Claire Coe and Steven Vaughan, 'Independence, Representation and Risk: An Empirical Exploration of the Management of Client Relationships by Large Law Firms' (Social Science Research Network 2015) SSRN Scholarly Paper ID 2679005 <https://papers.ssrn.com/abstract=2679005> accessed 17 July 2018.

distinctiveness as professionals and becoming 'mere service providers'. Cristopher Whelan and Neta Ziv's research shows that large corporate and institutional clients are 'privatising professionalism' through the terms of outside counsel guidelines; in this way, corporate clients exercise governance over their outside counsel, with these guidelines operating as an additional layer of regulation, on top of that imposed on lawyers by the state.[128] Coe and Vaughan concluded that the shift in the balance of power between lawyers and clients meant corporate lawyers had become 'prone to developing and normalising potentially risky and irresponsible practices'.[129]

An equally important strand of the literature seeks to examine the ethical inclination of large law firm lawyers, and the extent to which they exercise agency in their decision-making. This literature suggests that corporate lawyers tend to have a poor grasp of their professional duties, and that in any event, professional rules are mostly not front-of-mind factors which influence their actions. Lynn Mather and others note that professional rules do not significantly influence lawyer behaviour as they tend to be framed 'at a level of generality that crosses practice areas'; instead the practice area provides the 'cues and signals about appropriate behaviour and thus constitute crucial reference points for decisions'.[130] Richard Moorhead and Victoria Hinchley examined how corporate lawyers perceived their professional and ethical responsibilities.[131] Using the solicitor's obligation in England & Wales to uphold the rule of law and the proper administration of justice under the SRA Code of Conduct as the benchmark for their research into the ethical inclination of corporate lawyers, they found that 'professional ethics exert minimal, superficial influence over a more self-interested, commercially driven pragmatism.' Ethics were often equated by respondents with criminality, and unlawfulness assessed as a 'cost/benefit' decision about risk. Moorhead and Hinchley's respondents tended not to refer to notions of professional responsibility or duties under the SRA Code. Ethical issues were often reframed in business terms, as reputational issues, for instance. Contextual pressures were not found to be offset by significant counterbalances: for example, training on ethics or other ethical infrastructure. Instead, and consistent with Smigel's finding in New York decades previously, firms relied simply on hiring the 'right' people. This book emphasizes how this 'minimalism' and pragmatism exist but are variable across the different practice area contexts found in major international law firms.

128 Whelan and Ziv (n 116).
129 Coe and Vaughan (n 127).
130 Leslie C Levin and Lynn M Mather, *Lawyers in Practice: Ethical Decision Making in Context* (The University of Chicago Press 2012) 69, 70.
131 Moorhead and Hinchley (n 15).

1.4 The practice area context

The literature which considers the ethics of large international law firms mostly presents a picture of ethical inclination that is relatively homogenous regardless of practice specialty. For example, Steven Vaughan and Emma Oakley in their study of the independence of corporate lawyers in London 'found no real variation between different flavours of transactional lawyer'.[132] And Mitt Regan and Lisa Rohrer, in their recent US focussed book 'Big Law', reported that they did not 'find any systematic difference in viewpoints' based on practice area distinctions.[133] This book, on the other hand, sets out to consider the implications of the evolution of large international law firms into complex bureaucratic organizations divided into multiple organizational sub-units, typically based on their practice area specialization. It contributes fresh insights, recognizing that the proliferation in specialisms found in the modern corporate law firm means there is no such thing as an overall, homogenous firm culture.[134] The large law firm is instead a collection of practice areas, firms within the firm if you like, each with their own distinct culture that is shaped by clients and market dynamics as much as, if not more than, the culture of the firm, and certainly more than it is by professional regulation.[135]

Smigel, in his study of Wall Street firms in the 1950s, noted the emergence of specialist practice areas within large firms, making a connection between the degree of specialist knowledge of a practice area and its prestige within the firm.[136] A significant factor in the development of practice area groupings within large law firms on both sides of the Atlantic has been client pressure to offer ever more specialized advice.[137] The study of different fields of legal practice and their potential operation as a contextual factor indicating likely ethicality is also evident in Heinz and Laumann's study of Chicago lawyers.[138] They found that there were 'two hemispheres'; broadly two principal fields of legal practice based on client type—individuals and small businesses on the one hand, and corporations on the other.[139] Hanlon's work confirmed that the 'two hemispheres' polarization of the profession in the UK had been largely mirrored in the UK.[140]

This book hence underscores this importance of a lawyer's practice area context to their ethical-decision-making, which was the focus of Leslie Levin and Lynn

[132] Vaughan and Oakley (n 38) 72.
[133] Regan and Rohrer (n 113) 11.
[134] Regan (n 48) 8.
[135] Levin and Mather (n 130) 3.
[136] He asserted that banking and real estate, for example, were more routine and precedent-based practice areas where conformity was more prevalent, since these lawyers worked less in the 'grey areas' of the law, as compared to corporate and litigation lawyers, Smigel (n 108).
[137] A Francis, 'Legal Ethics, the Marketplace and the Fragmentation of Legal Professionalism' (2005) 12(2) International Journal of the Legal Profession 173.
[138] Heinz and Laumann (n 1)
[139] ibid.
[140] Hanlon (n 116).

Mather's excellent collection.[141] Mather and others, in their study of divorce lawyers, found that each practice setting will present particular challenges for lawyers working in that area of law, often deriving from the nature of the client and their legal problems.[142] Kimberly Kirkland's study of the situational norms of corporate lawyers focused on litigators because for her they represented 'an exceptionally influential paradigm of legal ethics'; exhibiting zeal even when not in a courtroom setting.[143] Kirkland found they developed distinctive 'practice norms'; for example, whether a reasoned or aggressive approach is adopted in dealings with opposing counsel. She found that lawyers adopted the norms of the practice area, and even of the partner in charge of a matter or client, applying a 'choice of norm' rule. These practice norms displaced professional rules and their own moral code, and they tended not to question the merits of the norms themselves. Kirkland concludes that if litigators can be influenced by their context, in the form of the bureaucratization of the firm environment, it follows that so can non-litigators.[144] Patrick Schmidt, in his research on transactional securities lawyers in US firms, supports this conclusion.[145] Similarly Mitt Regan, in his study of bankruptcy lawyers in New York, found that unique norms develop because of the situational and contextual factors presented by particular practice areas, leading him to argue that the explanation for ethical misconduct in large corporate law firms is more complex than simply being the result of 'bad apples' (a rogue lawyer) or a 'bad barrel' (a firm with a corrupt culture).[146]

If transactional corporate lawyers learn what is and isn't appropriate behaviour from their practical experience, including working with and observing others in their practice area, as opposed to the formal rules of professional conduct or their own moral code, we should not be surprised that what Mather and others term 'communities of practice' come into being which establish their own unique norms.[147] Building on Kirkland's findings, this book evidences the existence of multiple norms systems in large corporate law firms, each shaping the way lawyers think and act in the practice-based sub-units of the law firm, so that across the organization of the firm there is not one unified system of norms. Understanding this

[141] Leslie C Levin and Lynn Mather, *Lawyers in Practice: Ethical Decision Making in Context* (University of Chicago Press 2012).

[142] For divorce lawyers, 'messy human problems' and human emotion particular to advising divorcing couples were found to be a key influence on their ethical inclination, Levin and Mather (n 130) 63.

[143] Kimberly Kirkland, 'Ethics in Large Law Firms: The Principle of Pragmatism' (2004) 35 University of Memphis Law Review 631, 659–62.

[144] Kirkland (n 143).

[145] Patrick Schmidt, 'The Ethical Lives of Securities Lawyers', in Levin and Mather (n 130).

[146] A good example of a scholar adopting this approach, using a mix of qualitative methods, is Regan in his study of bankruptcy lawyers in large US law firms. Regan (n 48) 10. On the range of influencing factors see also Linda Haller, 'Regulating the Professions', in Peter Cane and Herbert Kritzer, *The Oxford Handbook of Empirical Legal Research* (OUP 2010) 227.

[147] Levin and Mather (n 130) 69, 70.

is key to explaining the way lawyers behave and make decisions, including with respect to questions of ethics.[148]

On the other hand, whilst accepting that each practice area has its own set of unwritten rules, or norms,[149] these are distinct from its internal logics.[150] A principal argument of this book is that the explanation for lawyer action is more complex than simply their puppet-like observance of social rules, or norms, and the focus of this book is consequently on the logics that govern their ethical decision-making, by providing the framework for their thought and action.

1.5 The structure of this book

This final section of the chapter sets out the remaining structure of this book.

Chapter 2 (Introducing the Case Study) introduces—and provides essential background and context to—the case study on which this book relies, a deep dive exploration of the leveraged finance practice setting found within most leading international law firms. I explore, often in granular detail, the practice area in which leveraged finance lawyers work, and the markets to which it is deeply connected. I begin by highlighting the questionable role of lawyers in a high value transaction that was heavily reported in the press. Next, I explain what led me to study leveraged finance lawyers. Finally, given the centrality of leveraged finance, leveraged buyouts, and private equity to the case study, Chapter 2 offers a detailed explanation of these markets, and their relationship to Big Law, for readers who might be less familiar with them.

Chapter 3 (Bank Lawyers: Practices and Logics) explores what the case study data reveal about the practices and logics of the lawyers that act for the banks which arrange and underwrite leveraged finance transactions, referred to throughout this book as the 'bank lawyers'. It begins by describing in detail a foundational but also controversial practice of the field: lawyer designation. Lawyer designation has spawned a series of referral relationships between bank lawyers and private equity lawyers across multiple large international law firms in London. I explain how these often deeply entrenched referral relationships led to the emergence of a survival logic, which leads bank lawyers to adjust their behaviour in order to continue as practitioners in the leveraged finance practice area. I also explore how the survival logic is closely connected to, and works in combination with, other key logics of the field. Bank lawyers are expected by the private equity lawyers who appoint

[148] Levin (n 64); Moorhead and others (n 21) 39.

[149] Which Pierre Bourdieu refers to as *habitus*, or, using a sporting metaphor, 'rules of the game', Townley (n 68) 49, 51; Loïc JD Wacquant, 'On the Tracks of Symbolic Power: Prefatory Notes to Bourdieu's "State Nobility"' (1993) 10 Theory, Culture & Society 1, 4; Karl Maton, 'Habitus', *Pierre Bourdieu: Key Concepts* (Second, Routledge 2014) 53. Vaughan and Oakley (n 38) 74.

[150] Similar to Pierre Bourdieu's concept of '*doxa*', Townley (n 68) 42–3; DiMaggio and Powell (n 68).

them to 'be commercial', or else they risk being boycotted for future work. I describe the series of often ethically dubious dispositions, practices, and strategies that bank lawyers have developed in response.

Chapter 4 (Bank Lawyers: Ethical Duties) considers the implications of the bank lawyer conduct which is described in the previous chapter for bank lawyers' ethical duties under the professional code of conduct to which they are subject. I put the case that the strategies and practices of bank lawyers which are revealed by the multiple-and-detailed examples in the data that I collected are likely to constitute breaches of Principle 3, of the SRA's Standards and Regulations, the duty to act 'with independence',[151] and the solicitor's related duty to disclose referral arrangements, as well as Principle 7 of the SRA's Standards and Regulations, which requires solicitors to act 'in the best interests of each client'.[152] I explore in some detail, for example, how these duties are engaged by the emergent, and ethically questionable, practice of what is commonly referred to as 'virtual trees', or 'trees in the head'.

In **Chapter 5 (Private Equity Lawyers: Practices and Logics)** the focus shifts to the private equity lawyers. It considers how a relentless strategy of contractual boundary pushing by private equity lawyers, taking advantage of the compromised independence of bank lawyers that is explored in Chapters 3 and 4, has been a material contributor to the dramatic evolution in leveraged loan terms. I describe and analyse how private equity lawyers have advocated for spurious 'add backs' in financial covenants that have significantly eroded their value to lenders, for example. We see how their contractual boundary-pushing strategies may—but will not always—align with a private equity lawyer's client's objectives, they tend to be primarily motivated by their own commercially pragmatic objectives of building their own personal profile and prestige for being perceived as the most aggressive in moving the market in leveraged loan terms.

Chapter 6 (Private Equity Lawyers: Ethical Duties) explores what the case study means with respect to the observance by private equity lawyers of their ethical duties under professional codes of conduct. I put the case that the contractual boundary-pushing strategies and practices of private equity lawyers which are revealed by my data may constitute breaches of the SRA's Principle 7, which requires solicitors to act 'in the best interests of each client'.[153] We see how the success of private-equity-lawyer strategies depend on the coercive authority they wield over bank lawyers. An example of this type of coercive boundary-pushing activity is

[151] The Standards and Regulations include the Principles and two Codes of Conduct, one for individual solicitors and one for firms. There is significant overlap between the two Codes, and for simplicity, and since the focus of this book is primarily on the logics and ethics of individual lawyers across different firms who happen to work in the same practice area, I have chosen to focus on the Code that applies to individual solicitors, as opposed to firms. Individual solicitors are personally accountable under this Code and are required to justify their decisions and actions, 'SRA Principles' (n 34).

[152] ibid.

[153] ibid.

then explored—the imposition on banks by private equity lawyers of new terms at the initial, 'commercial grid' stage of the transaction, which typically incorporates by reference the full financing terms of the transaction documents carried over from a previous transaction—at a moment when the banks tend not to be represented by designated legal counsel. I put the case that private equity lawyers are frequently in breach of the SRA's Principle 5, acting with integrity, and the related duty not to take unfair advantage of a third party.[154]

Chapter 7 (The Corruption of Markets by Big Law) explores one of the principal effects of the leveraged finance lawyer action described in the book up to this point: the significant uncertainty in the meaning of key terms in leveraged loan documents, and the potential for loophole lawyering that it creates. We see how transaction documents have become ambiguous to the extent where leverage finance lawyers and their clients tend not to fully understand them. I explore a series of examples in detail, including what is known as the 'J. Crew trapdoor', indecipherable and contradictory further indebtedness covenants and embedded defects in intercreditor and security sharing structures. We see how bank lawyers and private equity lawyers tend not to fix the multiple and often serious problems with leveraged loan documents that they encounter. Chapter 7 also explores what the case study means with respect to the observance by private equity lawyers of their ethical duties. I put the case that private equity lawyers are potentially in breach of their duty to act with integrity under Principle 5 of the SRA's Principles by pursuing 'loophole lawyering' when making the most of the uncertainty and defects in leveraged loan documents.[155] I further put the case that the case study raises serious question marks as to the competence of leveraged finance lawyers.

Chapter 8 (The Corruption of Big Law by Markets) explores how the case study reveals the way in which Big Law risks being corrupted by its deep connections to financial markets. The chapter identifies some of the potential market-based causes of the practice area logics driving the type of dubious ethical conduct revealed by the case study. We see that, contrary to the picture which tends to be presented in the literature that explores corporate lawyer ethics, the search for contextual factors influencing corporate lawyer ethics should not be confined to law firm-wide pressures and incentives, such as those which flow from 'eat what you kill' remuneration models, for example. I put the case that to identify and then evaluate the effect of the prevailing institutional logics that shape corporate lawyer action and ethical-decision-making, the range of a practice area's particular logics should be analysed, since these combine with law firm logics to create the pathways which facilitate individual lawyer action and ethical decision-making.[156]

[154] 'Acting with Integrity - Guidance' (25 November 2019) <https://www.sra.org.uk/solicitors/guidance/acting-with-integrity/> accessed 28 November 2020.

[155] 'SRA Principles' (n 34).

[156] Thornton, Ocasio, and Lounsbury (n 17) 9.

We see how a series of macro-economic forces and events, including the global financial crisis, a wave of new regulation directed at banks, a leveraged finance supply and demand disconnect, the blending of leveraged finance loan and bond investor markets, and a switch in bank lending and underwriting models in this market, together, shaped a distinct set of emergent logics that came to frame the ethical decision-making of leveraged finance lawyers. The result is that leveraged finance lawyers began to think and act differently to lawyers in other practice areas—even when compared to their colleagues within their own firm—because these logics came to comprise the most immediate framework within which they decided what was appropriate conduct in their daily work. I then consider an example. I show how real change to the conditions and logics of the leveraged finance practice area was effected by a sub-group of powerful private equity lawyers in particular, drawing on both the logics of their firm and the emergent logics of the markets in which they were operating.[157]

In **Chapter 9 (Conclusion)** I summarize what I consider to be the implications of this book for large international law firms. Next, I offer some reflections on the important questions this book raises about the 'value add' that major international law firms offer to clients, and ultimately also the extent to which clients and the wider public can and should continue to place their trust in these firms. Then, I consider what this book means for how regulators of the legal profession may better support lawyers who work in major law firms in acting ethically. In the final substantive section, I consider how leveraged finance lawyers—in creating, allowing to subsist, and taking advantage of pervasive uncertainty in loan documents—risk undermining key regulatory objectives such as the maintenance of fair and transparent markets, as well as contributing to the build-up of systemic risk in global financial markets.

Appendix 1 (Research Methods and Design) describes and critically analyses the case study's methodology and research design. I interrogate my initial hunches about what I thought was going on in the field of leveraged finance when I embarked on my research and reflect on the advantages and disadvantages for my research of my 'insider' status as a former international finance practitioner myself. I also present a detailed description of my approach to data collection and analysis and conclude with a critical analysis of the rigour of my research design, and the ethical questions arising out of this design.

157 ibid 177.

2
Introducing the Case Study

2.1 Introduction

The principal arguments made in this book are illustrated and supported by reference to a case study which draws on my own empirical research. It constitutes a deep-dive exploration of the leveraged finance practice setting found within most major international law firms to consider how its internal logics may influence individual lawyer action and ethical decision-making, and how in turn these dynamics are founded in, and can significantly influence and shape the conditions of, financial markets.[1]

The case study explores, often in quite granular detail, the practice area and connected markets in which leveraged finance lawyers work. In Chapter 3, for example, I explore the experiences of the lawyers that advise the arranging and underwriting banks in the financings of leveraged buyouts (the bank lawyers). And Chapter 5 explores the role of the lawyers that advise the private equity sponsors, effectively the borrowers of that financing (the private equity lawyers). Given the centrality of leveraged finance, leveraged buyouts, and private equity to what these lawyers experience in their everyday work, this chapter offers important background and context for readers who might be less familiar with them. Those readers who are familiar with the leveraged finance market, and the central role of large firms within it, may wish to pass over this chapter and move to the next.

This chapter begins by offering some context to the leveraged finance market, by reference to concerns expressed by domestic and international regulatory bodies, and in press reports concerning a high-profile transaction. It then explains in some detail the relationship between the leveraged finance and private equity markets and Big Law. Next, I explain in detail how these markets themselves operate, and the roles that lawyers play in them. The chapter then concludes.

2.2 The worst terms ever seen?

In January 2019, Mark Carney, the then Governor of the Bank of England, reported what he considered to be a new threat to global financial stability to a House

[1] Pierre Bourdieu, *The Social Structures of the Economy* (Polity 2005) 148; Patricia Thomson, 'Field', *Pierre Bourdieu: Key Concepts* (Second, Routledge 2014) 65.

of Commons committee: an acceleration in the global volume of leveraged debt with weak lender protections.[2] According to Carney, leveraged loans bore 'all the hallmarks' of the sub-prime mortgages that had caused the global financial crisis a decade before.[3] Around this time, the Financial Stability Board (FSB), an international body established in the wake of the global financial crisis to promote global financial stability, launched an investigation into the sector and concluded that the risks generated by weakness in creditor protections in leveraged loans were mostly not fully priced in by the lenders.[4] And in 2022, the European Central Bank issued a warning to the significant institutions it supervises over 'excessive risk taking' in the sector.[5]

The reports of the €7.1bn debt financing in support of the leveraged buyout of Thyssenkrupp's lifts business in 2020 are illustrative of this phenomenon. The protections for lenders under the proposed terms of the financing were described by market analysts as 'the worst ever seen'.[6] Two large international private equity funds had joined together to make a bid for the company, advised by one of the world's leading law firms, with a team based mainly in London and in Germany.[7] In this case, the proposed terms would give the new owners of the lifts business a 'trap door', effectively the right to move assets of the business out of the reach of the banks and other lenders who were financing the buyout, so that they would be unavailable in the event the business subsequently became insolvent and unable to service or repay the debt.[8]

This trap door feature was imported to Europe from the United States, where it had been controversially activated by the private equity sponsors in the restructuring of the financially distressed retailer, J. Crew.[9] For the assets being financed

[2] Philip Aldrick Editor Economics, 'Leveraged Loans at Pre-Crisis Levels — and I'm Worried, Says Carney' (The Times, 17 Janaury 2019) <https://www.thetimes.co.uk/article/leveraged-loans-at-pre-crisis-levels-and-i-m-worried-says-carney-r3s9qt59r> accessed 2 July 2022.

[3] ibid; John Cassidy, 'The Coronavirus Is Exposing Wall Street's Reckless Gamble on Bad Debt' *The New Yorker* (2020) <https://www.newyorker.com/business/currency/the-coronavirus-is-exposing-wall-streets-reckless-gamble-on-bad-debt> accessed 2 July 2022.

[4] 'Vulnerabilities Associated with Leveraged Loans and Collateralised Loan Obligations' (Financial Stability Board, 19 December 2019) <https://www.fsb.org/2019/12/vulnerabilities-associated-with-leveraged-loans-and-collateralised-loan-obligations/> accessed 2 July 2022.

[5] European Central Bank, 'Leveraged Transactions, - Supervisory Expectations Regarding the Design and Functioning of Risk Appetite Frameworks and High Levels of Risk Taking' (2022) <https://www.bankingsupervision.europa.eu/press/letterstobanks/shared/pdf/2022/ssm.2022_letter_on_leveraged_transactions.en.pdf>.

[6] Albeit the sponsors in this case did subsequently offer concessions to the terms originally proposed to lenders to ensure a successful syndication of the financing, 'Investors Rue Lack of Protections on €7.1bn Thyssenkrupp Debt' *Financial Times* (26 June 2020) https://www.ft.com/content/fae40c44-30af-4676-95ff-28feefa16890 accessed 23 June 2022. Nikou Asgari and Robert Smith, 'Thyssenkrupp Backers Improve €7.6bn Debt Terms after Lenders Balk' *Financial Times* (30 June 2020) <https://www.ft.com/content/81864124-e50c-4670-92c1-756582bb664b> accessed 9 August 2021.

[7] Asgari and Smith (n 6).

[8] 'Investors Rue Lack of Protections on €7.1bn Thyssenkrupp Debt' (n 6).

[9] Kenneth Ayotte and Christina Scully, 'J. Crew, Nine West, and the Complexities of Financial Distress Forum Collection: Bankruptcy and Restructuring in Response to Exogenous Shocks' (2021) 131 Yale Law Journal Forum 363; 'The J.Crew "Trap Door" and Its Implications for the Future of Leveraged Finance' Torys LLP (2019) <https://www.torys.com/Our%20Latest%20Thinking/Publi

to not be there to secure and support the financing was seen to represent something of a nadir for lenders in the balance of transaction terms in the European leveraged finance market. These reports emphasized the trend that was starting to worry international and domestic financial services supervisory bodies: that the loosening in loan covenants had moved well beyond simply the effects of 'covenant-lite' loan structures—loans with a limited number of financial covenants,[10] and where the borrower largely controls if and when they are tested—which had become the dominant form in large leveraged financings in Europe.[11]

The reports of the ThyssenKrupp transaction are striking for several reasons. Not least, for the large sums of money involved. For the purposes of this book, they are most notable for shining a light on the role of the law firm advising the private equity sponsors in advocating for these types of terms, which were widely considered to be highly aggressive when viewed from the lenders' perspective. The *Financial Times* reported that this firm had 'made a name for itself' by 'offering sponsors the greatest flexibility' in their loan and bond documentation on leveraged finance transactions across the European leveraged buyout market.[12]

To illustrate and support the arguments I make in this book, I draw heavily on a case study based on my empirical study of the practices and ethics of leveraged finance lawyers. I undertook a significant number of interviews with partners and senior associates at leading English and US firms in London. Most of the participants in my study were specialists in leveraged finance. So why did I select leveraged finance lawyers as the subject of my empirical study?

Before commencing the research for this book, I had a feeling that trends in loan terms in leveraged buyouts in Europe, of which the ThyssenKrupp financing is a prominent example, might be closely connected to the activity of lawyers. This hunch—and at this point it was no more than that—was primarily based on what I would describe as market chatter that had come to my attention during my time in legal practice. I had until the previous year been a solicitor specializing in international finance law. I had enjoyed a twenty-five-year career, the majority spent as an equity partner of a leading international law firm, based in London and in Asia. I had limited direct experience of this specialist area of legal practice, however. Casual conversations with colleagues and my contacts within banks had

cations//2019/05/the-j-crew-trap-door-and-its-implications-for-the-future-of-leveraged-finance/> accessed 23 June 2022.

[10] Covenant-lite loans tend to have two financial covenants instead of the four seen in 'LMA style' loans.

[11] 'Leveraged Loans Are Way Past "Cov-Lite"' *Financial Times* (16 November 2018); Sarah Paterson, 'The Rise of Covenant-Lite Lending and Implications for the UK's Corporate Insolvency Law Toolbox' (2019) 39 Oxford Journal of Legal Studies 654, 663–664. Charles-Henri Larreur, *Structured Finance: Leveraged Buy-Outs, Project Finance, Asset Finance and Securitization* (Wiley 2021) 43; John Gilligan and Mike Wright, *Private Equity Demystified: An Explanatory Guide* (Fourth Edition, OUP 2020) 217.

[12] Asgari and Smith (n 6).

alerted me to concerns surrounding the independence of lawyers when acting for the banks arranging leveraged finance loans. These concerns were connected to a practice generally known as 'lawyer designation' —where the lawyer and firm appointed to advise the banks is chosen (that is, designated), and paid for, by the private equity sponsor; effectively, the borrower of the loan chooses the lenders' lawyer and pays that lawyer's fees—which had become the norm in large-scale leveraged finance transactions in Europe.

I, hence, selected the leveraged finance practice area as my field of study for this book since I was aware, albeit at a relatively superficial level, of recurring practices adopted by lawyers which appeared to be relatively unique to the leveraged finance practices of large international law firms in London and which were causing ethical tensions. I felt these practices, and their causes and effects, merited further investigation.[13]

Upon commencing my research, I found that some of these concerns around the ethics of leveraged finance lawyering were already in the public domain, by virtue of articles in the legal and business press and in the correspondence of professional bodies.[14] A leading investment bank had reportedly ceased working with a large law firm on leveraged finance transactions over concerns that the firm's close relationships with certain private equity sponsors had compromised the independence of its lawyers, for example.[15] Most notably, concerns were highlighted in research undertaken for the Solicitors Regulation Authority (SRA) by Claire Coe and Steven Vaughan in 2015.[16] Coe and Vaughan had found that bank lawyers in leveraged finance transactions had relationships with private equity sponsors—which they vividly termed 'shadow clients'—which some of their participants felt might serve to constrain their professional autonomy.[17] Coe and Vaughan had thus highlighted in 2015 that leveraged finance was potentially a site of significant ethical tension in modern international law firms. This chimed with my own understanding from my time in practice.

[13] This type of direct personal experience of a social order can often be a starting point for qualitative research, David Silverman, *Doing Qualitative Research* (SAGE 2017) 101, 158.

[14] 'Goldman Sachs Leveraged Finance Group Loses Enthusiasm for Linklaters | The Global Legal Post' <http://m.globallegalpost.com/global-view/goldman-sachs-leveraged-finance-group-loses-enthusiasm-for-linklaters-43888593/> accessed 12 October 2019. Alex Newman, 'Linklaters Falls out of Favour with Goldman's City Leveraged Finance Team' (LegalWeek, 2014) accessed 12 October 2019. Colby Smith and Joe Rennison, 'Debt Machine: Are Risks Piling up in Leveraged Loans?' *Financial Times* (21 January 2019) <https://www.ft.com/content/64c9665e-1814-11e9-9e64-d150b3105d21> accessed 21 January 2019; City of London Law Society, 'Response of the CLLS Professional Rules and Regulation Committee to the SRA's Consultation "A Question of Trust"' (29 January 2016).

[15] 'Goldman Sachs Leveraged Finance Group Loses Enthusiasm for Linklaters | The Global Legal Post' (n 14); Newman (n 14).

[16] Claire Coe and Steven Vaughan, 'Independence, Representation and Risk: An Empirical Exploration of the Management of Client Relationships by Large Law Firms' (Social Science Research Network 2015) SSRN Scholarly Paper ID 2679005 <https://papers.ssrn.com/abstract=2679005> accessed 17 July 2018.

[17] ibid 59.

At the same time, my feeling was that there was a good deal more to discover and understand about what was going on in the leveraged finance practice areas of large international law firms in Europe. And the causes and effects of this activity. For example, I knew that the power to designate had, in effect, been delegated by the leading private equity sponsors to the law firms they usually engaged and the partners at those firms that were the relationship lawyers for those private equity clients. As a result, several partners at leading international firms in London who specialized in advising banks were sourcing most, if not all, of their work from referrals from those private equity lawyers. A series of referral relationships had consequently developed between bank-side and private equity lawyers across several leading international law firms in London that appeared to me to exhibit some of the typical characteristics of a lawyer/client relationship. My curiosity about the ethical implications of these relationships led ultimately to the writing of this book.

2.3 Big Law and leveraged finance

In this section, I describe the relationship between major international law firms and the private equity and leveraged finance markets that form the backdrop to the case study.

Standing back from leveraged finance for the moment, it is worth starting by looking—through a critical lens—at the global power of Big Law. It is well established that UK and US headquartered global law firms are, and have for more than three decades been, direct competitors in the global market for legal services.[18] John Flood attributes the global expansion and success of large UK and US international law firms to their global investment bank clientele, who were reliant on New York law and English law, being the laws and legal systems they were familiar with.[19] The corporate lawyer and law firm literature tends to assume that there is still what Flood describes as a prevailing colonial style, 'Anglo-American hegemony' in the global market for legal services.[20] Manuel Gomez and Marc Galanter, writing as recently as 2021, refer to New York and London as the 'global epicentres' of Big Law, for example.[21]

This book contributes an appreciation of the intra Anglo-American battle that is currently raging within Big Law for global superiority. It is the 'Anglo' firms that

[18] Joan Loughrey, *Corporate Lawyers and Corporate Governance* (CUP 2011) 19.

[19] John Flood, 'Transnational Lawyering: Clients, Ethics and Regulation', in Leslie C Levin and Lynn Mather (eds), *Lawyers in Practice, Ethical Decision Making in Context* (The University of Chicago Press 2012) 179.

[20] ibid.

[21] Manuel A Gomez and Marc Galanter, 'The Many Lives of Big Law: Three Decades in the Evolution of Large Law Firms' in Richard L Abel,Hilary Sommerlad, Ole Hammerslev, and Ulrike Schultz (eds), *Lawyers in 21st-Century Societies: Vol. 2: Comparisons and Theories* (Bloomsbury Publishing Plc 2022) 381.

are on the defensive; they are under severe competitive pressure from US firms and desperately fighting to maintain their elite status, not only in continental Europe and across the world, but also in their home market, London. Daniel Muzio and James Faulconbridge touched on this phenomenon when considering the effects of the deregulation of the legal services market in England and Wales in 1990.[22] US firms were able to recruit English lawyers for the first time, creating new competition for the Magic Circle and other leading English firms for the most lucrative corporate work.[23] The US firms went on a hiring spree of English partners and lawyers; with higher levels of profitability, the US firms were able to offer more attractive levels of remuneration to the 'star players' at the English firms.[24] More recently, we have seen another strategic response to this global competition: major transatlantic law firm mergers.[25]

The case study shines a light on one key facet of this global competition within Big Law: a battle in Europe both for the most lucrative private equity and related leveraged finance work and to hire and retain those lawyers who are seen as the leading specialists in this work. It is a battle that the US firms appear to be winning. The Magic Circle and other leading UK firms are losing out in a turf war in the leveraged finance practice area field for premium work, and talent, to the London and European offices of the more profitable US firms who can offer their lawyers higher remuneration, and because the US firms mostly control the relationships with the leading globally active private equity houses.

Perhaps, the most distinctive characteristic of the leveraged finance practice areas of major law firms is the nature of the borrower of the finance. It is not a large listed company, for example, but a special purpose vehicle (SPV) which is 'sponsored'—as in, the equity share capital of that SPV is owned, directly or indirectly—by a private equity fund. I hence adopt the market terminology of 'private equity *sponsor*' in this book. Private equity sponsors hold something of a magnetic attraction for Big Law. Firstly, private equity is now a massive global business, made up of thousands of private equity funds.[26] It constitutes a sizeable proportion of the global and domestic economy; and in the UK alone, over 2,000 companies count private equity sponsors among their investors, with those companies employing

[22] JR Faulconbridge and D Muzio, 'The Financialization of Large Law Firms: Situated Discourses and Practices of Reorganization' (2009) 9 Journal of Economic Geography 641, 653.

[23] ibid. 'Magic Circle' is a name adopted in the UK legal press in the 1990s to denote a group of five London-based law firms that are often considered to be the leading UK firms in the areas of corporate, banking and finance law, comprising Allen & Overy, Clifford Chance, Freshfields Bruckhaus Deringer, Linklaters, and Slaughter & May.

[24] ibid.

[25] 'A&O Shearman Merger Successfully Completed' <https://www.aoshearman.com/news/ao-shearman-merger-successfully-completed> accessed 27 December 2024.

[26] More than 3,500, with a 143 per cent increase in the number of firms in the period between 2000 and 2014. 'Number of Active PE Firms up 143% since 2000: A Global Breakdown | PitchBook' <https://pitchbook.com/news/articles/number-of-active-pe-firms-up-143-since-2000-a-global-breakdown> accessed 12 June 2019.

over 500,000 people and with an aggregate annual turnover of £87.4bn.[27] Just as importantly, relationships with private equity sponsors tend to be more profitable for large law firms than their relationships with large corporations.[28] This is because, not unlike investment banks, private equity sponsors are 'deal shops'. They primarily exist to buy, with a significant amount of money borrowed from banks and other lenders, and then, within a relatively short time horizon of three to five years, exit their investments in the businesses they acquire. In the meantime, private equity sponsors constantly experiment with adjustments to capital structures to enhance their returns. Many leveraged buyouts go on to experience financial difficulty and need to be restructured and managed through an insolvency process.[29]

A further significant attraction for Big Law is that private equity sponsors tend to be less sensitive to legal costs than other large corporate bank and institutional clients.[30] They mostly do not require firms to bid for a place on a multi-firm panel, which these days feature in most large law firm relationships with international banks, for example. The typical price for admission to these panels is to offer billing rate discounts, volume fee rebates, free associate secondments, and other financially onerous concessions.[31]

In 'Eat what You Kill', Mitt Regan charts how large New York firms were drawn to the practice area of bankruptcy in the 1980s because of the pressure to generate higher profits, resulting from intense inter-firm competition, merit-based partner remuneration models, and an explosion in lateral hiring.[32] Given the scale of the transactions and the lucrative fees on offer, it was inevitable that large international law firms would similarly be drawn to this new and emerging market of leveraged finance because of the increasing focus of law firm leaders and managers on driving ever greater profitability.[33]

Marc Galanter and William Henderson observed that in the 1970s, established high- status law firms in New York were initially reluctant to enter the lucrative market for mergers and acquisitions (M&A) work, especially involving hostile

27 'BVCA Private Equity and Venture Capital Map' <http://www.privateequitymap.co.uk/> accessed 12 June 2019.

28 Sujeet Indap, Barney Thompson, and James Fontanella-Khan, 'How a Private Equity Boom Fuelled the World's Biggest Law Firm' *Financial Times* (6 June 2019) <https://www.ft.com/content/13696928-86d5-11e9-a028-86cea8523dc2> accessed 7 June 2019.

29 'Kirkland Secures $56M in Fees for Toys "R" Us Bankruptcy' *Legal Week* (10 June 2019). Paul Hodkinson, 'Why Buyout Firms Are Becoming More Attractive Clients than Banks' *Legal Week* (2 June 2019)<https://www.law.com/legal-week/2019/02/06/why-buyout-firms-are-becoming-more-attractive-clients-than-banks/> accessed 7 February 2019. Indap, Thompson and Fontanella-Khan (n 28).

30 'Why Buyout Firms Are Becoming More Attractive Clients than Banks' (n 29).

31 DB Wilkins, 'Team of Rivals? Toward a New Model of the Corporate Attorney/Client Relationship' (2009) 62 Current Legal Problems 478, 2071; Russell G Pearce and Eli Wald, 'The Relational Infrastructure of Law Firm Culture and Regulation: The Exaggerated Death of Big Law' (Social Science Research Network 2013) SSRN Scholarly Paper ID 2627733 128 <https://papers.ssrn.com/abstract=2627733> accessed 5 December 2018.

32 Milton C Regan, *Eat What You Kill: The Fall of a Wall Street Lawyer* (University of Michigan Press 2004) 10.

33 Faulconbridge and Muzio (n 22) 650.

takeovers, which allowed 'upstart' new entrant firms like Wachtell Lipton and Skadden Arps to develop a market-leading position.[34] The Magic Circle firms were similarly slow to recognize the potential of the private equity and leveraged finance market in Europe. Bank lawyer [#32] said:

> Originally it was quite a small ticket and then the market grew through the 90s. Initially I think some of the big law firms had not been too bothered about the sector because it was quite small scale, and the deals were not huge.

Russell Pearce and Eli Wald observe that 'the history of law firms providing legal services to corporate clients is one of change and evolution'; these firms have in recent years developed 'innovative and successful models of Big Law practice'.[35] This involves firms being 'strategically opportunistic', making targeted investments through the promotion and lateral hiring of partners in new practice areas and markets where the firm considers it will have—or can build—a competitive advantage.[36] The successful large international law firms now tend to adopt a strategy of what Wald calls 'smart growth'.[37] Kimberley Kirkland describes how modern law firms make 'decisions about which practice group to emphasise' based on 'predictions about the future market for and likely profitability of those practices and the reputation and image management hopes to create for the firm.'[38] This impacts the level of investment by the firm, in particular, the promotion of new partners, and the lateral hiring of partners from other firms.[39]

Until the late 1990s, according to bank lawyer [#32], the field was dominated by what might be referred to as 'mid-tier' UK firms, like Wilde Sapte and Ashurst. At this point, Magic Circle and other leading UK firms embraced the opportunities thrown up by the growth in scale and importance in international capital markets of private equity funds. As European leveraged buyouts got larger, more complex, and increasingly involved multiple jurisdictions, they found themselves playing catch up with mid-tier English firms, however.

James Faulconbridge and Daniel Muzio have noted how an important element of the financializaton of large law firms in this period, evidenced by their increasing focus on increasing the critical metric of profit per partner, or PEP, was the lateral hire of 'rainmaker' partners from other firms, a strategy that is effectively seen as a

[34] Marc Galanter and William D Henderson, 'The Elastic Tournament: The Second Transformation of the Big Law Firm' (Social Science Research Network 2008) SSRN Scholarly Paper ID 1104711 1895 <https://papers.ssrn.com/abstract=1104711> accessed 6 December 2018.

[35] Pearce and Wald (n 31) 126.

[36] Eli Wald, 'Smart Growth: The Large Law Firm in the Twenty-First Century Colloquium: Globalization and the Legal Profession' (2011) 80 Fordham Law Review 2867, 2883, 2912.

[37] ibid 2893; Marc Galanter and Thomas Palay, *Tournament of Lawyers: The Transformation of the Big Law Firm* (University of Chicago Press 1991).

[38] Kimberly Kirkland, 'Ethics in Large Law Firms: The Principle of Pragmatism' (2004) 35 University of Memphis Law Review 631, 669–670.

[39] ibid.

shortcut to enhanced profitability by poaching those who generate the most profit at competitor firms.[40] To increase their market share of leveraged finance work, large law firms have mostly pursued a strategy of aggressive lateral hiring. This has happened in two phases. First, the hiring by the Magic Circle and other leading UK firms of partners from the mid-tier of UK firms in the late 1990s and early 2000s.

Lateral hiring in the field then entered a second phase. This time, US firms, who were busy building their presence in London and across Europe, sought to hire rainmaker partners who were specialists in leveraged finance from the Magic Circle and other leading UK law firms. Often these were partners who had been hired in from mid-tier UK firms in the first phase. US firms in London that felt underrepresented in the field transformed their business models and undertook significant lateral partner, associate, and team hires to better position themselves to secure work from private equity sponsors.[41]

The result of this second phase of lateral hiring is that Magic Circle and other leading UK firms are losing out in the turf war in leveraged finance practice area for premium work, and talent, to the more profitable US firms.[42] US firms have been able to offer potential lateral hires remuneration at levels materially above what most UK firm remuneration models can tolerate.[43] Leading UK firms have experienced difficulties in retaining their rainmaker private equity and leveraged finance partners due to the inflexibility of their lockstep models—where partner remuneration is based on years spent as a partner—in the face of the US firms' largely merit-based 'eat what you kill' models.[44] This has led many UK firms to adjust, and even discard, lockstep, a reflection of how leveraged finance has become so central to their business models.[45] UK firms have, however, nevertheless found it difficult to hire and retain rainmaker partners given the strength of the US dollar against sterling in recent years.[46] As a consequence, US firms, on the whole, have increased their prominence in the field, whilst the status of the Magic Circle and other UK firms in the field has diminished following a sustained onslaught on their principal resource—their most profitable partners.[47]

[40] Faulconbridge and Muzio (n 22) 650.

[41] 'Global London: The Big Long – Inside Sidley's Daring Attempt to Relaunch as a Private Equity Leader' (*Legal Business*, 8 April 2019) <https://www.legalbusiness.co.uk/analysis/the-big-long/> accessed 9 April 2019; Indap, Thompson, and Fontanella-Khan (n 28).

[42] 'Linklaters Becomes Latest Law Firm to Phase out "Lockstep" Pay Model | Financial Times' <https://www.ft.com/content/eed76b45-cca4-474e-a451-127fc62eb702> accessed 17 July 2023.

[43] Indap, Thompson, and Fontanella-Khan (n 28).

[44] James Fontanella-Khan, Sujeet Indap, and Barney Thompson, 'The Dawn of the Superstar Lawyer' *Financial Times* (9 April 2018) <https://www.ft.com/content/b9c96d04-376c-11e8-8eee-e06bde01c544> accessed 30 July 2018.

[45] 'Blame Private Equity for the End of London Lawyers' Lockstep' *Financial Times* (5 January 2022).

[46] 'UK's "Magic Circle" Law Firms Struggle to Grow in US amid Sinking Pound' *Financial Times* (11 October 2022) <https://www.ft.com/content/fab70e6e-52fb-4f70-ba82-5f4880545426> accessed 17 July 2023.

[47] James Fontanella-Khan, Sujeet Indap, and Barney Thompson, 'How a Private Equity Boom Fuelled the World's Biggest Law Firm' *Financial Times* (6 June 2019) <https://www.ft.com/content/

That US firms are winning the turf war is not simply due to their ability to offer higher levels of remuneration, however. US firms have taken strategic advantage of the new field conditions created by macro-level forces and events impacting the field since the mid-2000s, particularly the convergence in loan and bond market terms that I explore in Chapter 8. US firms were historically more familiar with US high-yield-bond terms and structures, and they have been able to successfully sell this expertise in a new market, Europe. Further, they mostly control the relationships with the dominant US private equity houses—the US market has historically dominated global transaction volume in terms of its size, and its largest players have now themselves gone global.[48] The US firms had long established relationships with these private equity sponsors in the US and when these sponsors became more active in the European market from the mid-2000s, US law firms successfully transported these relationships to Europe.[49] From this platform, they have been able to develop close relationships with many of the major European and other non-US private equity sponsors.

The turf war in this field of practice is evidenced by the schism that has appeared in who acts for who in the leveraged finance practice area field. As recently as 2009, John Flood observed that law firms constantly switched between acting for bank lenders and their borrowers.[50] However, this is no longer the case in the leveraged finance practice area field. A bifurcation of the field has occurred where lawyers, and increasingly firms, tend to act only ever for the private equity sponsors.

The bank lawyers are mostly concentrated in the Magic Circle firms, plus a small number of other leading UK firms (as well as a handful of US firms with offices in London who have decided not to compete with the elite US firms for sponsor-side work).[51] The private equity lawyers that act for the most powerful private equity sponsors, on the other hand, many of whom trained with Magic Circle and other large English firms, are mostly situated in a handful of elite US firms.[52]

Due to the economic, skill set, and client relationship deficiencies I have noted, the Magic Circle and other leading UK firms are almost entirely excluded from the competition for sponsor-side work, and hence have been deprived of the

13696928-86d5-11e9-a028-86cea8523dc2> accessed 9 August 2021; Fontanella-Khan, Indap, and Thompson (n 44).

[48] Gilligan and Wright (n 11) 45,70.

[49] Although the largest US private equity sponsors began to establish offices in London in the 1990s, Gilligan and Wright (n 11) 45,70.

[50] John Flood, 'Ambiguous Allegiances in the Lawyer-Client Relationship: The Case of Bankers and Lawyers' https://www.researchgate.net/publication/228135498_Ambiguous_Allegiances_in_the_Lawyer-Client_Relationship_The_Case_of_Bankers_and_Lawyers accessed 9 june 2023.

[51] This is a generalization; some US firms do focus on bank-side work. However, in the large-cap market in Europe, no UK firm has been able to focus solely on acting for the leading private equity sponsors.

[52] Often having been hired on remuneration packages exceeding what is on offer at English firms, see Fontanella-Khan, Indap, and Thompson (n 44).

opportunity for prestige and elite status in this field, as well as for the most lucrative work. Their choice has been to accept the less prestigious and remunerative role as designated counsel for the arranging banks or leave the field entirely. This outcome is encapsulated by private equity lawyer [#35]'s observation that the US firms have 'cannibalised the Magic Circle's business'.

2.4 Leveraged buyouts explained

The term 'leveraged finance' broadly denotes the purchase of assets where a significant proportion of the purchase price is funded by debt, or 'leverage', as opposed to equity or cash.[53] In a leveraged buyout, or LBO, the leverage is applied, together with a relatively small amount of equity, in the purchase of an established business, with the private equity sponsor commonly taking a controlling interest in the business, or at least a substantial minority shareholding, by buying out the existing shareholders.[54] These loans may finance anywhere between 50 per cent and 90 per cent of the purchase price of the target business and are typically arranged and underwritten by investment banks.[55] These acquisition loans typically become the obligation of the acquired business to repay.

So, what are private equity sponsors? Their typical legal structure is shown in Figure 2.1. They tend to be funds which are legally organised as limited partnerships (LPs) to maximise tax advantages from the perspective of the managers and the investors of the LP. The general partner of the LP is usually a corporate entity. The investors, typically comprising banks, insurance companies, sovereign wealth funds, high net-worth individuals, and other sophisticated investors, invest as limited partners in the limited partnership and have limited rights to influence the choice of investments and other strategic decisions made by the managers of the fund acting through the general partner.[56]

Private equity sponsors typically invest in the common equity, the ordinary shares, of private and public companies[57] in leveraged buyouts.[58]

[53] Or the leverage can be added later i.e., used to 'refinance' existing assets, originally purchased with equity.

[54] As distinguished from venture or growth capital which is an investment aimed at funding a fledgling business—or a large publicly listed company which is then converted into a private company—'taken private'. Most leveraged buyouts around the world are of private companies, however, Gilligan and Wright (n 11) 2.

[55] 'Leveraged Loan Primer' (*S&P Global, 2020*) 9 <https://www.spglobal.com/marketintelligence/en/pages/toc-primer/lcd-primer> accessed 26 July 2022.

[56] Gilligan and Wright (n 11) 4.

[57] They hence engage in a narrower range of investment activities than hedge funds.

[58] A leveraged buyout need not necessarily feature a private equity sponsor. A listed or private company may also decide to use a significant proportion of bank or other debt to acquire a target company. The purchase of a controlling interest in Manchester United by the Glazer family in 2005 was structured as a leveraged buyout, for example, Ola Olatawura, 'The Theatre of Dreams - Manchester United FC, Globalization, and International Sports Law' (2005) 16 Marquette Sports Law Review 287.

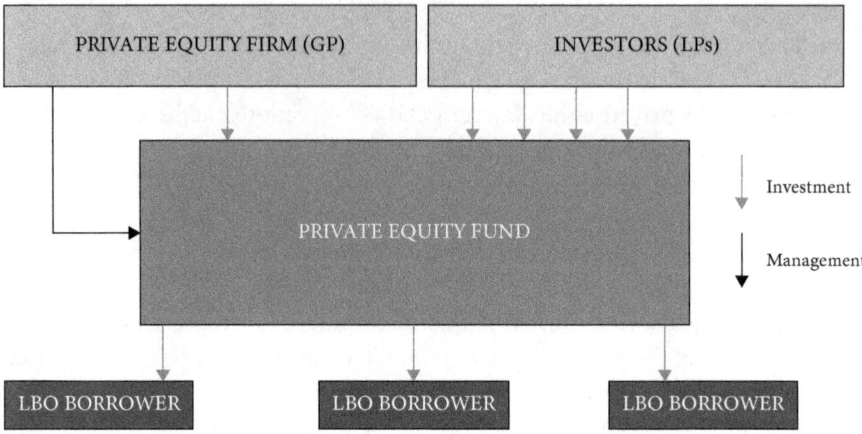

Figure 2.1 The legal structure of a private equity fund.

LBOss hence result in the acquired business taking on high levels of indebtedness, typically measured by reference to a ratio of gross debt to earnings before interest, tax, depreciation and amortisation (EBITDA) of around three times or higher, often many times higher.[59] In the United Kingdom, LBOs do not have an especially long history. Their emergence can largely be traced to changes introduced by the Companies Act 1981. For the first time, private equity sponsors were able to grant their lenders security over a target group's assets and cashflows, and offer guarantees from the target group, in each case to support the acquisition finance.[60] This meant banks were willing, given their first-ranking, 'senior secured' status, to lend a significant proportion of the purchase price for what would become, post-buyout, a highly leveraged, and thus relatively high risk, business.[61] Over in the US, probably the most famous private equity-backed leveraged buyout—Kohlberg, Kravis, Roberts' (KKR) US $24 billion buyout of the tobacco and foods group RJR Nabisco in 1988—brought this emergent deal type to the world's attention.[62]

[59] Gilligan and Wright (n 11) 172, 192, 194. Leveraged loans may be applied for other purposes, such as refinancing and dividend recapitalizations (where the debt is drawn to fund the payment of a dividend to the private equity sponsor). There is no accepted definition of a leveraged loan. 'Vulnerabilities Associated with Leveraged Loans and Collateralised Loan Obligations' (n 4) 5. Other features of leveraged loans might also be a sub-investment grade rating of the loan (below BBB) and high interest pricing (a margin of 125 basis points and above). ibid. 'Leveraged Loan Primer' (n 55).

[60] This 'financial assistance' had previously been illegal. Albeit to be legal, such financial assistance was subject to a series of conditions. Gilligan and Wright (n 11) 22.

[61] In a leveraged buyout the senior secured lenders are those lenders which are entitled to get paid first in an insolvency scenario, with the equity providers paid last, potentially with a range of junior creditors ranked hierarchically in between. They are thus 'first ranking'.

[62] See Bryan Burrough and John Helyar, '*Barbarians at the Gate: The Fall of RJR Nabisco*' (Harper 1989).

The focus of this book is on large-scale—commonly referred to as 'large-cap' (as in large capital) —leveraged buyout transactions in Europe, featuring upwards of US$500 million of debt and which are arranged and underwritten by leading investment banks and then widely syndicated to other banks and institutional investors. These transactions tend to involve the world's leading international law firms acting for either the private equity sponsor or its banks. Although transactions with a value over £100m make up around a tenth of total leveraged buyouts by number, they constitute over 90 per cent by value.[63] Media coverage and even academic research has been biased towards this segment of the market, especially 'public to private' transactions (public company acquisitions).[64] The majority of the participants in this book were most actively involved in the large-cap market.

Given the focus on large-cap transactions, the examples I evaluate in this book may not be entirely reflective of other segments of the market, where practices and documentary approaches may be different. 'Mid-market' transactions are smaller, say US$30 million to US$500 million, and tend not to be widely syndicated to a broader range of investors. Further, arrangers and lenders in the mid-market often comprise smaller commercial, as opposed to investment, banks, and 'direct lenders', such as private credit funds who tend to 'take and hold' the loan exposure, as opposed to arranging, underwriting, and then selling down their exposure under the loan, although a smaller scale syndication may occur.[65] The participants in my study that had some experience of the mid-market reported that typical documents seen in this segment of the market tended to look and feel different to those in the large-cap market, for example, being more balanced between the interests of lenders and borrowers.

Leverage plays a critical role in a buyout. It broadly achieves two objectives: enhanced returns for, and a transfer of risk away from, the private equity sponsor.[66] The LBO can thus be seen as a financing technique: enhanced returns using significant leverage, plus the adoption of a tax efficient structure, which delivers both financial and risk benefits for the equity holder, the private equity sponsor.[67]

The first purpose of leverage is to amplify the potential returns for the private equity sponsor as the equity investor; provided the purchased assets increase in value, the equity investor, not the lender, captures most of the upside.[68] Put simply, the more debt that is used the less equity the private equity sponsor needs to invest

63 Gilligan and Wright (n 11) 29–30.

64 ibid 30, 37–39.

65 Having said that, more recently direct lenders have participated more actively in the large cap market. See eg the US$3.5bn financing of the Access Group in 2022, 'Lenders Aren't Happy - and Lawyers Are in the Ethical Firing Line' (*The Lawyer | Legal insight, benchmarking data and jobs*, 6 October 2022) <https://www.thelawyer.com/lenders-arent-happy-and-lawyers-are-in-the-ethical-firing-line/> accessed 6 October 2022.

66 For a succinct summary, see Paterson (n 11) 658.

67 Larreur (n 11) 4–7, 13.

68 Gilligan and Wright (n 11) 21; Elisabeth de Fontenay, 'Do the Securities Laws Matter - The Rise of the Leveraged Loan Market' (2013) 39 Journal of Corporation Law 725, 739.

from its own resources. Since the debt provided by lenders is cheaper than equity, it provides enhanced returns for the private equity sponsors as equity holders because the return on debt is fixed, meaning the equity investor captures pretty much the entirety of the capital gain in the value of the investment.[69]

The private equity sponsor will seek to generate an annual return on its investment (the 'internal rate of return' or 'IRR') of 20% or more, sufficient to meet interest payments on the debt used to acquire the target business and refinance any existing bank facilities the target has, and to pay itself an ongoing dividend. Ultimately, the private equity sponsor's goal is to exit its investment in the target company in a time frame of between three and ten years, having made a significant profit on its investment, through a sale or listing of the target company on a recognized stock exchange.[70] To make a profit on exit, the price received by the private equity sponsor must be higher than the cost of the private equity sponsor 's equity plus the interest costs of the borrowed funds.[71]

The tax treatment of the private equity sponsor's return, or 'carried interest', where it is treated as capital and not income in many jurisdictions and thus benefits from lower tax rates, is controversial.[72] Private equity is also widely perceived as deliberately short term, with strategies focussed on loading the target company with significant amounts of debt and then 'asset-stripping'—selling off assets and 'spinning-off' businesses in order to pay down the acquisition debt—as opposed to strategies aimed at generating long-term growth.[73] John Gilligan and Mike Wright argue that the empirical evidence suggests that the profits made by private equity investment tend to come from improvements in management and operational aspects of the business, as opposed to from the use of leverage, however.[74] Marc Moore argues that the view of private equity sponsors as asset strippers is outdated; from the 2000s, private equity sponsors developed their industry-specific, as opposed to purely financial, expertise in order that they might promote growth not through financial engineering but rather by addressing 'latent deficiencies that constrain the development of a portfolio company's business' or by simply offering 'an alternative entrepreneurial perspective on any one or more strategic issues'.[75]

[69] Gilligan and Wright (n 11) 16. Larreur (n 11) 4–7, 13.

[70] John Armour and others, *Principles of Financial Regulation* (OUP 2016) 492. Gilligan and Wright (n 11) 4, 237.

[71] See 'Leveraged Finance - How Leverage Is Used to Increase Equity Returns' (*Corporate Finance Institute*) <https://corporatefinanceinstitute.com/resources/knowledge/finance/what-is-leveraged-finance/> accessed 12 June 2019.

[72] See eg 'Reviled Tax Break for Private Equity Proves Hard to Kill Off' *Financial Times* (30 July 2022).

[73] Although Gilligan and Wright point out there is little evidence to support this claim. Gilligan and Wright (n 11); Marc T Moore, 'Private Equity Buyouts and Corporate Governance: Contrasting the "80s and 00s"' 13 <https://sites.uclouvain.be/cpdr-refgov/publications/Working%20Papers/Corporate%20Governance%20-%20CG_(10.08.2007_19h08)_WP-CG-17.pdf>.

[74] Gilligan and Wright (n 11) 284.

[75] Moore (n 73) 13.

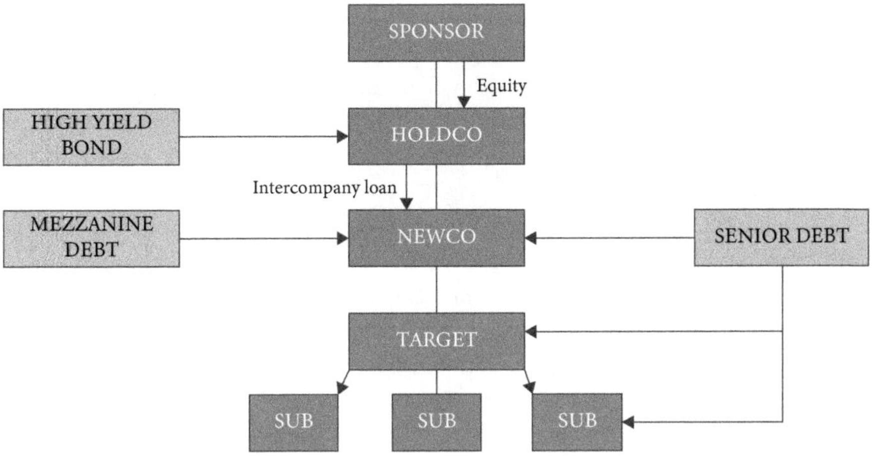

Figure 2.2 A leveraged buyout presented diagrammatically.

In employing leverage, a private equity sponsor is not only seeking to enhance its returns but also to transfer risk to its lenders. Because the lenders are funding the bulk of the purchase price, the risk of the LBO failing is largely transferred to them.[76] This is because of the non-recourse nature of the financing structure. This isolates those equity holders from the risk of the non-performance of those assets.[77] The private equity sponsor is only risking its own equity investment and puts up no other collateral for the debt. The lenders are exposed to the performance of the underlying asset, the target group, and its business, so that the repayment of the loan depends on those underlying assets, and they typically have no recourse back to the private equity sponsor if the target group fails. The lender, therefore, must assess the likelihood that the business of the target company will be successful and generate enough cash to service the interest payments, whilst also considering the reputation and track record of successful versus failed investments the private equity sponsor has previously made.

To achieve this non-recourse structure, which transfers most of the risk to the lenders, the private equity sponsor (shown in Figure 2.2 as 'Sponsor') will, often via one or more layers of offshore investment vehicles, invest in an SPV (presented in Figure 2.2 as 'Holdco') which itself owns all the shares in the SPV borrower (shown in Figure 2.2 as 'Newco'). Newco makes the bid for the target company and is 'sponsored' (i.e., owned and funded) by the private equity sponsor.[78]

[76] 'Leveraged Loan Primer' (n 55) 9.

[77] The advantage for the lenders in that they are not exposed to the risks of the other assets and liabilities of the sponsors.

[78] Gilligan and Wright (n 11) 135. The borrower may in fact be a separate 'debtco', a subsidiary of Newco, to allow share security over the shares on the debtco to be granted by the newco. ibid.

This layering of companies, usually incorporated in low-tax jurisdictions, ensures that the lenders will have no recourse back to the private equity sponsor in the event the financing defaults, which will usually be because the target group has not met financial projections. The borrower SPV acquires the target company in the buyout, which (together with any subsidiaries, shown in Figure 2.2 as 'Sub') in turn becomes its subsidiary.

The make-up of the debt facilities for large leveraged buyouts has changed significantly since the mid-2000s. Prior to this, buyouts were mainly financed by a single senior facility, although it was not uncommon for the leveraged loan contract to split the debt into senior and junior tranches, with the senior debt paid out first in the event of the insolvency of the target company. The junior tranche was typically referred to as 'mezzanine debt' (shown in Figure 2.2 as 'Mezzanine Debt') because of its ranking upon an insolvency between the senior debt and the equity in the target company's capital structure.

As well as senior secured loans and mezzanine debt, leveraged buyout financings in the large-cap market in Europe have, since the mid-2000s, commonly included a bond component (shown in Figure 2.2 as 'High Yield Bond').[79] High yield bonds are publicly traded debt instruments with a higher rate of interest than 'investment grade' bonds (those rated as low risk by a recognised credit rating agency such as Standard and Poor's or Moody's), and that often do not share in the transaction's security package. Facilities may now also include a secured, subordinated tranche, often referred to as 'second lien', either in bond or loan form.[80]

European leveraged loans are traditionally considered senior secured, or 'first lien', instruments, ranking them above other creditors of the borrower and its subsidiaries.[81] Senior secured debt, distinguished from junior and subordinated debt, denotes lenders which are first ranking in all respects; they enjoy priority over the borrower group's other debt in the ordinary course, including in the receipt of interest and other payments, and then priority over the proceeds of security enforcement, including asset sales, in a distressed scenario and have a driving seat in any restructuring negotiations. These priority relationships are normally recorded in a legally enforceable contract, the intercreditor agreement.[82]

So, as well as advising their clients on the terms of the loan documents, leveraged finance lawyers will also advise their clients on the terms of the security and

[79] High yield, or 'junk' bonds, trace their roots back to the 1980s in the US where they were introduced—by Michael Milken at now defunct Drexel Burnham Lambert, Glenn Yago, *Junk Bonds: How High Yield Securities Restructured Corporate America* (Illustrated edition, OUP 1990). Cited in de Fontenay (n 68) 741. Gilligan and Wright (n 11) 172–173.

[80] Larreur (n 11) 45–46.

[81] See eg Ares, 'European Leveraged Loans: An Allocation That's Here to Stay' (2022) 3, 9 <https://www.aresmgmt.com/sites/default/files/2022-06/TCE-00171_Euro-Loans-White-Paper-vF.pdf>. Some leveraged loan structures even feature senior term loans and revolving credit facilities which enjoy 'super senior status'. Here, the revolving facility lender will be paid out from security enforcement recoveries before the term loan lenders, ibid 9; Gilligan and Wright (n 11) 211.

[82] Gilligan and Wright (n 11) 171.

intercreditor documents. The security package may include, for example, mortgages and charges over shares, real property, bank accounts, and revenue streams. These security interests will be recorded in the security documents. The banks were traditionally granted comprehensive security over all, or substantially all, the borrower group's assets, though this is no longer the case, for the reasons considered in Chapter 7. The secured assets—of significantly greater value than the loans they were making—could then be realized if necessary upon the borrower's insolvency to repay the loan. This security package hence impacted both the size of the loan the banks were willing to make and its pricing.[83]

Large-scale LBOs often involve an auction process, with multiple and intense work streams, where private equity sponsors are invited to submit bids for a target company and its subsidiaries, with vendors commonly pressing for a swift conclusion at the highest achievable sale price.[84] M&A lawyers advise the private equity sponsor on the acquisition aspects, which will include the drafting and negotiation of the share purchase agreement and legal due diligence with respect to the target group. The bank lawyers and the private equity lawyers will typically advise their respective clients on the financing aspects of the transaction structuring, its legal risks, and the suite of finance, security and intercreditor documents, often working to short transaction timelines, as the debt financing which supports the bid must usually be in place when the bid is submitted.

Notwithstanding their senior secured position, LBOs have always involved significant credit risk for lenders. In 'Eat What You Kill', Mitt Regan describes an LBO that went wrong as 'typical of buyouts in the 1980s' because the interest payments drained the company 'of the funds it needed for working capital and long-term investment.'[85] It is not uncommon for a target company to experience financial difficulties after being the subject of an LBO since it is typically left with high levels of debt to service.[86] These high interest payment burdens are what make LBOs risky for lenders; they are highly sensitive to any deterioration in the revenues of the target company. In a distressed sale or insolvency procedure of a company acquired by way of an LBO, the lenders will often fail to recoup the total amount they have lent.[87] With the emergence of covenant-lite structures in the period immediately prior to the global financial crisis, in 2005-07, the risks of LBOs increased even further for lenders.[88] According to Elisabeth de Fontenay, 'the adoption and

[83] Gilligan and Wright (n 11) 171, 189, 249; Sarah Paterson and Rafal Zakrzewski, *McKnight, Paterson, & Zakrzewski on the Law of International Finance* (Second, OUP 2017) 733, 815–816.

[84] Gilligan and Wright (n 11) 141–142.

[85] Regan (n 32) 78.

[86] Gilligan and Wright (n 11) 284.

[87] See generally, Paterson (n 11).

[88] Paterson suggests there were no covenant-lite deals in Europe before the global financial crisis, ibid 659. However, it appears there were at least some 'covenant-loose' deals, with perhaps one maintenance covenant, a ratio of debt to EBITDA. Eg, KKR's £11.9bn bid for Alliance Boots in 2007, see 'KKR Presents Mouth-Watering Boots Debt' *Financial Times* (6 July 2007); 'RLPC-Boots LBO Loans Test Covenant-Lite Model ' *Reuters* (30 March 2007) <https://www.reuters.com/article/

rapid proliferation of "covenant-lite" loans is the most discussed (and criticized) manifestation of the loosening of covenants in leveraged loans'.[89]

Arguably, the most important loan terms are the financial covenants. Chief among them is the leverage ratio, effectively an obligation on the borrower group to ensure its net debt does not exceed an agreed multiple of its EBITDA (meaning the borrower group's earnings before interest, tax, depreciation and amortisation).[90] Prior to the mid-2000s, these typically took the form of 'maintenance covenants' that were tested periodically, for example, every three months, allowing lenders to monitor the borrower's financial health.[91] Banks were specialists in monitoring the credit and other risks associated with borrowers, seeing it as part of their ongoing relationship.[92] In any event, as banks are heavily regulated and supervised, close monitoring of their loan exposures was necessary, and the costs of doing so factored into their business model.[93]

The covenant-lite loan structure has limited the number, and frequency of testing, of the financial covenants typically included in European leveraged financings. Prior to the emergence of covenant-lite loan structures, the real benefit for lenders of a breach of covenant was not the acceleration and enforcement right itself, but the early warning signal it gave them, and the incentive the triggering of these rights gave to the borrower to negotiate a financial and/or operational restructuring of the target group with the lenders to stave off insolvency. Covenant-lite structures mean that lenders can no longer rely on the early warning signals and enforcement rights they once had when the borrower is spiralling towards insolvency.[94] According to de Fontenay, covenant-lite loans mean the lenders 'entirely relinquish this control over the borrower'.[95] This conclusion is supported by emerging empirical evidence that covenant-lite loans leave lenders facing the risk of lower recoveries in the event of the borrower's default.[96]

alliance-boots-takeover-loan-idUKL3048613020070330> accessed 20 February 2023. On the increase in lender risk, see Matthew T Billett and others, 'Bank Skin in the Game and Loan Contract Design: Evidence from Covenant-Lite Loans' (2016) 51 Journal of Financial and Quantitative Analysis 839, 840; Mitchell Berlin, Greg Nini, and Edison G Yu, 'Concentration of Control Rights in Leveraged Loan Syndicates' (2020) 137 Journal of Financial Economics 249; de Fontenay (n 68) 745.

89 de Fontenay (n 68) 745.
90 Larreur (n 11) 42.
91 Paterson (n 11) 657–659. de Fontenay (n 68) 736.
92 de Fontenay (n 68) 736.
93 ibid 727.
94 Paterson (n 11).
95 de Fontenay (n 68) 745.
96 'Leveraged Finance: Lenders Blinded By Covenant-lite? Highlighting Data On Loan Covenants And Ultimate Recovery Rates' <https://www.spglobal.com/ratings/en/research/articles/180412-leveraged-finance-lenders-blinded-by-covenant-lite-highlighting-data-on-loan-covenants-and-ultimate-recovery-rates-10493116> accessed 2 July 2022. Cited in 'Vulnerabilities Associated with Leveraged Loans and Collateralised Loan Obligations' (n 4) 8.

The principal problem with loans featuring covenant-lite are twofold: they do not address the risk to lenders of excessive borrowing, and, as Sarah Paterson has observed, they lead to financially distressed borrowers holding lenders 'at bay long after they should have begun a restructuring process'.[97] Covenant-lite involves 'incurrence'—as opposed to maintenance—testing. This means the financial metric in the covenant is only tested upon the borrower choosing to take a given action, for example, when incurring further debt, paying a dividend, making an acquisition, or other specified event. Since these are events within the control of the borrower, it can ensure the covenant is not tested at an inconvenient moment.[98] This follows the approach traditionally seen in high yield bonds.[99] Paterson notes there is a paradox here; leveraged loans are highly sensitive to any deterioration in the borrower's financial condition and ability to service a heavy-interest payment burden, as compared to more conventional, less highly leveraged, corporate loans.[100] Yet under less-risky corporate loans, the borrower is subject to the more rigorous testing regime than in high-risk leveraged lending. This problem for lenders is typically compounded by private equity sponsors insisting on significant 'headroom', often in the region of 20–40 per cent, so even when the covenant is tested the financial metric is set so high that the borrower's EBITDA can drop significantly without breaching the covenant.[101]

Covenant-lite loans have become the dominant form adopted in large-cap leveraged buyouts.[102] Concerns as to the resulting weakening of lender protections have been raised by the Bank of England.[103] However, this book shows how the loosening of loan covenants that is exemplified by covenant-lite is not simply the consequence of market conditions. Lawyers have played a critical role in, first, ensuring that covenant-lite became the dominant loan structure seen in large scale leveraged buyouts in Europe, and then by further undermining the protections for lenders in leveraged finance documents and structures.

[97] Paterson (n 11) 665.

[98] Often also referred to as a 'springing covenant', 'Vulnerabilities Associated with Leveraged Loans and Collateralised Loan Obligations' (n 4) 8.

[99] ibid 7–8.

[100] Paterson (n 11) 658.

[101] Gilligan and Wright (n 11) 216.

[102] Between 2015 and 2018, covenant-lite loans increased from 27.2 per cent to 83.3 per cent of the market, Jimmie Franklin, 'Covenant-lite Leaves Borrowers Happy and Lenders Gloomy' [2019] International Financial Law Review <https://www.proquest.com/docview/2286662340/abstract/C5A29494C3504C9BPQ/1> accessed 2 July 2022.

[103] 'House of Commons - Treasury - Tenth Report', 24 July 2007 <https://publications.parliament.uk/pa/cm200607/cmselect/cmtreasy/567/56702.htm> accessed 18 July 2022. Cited in Joanna Gray, 'Lawyers and Systemic Risk in Finance: Could (and Should) the Legal Profession Contribute to Macroprudential Regulation?' (2016) 19 Legal Ethics 122, 126.

2.5 Conclusion

Having now provided important background and context as to the markets in which leveraged finance lawyers work, and introduced the roles that they play in them, in the next chapter I introduce my case study data and explore what it demonstrates as to the practices and logics of bank lawyers in the leveraged finance practice setting.

3
Bank Lawyers: Practices and Logics

3.1 Introduction

In this chapter, I explore what my empirical data reveals about the practices and logics of the lawyers that act for the banks which arrange and underwrite leveraged finance transactions, which I refer to as the 'bank lawyers'. Robert Rosen has stated that sophisticated clients of large firms want their lawyers to 'add value' by acting as hybrid legal and business consultants, with a key element of this role being assessing and then managing risk for the client.[1] In the leveraged finance practice area, bank lawyers are mostly not performing this role; they tend not to undertake a comprehensive assessment of the potential weaknesses in the loan terms drafted by the private equity lawyers which they review on behalf of their bank clients. They may not flag and then challenge, for example, terms that materially erode lender protections and/or which might contain loopholes for private equity lawyers to take advantage of in the future. To understand the factors driving this phenomenon, it is necessary to explore a foundational, and controversial, practice of the leveraged finance practice area: lawyer designation, and the unique practice area logics of which it is a tangible expression.

This chapter reveals how the practice of designation is evidence of a key logic of the leveraged finance practice area field. Bank lawyers and private equity lawyers share an understanding that a perceived misstep by a bank lawyer might lead to them being boycotted for future designation work. The bank lawyers have adjusted their behaviour in response to this *survival logic,* and this chapter explores the series of subtle dispositions, practices, and strategies that bank lawyers have developed. They are expected, for example, to be 'commercial', but whether they meet this expectation is subjectively determined by the private equity lawyers. Private equity lawyers get to decide because they are seen as the owners of this market and, under this *owns-the-market* logic, they get to define the boundaries of the bank lawyers' role.

The survival logic is closely connected to, and works in combination with, another key logic of the field, the *cleared-the-market* logic. Influenced by this logic, bank lawyers narrowly interpret their role, confining themselves to contesting

[1] Robert Eli Rosen, 'We're All Consultants Now: How Changes in Client Organizational Strategies Influences Change in the Organization of Corporate Legal Services' (2002) 44 Arizona Law Review 637, 658–60.

terms proposed by the private equity lawyers which can clearly be considered to present a distribution risk, in that the inclusion of the term may obstruct a successful distribution (syndication) of the loan, as opposed to identifying the range of credit and other risks for lenders which may lurk in the proposed terms. Whilst the survival logic constrains the bank lawyers' inclination to offer robust challenge to the terms proposed by the private equity lawyers, the cleared-the-market logic provides them with a convenient self-justification for adopting this stance.

This chapter is arranged as follows. It begins with a description of what lawyer designation is, and how it has spawned a series of referral relationships between bank lawyers and private equity lawyers. I explain how these dynamics have led to the emergence of the survival logic. There follows a description of how bank lawyers adjust their behaviour in response to this logic, adopting strategies designed to 'manage the banks' towards acceptance of the private equity sponsors' terms. The chapter then concludes.

3.2 The lawyer designation model

> I always have influence. I am literally picking the banks' lawyers. In reality, if you want to track where their mandate comes from, it's me.

Private equity lawyer [#36]'s observation reflects how, because of the lawyer designation model, private equity lawyers now play a pivotal role in the bank lawyer selection process. In this section, I describe this foundational practice of the field in detail; I explain what the lawyer designation model is, and why it can be seen as evidence of the survival logic.

(a) The model explained

Historically, bank lawyers sourced their work via their own and their firm's relationships with banks. Since the mid-2000s, due to the emergence of the lawyer designation model, they now source their work through their relationships with private equity sponsors, and/or the private equity sponsor's regular legal counsel, who effectively appoint them to act for the banks on leveraged buyout transactions. Under the designation model, the banks typically have little or no influence over the choice of the law firm or lawyer that will act for them on a transaction.[2]

[2] Alex Newman, 'Linklaters Falls out of Favour with Goldman's City Leveraged Finance Team' (*LegalWeek*, 2014) <https://www.law.com/legal-week/2014/08/04/linklaters-falls-out-of-favour-with-goldmans-city-leveraged-finance-team/> accessed 12 October 2019.

Private equity lawyer [#37] said 'the banks don't really have any say. They perhaps have a veto right. Maybe. But not really, to be honest.'

Designation has its roots in the long-standing convention that a borrower pays a bank lender's legal fees.[3] This 'borrower pays' convention is common across lending markets.[4] The continued existence of this convention in the leveraged finance field is anachronistic, reflecting a time when the arranging banks held the balance of power over private equity-owned borrowers in the negotiation of leveraged loan terms. This balance of power has since been reversed. As market conditions shifted in their favour from the mid-2000s onwards, rather than refusing to continue to pay, private equity sponsors instead insisted that if they were expected to pay for the bank's lawyers, then they—or more often their lawyers on their behalf—should also be able to choose them. Private equity lawyer [#7] said:

> It was the KKRs[5] of the world that started to say to banks, 'Well, if we're paying the fees on a leveraged finance transaction for your lawyers, then we want to know that they are sensible lawyers. We want people that are going to work with us.'

This observation encapsulates the dominant practice area logics of which designation is a tangible expression: that private equity sponsors and their lawyers expect something in return from the bank lawyers they select. Bank lawyers, for their part, understand and accept this bargain. They have adjusted the way in which they think about and carry out their role to match the expectations of the private equity sponsors and their lawyers who designate them.

Designation by private equity lawyers, where the private equity sponsor effectively delegates the choice of bank lawyer to its external legal counsel, appears to be the more common variant of the practice.[6] Some private equity sponsors, those with an internal, well-resourced financing-focussed team,[7] for example, may take a more prominent role in the bank lawyer selection process, and might initially propose a bank lawyer to act for the banks on a transaction. But mostly, the power to designate is exercised by private equity lawyers, as opposed to private equity sponsors. Even where the private equity sponsor takes the lead in proposing a lawyer or firm to act for the banks, private equity lawyers generally still exercise a veto right

[3] Strictly, the arranging banks pay the legal fees of their legal counsel and are reimbursed by the borrower in an amount equal to those fees pursuant to a costs indemnity in the loan agreement.

[4] It is seen in the corporate lending world, and even in the residential mortgage market, for example.

[5] KKR is a leading global private equity sponsor, headquartered in the US, 'KKR Today' (*KKR*, 2 June 2014) <https://www.kkr.com/kkr-today> accessed 26 June 2023.

[6] At least in the large-cap market, see eg, 'The Powerful City Lawyer at The Center of a Private Equity Storm' (*Bloomberg.com*, 16 February 2023) <https://www.bloomberg.com/news/articles/2023-02-16/the-powerful-city-lawyer-at-the-center-of-a-private-equity-storm> accessed 16 February 2023.

[7] Larger private equity sponsors may have a 'capital markets' team that leads the financing, as opposed to the M&A aspects of the transaction. Members of this team may have developed their own relationships with banks lawyer (they are often former bank lawyers themselves).

over the appointment, reflected in this comment by private equity lawyer [#36]: 'If I had concerns, I could still blackball them.'

(b) The resulting referral relationships

Because of this lawyer-led form of designation, a series of preferred working relationships between private equity lawyers and firms, on the one hand, and bank lawyers and firms, on the other, have developed. These referral relationships are now an established structural characteristic of the leveraged finance practice area.[8] Individual bank lawyers have built long-standing and often highly lucrative designation relationships with individual private equity lawyers, who in some cases are equivalent, in terms of annual billings, to major corporate or financial institution clients of the bank lawyer's firm.[9]

The effects of these referral relationships can be seen in bank lawyer marketing strategies. Mitt Regan and Lisa Rohrer argue that corporate lawyers increasingly adopt selling skills to secure work from clients, in response to firm-level (meso) logics, such as the pressure to meet profit targets.[10] In the leveraged finance practice area field, bank lawyers are focussed on deploying these skills in developing close relationships with private equity lawyers, as if they were clients. Bank lawyer [#22] depicted these referral relationships as a direct consequence of designation: 'it's natural, all lender counsel will make a point of going around the market and just chatting and just being friends with the sponsor lawyers.'

On the other hand, bank lawyers do not spend much time building and maintaining their relationships with banks, which they see as a poor use of their time and other resources, even though these banks will be their direct clients on leveraged buyout transactions. They calculate that marketing activities directed at banks mostly do not help them win work, which they largely source through their referral relationships with private equity lawyers. Bank lawyer [#15] explained:

> You prioritise marketing to sponsors, and then to sponsor law firms, over banks. The odd bank is worth having a good relationship with on the basis they do have mandates to give out on occasion. Only the really big, most successful underwriting banks, the top three, probably fall into that category.

[8] A referral is broadly where a person has provided information to a solicitor which enables the solicitor to make an offer to the client to provide legal services, where the source of the information is not the client, see, 'Legal Aid, Sentencing and Punishment of Offenders Act 2012' s 56 (5) <https://www.legislation.gov.uk/ukpga/2012/10/section/56/enacted> accessed 27 February 2023.

[9] 'The Powerful City Lawyer at The Center of a Private Equity Storm' (n 6).

[10] Mitt Regan and Lisa H Rohrer, *BigLaw: Money and Meaning in the Modern Law Firm* (The University of Chicago Press 2020) 1.

The larger global investment banks, then, may hold—at best—a final veto power. Although in one reported instance, a major investment bank indicated it would no longer allow a particular firm to be designated to act for it,[11] banks rarely exercise such a veto right, mindful of jeopardizing their own relationship with the private equity sponsor.

Bank lawyers mostly market their services to the private equity lawyers with whom they have a referral relationship, or with whom they wish to establish a relationship. These private equity lawyers tend to be concentrated in the handful of private equity-focussed US law firms who largely control the award of designations for larger leveraged buyouts in Europe. These marketing activities can be both sporadic, ranging from a post-deal 'thank you lunch' or a game of golf, or a trip to a football match. But bank lawyer marketing also takes the form of something more akin to sophisticated and strategic client relationship management style initiatives. According to bank lawyer [#44]:

> There's a lot of marketing to sponsors and sponsor law firms. It will be lawyer to lawyer. Each sponsor law firm has probably got three or four top lawyers. And for each of those top lawyers we have a person within our firm who is responsible for that relationship.

Marketing activities like this between private equity lawyers and bank lawyers demonstrate how the referral arrangements at the heart of the lawyer designation model often share characteristics common to traditional lawyer-client relationships. Private equity lawyers can hence be considered as the bank lawyers' quasi-clients.

3.3 Logics evident in practices

The sections that follow explore how a series of interrelated logics can be discerned in the range of sometimes subtle and nuanced dispositions, practices, interactions, and strategies routinely adopted by bank lawyers.[12]

(a) The survival logic

Bank lawyers understand the nature of the bargain they have struck with the private equity lawyers who designate them. They mostly implicitly, but

[11] Newman (n 2).

[12] Patricia H Thornton, William Ocasio, and Michael Lounsbury, *The Institutional Logics Perspective: A New Approach to Culture, Structure, and Process* (OUP Oxford 2012) 132.

sometimes explicitly, agree not to be 'difficult', and to take a 'commercial' stance, in the negotiations of loan terms. They understand that the flow of designated work through their referral relationship with a given private equity lawyer may be temporarily or permanently interrupted if they do not hold up their end of the bargain. The private equity lawyer will simply go elsewhere on the next transaction.

In common with all institutional fields, the leveraged finance practice area has its own internal logics.[13] These are field-specific frames of reference which influence the behaviour of the actors situated within it.[14] These prevailing logics shape how bank lawyers make sense of their day-to-day practice context and then decide what is appropriate and legitimate conduct.[15] The field's logics provide both a constraint on bank lawyer action, and at the same time constitute the contextual framework within which they sense-make and make choices.[16] Bank lawyer activity in the field is hence regulated by these logics.[17]

The emergence of designation as an established practice prompted a shift in logics at the micro level which has fed directly into bank lawyer sense-making.[18] This is neatly reflected in private equity lawyer [#23]'s comment:

> Anybody who is bank-side these days knows, if they are problematic, if they cause unnecessary delay or problems for the sponsor, then they will not be instructed again.

That bank lawyers accept this bargain and consider that the private equity lawyers 'own the market' is reflected in how in my interviews they sometimes indicated a degree of sympathy with the private equity sponsors' and their lawyers' objectives; for example, bank lawyer [#30] said:

> You can see if you're paying for it you could feel with some justification that you don't want difficult, awkward people running up bills at your expense.

13 Barbara Townley, 'Bourdieu and Organizational Theory: A Ghostly Apparition?', *The Oxford Handbook of Sociology, Social Theory, & Organization Studies* (OUP 2014) 42–43; Paul J DiMaggio and Walter Powell W, 'Introduction', *The New Institutionalism in Organizational Analysis* (The University of Chicago Press 1991).

14 Thornton, Ocasio, and Lounsbury (n 12); Townley (n 13) 54. Thornton, Ocasio, and Lounsbury (n 12) 134–9. Richard Moorhead, Steven Vaughan, and Cristina Godinho, *In-House Lawyers' Ethics, Institutional Logics, Legal Risk and the Tournament of Influence* (Hart 2018) 207–08.

15 Royston Greenwood and CR Hinings, 'Radical Organizational Change', *The SAGE Handbook of Organisation Studies* (Second, SAGE Publications 2013) 819.

16 Thornton, Ocasio, and Lounsbury (n 12) 53–54.

17 Greenwood and Hinings (n 17) 819; Roger Friedland and Roger R Alford, 'Bringing Society Back In: Symbols, Practices, and Institutional Contradictions', *The New Institutionalism in Organizational Analysis* (The University of Chicago Press 1991).

18 Thornton, Ocasio, and Lounsbury (n 12) 129.

Here we see a practice—designation—accorded a common, shared understanding by actors in this practice area field. The survival logic can be seen, both, in how bank lawyers act and in how they express their motivations for that action.[19] This logic is manifested in the cultural identity of bank lawyers, the characteristics of which have evolved to enable them to continue to receive designated work from the private equity lawyers with whom they have established referral relationships.[20]

Bank lawyers are not simply responding to the structural conditions of their field, but also creatively influencing them, through their deliberate and strategic action.[21] Bank lawyers have adopted a series of dispositions, practices, and strategies in response to this survival logic, which together demonstrate that these referral relationships are founded in a tacit and commercially pragmatic recognition on the bank lawyer side that there is business merit in being on friendly terms with, and even potentially being viewed as accommodating towards, the private equity sponsors and their lawyers, in order to secure a continuing stream of designation work. I consider these dispositions, practices, and strategies in the next section.

(b) Being commercial

Historically, bank lawyers reviewed and evaluated the complex and lengthy terms of the loan, intercreditor, security and other finance documents, identifying and mitigating any credit and other risks for their bank clients arising from them. In practical terms, they no longer do so. Instead, there is a tacit understanding between bank lawyers and private equity lawyers that the bank lawyers will 'manage the banks' towards an acceptance of the private equity sponsor's proposed terms. Bank lawyers have absorbed the private equity lawyers' interpretation of the scope of their role, which is to ensure that the banks do not put up too much resistance in the negotiation of the loan terms proposed by the private equity lawyer. Private equity lawyer [#35] said:

> We expect deal management. And what I mean by that is, and I use the phrase advisedly, is managing their clients.

This is understood by bank lawyers to be the central element of their role. Future designated work depends on the bank lawyer successfully executing their end of the bargain, as demonstrated by this comment from bank lawyer [#38]:

[19] ibid 54.

[20] I use the term 'cultural identity' here to indicate members of a group who share a common understanding of their social context, David Matsumoto, 'Culture, Context, and Behavior' (2007) 75 Journal of Personality 1285, 1285.

[21] Thomas B. Lawrence and Roy Suddaby, 'Institutions and Institutional Work' in Stewart R Clegg,Cynthia Hardy, Thomas B Lawrence and Walter R Nord (eds), *The SAGE Handbook of Organization Studies* (SAGE 2006) 215 .

> Sponsors' counsel will say, 'you're not doing your job, you're supposed to be getting the banks over the line on this, this is why we hired you'.

A central expectation of private equity lawyers is that bank lawyers adopt a 'commercial' stance during negotiations. Sometimes, in my interviews other similar terms were used, such as 'constructive', and 'collaborative'. In response, the bank lawyers signal that they will not obstruct the swift progress of the transaction. Bank lawyer [#5] said the standard bank lawyer pitch to sponsors and their lawyers when seeking designations is 'We're sensible. We're commercial'.

It is understood on both sides that it is not a question of whether a bank lawyer has been objectively commercial; this question is subjectively determined by the private equity lawyer. They are seen as the owners of this market; under this owns-the-market logic, they define the boundaries of the bank lawyers' role. 'Being commercial' is hence a proxy for the bank lawyers adopting the dispositions and strategies I explore in this section that are designed to ensure they continue to receive a stream of designation work from the private equity lawyers they have referral relationships with.

Central to this shared understanding that bank lawyers are to be commercial is an expectation that bank lawyers will not raise, or permit their bank clients to raise, more than a handful of comments on the proposed terms. Private equity lawyer [#26] said the 'good' banking lawyers, the ones they liked to work with, will send an issues list to their bank clients formed of three segments:

> The list of points which are completely new, non-standard, off market or bespoke, the list of points which we see people regularly debating, and the list of points which for this and for a number of other sponsors have just cleared the market'.

They want bank lawyers to present their clients with lists, the shorter the better. Not advice. Bank lawyers should, according to private equity lawyer [#26], leave it to their client to decide whether to raise the issues with the private equity sponsors and their lawyers.

> That to us is the most important aspect of why people in places like [names two bank focussed firms] do a good job.

Bank lawyer [#15] said there is a shared understanding with private equity lawyers that they 'can only raise five or ten points'. Keeping the banks' list of issues on the documents short is understood by bank lawyers to match the expectations of private equity sponsors and their lawyers. It is thus a practice which demonstrates the powerful influence of both the survival and owns-the-market logics.

Keeping the issues list short requires that bank lawyers deploy subtle skills of persuasion in their dealings with their own bank clients. In 'The Practice of Law as a Confidence Game', Abraham Blumberg argued that the US defence attorneys he studied in the 1960s frequently achieved their self-interested objectives by employing 'a measure of sales-puff, which may range from an air of unbounding self-confidence, adequacy, and dominion over events, to that of complete arrogance'.[22] Bank lawyers are similarly engaged in a constant campaign to get their clients comfortable with the terms proposed. They deploy selling skills to do so. In my interviews with them, some bank lawyers were open about how they win designation work from the private equity lawyers they then face across the negotiation table on leveraged buyout transactions. They admitted they need to sell the terms proposed by the private equity lawyers to their bank clients as the price of survival in this market. Bank lawyer [#31] said they commonly adopt a stance with their bank clients of 'these are the reasons why you should be ok to do this'; in other words, according to bank lawyer [#31] 'I need to act as a salesman.'

Private equity lawyer [#35]'s observation indicates the shared understanding that this is an appropriate approach for bank lawyers to adopt:

> The better firms don't tell clients not to make points if they want to, if they're important, but I think they probably work with their clients to try and help them identify what are the 'most important points', put it like that.

On the other hand, it will often be in the interests of the bank client to keep its comments list short; it might present them in a more favourable light to the private equity sponsor, making them look helpful and cooperative, and so help them win the arranging and underwriting mandate, for example. Bank lawyers might appropriately consider it part of their role to assess whether the bank—when competing with other banks for the arranging mandate—is more likely to win the arranging mandate by making as few comments as possible on the transaction terms drafted by the private equity lawyers. Often these strategies and practices will reflect an appropriate exercise of professional judgement by the bank lawyer. Bank lawyers may point out other provisions in the documents that may give the bank some comfort on the relevant issue. Bank lawyer [#44] said:

> Getting a bank comfortable means you can offer another mitigant elsewhere in the document or you can explain how if you look at certain provisions together, in the round, you have a fair degree of protection.

However, amidst the cut-and-thrust of negotiations, such client-centred motives become intertwined and confused with the bank lawyer's wish to present themselves as accommodating and helpful to the private equity lawyers. When

[22] Abraham S Blumberg, 'The Practice of Law as Confidence Game - Organizational Cooptation of a Profession' (1966) 1 Law & Society Review 15, 26.

judgements are finely balanced, and perhaps also when they are not, the survival logic will likely exert influence in framing how bank lawyers exercise their discretion. The risk is that this objective of appearing to be 'commercial' assumes priority in the governing framework in which the bank lawyer makes decisions, and prevails over other, more client-centred and/or ethical objectives. This is particularly so when the survival logic works in combination with another powerful logic in persuading bank lawyers that being commercial and keeping the banks' comments on the proposed loan terms to a minimum is a legitimate objective in its own right.

(c) The cleared-the-market logic

Leslie Levin observes that lawyers are as vulnerable to confirmation bias, where they point to information that supports the propriety of their conduct and decision-making, and ignore information that suggests the opposite, as non-lawyers.[23] It is understood by bank lawyers and private equity lawyers, alike, that bank lawyers should not raise, or permit their bank clients to raise, comments which are perceived by the private equity lawyers to be outside the narrow range of points 'normally' raised on transactions.

What is normal is mostly determined according to a shared understanding of which terms have previously 'cleared the market'. Bank lawyer [#34] explained their approach:

> The starting point is, is this something that's in a previous precedent, and if that point has previously cleared the market, it becomes much harder to argue that this time around you should change it.

Once a 'new' term clears the market—where participations in the loans are successfully sold down by the initial arranging and underwriting banks to the long-term lenders via the syndication process—they become viewed by private equity and bank lawyers, alike, as market standard and consequently unchallengeable.

This cleared-the-market logic operates as a signal to bank lawyers that a term, however aggressive or uncertain it might first have appeared, or detached from the circumstances of the proposed transaction, need not, indeed should not, be challenged.[24] This is notwithstanding that the core business, legal and other characteristics of transactions tend to vary, often quite significantly. What lenders might have felt it appropriate to previously agree to on a large German buyout might not be appropriate for a small Eastern European deal,

[23] Leslie C Levin, 'Bad Apples, Bad Lawyers or Bad Decision-making: Lessons from Psychology and from Lawyers in the Dock Book Review Essay' (2009) 22 Georgetown Journal of Legal Ethics 1549, 1583–84, 1566; Loughrey (n 46) 746.

[24] Thornton, Ocasio, and Lounsbury (n 12) 149–50, 152.

for example. Or where one borrower is situated in a cyclical industry, versus another which is in a more stable sector. Although it might be appropriate in the context of deal *x* to include the term in question, it may be inappropriate in the context of deal *y*. In other words, whilst the survival logic constrains the bank lawyers' inclination to offer robust challenge in these circumstances, the cleared-the-market logic provides them with a convenient self-justification for this stance.

As I have already noted, private equity lawyers are seen as owners of this market; they define the boundaries of the bank lawyers' role. Here they define the narrow universe of issues that may be raised by bank lawyers on transactions. The cleared-the-market logic is apparent in this observation by private equity lawyer [#12], who described the process of negotiating terms as 'it's a case of "well, this has cleared the market, what else is left to discuss?"' Private equity lawyer [#23] said that when a bank lawyer challenges a provision in the documents because they believe it creates a material risk for the banks, but that provision has been seen in a previous successful transaction in the market, private equity lawyers tend to just say 'this has cleared the market', and 'we're not going to spend time fixing a document that has been agreed many times before'.

It is understood that a term which has previously cleared the market should not be challenged because its inclusion will not jeopardize the successful syndication of the loan. Bank lawyers do not tend to draw a clear distinction between a term which presents a 'distribution risk' issue—a term which presents a risk that the loans will not be successfully syndicated—versus terms which imply credit and other risks for the lenders. Often, this is because it is hard to distinguish them. Even if it has previously cleared the market in one deal, a provision that allows the borrower to raise more debt without the consent of the lenders is a credit risk issue that might become a distribution risk issue if it means potential lenders will be less inclined to buy participations in the loan when it is syndicated. Even where bank lawyers do review the documents from a credit-focussed position, according to bank lawyer [#24] 'it's a secondary consideration'. This creates a potential grey area where the exercise of a lawyer's discretion framed in the prevailing logics of their practice area might mean they fail to match their client's expectations in a particular instance. For example, the banks might expect to be clearly advised if there was an issue in the loan terms that could obstruct lender enforcement rights because of the insolvency regime in the target's local jurisdiction. But the bank lawyer may not highlight this provision to their bank client if that term has cleared the market in a previous transaction.

This narrowing in the bank lawyer's understanding of the scope of their role, driven by the cleared-the-market logic, can be viewed more as a shift in emphasis, rather than as an absolute shift away from their traditional, more substantive role of identifying the range of credit and other risks inherent in the proposed terms. In my interviews with them, they often appeared unsure of the precise scope of their role. It is in this grey area that bank lawyer sense-making is most susceptible to the influence of the survival, owns-the-market and cleared-the-market logics working in combination. These are the logics most readily accessible to them.

What is in the best interests of the client is, of course, context-dependent. Bank lawyers exercise significant discretion in determining which issues to report to clients, and/or to raise with the private equity lawyers in the negotiations, and which to allow to pass unreported and/or unchallenged. If a bank lawyer determines that a proposed term poses a potential distribution risk, they might consider it in the best interests of the client to raise it. But the survival logic will also kick in; they will also factor into their sense-making any risk that they might antagonize the private equity lawyer with whom they have a referral arrangement. Here the cleared-the-market logic is likely to influence their decision as to how to proceed. Bank lawyers understand that private equity lawyers are less likely to be antagonized by their raising an issue that is clearly one of distribution—as opposed to credit—risk. Bank lawyer [#27] gave the example of a tax issue they had identified in the terms proposed by the private equity lawyer that meant:

> Some of the deal was going to get less credit support from the target group than another bit of the deal, and I was saying, 'it's going to be obvious in the documentation and then investors aren't going to want to come into that bit of the deal'.

Here the bank lawyer had to decide whether to raise this issue with the private equity lawyer. Their discretion was ultimately exercised in favour of raising it on the basis that it was considered by the bank lawyer to be, and was communicated to the private equity lawyer as, a distribution, as opposed to credit, risk issue but also, and perhaps just as importantly, since the bank lawyer felt it was also an 'obvious' distribution risk issue. The bank lawyer felt the need to satisfy themselves that the issue would be clearly understood as a distribution risk issue by the private equity lawyer. The risk is that a less 'obvious' distribution risk issue may not have been raised at all, even if that meant the banks and lenders being subjected to increased distribution (and credit) risk as a result. This blending of logics means bank lawyers are less likely to raise an issue if in their judgement they might appear to the private equity lawyer not to be acting 'commercially'. The cleared-the-market logic operates to reassure them that this narrow interpretation of the scope of their role aligns with their client's wishes. But does it?

(d) The mismatch with client expectations

An important question is whether bank clients fully appreciate that bank lawyers mostly do not consider it part of their work scope to identify the broader credit and other risks that might negatively impact the interests of lenders when reviewing transaction documents. This limited scope is not made explicit in formal client terms of engagement, for example.[25] It might be argued that bank lawyers have simply narrowed the scope of their role to more closely align themselves with their arranger and lender clients' interests and their reduced bargaining power. This could mean, as Simon Salzedo KC and Tom Wood have suggested:

> The extent to which lawyers acting for lenders are prepared to be accommodating (with a view to the future relationship with the sponsor's firm) will often mirror the extent to which the lender is prepared to be accommodating (with a view to future investment opportunities with the same sponsor).[26]

To address this question and potential counter argument, it is helpful to assess the bank lawyers' dispositions and strategies against an 'ideal type'; in this case, how a bank lawyer might be expected by their arranger clients to approach their role.

Here it is worth noting how this question is complicated by the internal dynamics of large investment banks. Participants frequently referred to the various teams within banks having different motivations and objectives which were often in tension. Bank lawyer [#18] for example, said:

> If you send them a list and say 'these are 15 points we think are the most important points to negotiate and fight about', while the origination team and the business team would be very pleased with you, there may be other teams such as credit teams and execution teams who, when they receive the list, might be completely shocked because there are only 15 points to care about in a 150 page term sheet.

The origination teams have the closest relationship with the private equity sponsor and so might be more prepared to overlook credit, distribution, and other risks in deal structures and documents where it helps them to maintain a positive relationship with the sponsor. Whereas the credit, legal, and/or execution teams are mostly focussed on ensuring these risks are identified, challenged, and/or mitigated. Bank lawyers must balance the wishes of these different factions within their bank clients, as well as balancing those interests collectively against the interests of the private equity lawyers with whom they have referral relationships. Even allowing for these internal distinctions and tensions, bank lawyers are frequently not raising,

[25] The SRA has warned solicitors of the importance of ensuring clients have given genuine consent to any such limited retainer. Especially where the client is unsophisticated, 'Investment Schemes - Warning Notice' (17 August 2020) <https://www.sra.org.uk/solicitors/guidance/investment-schemes-including-conveyancing/> accessed 2 March 2023; 'Conflicts of Interest - Guidance' (3 February 2020) <https://www.sra.org.uk/solicitors/guidance/conflicts-interest/> accessed 27 October 2020.

[26] Simon Salzedo and Tom Wood, 'Improper Leverage? Own Interest Conflicts and the Designation Model in Leveraged Finance Transactions' (2023) 4 Journal of International Banking and Financial Law 209, 211.

and/or clearly advising on, all the relevant risk issues, so that the various teams within the bank are not afforded the opportunity to collectively decide how they wish to proceed.

According to bank lawyer [#15] —who was able to offer a client perspective, as they had witnessed a variety of approaches adopted by bank lawyers when on secondment to a bank client—the 'best possible work product' for a bank client is where the bank lawyer has 'thought about' the terms proposed by the private equity lawyer, including 'from a logical and credit standpoint'. This should then lead to clear advice being given to the client on whether it is in fact an issue that they should be pushing back on. This is the ideal type approach.

In-house lawyer [#17] —an in-house counsel at an arranging and underwriting bank—said this is not the work product they were most used to receiving, however, and in 'the worst case' bank lawyers frequently 'miss out points entirely'. I am going to draw on my interview with this participant quite heavily in this section, given they offered a valuable and detailed client perspective on the nature and tone of the typical bank lawyer advice to their clients.

According to bank lawyer [#15], the most common approach was somewhere in between these ideal type and worst cases. Bank lawyers would often simply provide a 'summary of the changes' in the draft documents prepared by the private equity lawyer 'versus what the last deal that that sponsor did'. In other words, the bank lawyer simply runs a redline comparison of the current and previous documents, and then sends it to the bank, together with a descriptive summary of the differences. A step up from this minimalist approach is to provide this summary together with some limited advice, an overlay as to which terms look, on the face of it, problematic from a credit or other risk perspective, but which have nonetheless cleared the market in a previous transaction. But here the bank lawyers deploy subtle strategies, the effect of which is to obscure the importance of the issue to the banks.

According to in-house lawyer [#17], bank lawyers might offer their client mere 'anodyne descriptions' of issues. So, a material issue—which might involve additional credit and/or distribution risk for their bank clients were it to be accepted—is identified but its significance underplayed because all the bank lawyer's comments are presented in the same neutral tone. According to in-house lawyer [#17]:

> They sort of just describe … 'the language says this, the language says that' - they don't tell you what's wrong with it.'

In-house lawyer [#17] described a more sophisticated version of this approach, which is adopted by the firms that are perceived as the most successful in securing designation work: this was 'harder for us to complain about, because it's not bad enough to get us to complain, but it's also not enough to really deliver effective pushback'. In-house lawyer [#17] explained that these bank lawyers:

> Won't use anything like, 'this is off market', 'this is unprecedented', 'this shouldn't be your risk'. It will not be so categorical. It will be very soft. Like 'you might want to consider this', 'you might want to consider asking for this', 'sometimes we've seen banks do this'. Very mild, you know, 'no big deal, but hey, here's something you might want to think about' kind of stuff.

Here bank lawyers are flagging up an issue to their bank client. They are also, if one is being cynical, creating an audit trail that they can point to in the future if necessary to show they did so. But they are at the same time downplaying what might be material risk issues for their client. Here there appears to be a mismatch between what the bank client expects in terms of advice, or at least the legal and/or credit team at the bank, and the service that bank lawyers deliver. They are not clearly advising whether the issue is serious and should be robustly challenged. They are perhaps even implying, through their tone, the opposite.

In-house lawyer [#17] said this approach frequently leaves the bank, as client, unsure of the extent to which the issue is of sufficient importance that it should be raised in the negotiations with the private equity sponsor and its lawyers:

> A lot of banks sometimes have quite junior people, with no experience of documentation, no legal background, they're looking for, 'what should I care about?' 'what should I say 'no' to?'

In-house lawyer [#17] observed that bank lawyers might reflect on the contrast between the tone and substance of their advice and that of the advice the private equity sponsor is typically receiving from its lawyers on the other side of the transaction—again this is seen as a key component of the 'ideal type' approach:

> It's very clear, it's very exact. It's 'you cannot accept this, it exposes you to this liability or this risk', or 'it completely undermines the concept that is otherwise trying to be created', those sorts of strong descriptions.

Banks are thus getting a materially different, and when assessed against this ideal type, poorer, level of service than private equity sponsors receive from their lawyers. Bank clients are frequently left to decide themselves whether to pursue an issue, without clear advice from their external legal counsel.

Here we see the survival logic in action. The approach adopted by bank lawyers aligns more with what private equity lawyers want from the bank lawyers, with whom they have referral relationships, than what the banks want from their lawyers. The survival logic works in combination with the owns-the-market and cleared-the-market logics to justify in the mind of the bank lawyer the narrowing of the list of issues raised. By playing down the significance of those issues through the tone of the language used to describe them, and not providing clear advice, the bank lawyer, consciously or subconsciously, theorizes that this approach will lead to fewer comments being raised by the banks on the documents. This serves a self-interested objective, being seen as commercial in the eyes of the private equity lawyers with whom they have an established referral relationship.

Bank lawyer [#15] felt that lawyers who did this had persuaded themselves that this is what their clients wanted:

> I'm sure that some of the law firms that produce notes on that basis did so because that's what they thought was helpful.

Joan Loughrey has argued that lawyers frequently exhibit blindness to corporate misconduct, but as opposed to being conscious and strategic, it may simply be due to cognitive bias; this 'is particularly likely to be the case if everyone else is behaving as if nothing is wrong'.[27] The cleared-the-market logic similarly reinforces and makes more effective the survival logic in the theorizing of the bank lawyers by enabling bank lawyers to maintain a positive self-image. They delude themselves that their narrow interpretation of their role aligns with their client's expectations.

(e) The normalization of practices

These strategies and dispositions of the bank lawyers have become established and relatively normalized practices of the field. What institutional theorists often refer to as 'institutional work' has hence emerged from the bank lawyers' 'practical work', meaning their everyday behaviours.[28] Thomas Lawrence and Roy Suddaby define institutional work as 'the purposive action of individuals and organisations aimed at creating, maintaining and disrupting institutions'.[29] Michael Smets refers to this process as the 'paradox of embedded agency'.[30] A micro-level process—here, the bank lawyers' day-to-day work—has become embedded as normalized and accepted behaviour. In other words, it has become a structural condition of the field due to the discretionary and often deliberate behaviour of the bank lawyers.[31] Bank lawyers have affected what Wanda Orlikowski refers to as 'situated change' to the conditions of the field, by making frequent adaptions to their existing practices.[32]

27 Joan Loughrey, *Corporate Lawyers and Corporate Governance* (CUP 2011) 5–6.

28 Michael Smets, 'Institutional Work Taken Literally: How Logics Shift as Banking Lawyers "Get the Deal Done"' (2009 Academy of Management annual meeting, USA, 2009) 7 <http://publications.aston.ac.uk/id/eprint/18544/> accessed 20 May 2021.

29 Lawrence and Suddaby (n 21) 247.

30 Smets (n 28) 7.

31 ibid 8.

32 Wanda J Orlikowski, 'Improvising Organizational Transformation Over Time: A Situated Change Perspective' (1996) 7 Information Systems Research 63.

Lawrence and Suddaby argue that theories of institutional work are closely connected to theories of power.[33] The English banking lawyers in Smets' study negotiated the range of available options for the practices and meanings of their field with their German colleagues because there was no significant disparity in their respective power.[34] The English lawyers hence sought to accommodate the contradictions between their common law framework and the German lawyers' legal and professional norms which were rooted in the legal traditions of the civil law system.[35] Unlike Smets' English banking lawyers, who continually negotiated adjustments to their practices with their German colleagues in an attempt to seek compromise, so that they could collectively position themselves as 'one firm', private equity lawyers do not encounter such barriers to task accomplishment from the bank lawyers they negotiate with, and are mostly able to impose their meanings on their counterparts.[36] Unlike the English banking lawyers in Smets' study, they could usually count on the cooperation of their bank lawyer counterparts to be accommodating of the terms that they propose, without needing to negotiate compromises.[37]

The result is a relatively weak dialectic struggle between contradictory practices and meanings of the private equity lawyers and their bank lawyer counterparts, leaving private equity lawyers mostly free to set the terms of transaction processes, structures, and documents independently of the bank lawyers.[38] The result is the contractual boundary-pushing strategies of the private equity lawyers explored in Chapter 5, which are facilitated by this collective acquiescence of the bank lawyers.[39]

3.4 Conclusion

Perhaps the most important element of a leveraged finance lawyer's role is to advise their client on the negotiation of the detailed financing terms. Because of the referral relationships that flow from the designation model, pursuant to which

33 .

34 Smets (n 28) 3.

35 ibid.

36 ibid 8–10.

37 ibid 3.

38 Royston Greenwood, Roy Suddaby, and CR Hinings, 'Theorizing Change: The Role of Professional Associations in the Transformation of Institutionalized Fields' (2002) 45 The Academy of Management Journal 58; Myeong-Gu Seo and WE Douglas Creed, 'Institutional Contradictions, Praxis, and Institutional Change: A Dialectical Perspective' (2002) 27 The Academy of Management Review 222. Smets (n 28) 5.

39 Huseyin Leblebici and others, 'Institutional Change and the Transformation of Interorganizational Fields: An Organizational History of the U.S. Radio Broadcasting Industry' (1991) 36 Administrative Science Quarterly 333; Christine Oliver, 'Strategic Responses to Institutional Processes' (1991) 16 Academy of Management Review 145, 145; Thomas B. Lawrence and Suddaby (n 21) 217.

private equity lawyers have the power to select and ultimately block bank lawyers from designated work, a survival logic has emerged which has diminished the inclination of bank lawyers to oppose the terms proposed by those private equity lawyers in loan documents, which often leads to additional risks for their bank clients. These logics act together to exert a powerful influence on the exercise of bank lawyer judgement and discretion. The bank lawyers' dispositions, practices, and strategies, which they have developed in response to these logics, have become embedded in the structural conditions of the field as ordinary, or institutional, modes of working in the leveraged finance practice area field.[40] The effect is that when in the past bank lawyers might have undertaken a comprehensive review of transaction documents, challenging problematic provisions carried over from previous transactions, especially if the business context of the previous transaction was markedly different, bank lawyers no longer tend to do so.

The ways in which the bank lawyers have chosen to respond to these logics has created a perception that bank lawyers may not always be acting in accordance with their ethical duties under the professional code of conduct to which they are subject. I explore whether there is substance to this perception in the next chapter.

[40] Smets (n 28). Karin Knorr Cetina, Theodore R Schatzki, and Eike von Savigny, *The Practice Turn in Contemporary Theory* (Routledge 2005); Lawrence and Suddaby (n 21) 219.

4
Bank Lawyers: Ethical Duties

4.1 Introduction

In this chapter, I explore the implications of the case study for bank lawyers' ethical duties, the most applicable being, first, the duty to act with independence, second, the solicitor's duty to disclose referral arrangements, and third, the solicitor's duties to avoid conflicts of interest and to maintain client confidentiality. I explore how these latter duties are engaged, in particular, by the emergent practice of what is commonly referred to as 'virtual trees', or 'trees in the head'. As I have already noted, the terminology used to describe this practice is in and of itself both misleading and verging on the ridiculous; its use serves to undermine bank lawyers' collective ethical credibility. Bank lawyer [#27] agreed: 'I don't think you can have a tree in the head. It's a misnomer.'

4.2 The duty to act with independence

The solicitors' duty to act with independence has not been a major site of scholarly or practitioner interest or research, as compared to say, the duty to avoid conflicts of interest. It is perhaps telling that in an insightful article written by leading barristers Simon Salzedo KC and Tom Wood (which I shall return to later in this chapter) exploring the professional conduct issues raised by an article I had written with respect to designation in leveraged finance, the authors chose to focus in detail on the issues designation raises with respect to conflicts of interest, whilst mentioning independence only in passing.[1]

It is clear from my data, as set out in detail in the previous chapter, that private equity lawyers clearly exert a powerful influence over the judgement of bank lawyers. Occasionally, a bank lawyer was prepared to admit to offering to be supine in their negotiations with private equity lawyers. For example, bank lawyer [#13] said:

[1] Simon Salzedo and Tom Wood, 'Improper Leverage? Own Interest Conflicts and the Designation Model in Leveraged Finance Transactions' (2023) 4 Journal of International Banking and Financial Law 209. Salzedo and Wood were commenting on Trevor Clark, 'The Pendulum Swing in Leveraged Finance Loan Terms: The Role of Designation' (2023) 38 Journal of International Banking Law and Regulation 45.

> I go to the sponsor lawyer and say 'can we be your stuffee? We'll be completely supine.' And then I try and develop a backbone on the transaction itself.

This risk of third-party interveners in the large firm lawyer/client relationship negatively impacting lawyer autonomy has been identified in two studies by leading legal ethicists. First, it can be seen in John Flood's work on corporate lawyer/bank relationships; he shows how lawyers working in international financial markets for a corporate client taking a loan, or issuing securities, may feel pressure to take into account the interests of third parties, most notably, banks, in addition to those of their own client.[2] Flood found that investment banks commonly referred their corporate clients to a large law firm when they considered it had outgrown its previous firm, for example.[3] Flood reports that the relationship became 'tripartite between bank-lawyer-client', raising the question for the lawyer 'who is the client?'[4] Flood implies that this means the lawyer may feel some loyalties to the bank, some ethical pressure, and challenges to their autonomy: 'To whom, therefore, is the actual loyalty owed? Codes of professional conduct give obvious answers, but the reality is otherwise. The true allegiance is between law firm and bank.'[5] Steven Vaughan' and Claire Coe's research can similarly be seen as raising an important red flag about the threats to lawyer independence of these types of relationships in the corporate sphere.[6] They found, in 2015, that bank lawyers in leveraged finance transactions had relationships with private equity sponsors who were paying their fees which served to constrain their professional autonomy.[7]

Coe and Vaughan were not, however, given any examples and so were unable to assess whether these bank lawyers had breached their ethical duties under the professional code of conduct to which they were subject. My data, on the other hand, does serve up a series of transaction-based examples on which to more forensically explore solicitor compliance with the duty to maintain independence.

In this section, I put the case that the strategies and practices of bank lawyers which are revealed by the multiple detailed examples in the data that I collected should be considered breaches of Principle 3, of the SRA's Standards and

[2] John Flood, 'Transnational Lawyering: Clients, Ethics and Regulation', in Leslie C Levin and Lynn Mather (eds), *Lawyers in Practice, Ethical Decision Making in Context, Edited by Leslie C. Levin & Lynn Mather* (The University of Chicago Press 2012) 181; John Flood, 'Ambiguous Allegiances in the Lawyer-Client Relationship: The Case of Bankers and Lawyers' 24, https://www.researchgate.net/publication/228135498_Ambiguous_Allegiances_in_the_Lawyer-Client_Relationship_The_Case_of_Bankers_and_Lawyers accessed 9 june 2023.

[3] Flood, 'Transnational Lawyering: Clients, Ethics and Regulation' (n 2) 181; Flood, 'Ambiguous Allegiances in the Lawyer-Client Relationship' (n 2) 24.

[4] Flood, 'Transnational Lawyering: Clients, Ethics and Regulation' (n 2) 181.

[5] Flood, 'Ambiguous Allegiances in the Lawyer-Client Relationship' (n 2) 24.

[6] Claire Coe and Steven Vaughan, 'Independence, Representation and Risk: An Empirical Exploration of the Management of Client Relationships by Large Law Firms' (Social Science Research Network 2015) SSRN Scholarly Paper ID 2679005 <https://papers.ssrn.com/abstract=2679005> accessed 17 July 2018.

[7] ibid 59.

Regulations, the duty to act 'with independence',[8] as well as Principle 7 of the SRA's Standards and Regulations, which requires solicitors to act 'in the best interests of each client'.[9]

The SRA does not, however, provide formal guidance as to what the duty to act with independence involves.[10] Neither is there much guidance to be found on what independence means in the decisions of the courts of England and Wales or in those of the Solicitors Disciplinary Tribunal.[11] The SRA confirmed to me in correspondence that the omission of specific guidance on the meaning of Principle 3 is deliberate:

> The StaRs provide a more flexible model for the regulatory framework and one in which we put more trust in professionals to use their own judgement. We think the duty to act with independence is relatively clear and therefore did not think it necessary to produce further guidance on the topic.[12]

The scope of the duty is not clear, however. Coe and Vaughan describe lawyer independence as 'complex, contested and nuanced'.[13] The onus is on solicitors to use their own professional and ethical judgement in determining how the duty to act with independence applies to their work but with little to guide them as to the parameters within which they are to exercise this judgement.[14]

For background and context, it is necessary to investigate the regulatory objectives of the SRA's governing legislation. In its paper explaining the regulatory objectives of the Legal Services Act 2007 (LSA), the Legal Services Board noted that a lawyer's advice 'should be independent of inappropriate influence'.[15] Whilst acknowledging that most legal work is undertaken for profit, the LSA's regulatory objectives were aimed at protecting the client from 'lawyers acting in their own financial interests'; notably the LSB emphasized that lawyers were to be 'mindful of the source of payment for their services ... so that they can identify and manage

[8] 'SRA Principles' (25 November 2019) <https://www.sra.org.uk/solicitors/standards-regulations/principles/> accessed 6 July 2020.

[9] ibid.

[10] The SRA provides guidance with respect to other Principles, such as the duty to act honestly, and the duty to act with integrity. There are, however, a series of case studies, 'Lack of Independence - Case Studies' (25 November 2019) <https://www.sra.org.uk/solicitors/guidance/lack-independence/> accessed 23 November 2020. https://www.sra.org.uk/solicitors/guidance/acting-with-integrity/, https://www.sra.org.uk/solicitors/guidance/general-dishonesty/

[11] See Emma Oakley and Steven Vaughan, 'In Dependence: The Paradox of Professional Independence and Taking Seriously the Vulnerabilities of Lawyers in Large Corporate Law Firms' (2019) 46 Journal of Law and Society 83, 90. Oakley and Vaughan note some of the relevant SDT decisions in footnote 29.

[12] Email to the author from the SRA, 4 December 2020.

[13] Coe and Vaughan (n 6) 44.

[14] Oakley and Vaughan (n 11) 90.

[15] LSB, 'The Regulatory Objectives – Legal Services Act 2007' (p11) – http://www.legalservicesboard.org.uk/news_publications/publications/pdf/regulatory_objectives.pdf; Coe and Vaughan (n 6) 44,45.

the potential threat to their independence.'[16] The guidance to the principle that existed in the SRA's handbook which preceded the SRA's current Standards and Regulations, which was slightly differently worded—it required a solicitor not to 'allow [his/her] independence to be compromised'—emphasized the lawyer's independence both from the state and from clients.[17]

Beyond these limited sources there is little guidance, so it is difficult to state with any certainty what the regulatory concept of independence in Principle 7 means for solicitors in England and Wales. From the literature that has considered lawyer independence, it appears independence likely encompasses a series of quite disparate elements, including the independence of lawyers from the influence of: the state; clients; regulators of the legal profession/the regulatory framework; the legal profession itself; their own self-interest; the firm's income generation demands; and third parties.[18] For bank lawyers, it is their duty to remain independent from the influence of third parties that is most applicable. In this section, I explore what my data reveals about whether leveraged finance lawyers are adequately managing these types of threats to their independence.

The International Organization of Securities Commissions (IOSCO)—which describes itself as 'the international body that brings together the world's securities regulators and is recognized as the global standard setter for financial markets regulation'[19]—reported in late 2023 that through industry roundtables it had heard concerns from market participants that the practice of lawyer designation in leveraged finance 'may not serve to ensure the advice that [underwriting banks] receive is independent' and that 'conflicts of interest may arise whereby lawyers representing the banks might be reluctant to push back against sponsor lawyers due to the risk that they could be excluded from the market for lender-side work'.[20] IOSCO encouraged both underwriting banks and the lenders to obtain independent legal advice, on the basis that the advice of designated counsel is *not independent*, and that banks are not receiving legal advice that promotes and defends their interests.[21] It is striking that IOSCO connected market conduct risks—specifically, a lack of transparency—in the European leveraged finance market so directly to a lack of lawyer independence in this way.[22] Press reports also suggest

16 ibid.

17 See Coe and Vaughan (n 6) 45.

18 See for example, ibid 45; Ronit Dinovitzer, Hugh Gunz, and Sally Gunz, 'Unpacking Client Capture: Evidence from Corporate Law Firms' (2014) 1 Journal of Professions and Organization 99. Hugh Gunz, Sally Gunz, and Ronit Dinovitzer, 'Professional Ethics' [2015] The Oxford Handbook of Professional Service Firms 123.

19 'About IOSCO' <https://www.iosco.org/v2/about/?subsection=about_iosco> accessed 19 December 2024.

20 International Organisation of Securities Commissions, 'Leveraged Loans and CLOs, Good Practices for Consideration, Consultation Report CR05/2023' (September 2023) 34 <https://www.iosco.org/library/pubdocs/pdf/IOSCOPD746.pdf>.

21 ibid 34–35.

22 'Regulators Turn Attention to Designated Counsel in Leveraged Finance Deals' (*Law.com International*, 9 February 2023) <https://www.law.com/international-edition/2023/02/09/financial-

that bank lawyers are widely perceived both (i) not to be acting in the best interests of their bank clients and (ii) to lack independence from the influence of private equity sponsors and their lawyers, in each case due to the effects of the lawyer designation model.[23] My data suggest that there is substance to this perception; that threats to their independence both exist and are not being adequately managed by them.

In my research interviews with leveraged finance lawyers, a majority moved quickly to talking about the lawyer designation model, usually without first being prompted by me. The frequency with which this occurred indicates that designation was widely perceived amongst the body of practitioners to be a central characteristic of the field. Perhaps more emphatically, the nature and tone of their observations signalled to me that they were also conscious that designation, and the lawyer practices and stances flowing from it, were unethical. This aligns with Coe and Vaughan's study; a number of their participants, when asked general questions about threats to large firm lawyer independence that they had experienced or were aware of, referred to bank lawyers in leveraged finance transactions and their relationships with private equity sponsors.[24] Similarly, and although my participants did not specifically use the terms 'independence' or 'autonomy', it became clear to me that their principal ethical concern with designation centred around the challenges it presented to bank lawyer independence from the inappropriate influence of third parties. Here, and this is a finding which extends our understanding beyond Coe and Vaughan's illuminating work, we need to consider the influence not only of private equity sponsors but also of their regular legal counsel.

A clear illustration of how designation raises clear questions as to bank lawyer independence is their marketing strategies; these openly target private equity lawyers, sometimes alongside marketing to the private equity sponsors, but also often exclusively. Several participants were prepared to acknowledge the ethical aspects of these marketing strategies. For example, bank lawyer [#28] told me:

> There are partners at my firm that will go to football matches with partners at sponsor firms who should be their rivals, and they shouldn't even be talking.

regulators-turn-attention-to-designated-counsel-in-leveraged-finance-deals/> accessed 28 March 2023. I am cited in this article.

[23] See eg Alex Newman, 'Linklaters Falls out of Favour with Goldman's City Leveraged Finance Team' (*LegalWeek*, 2014) <https://www.law.com/legal-week/2014/08/04/linklaters-falls-out-of-favour-with-goldmans-city-leveraged-finance-team/> accessed 12 October 2019; 'Private Lenders Lawyer up as Unease Grows over Appointed Counsel' (*BusinessLIVE* 5 July 2022) <https://www.bloomberg.com/news/articles/2022-07-05/private-lenders-lawyer-up-as-unease-grows-over-appointed-counsel> accessed 21 September 2022; 'Lenders Aren't Happy - and Lawyers Are in the Ethical Firing Line' (*The Lawyer | Legal insight, benchmarking data and jobs*, 6 October 2022) <https://www.thelawyer.com/lenders-arent-happy-and-lawyers-are-in-the-ethical-firing-line/> accessed 6 October 2022.

[24] Coe and Vaughan refer to the private equity firms as the bank lawyers' 'shadow clients', ibid 59.

Even more notably, several participants identified to me by name individual bank lawyers, partners of leading City law firms, who had pursued a conscious strategy over a period of years of cultivating close relationships with private equity lawyers. According to these accounts, these bank lawyers had recognized that they could make themselves indispensable to private equity lawyers by indicating, either explicitly or by tacit understanding, that they would be willing to accommodate them on a wide range of issues arising on transactions. For example, private equity lawyer [#36] said:

> With [names a bank lawyer] or [names another bank lawyer] I know they are not going to ever raise anything I don't want them to raise. I know they're probably not going to read the structure paper or even the loan document very closely.

Several participants reported that banks frequently complained about law firms that advised them on leveraged finance transactions lacking independence. Private equity lawyer [#12] said:

> It's not a secret in the market that certain banks have had problems with certain firms that are perceived to just roll over for the sponsors without properly negotiating points.

Although there has yet been no (public) regulatory complaint and hence no public regulatory action, that banks and other lenders complain to law firms is apparent from media reporting.[25] In other words, 'it's no secret', according to bank lawyer [#13]:

> We've had our run-ins with banks where they have been very vocal that we haven't been acting in their best interests.

That bank lawyers were generally aware of the ethical challenges to their independence arising from the lawyer designation model was also evident in the frequency of the self-justifications that bank lawyers offered up in my interviews with them. These generally appeared to be driven by a desire to preserve a positive moral self-image.[26] On lawyer self-image as a motivation for conduct, Joan Loughrey has observed that lawyers:

> are just as vulnerable to the effects of egocentrism which causes people to interpret information in ways to favour themselves, and to confirmation bias whereby

25 Newman (n 23); 'Private Lenders Lawyer up as Unease Grows over Appointed Counsel' (n 23).
26 Yuval Feldman, *The Law of Good People* (CUP 2018) xiii.

people look for information that confirms the correctness of their view and disregard negative information.[27]

There is empirical evidence that supports this contention. Donald Langevoort, for example, explored the individual characteristics of in-house lawyers working in large business organizations in the United States, finding that they were often ambitious and driven by their own promotion prospects.[28] In-house lawyers were consequently prone to developing a 'flexible' cognitive style when evaluating risk when they were immersed in an organizational culture of competitive success.[29] Langevoort concluded that in-house lawyers had channelled the values, language, and mindset of the outside lawyer, with little to separate them.[30]

In my interviews, these types of retrospective justifications were frequently the basis on which bank lawyers made sense of their continued commitment to behaviours that can be seen as inappropriate or unethical, and these enabled them to maintain their positive moral self-image.[31] Albeit bank lawyers appeared to care quite deeply about their moral self-image, and/or—for business reasons—their reputation for integrity, this goal did not seem, however, to have countered or even mitigated in any material way the situational pressures and incentives on them to act unethically.[32] This indicates that the bank lawyers are what Yuval Feldman has described as 'situational wrongdoers'; actors who 'behave badly in a situation that allows them to self-justify their behaviour'.[33] The data I collected contain a series of examples of these types of self-justifications.

For example, in my interviews with them, bank lawyers tended to shift responsibility for their lack of independence to their bank clients. These sorts of self-justifying narratives were often founded in a perception that large bank clients needed less 'looking after' from their lawyers, and/or distorted notions of the expertise their clients required from them, allowing them to narrow the scope of their role to fit with what, in their minds, the private equity lawyers expected of them.

This bank lawyer world view supported a 'blame the client' logic which enabled bank lawyers to both give meaning to, and in their own sense-making process,

27 Joan Loughrey, 'Accountability and the Regulation of the Large Law Firm Lawyer' (2014) 77 The Modern Law Review 732, 746. See also Leslie C Levin, 'Bad Apples, Bad Lawyers or Bad Decision making: Lessons from Psychology and from Lawyers in the Dock Book Review Essay' (2009) 22 Georgetown Journal of Legal Ethics 1549, 1549, 1583–84, 1566.

28 Donald Langevoort, 'Getting (Too) Comfortable: In-House Lawyers, Enterprise Risk and the Financial Crisis' [2011] Georgetown Law Faculty Working Papers 7–8 <http://scholarship.law.georgetown.edu/fwps_papers/154>.

29 ibid 11.

30 ibid 3.

31 Feldman (n 26) xiii, 61, 66. Patricia H Thornton, William Ocasio, and Michael Lounsbury, *The Institutional Logics Perspective: A New Approach to Culture, Structure, and Process* (OUP 2012) 133. Jennifer K Robbennolt, 'Behavioral Ethics Meets Legal Ethics' (2015) 11 Annual Review of Law and Social Science 75, 76.

32 Robbennolt (n 31) 76.

33 Feldman (n 26) 61, 66.

legitimize, their actions.[34] In my interviews, bank lawyers frequently presented their bank clients as having created the environmental conditions which made it increasingly challenging, if not nigh on impossible, for bank lawyers to act with independence. This positioning is understandable, given the collective acquiescence of the bank community to the lawyer designation model which has created material challenges to bank lawyer independence. Banks could, in an instant, remove the ethical challenges for their lawyers which are evident in the data I collected by instead paying for, or at least restoring their ability to select, their own legal counsel. Or they could appoint and pay for another law firm to act as 'shadow counsel' to look over the shoulder of designated counsel if they do not trust them to do a proper job, something which is already seen in the market.[35] Or banks could, either individually, or collectively, make a formal complaint to the SRA, that the independence of their lawyers has been severely compromised. That they do not do so is likely motivated by a desire to avoid jeopardizing their own relationships with private equity sponsors and the opportunity to earn the lucrative fee and other income that they derive from arranging and underwriting the financings of leveraged buyouts.

This collective bank community stance provides a basis on which bank lawyers choose to interpret their activities as aligned with their clients' objectives, and hence bank lawyers feel empowered to interpret their own strategies and depositions as evidence of their compliance with Principle 7, the duty to act in the best interests of their client. There is evidence of a misalignment in the case study data which contests this assertion, however, which I have included in this and the previous chapter. This data means, in contrast to their own self-perception, that the bank lawyers are not absolved of responsibility for breaching their ethical duty to act with, and to manage threats to their, independence under Principle 3. And in any event, there is a broader point; these are minimum standards. Whether any rules of professional practice have been breached is not necessarily the only issue. The solicitors' branch of the legal profession in the UK is itself clear that lawyers are required to observe high standards of conduct; The Law Society states prominently on its web page that 'the commitment to behaving ethically is at the heart of what it means to be a solicitor'.[36] Many of the lawyers I spoke to, on both sides of the lender/borrower divide, were uneasy about the ethical aspects of their day-to-day work in this market. The designation model and the practices and stances it engenders create significant tension, pressure, and stress for many, perhaps most, of

[34] Patricia H Thornton and William Ocasio, 'Institutional Logics and the Historical Contingency of Power in Organizations: Executive Succession in the Higher Education Publishing Industry, 1958-1990' (1999) 105 American Journal of Sociology 801, 155, 159.

[35] 'Private Lenders Lawyer Up as Unease Grows Over Appointed Counsel' *Bloomberg.com* (5 July 2022) <https://www.bloomberg.com/news/articles/2022-07-05/private-lenders-lawyer-up-as-unease-grows-over-appointed-counsel> accessed 21 September 2022.

[36] 'Professional Ethics' <https://www.lawsociety.org.uk/topics/ethics/> accessed 21 December 2024.

them; not least because they know, from the outside looking in, their professional integrity and independence is questionable, and is now actively being questioned.

A counterargument could perhaps be mounted that the public interest is best served by bank lawyers continuing to adopt an accommodating stance to enable financial markets to function as they currently do, overriding the public interest in the banks receiving independent advice, for example. However, when balanced against other public interests, for example, maintaining public trust in the legal profession, and the transparency and stability of financial markets, this argument is not at all compelling.[37]

4.3 The duty to disclose referral arrangements

In addition to the effect the bank lawyers' referral arrangements with private equity lawyers have on their observance of duties to act in the best interest of their client, and with independence,[38] there are also rules which apply specifically to the referral arrangements themselves. Formal arrangements for the referral of work to solicitors in England & Wales have only been permitted since 1990, an indication that referral arrangements bring with them potential ethical challenges for the lawyers involved;[39] in particular, they bring the risk that a solicitor might allow a referral arrangement to undermine their independence.[40] The SRA has historically focussed its enforcement strategy on referral arrangements that involve the payment of a fee; and referral arrangements with respect to claims following personal injury or death are now prohibited.[41] The referral relationships at the heart of lawyer designation, although they do not involve the payment of a fee, should nonetheless be disclosed by bank lawyers to their prospective bank clients

[37] For the potential for this type of lawyer action to contribute to the build-up of systemic risks, see the next chapter.

[38] Andrew Boon, *The Ethics and Conduct of Lawyers in England and Wales* (Bloomsbury Publishing 2014) 28.

[39] Under the Solicitors' Introduction and Referral Code 1990, see Tasha Keen, 'Referral Fees and Fee Sharing – Where Are We Now?' (*Birmingham Law Society. One Profession. One Region. One Voice*, 1 June 2021) <https://birminghamlawsociety.co.uk/referral-fees-and-fee-sharing-where-are-we-now/> accessed 27 February 2023.

[40] The literature on lawyer referral is mostly focussed on the ethical issues arising from the payment of referral fees, Heather M Field, 'Offshoring Tax Ethics: The Panama Papers, Seeking Refuge from Tax, and Tax Lawyer Referrals The Sanford E. Sarasohn Conference on Critical Issues in Comparative and International Taxation II: Taxation and Migration' (2017) 62 Saint Louis University Law Journal 35, 36.

[41] 'Referral Fees LASPO and SRA Principles - Warning Notice' (25 November 2019) <https://www.sra.org.uk/solicitors/guidance/referral-fees-laspo-sra-principles/> accessed 27 February 2023. The payment of a referral fee for work involving claims following personal injury or death is prohibited, 'Legal Aid, Sentencing and Punishment of Offenders Act 2012' s 56 <https://www.legislation.gov.uk/ukpga/2012/10/section/56/enacted> accessed 27 February 2023; 'The Prohibition of Referral Fees in LASPO 56 60 - Guidance' (25 November 2019) <https://www.sra.org.uk/solicitors/guidance/prohibition-of-referral-fees-in-laspo-56-60/> accessed 27 February 2023. See further Andrew Higgins, 'Referral Fees - The Business of Access to Justice' (2012) 32 Legal Studies 109.

pursuant to Rule 5.1 of the SRA's Code of Conduct for Solicitors (Individuals), which provides that clients are to be informed about any referrer which has any interest in making an introduction, financial *or otherwise*.[42] The objective here is that there should be transparency for the client where any arrangement—which does not need to be financial—gives a law firm a benefit.[43]

The SRA has stated that it would expect disclosure to be made where there is a pre-existing referral contract.[44] Typically, there will not be a written agreement between bank lawyers and private equity sponsors and/or their lawyers. On the other hand, the referral relationships between bank lawyers and private equity lawyers tend to be relatively well established and long-standing, even if unwritten, so it is consistent with the SRA's publicly stated stance for bank lawyers to disclose details of them to their bank clients in any event.[45] Since these preferred working relationships are opaque, and because of the independence and other ethical questions they provoke, disclosure is required in order that bank lawyers may demonstrate their observance of their broader duties, such as the duty to maintain trust and confidence in solicitors and in legal services, under Principle 3.[46] Further, lawyers owe a duty of loyalty to the client, as fiduciaries, over and above what the SRA's Code requires, which means solicitors may not act in their own interests without the informed consent of their client.[47]

Disclosure should occur prior to bank lawyers commencing work on a matter, so that the client can decide if they wish to proceed; this disclosure of the referral arrangement could be made clear in their terms of engagement with the client, for example. Bank lawyers should then keep written records of these referral arrangements, so that they can demonstrate compliance with these broader duties under the SRA Principles and the common law if called upon.[48] Several participants confirmed to me that this type of formal disclosure of referral arrangements in engagement terms did not take place.

[42] 'SRA Code of Conduct for Solicitors, RELs and RFLs' (25 November 2019) <https://www.sra.org.uk/solicitors/standards-regulations/code-conduct-solicitors/> accessed 15 November 2020; 'Conflicts of Interest - Guidance' (3 February 2020) <https://www.sra.org.uk/solicitors/guidance/conflicts-interest/> accessed 27 October 2020.

[43] Keen (n 39).

[44] 'Solicitor Referral Arrangements: How to Maintain Independence and Compliance' <https://www.theaccessgroup.com/en-gb/blog/lgl-solicitor-referral-arrangements/> accessed 27 February 2023.

[45] 'The Powerful City Lawyer at The Center of a Private Equity Storm' *Bloomberg.com* (16 February 2023) <https://www.bloomberg.com/news/articles/2023-02-16/the-powerful-city-lawyer-at-the-center-of-a-private-equity-storm> accessed 16 February 2023.

[46] 'SRA Principles' (n 8).

[47] Per Millet LJ, *Bristol and West Building Society v Mothew* [1998] EWCA Civ 533 at 18. Cited by Coe and Vaughan (n 6) 31.

[48] In the past, solicitors were required to keep written records of any referral arrangements, whether or not they required payment of a fee, 21 October 1998, 'Solicitors' Referral Code 1998 -- Review of the Introduction and Referral Code' (*Law Gazette*, 21 October 1998) <https://www.lawgazette.co.uk/news/solicitors-referral-code-1998-review-of-the-introduction-and-referral-code-/20839.article> accessed 27 February 2023.

4.4 The duties to avoid conflicts of interest and to maintain client confidentiality

In this section, I consider how bank lawyers might also be in breach of their duties to avoid conflicts of interest and to maintain client confidentiality.

A solicitor's duty to avoid conflicts of interest is founded in their fiduciary duty to their client.[49] The rules against conflicts of interest serve to protect a client's autonomy, requiring lawyers to act without regard to their own interests.[50] The applicable rules are found in Rules 6.1 and 6.2 of the SRA's Code of Conduct for Solicitors (Individuals).[51] Conflicts rules are especially front of mind for lawyers in large City firms because their application may mean they have to forgo work. It is perhaps unsurprising then that Janine Griffiths-Baker found that corporate lawyers routinely evaded these rules; or that large City firms have actively lobbied for conflicts of interest rules to be loosened.[52] Mitt Regan has observed that these rules tend to create:

> considerable opportunities for self-serving rationalisation. Under conditions of uncertainty, even well-intentioned individuals tend to interpret events consistent with their own self-interest. Lawyers whose compensation and prestige depend largely on keeping clients will naturally be disposed to conclude in a given situation that there is no problematic conflict unless its unmistakeably clear.[53]

In other words, lawyers are inclined to seek reasons to justify taking on work whenever they can. This bias towards finding the 'right' answer when a potential conflict of interest arises is, as I will explore below, aided by a degree of ambiguity in the rules themselves. The sections that follow explore two specific potential breaches of the duty to avoid conflicts of interest. First, I consider the practice of lawyer designation. Then, I explore the practice of virtual trees, also known as trees in the head.

(a) Own interest conflicts: designation

I have already argued that the lawyer designation model negatively affects bank lawyer compliance with their duties to act in the best interests of the client, and

[49] Another specific duty is the duty to maintain client confidentiality, Boon (n 38) 296, 376.
[50] ibid 377.
[51] 'SRA Code of Conduct for Solicitors, RELs and RFLs' (n 42).
[52] Boon (n 38) 376; Janine Griffiths-Baker, *Serving Two Masters: Conflicts of Interest in the Modern Law Firm* (Hart Publishing 2002); Joan Loughrey, *Corporate Lawyers and Corporate Governance* (CUP 2011).
[53] Milton C Regan, *Eat What You Kill: The Fall of a Wall Street Lawyer* (University of Michigan Press 2004) 319.

with independence. In this section, I analyse designation, and the referral relationships that flow from it, against the solicitors' duty to avoid own interest conflicts of interest.

Under Rule 6.1 of the SRA's Code of Conduct, a solicitor may not act if there is an 'own interest conflict' or a significant risk of such a conflict.[54] There are no exceptions to this rule; it cannot be contracted out of in lawyer/client terms of engagement, and neither can the client give express or implied consent to the conflict.[55]

This rule reflects the fiduciary relationship that exists under common law between lawyer and client: they must not let their own interests conflict with those of their client and must always put the client's interests ahead of their own.[56] The fiduciary duty is to ensure that a person in a position of trust does not use information to their own advantage or that of a third party.[57] It is sometimes referred to as the 'fair dealing' rule and covers solicitors receiving gifts and benefiting from appointments, for example.[58]

The SRA's Glossary defines an own interest conflict as 'any situation where your duty to act in the best interests of any client in relation to a matter conflicts, or where there is a significant risk that it may conflict, with your own interests in relation to that or a related matter.'[59] Most examples of solicitor own interest conflicts that have led to court cases relate to their own separate business interests; for example, where a solicitor has a personal interest in a business venture which stands to profit from a transaction undertaken by the client.[60] And these types of conflict feature in the examples given in the SRA's own guidance note on conflicts of interest.[61] The leading case is *Boardman v Phipps*.[62] A solicitor who was a trustee of a trust that held shares in a company purchased the remaining shares in that company in his own name when the trust decided not to buy them. The solicitor was held liable to account for the profits made from the increase in value of the shares. The question of conflict of interest was not straightforward—the trust did not want to buy the shares—but a majority of the House of Lords nonetheless took the view that there was a conflict of interest as the trust may have changed its mind.[63] Paul Todd notes that the case:

54 'SRA Code of Conduct for Solicitors, RELs and RFLs' (n 42).
55 Salzedo and Wood (n 1); 'Conflicts of Interest - Guidance' (n 42).
56 Janine Griffiths-Baker (n 52) 17.
57 ibid 24.
58 ibid 17.
59 'SRA Glossary' (11 March 2021) <https://www.sra.org.uk/solicitors/standards-regulations/glossary/> accessed 2 August 2023.
60 See, for example, *Solicitors Regulation Authority v Dennison* [2012] EWCA Civ 421; Jonathan Herring, *Legal Ethics* (OUP 2017) 185.
61 'Conflicts of Interest - Guidance' (n 42).
62 [1967] 2 AC 46.
63 P Todd, *Textbook on Trusts* (4th edn, Blackstone Press 1999) 340. Cited in Janine Griffiths-Baker (n 52) 17 fn 3.

demonstrates how willing the courts are to find even the most theoretical possibility of a conflict of interest where a solicitor's interests conflict with the interests of his clients.[64]

On the other hand, as Coe and Vaughan noted, lawyers are subject to a range of pressures, and professional rules on conflicts of interest do not try to regulate all of them.[65] As Christine Parker and Adrian Evans point out, it would be naive to assume that lawyers are always completely devoted to the interests of their clients to the exclusion of all other influences.[66] Lawyers face a series of conflicts of interest in their day-to-day work. It is of course appropriate for lawyers to seek to make a profit from charging fees for a matter, for example.[67] Further, according to Voss J. in *Dennard v PricewaterhouseCoopers LL,* where a professional seeks to obtain further work from a client by pointing to their work for another client, this is not a conflict of interest at common law unless the professional has a 'perverse incentive to achieve a result that may be at odds with the interests of their client'.[68] A conflict of interest hence arises where a profit motivation negatively impacts a solicitor's ability to properly and independently represent the interests of their clients on a transaction.[69]

When it comes to designation, there are two possible own interest conflicts of interest facing bank lawyers. First, that the referral relationship with a private equity lawyer/firm could be seen as a business in which the bank lawyer is interested. The second is that the bank lawyer's law firm could be seen as a business in which the bank lawyer is interested. I will now consider each of these possibilities in turn.

As noted already, Simon Salzedo KC and Tom Wood considered the ethical implications for lawyers of an article I had written on lawyer designation.[70] They offer a valuable analysis of the potential for conflicts of interest to arise in breach of the SRA's Rule 6.[71] Focussing on designation and the network of referral relationships between lawyers and law firms that flow from it which I had identified in my article, they methodically consider what relevant case law, including the leading case of *Marks & Spencer Plc v Freshfields*[72] precisely requires as to the closeness of the connection between two related matters so that a 'two client conflict' can arise.[73] Salzedo and Wood develop the argument that a lender-side firm's referral

[64] Todd (n 63) 340. Cited in Janine Griffiths-Baker (n 52) 17 fn 3.
[65] Coe and Vaughan (n 6) 31.
[66] Christine Parker and Adrian Evans, *Inside Lawyers' Ethics* (CUP 2018).
[67] Herring (n 60) 181–82.
[68] [2110] EWHC 812 (Ch). See also Salzedo and Wood (n 1).
[69] See Lord Neuberger of Abbotsbury, 'Lord Upjohn Lecture 2012: Reforming Legal Education' (2013) 47 The Law Teacher 4, 7; cited in Coe and Vaughan (n 6) 46.
[70] Salzedo and Wood (n 1); Clark (n 1).
[71] Clark (n 1).
[72] [2204] EWCA Civ 741.
[73] The Law Society, 'Conflict of Interests Practice Note' (2023) <https://www.lawsociety.org.uk/topics/client-care/archive/conflict-of-interests-july-2023> accessed 19 December 2024; Solicitors Regulation Authority, *SOLICITORS' CODE OF CONDUCT 2007* (The Law Society 2009). Salzedo and

relationship with a private equity sponsor-side firm has the potential to be 'a personal or business relationship' for the purposes of the SRA's Guidance on conflicts of interest, where the solicitor might obtain 'a personal interest or benefit' by being accommodating to the sponsor-side firm when negotiating the terms of a transaction. Salzedo and Wood stop short of concluding that a conflict of interest arises in these circumstances; for this there would need to be, they say, evidence that:

> in the course of negotiations on a particular deal a sponsor firm were to link a lender's position on a particular contract clause to whether that lender firm would be designated on a future deal.[74]

There is indeed evidence to this effect in my data. Bank lawyers frequently reported to me in my interviews with them that they were warned by the private equity lawyer they were negotiating with on a transaction not to raise a particular issue on a clause in the documents, or to drop issues they had already raised. Bank lawyer [#22] described how a private equity lawyer called them after one negotiation session and said, 'with that sort of approach you're never going to get another referral from us.' Bank lawyer [#22] confirmed that the private equity lawyer then followed through with the threat; they missed out on subsequent deal opportunities because they were boycotted by that private equity lawyer and their firm. This phenomenon was also confirmed by private equity lawyers themselves. For example, private equity lawyer [#41] told me they would often say amid a negotiation with a bank lawyer:

> 'Hey, you're raising stupid points that are wasting time. If you continue to do that, you'll never get chosen again.'

As I noted in the previous chapter, as well as this evidence of explicit threats from private equity lawyers to blacklist bank lawyers, and even evidence that actual blacklisting occurred, the *implicit* threat is sufficient to affect the bank lawyer's judgement in the negotiation of loan terms. Bank lawyers understood that the flow of designated work through their referral relationship with a given private equity lawyer could be temporarily or permanently interrupted if they did not hold up their end of the bargain. This is evidence of the existence of a 'perverse incentive'

Wood also cite persuasive but admittedly non-binding sources; the Law Society Guidance on conflicts of interest, which suggests the solicitor faces a potential conflict of interest where they have or 'might obtain, any personal interest or benefit in a transaction in which they act for the client', and the 2007 iteration of the SRA's Code of Conduct which was more specific on the question of two client conflicts than the current Standards and Regulations that came into effect in 2019, which refers to, quoting Salzedo and Wood, an 'indirect interest' in a 'specific business concern in which a solicitor is interested which they then recommend a client invest in'. Salzedo and Wood (n 1).

[74] Salzedo and Wood (n 1).

to achieve an outcome which conflicts with the interests of their client, referred to by Voss J. in *Dennard v PricewaterhouseCoopers LLP*.[75] My data hence supports the conclusion that there was frequently actual conflict; and not simply the potential for conflict. The bank lawyers' divided loyalties that arise from the designation model and the referral relationships that flow from it are thus improper conflicts, in that they materially affect the exercise of a bank lawyer's judgement, both consciously and subconsciously, in their everyday work for their clients in a manner which prioritizes their own interests over those of their client.[76]

The bank lawyer's law firm could also be seen as a business in which the bank lawyer is interested, which, given the perverse incentives associated with lawyer designation and the firm's business logics, materially affect the exercise of a bank lawyer's judgement in a manner which prioritizes their own interests over those of their clients. It is clear from the cases that a conflict of interest can arise in relation to the future interests of the lawyer, provided it is not a mere theoretical possibility that those interests might arise.[77] When considering the referral relationships that flow from designation, the potential for conflict here is between the bank client's interests with respect to the matter at hand, and the bank lawyer's—and their firm's—future commercial interests. Bank lawyers who are equity partners of large law firms have a direct personal interest in a business venture that stands to directly benefit from their securing lucrative designation work: their firm. Corporate law firms adopt corporate style business models and tightly monitor and enforce partner productivity and firm profitability.[78] Partners are now typically partly, and sometimes mostly, remunerated on a basis which reflects their individual contribution to the firm's billings to clients. The designation model means bank lawyers sometimes work against their client's interests to secure future work for themselves and for their firm from a third party, the private equity lawyer and/or sponsor. This future work will generate further income for their firm, in which they, if they are equity partners, will directly participate, in the form of profit distributions.[79] Perceived success in generating profit for the firm brings indirect financial benefits too; it consolidates and protects their status, and therefor income, as a partner.[80] Partners who are not able to generate required levels of income increasingly risk being sacked, or they may be de-equitised, or have a reduced profit share imposed

75 [2110] EWHC 812 (Ch). See also ibid.

76 Herring (n 60) 181–82.

77 *Marks & Spencer plc v Freshfields Bruckhaus Deringer* [2004] EWHC 1337 (Ch); ibid 186.

78 Laura Empson, *Managing the Modern Law Firm* (OUP 2007).

79 Ronald J Gilson and Robert H Mnookin, 'Sharing among the Human Capitalists: An Economic Inquiry into the Corporate Law Firm and How Partners Split Profits Symposium on the Corporate Law Firm' (1984) 37 Stanford Law Review 313. Mitt Regan and Lisa H Rohrer, *BigLaw: Money and Meaning in the Modern Law Firm* (The University of Chicago Press 2020) 96–120, 121–77. Non-equity partners may also benefit through enhanced salary and bonus payments.

80 JR Faulconbridge and D Muzio, 'The Financialization of Large Law Firms: Situated Discourses and Practices of Reorganization' (2009) 9 Journal of Economic Geography 641, 642.

on them.[81] Further, it is increasingly recognized in the literature that individual lawyers may be just as much, if not more, committed to the pursuit of personal and commercial objectives, such as promotion and job retention, than they are with those of their clients.[82]

It might be argued that provided that the referral relationship that leads to the potential for conflict is identified and disclosed to the client, it should be allowed, provided no harm flows to the client.[83] As I have already noted, bank lawyers did not disclose, and seek prior written consent for, their referral arrangements with private equity lawyers and sponsors, albeit banks may in some instances be aware, at least on a superficial level, that they exist. Bank lawyers often sought to justify their conduct by presenting banks as being fully aware of the ethical risks and challenges flowing from the designation model. In other words, their clients were presented as knowing enablers. In this way, bank lawyers portrayed their clients as having implicitly, even if not explicitly, provided their informed and advance consent to their external legal counsel having waived this potential for conflict of interest. As a result, banks were presented as, in effect, estopped from complaining when their lawyers showed themselves to lack independence from private equity sponsors and their lawyers. Bank lawyer [#28]'s observations were representative of this type of 'blame the client' logic:

> You have banks complaining, but the banks are aware of it, it is not going on behind the scenes, they are not being duped into thinking they have got fully independent counsel acting for them. They know, and everyone knows, that's just the way it is.

As I have previously mentioned, as far as I am aware, the banks have not, individually, or collectively, raised these complaints formally and publicly with the SRA. However, since several of my participants told me that banks complain to them about the behaviour of bank lawyers in leveraged buyouts, it is difficult to support an argument that they have implicitly waived their rights, even if such a client waiver of fiduciary and professional duties with informed consent were possible, which it is not. As fiduciaries, owing a duty of loyalty to the client, over and above what the SRA's Code requires, solicitors may not act in their own interests without the informed consent of the client.[84]

[81] ibid 649–55. See Regan and Rohrer (n 79) 16–22.

[82] Marc Galanter and William D Henderson, 'The Elastic Tournament: The Second Transformation of the Big Law Firm' (Social Science Research Network 2008) SSRN Scholarly Paper ID 1104711 <https://papers.ssrn.com/abstract=1104711> accessed 6 December 2018; Gunz, Gunz, and Dinovitzer (n 18) 129.

[83] Herring (n 60) 183–84.

[84] Per Millet LJ, *Bristol and West Building Society v Mothew* [1998] EWCA Civ 533 at 18. Cited by Coe and Vaughan (n 6) 31.

In any event, the SRA's guidance on conflicts of interest makes clear that a client cannot consent to a solicitor's own interest conflict.[85] Given the rules against conflicts exist for public interest purposes, conflicts of interest are not merely matters of private contract that bank lawyers are able to contract out of.[86]

(b) Same matter conflicts: virtual trees, trees in the head

The rules against conflicts of interest also prohibit lawyers from acting for two clients on the same matter whose interests conflict.[87] Rule 6.2 of the SRA's Code of Conduct for Solicitors (Individuals) requires that they must not act in a situation where their separate duties to act in the best interests of each client conflict or there is a significant risk of such conflict, albeit there are prescribed exceptions.[88]

In a leveraged buyout, it might be argued that because of the designation model and the resulting survival logic, the bank lawyers, in practical effect, have two clients whose interests conflict (as arrangers/lenders and borrowers of a syndicated loan). Bank lawyers have divided loyalties; to their direct clients, the banks, and to a third party, the private equity sponsor, and their lawyer on whom they rely for future work. However, because the bank lawyers do not technically act for the private equity lawyers or sponsors on a transaction, so that they are not a 'client', Rule 6.2 does not apply as a basis on which to assess the effects of the lawyer designation model. So Coe and Vaughan concluded that under the SRA's regulations, conflicts of interest would only be relevant if the 'shadow client' was 'technically' a client of the firm on the matter.[89] They therefore examined these issues in the context of lawyer independence (I have also argued that the referral relationships arising from designation potentially constitute an own-interest conflict of interest).[90] In other words, what is a clear 'commercial' conflict is not a 'legal' conflict for the purposes of the SRA's Code of Conduct.[91] As Coe and Vaughan observe:

> It strikes us that much of the emphasis in the SRA's conflicts rules is on lawyers' obligations in relation to given matters rather than the complex relationships between firms and their suite of clients within and without the context of specific matters.[92]

[85] 'Conflicts of Interest - Guidance' (n 42).
[86] Coe and Vaughan (n 6) 8, 42; Loughrey (n 52) 230.
[87] Janine Griffiths-Baker (n 52) 2. See Rule 6.2 of the SRA Code, 'SRA Code of Conduct for Solicitors, RELs and RFLs' (n 42).
[88] 'SRA Code of Conduct for Solicitors, RELs and RFLs' (n 42).
[89] Coe and Vaughan (n 6) 61.
[90] ibid.
[91] On the difficulty in defining conflicts of interest, see Donald Nicolson and Julian S Webb, *Professional Legal Ethics: Critical Interrogations* (OUP 1999) 129. Cited in Coe and Vaughan (n 6) 31.
[92] Coe and Vaughan (n 6) 32.

Rule 6.2 is, however, engaged by the emergent practice of what is commonly referred to as 'virtual trees, or 'trees in the head'. Until relatively recently, around 2018, each bank competing for the arranging mandate on a syndicated deal would be advised by a separate team, or (physical) 'tree', a partner supported by one or more associates of the same firm, with information barriers erected between the teams. There might be a 'common carrier' team undertaking generic work on behalf of the banks as a whole to avoid, for example, multiple teams producing the same summary of what the sale and purchase agreement says or negotiating reliance letters for due diligence report providers. However, the practice has now changed; now all the competing banks tend to be advised by a single partner/team at the same firm.

As there are no 'physical' trees anymore, this new practice was hence often referred to by my participants as a 'virtual' tree. It was also often commonly referred to as a 'tree in the head'—in other words, the individual lawyer or lawyers advising the banks, which are competing against each other for the same objective, the award by the private equity sponsor of the financing mandate—erect barriers 'within their head'. Whilst they may receive sensitive and confidential information from one bank in the group, which might include the proposed pricing and other core terms they intend to offer to the sponsor, they are expected not to share this information with any other bank. Private equity lawyer [#28] lawyer explained the purpose of these trees:

> The whole point of having these trees is being able to have separate negotiations, we don't want the lenders to talk to each other, we want to get the best possible terms they will offer individually.

However, private equity lawyer [#36] said the hardest thing for the bank lawyers:

> is to do trees in the head and do it well. Because 'well' means keeping the sponsor and their lawyers happy and all the banks happy. You've got this extreme time pressure and you're meant to be representing multiple banks. It's really tough.

A picture emerges of overstretched partners and associates struggling to manage the demands of the transaction process, advising multiple clients, and working to tight deadlines, and constantly fearing divulging one bank's confidential information to another bank by mistake. The bank lawyers are often given two to three days by the private equity lawyers to respond with an issues list individualized for each of the banks. A set of 'common observations' on the documents is also sent out to each bank. Bank lawyer [#34] said they would often have to be blunt with individual bank clients to manage expectations as to their availability:

> I will say 'Look, I have time for a two-hour call with you. This is the window'. They kind of get that that's just physically the only way you can manage a 48-hour process with that many different trees.

Bank lawyer [#34] said that the pressure to ensure that there were no leaks of confidential information also detracted from their ability to properly serve each client:

> Your first priority when you're running a tree process is just don't mess anything up. Don't send anything to the wrong person, don't breach confidentiality.

As a second priority, bank lawyers undertake a minimalized review of the documents. Guided by the survival and cleared-the-market logics they mostly seek to ensure the proposed terms do not include terms that have not cleared the market in a previous transaction. The individual bank's specific aims and objectives are, according to bank lawyer [#34], 'very much third on the list'. They also narrowly interpret what the individual banks might care about. Bank lawyer [#18] said they mostly focus on 'deviations' of the terms in the commitment papers from that bank's initial outline term sheet positions. They might also seek to reflect any 'bank specific' points. For example, banks might, as a 'house' position, require the flexibility to transfer the debt to another entity within its corporate group.

What is notable here is that there is no expectation that the bank lawyer will undertake a substantive review of the documents as a whole, to identify potential credit and other risks that may be lurking in those documents, given the particular business context of the transaction. Not even as a fourth priority. This appears to be because a core objective of the bank lawyers at this stage is not to be seen to be making any points themselves, but rather to be seen as a mailbox, simply passing on the comments of their bank clients to the private equity lawyers. Otherwise, they risk being perceived by the private equity lawyers with whom they have referral relationships as uncommercial. Bank lawyer [#27] said:

> What I'm not there to be is a roadblock to a transaction or to build momentum behind certain points.

Bank lawyer [#27] said that if any material commercial points appear on several banks' issues list so that it looks like there is some consistency of view, this could result in them getting boycotted for future work:

> The sponsor's lawyers will point the finger at us and say, well, you guys are being difficult here. And these are not points being made by the bank they're points being made by you.

In the interviews, bank lawyers frequently appeared almost relieved. Bank lawyer [#41] said these dynamics:

> make our lives easier because if we're not reviewing a document from scratch and trying to build back in anything that's not in there, that cuts down the time, and potentially the costs, involved.

So—according to private equity lawyer [#23] —bank lawyers absolve themselves of responsibility for challenging problematic terms by saying 'this is something that other people have signed off on'.

The effect is that bank lawyers are not minded to undertake a comprehensive review of the terms proposed by the private equity lawyers and where appropriate offer robust challenge. Firstly, because of the pressures and challenges implicit in the trees in the head practice, they typically do not have the time and the bandwidth to do so. Secondly, the bank lawyers' goal is to ensure each bank minimizes the number of points on their issues list; this is further evidence of the influence of the survival logic. They may also do this in part because they consider this will help the bank win the mandate. But it is likely their motivation is also—perhaps even primarily—to avoid antagonizing the private equity lawyer with whom they have an established referral relationship.

Leading textbooks on legal ethics do not anticipate the possibility of one solicitor acting for more than one client on the same matter where it is understood at the outset that their interests will inevitably conflict; the closest they come is to examining cases where a husband and wife instruct a solicitor on a 'joint retainer' basis but where a solicitor subsequently discovers that their interests conflict.[93] With trees in the head, leveraged finance lawyers appear to have developed a practice that is relatively unique amongst lawyers in practice in England and Wales. However, in this instance this practice has been considered, and given the green light, by the SRA, as I consider later.

The ethical risk with trees in the head starts with an acknowledgement that the banks' interests conflict, since they are competing to offer best terms to the private equity sponsor in order to win the underwriting and arranging mandate. During this process, each of the banks share their proposed pricing and other sensitive and confidential information with the bank lawyer advising them and each of the other banks. Leaking information with respect to a bank's pricing can be to their detriment, as it would allow another bank to match that pricing, if it is more competitive than theirs, to continue in the process. If the leak related to, for example, flexibility for the borrower under the deal's negative covenants, then a bank learning that another bank is offering greater flexibility could, again, decide

[93] See, for example, Boon (n 38) 366; Herring (n 60) 110.

to match that flexibility to continue in the deal. In both examples, the leaking of the more competitive bank's information is detrimental to their chances of winning the arranger mandate at the expense of the bank to whom that confidential information has been disclosed. The case study shows, as I explore below, that it is not just that this practice generates heightened risks of leaks; actual leaks do take place.

Under Rule 6.2 (b), acting for two clients competing for the same objective is permissible where the objective is a contract or business opportunity, a requirement which acting for two or more banks competing for a financing mandate on a leveraged buyout satisfies. However, there are three provisos to Rule 6.2 (b). First, the clients must have provided prior written and informed consent. Second, the solicitor must 'put in place effective safeguards' to protect each client's confidential information. Third, the solicitor must be satisfied that it is 'reasonable to act for all of the clients'.

The year after the SRA's Standards and Regulations, which contained Rule 6.2 (b) were issued, the SRA issued guidance, in March 2020, which effectively waived the second proviso, effective safeguards (that is, information barriers). This was in response to lobbying by large law firms. The changes made to the SRA's Guidance to Rule 6.2 on 2 March 2020, included the following:

> It may not be "appropriate" for effective safeguards to be put in place. This might arise, for example, where your clients consider it desirable for the same lawyer(s) to represent them, and they agree with you which information can and cannot be shared, and therefore that structural safeguards to protect their confidential information are not required.[94]

Solicitors wishing to rely on this waiver of information barriers in the guidance to Rule 6.2 (b) need to 'obtain informed consent from each client that no structural safeguards are needed'.[95] In their agreement with each client, the solicitor must agree 'not to share with them material information which is confidential to the other client/s (and which those client/s have not consented to the disclosure of)'.[96] The solicitor 'must also be satisfied that your clients understand what sort of information you will not be able to disclose'.[97] Finally, the solicitor must remain satisfied that it is in 'the best interests of each client to act on this basis'.[98]

At this point I might make two tangential observations. Firstly, the SRA's rules and guidance appear to diverge with the common law. This itself could be problematic. According to Andrew Boon, in his leading work on legal ethics, the rules of professional conduct for solicitors should not be less onerous than the

[94] 'Conflicts of Interest - Guidance' (n 42).
[95] ibid.
[96] ibid.
[97] ibid.
[98] ibid.

standards set at common law.[99] The potential consequence is that a solicitor may find themselves in compliance with the SRA's rules, but liable to a civil action from their client for misuse of confidential information.[100] The leading cases on the duty of confidentiality have considered the duty to maintain the confidentiality of the information of *past* clients when taking on a *new* client in relation to a different matter. Here the courts, in a series of cases including both accountants and lawyers,[101] have emphasized that a solicitor may only act for the new client upon two conditions: first, the new client has waived their right to the disclosure of the confidential information of the past client, and second, information barriers[102] are erected to ring-fence the confidential information of the past client, minimizing the risk that the information 'leaks', whether by error or otherwise, to the new client.[103] The test is whether a reasonable person would anticipate that a breach of confidence might occur under the arrangements that are being contemplated.[104] With respect to trees in the head, however, there is no past nor new client; the same solicitor, or team of solicitors, acts for two or more clients concurrently. This means there are no information barriers—which typically involve separate solicitors and/or teams acting for each client with information barriers erected between them—to protect each client from the risk that their confidential information is leaked to another.

Secondly, the issuing by the SRA of the March 2020 guidance, effectively waiving the requirement for information barriers provided the client consents, appears to be an example of large law firms adeptly influencing professional regulation in ways which align with their interests.[105] The guidance was issued specifically to ensure the practice of trees in the head could continue.[106] When the Code was updated in 2019, concerns were expressed that the trees in the head practice conflicted with the requirement in Rule 6.2 (b) to erect information barriers when acting for more than one client on the same matter.[107] At least one firm decided for this reason that it would no longer participate in the practice. Bank lawyer [#29] said:

[99] Boon (n 38) 358.

[100] 'Confidentiality of Client Information - Guidance' (30 June 2022) <https://www.sra.org.uk/solicitors/guidance/confidentiality-client-information/> accessed 24 March 2023.

[101] Although the leading case of *Bolkiah v KPMG* [1999] 1 All ER 517 concerned accountants, the court held that the principles apply equally to lawyers.

[102] Often referred to as Chinese Walls', 'Harry McVea, '"Heard It through the Grapevine": Chinese Walls and Former Client Confidentiality in Law Firms' (2000) 59 The Cambridge Law Journal 370.

[103] See eg, Re a Firm of Solicitors [1992] 1 All ER 353 (CA); Herring (n 60) 336.

[104] ibid 337; Re a Firm of Solicitors [1992] 1 All ER 353 (CA).

[105] For other examples of this, see Loughrey (n 52) 48–49; Janine Griffiths-Baker, *Serving Two Masters: Conflicts of Interest in the Modern Law Firm* (Hart Publishing 2002); Chris Perrin, 'City of London Law Society, Letter to the Review of the Regulation of Corporate Legal Work' (8 January 2009) http://www.citysolicitors.org.uk/storage/2013/07/Hunt-Review-Final-Signed-Copy.pdf.

[106] Email to the author from the SRA on 2 July 2020.

[107] 'SRA Standards and Regulations' (25 November 2019) <https://www.sra.org.uk/solicitors/standards-regulations/> accessed 21 June 2022.

> When the uncertainty got raised, we as an institution decided to take the most conservative path and we decided that we had to do physical trees.

In correspondence, the SRA confirmed to me that that the changes to the Code implemented in 2019:

> did not take all relevant situations into account, for example, if clients consider it desirable for the same lawyer(s) to represent them.[108]

A group of law firms, acting under the umbrella of the City of London Law Society (CLLS), had asked the SRA for a clarification to be made to the guidance; but this was done, according to in-house lawyer [#17], without consultation with their bank clients. The SRA has confirmed to me in correspondence that it updated its guidance on Rule 6.2 in March 2020 following these representations from the CLLS.[109]

Although the SRA's March 2020 guidance to Rule 6.2 (b) dispenses with the need for information barriers, the remaining two provisos still apply. In other words, trees in the head are still subject to the client providing informed consent, and the solicitor still believing that it is reasonable to act. My conclusion is that these two provisos cannot be satisfied given that my data shows that confidential information about one bank's economic and other proposed terms is frequently disclosed to other banks. That leaks occur frequently became clear in my interviews. According to private equity lawyer [#43], for example, 'the trees are very leaky, that's for certain' and the suggestion that one bank's information is not ever leaked to other banks is a 'fiction'. Private equity lawyer [#43] provided an example:

> We got a new bank involved in this process who told us from the outset that they can only be involved if the minimum equity was x, and then two other banks who'd never had that as an issue suddenly wanted that.

My data discloses several potential reasons why these leaks occur. The high-pressure conditions under which bank lawyers work make leaks of confidential information likely to occur inadvertently. Bank lawyers need to prepare multiple but identical emails to the separate banks' email distribution lists, for example. Bank lawyer [#37] said:

> There are times when an associate will write a wayward email that was intended for a different bank. I think it's happened at every firm I've worked at. I mean, you do your best to make sure it doesn't happen. But the reality is it does happen.

108 Email to the author from the SRA on 2 July 2020.
109 ibid.

A lot of time is spent by associates, in particular, trying to avoid this type of 'cross contamination'; and there is a 'fear factor' amongst them, in case they 'screw up the deal' according to bank lawyer [#40]. But leaks still happen. Private equity lawyer [#36] said, referring to the bank lawyers they commonly dealt with:

> It's never nice when an associate says or sends something that they shouldn't have. It's just that people make mistakes.

Or disclosure might be in response to client pressure to disclose one bank's information to another bank. Associates are recognized as particularly susceptible to this pressure. According to bank lawyer [#29], a partner:

> We constantly get asked the question from banks 'has anyone else raised this issue?' I say, 'I can't tell you that'. If there was a proper tree, I wouldn't know at all, but they know that I do and so they're trying to get the information out of me. I'm constantly trying to drill into the team 'don't mention the views of other banks, really be careful, if a banker asks you, "what are the people saying on this point?" you can talk to them generically'. We can say 'we know that people in the market will have an issue with blob'. But we can't say 'another bank didn't like this point. So yes, you too can not like that point'.

Leaks may also occur because bank lawyers are not fully cognisant of their professional duty to keep a client's information confidential. Private equity lawyer [#28] offered an example:

> The partner acting for the banks had put an associate on it who was meant to be senior but just clearly didn't know what he was doing. And every step of the way there were issues; this guy kept revealing terms that one bank was asking for, to another one.

Further, bank lawyers might, in the exercise of their judgement in advising an individual bank, be influenced, consciously or subconsciously, by their knowledge of the position of other banks in the group on a particular issue. Bank lawyer [#34] referred to this as 'cross-pollution':

> On occasion you might guide in a way that you think is going to be helpful. Like, if they're on the fence about a point and you know, in your tree'd head, that every other bank is pushing it, you might think, well, they're not going to get in trouble for raising this. So, it is probably on balance not a problem if they do.

Bank lawyer [#42] said they also deploy their knowledge of other banks' positions to talk banks out of raising issues, for example:

> There's a degree to which, without particularising exactly what other lenders are saying about things, you can help a bank to arrive at more of a consensus position in that bank's interest and everyone else's interests by pointing out to them that they're an outlier.

The SRA included guidance in its previous Code of Conduct, in Rule 3.5, as to what is now the third proviso to the current Rule 6.2 (b) – reasonableness—meant in practice: the solicitor should not act for both clients where there was a real risk that the clients might be prejudiced by not being represented separately.[110] As already noted in Chapter 3, banks frequently complain about the level of service they receive, and this puts pressure on the already precarious relationships these firms have with the banks. Bank lawyer [#34] said:

> You'll have at least one or two people at the bank who will say 'oh, you weren't very helpful, you gave me one call slot time and said we can only speak to you in that time. We expect our lawyers to be more generally available'.

Further, the guidance to the previous rule also provided that the solicitor should not act for both clients where there was a real risk that the lawyer could not act for both clients even handedly.[111] Although bank lawyers may view banks as sophisticated users of legal services—and this is a valid consideration—it is also relevant that the bank clients may have been placed under commercial pressure to agree to this arrangement by the private equity sponsor; here, if they do not agree to this arrangement it is likely they will be excluded by the private equity sponsor from the competition for the financing mandate.[112]

Further, it is clear from case law that it is not reasonable for a solicitor to act for multiple clients in relation to the same matter where the risk of inadvertent disclosure of information confidential to one client to another is high. Relying on *Bolkiah v KPMG,* the SRA has emphasised that clients:

> should be protected from any real risk of the disclosure. A real risk does not have to be substantial - but must be more than merely fanciful or theoretical.[113]

This is particularly so given that solicitors are bound by other mandatory ethical principles, such as the duty to act in the best interests of the client, and to act with integrity.[114] My data show not only that the risk of unauthorized disclosure is high, but it also actually frequently occurs.

[110] Herring (n 60) 192, fn 37.
[111] ibid.
[112] ibid 192.
[113] 'Confidentiality of Client Information - Guidance' (n 100); *Bolkiah v KPMG* [1999] 2 AC 222.
[114] 'SRA Principles' (n 8).

It is also likely the practice of trees in the head falls foul of Rule 6.3, which requires solicitors to 'keep the affairs of current and former clients confidential unless disclosure is required or permitted by law or the client consents.'[115] Although conflicts of interest rules are separate from the confidentiality principle, they are connected when a lawyer advises two clients on the same matter.[116] It is likely that the rules have developed in parallel because conflict of interest is seen as less of an issue where there is a past and present client—in this case the ethical question will be centred around the duty to maintain the confidentiality of the past client.[117] However, where a solicitor advises two clients concurrently the question is also about divided loyalties. Hence conflict of interest, as well as confidentiality, rules are engaged.

Lord Scott, in *Three Rivers District Council v Governor and Company of the Bank of England (No.6)* described confidentiality as a 'central pillar' of legal ethics.[118] According to Jonathan Herring, 'lawyers have a special obligation flowing from their position in society and the trust imposed on them by their clients to keep information private.'[119] The duty of confidentiality is seen as a social good, in that it allows clients to seek the advice of solicitors on their most sensitive matters, without fear of the information being disclosed to a third party.[120] It is critical that lawyers take the duty to maintain a client's confidentiality seriously, and not handle confidential information casually.[121] Per Lord Millett in *Bolkiah v KPMG*:[122]

> It is of overriding importance to the administration of justice that a client should be able to have complete confidence that what he tells his lawyer will remain secret. This is a matter of perception as well as substance.

In summary, then, although a bank lawyer may agree with each bank to keep its information confidential and to not share it with the other banks, my data reveals that there is not only a significant risk that this information will be disclosed but that in practice unauthorised disclosure does occur. I have, hence, concluded that the practice of virtual trees, trees in the head, does not comply with the SRA's rules.

[115] 'SRA Code of Conduct for Solicitors, RELs and RFLs' (n 42).
[116] Herring (n 60) 181.
[117] Boon (n 38) 379.
[118] *Three Rivers District Council v Governor and Company of the Bank of England (No.6)* [2005] 1 AC 610 [34], per Lord Scott.
[119] Herring (n 60) 151.
[120] Boon (n 38) 334.
[121] David F Chavkin, 'Why Doesn't Anyone Care about Confidentiality - (And, What Message Does That Send to New Lawyers)' (2012) 25 Georgetown Journal of Legal Ethics 239; Herring (n 60) 173.
[122] [1999] 2 AC 222, 240; Herring (n 60) 151.

4.5 Conclusion

In this chapter, I explored the implications of the case study for bank lawyers' ethical duties, the most applicable being, first, the duty to act with independence, second, the solicitor's duty to disclose referral arrangements, and third, the solicitor's duties to avoid conflicts of interest and to maintain client confidentiality. I have concluded that bank lawyers will frequently breach each of these duties.

The next chapter explores how the prevailing logics of the leveraged finance practice area have emboldened private equity lawyers to pursue a contractual boundary-pushing strategy which has led to materially looser and uncertain loan covenants becoming a pervasive feature of European leveraged loans.

5

Private Equity Lawyers: Practices and Logics

5.1 Introduction

In this chapter, I explore what my empirical data reveals about the practices and logics of the lawyers that act for the private equity sponsor-backed borrowers in leverage finance transactions, the private equity lawyers. Specifically, this chapter considers the profound impact that discretionary private equity lawyer activity has had on the evolution of leveraged loan terms in Europe.

Since the mid-2000s, there has been an inexorable, uni-directional shift in the balance in leveraged loan terms away from providing core protections for banks and other lenders.[1] Bank lawyer [#34] noted:

> If you look at documents from even two years ago, they look very different; the market is always evolving. And they only tend to evolve one way, which is getting more and more sponsor friendly.

Press commentary of the ThyssenKrupp transaction in 2020, for example, noted the 'steady erosion of protections for investors over recent years as the market appeared to have moved to embrace aggressive sponsor features'.[2] These reports also shine a light on the contractual boundary pushing of the law firm advising the private equity sponsors in advocating for these types of terms, which were widely viewed as highly aggressive from the lenders' perspective.[3]

The strategy of contractual boundary pushing, motivated by a 'move the market' logic—which appears to have become the most available logic to private equity lawyers when deciding what is appropriate conduct—is a material

[1] 'Hot Leveraged Loan Market Puts Ebitda "Add-Backs" under Scrutiny' *Financial Times* (10 February 2017) <https://www.ft.com/content/ce5d0eee-eea0-11e6-930f-061b01e23655> accesed 15 February 2023; 'When The Cycle Turns: The Continued Attack Of The EBITDA Add-Back' <https://www.spglobal.com/ratings/en/research/articles/190919-when-the-cycle-turns-the-continued-attack-of-the-ebitda-add-back-11156255> accessed 2 July 2022.

[2] 'Investors Rue Lack of Protections on €7.1bn Thyssenkrupp Debt' *Financial Times* (26 June 2020) <https://www.ft.com/content/fae40c44-30af-4676-95ff-28feefa16890> accessed 23 June 2022.

[3] Nikou Asgari and Robert Smith, 'Thyssenkrupp Backers Improve €7.6bn Debt Terms after Lenders Balk' *Financial Times* (30 June 2020) <https://www.ft.com/content/81864124-e50c-4670-92c1-75658 2bb664b> accessed 9 August 2021.

contributor to this dramatic evolution in loan terms. Private equity lawyers are here effectively 'making law', in that their actions have been a material contributing factor to the way in which leveraged finance contracts have developed.[4] In other words, the major loosening in loan covenants is not purely a byproduct of shifting market conditions. At the same time, private equity lawyers have been greatly assisted by an absence of robust challenge from bank lawyers. Due to lawyer designation and the survival logic, bank lawyers seek to placate private equity lawyers by providing a less diligent standard of document evaluation than would otherwise be the case. Private equity lawyers have hence found themselves pushing at something of an open door when negotiating leveraged loan terms with the bank lawyers. This bank lawyer acquiescence has been critical to the effectiveness of the private equity lawyers' contractual boundary-pushing strategies that are explored in this chapter.[5] Whilst their contractual boundary-pushing strategies may—but will not always—align with a private equity lawyer's client's objectives, they tend to be primarily motivated by their own commercially pragmatic objectives.[6] Private equity lawyers and firms engage in intense competition with each other to be perceived as the best at 'moving the market', in documentary terms, further towards private equity sponsors. The firms build their profile and attract work by pursuing this strategy of improving terms on each transaction.

This chapter is arranged as follows. It first sets the scene by describing the key transactional battleground between private equity lawyers and their bank lawyer counterparts: leveraged loan covenants. Next, it describes the private equity lawyers' core strategy: how they approach this battle, which is to continually push contractual boundaries on each transaction in a manner which is often disconnected from the precise jurisdictional and business context of the transaction, and sometimes also the interests of their client. This strategy has resulted in a 'race to the bottom' and played a major role in the contagion of looser loan covenants across the market. An example of this strategy, the spurious and ambiguous 'add backs' in financial covenants, is examined in detail. The chapter then concludes.

[4] Michael J Powell, 'Professional Innovation: Corporate Lawyers and Private Lawmaking' (1993) 18 Law and Social Inquiry 423. Joan Loughrey, 'Accountability and the Regulation of the Large Law Firm Lawyer' (2014) 77 The Modern Law Review 732.

[5] Huseyin Leblebici and others, 'Institutional Change and the Transformation of Interorganizational Fields: An Organizational History of the U.S. Radio Broadcasting Industry' (1991) 36 Administrative Science Quarterly 333; Christine Oliver, 'Strategic Responses to Institutional Processes' (1991) 16 Academy of Management Review 145, 145; Thomas B. Lawrence and Roy Suddaby, 'Institutions and Institutional Work' in Stewart R Clegg, Cynthia Hardy, Thomas B Lawrence and Walter R Nord (eds), The SAGE Handbook of Organization Studies (SAGE 2006) 217.

[6] Richard Moorhead and Rachel Cahill-O'Callaghan, 'False Friends? Testing Commercial Lawyers on the Claim That Zealous Advocacy Is Founded in Benevolence towards Clients Rather than Lawyers' Personal Interest' (2016) 19 Legal Ethics 30.

5.2 Contractual boundary pushing

Private equity lawyer [#43] explained how they seek to push the boundaries of contractual terms on each and every transaction:

> We take the last deal where we got the best terms, we look at the market, at what other sponsors are getting, and then we update our precedent [loan documents]. Then we use that as the new precedent.

Loan covenants in leveraged finance documents operate as a form of private law governing cross-border leveraged buyout transactions, allocating risk between lenders and borrowers.[7] The covenants either require the borrower to take positive steps (positive covenants), such as to deliver financial information to the lenders on a recurring basis, or restrict the borrower from taking action (negative covenants).[8] Through this mechanism, leveraged loan agreements historically offered the lenders a veto right over the range of major corporate and financial steps the target group might propose to take during the life of the loan; for example, the borrowing of further debt, the making of significant disposals or acquisitions, and the payment of dividends to its shareholders.[9]

Private equity sponsors, on the other hand, seek as much flexibility as possible to pursue their various operational and financing strategies which are aimed at maximizing their return from the purchase of the business, without the need to obtain the lenders' consent (or waiver) each time. This might be for legitimate reasons. Borrowers might wish to undertake sensible operational and strategic steps for the business, for example, the disposal of some 'non-core' assets, or a reduction of debt.[10] Waivers of covenants, if forthcoming, can take time to obtain. Lending syndicates can comprise tens and sometimes hundreds of lenders, and waivers typically require a two-thirds majority, and sometimes even unanimous, lender consent. Further, the consent or waiver might come with 'strings attached': for example, a requirement that the proceeds from non-core asset sales must be wholly or partly applied in the prepayment of the loan, rather than used for investment in the core business, or to fund a dividend payment to the private equity sponsor.

The broad aim of the covenants, taken as a whole, is to mitigate the lenders' primary risk, that of the borrower's insolvency, or credit risk. A breach of

[7] Similar to collateral in the over-the-counter derivatives market, see Annelise Riles, *Collateral Knowledge: Legal Reasoning in the Global Financial Markets* (University of Chicago Press 2011) 224–25.

[8] Charles-Henri Larreur, *Structured Finance: Leveraged Buy-Outs, Project Finance, Asset Finance and Securitization* (Wiley 2021) 41–42.

[9] Elisabeth de Fontenay, 'Do the Securities Laws Matter - The Rise of the Leveraged Loan Market' (2013) 39 Journal of Corporation Law 725, 736.

[10] Sarah Paterson, 'The Rise of Covenant-Lite Lending and Implications for the UK's Corporate Insolvency Law Toolbox' (2019) 39 Oxford Journal of Legal Studies 654, 661.

covenant typically results in the triggering of rights and entitlements for the lenders, including the ability to accelerate the maturity of the loan and seek its immediate repayment.[11] The lenders are granted these rights so that they may take steps to mitigate their risk of loss before the borrower's financial position deteriorates too drastically. One issue is what Michael Jensen and William Meckling identify as the 'creditor director agency problem in distress'.[12] This is the risk that when a company is in financial distress, the directors may take ever increasing risks to save the company, and their own jobs. But this activity may negatively impact creditors by, for example, reducing available cash and hence the amount lenders may recover.[13] Covenants in loan agreements traditionally mitigate this risk.

The protection loan covenants once offered to lenders has been severely diluted by the shift to covenant-lite loan structures that I described in Chapter 2. But covenant weakening did not stop there. Covenants have continued to be loosened by the relentless contractual boundary pushing of private equity lawyers that I explore in the next section.

According to bank lawyer [#44] because of the loosening of loan covenants a lender's lending decision has been reduced to whether they 'trust this sponsor to run this business in a way that is going to be income generative?' Bank lawyer [#5] said 'these loan documents are the most complicated IOUs in the history of the world, because the borrowers can pretty much do what they want'.[14] Private equity lawyer [#24] reflected a recurring theme in my interviews, that 'the terms are being driven by the lawyers rather than by the sponsor'. In-house lawyer [#19] said the shift in the balance of loan terms was 'being driven by sponsor-side counsel in a race to the bottom'.

This section considers how the strategic action of private equity lawyers, motivated by a 'move the market' logic—the most available logic to private equity lawyers when deciding what is appropriate conduct—has been a material contributor to the dramatic weakening in global leveraged loan covenants. Private equity lawyers and firms are engaged in intense competition with each other to be perceived as the best at 'moving the market', in documentary terms, in leverage finance transactions, further towards private equity sponsors. For example, private equity lawyer [#43] indicated that:

[11] Larreur (n 8) 41.

[12] Michael C Jensen and William H Meckling, 'Theory of the Firm: Managerial Behavior, Agency Costs and Ownership Structure' (1976) 3 Journal of Financial Economics 305. Cited in Paterson (n 10) 657.

[13] Jensen and Meckling (n 12). Cited in Paterson (n 10) 657.

[14] IOU is anacronym for 'I owe you'. The IOU is an informal record of a debt where there is uncertainty as to whether it is legally binding and enforceable as a matter of contract, 'IOU: What It Is, How It Works, and Examples' (*Investopedia*) <https://www.investopedia.com/terms/i/iou.asp> accessed 12 March 2023.

> The usual approach we take is to always go for the best terms we can, often pushing the boundaries of every deal, to make it even better for sponsors in some new way.

This strategy of contractual boundary pushing has become an organizational routine, where private equity law firms draw on their collective experience and knowledge and make it available to their clients, as what Michael Smets and others have called a 'template of knowledge'.[15] Elisabeth de Fontenay describes how leveraged finance lawyers have developed digital data bases with extensive 'side by side' comparisons of terms seen in other transactions.[16] Private equity lawyer [#28] noted that these databases have become quite sophisticated, often involving 'a precedent bank for a particular sponsor on a particular term with different lenders.' Private equity lawyers and firms keep their loan document templates constantly updated, with the help of their firm's knowledge professionals. Private equity lawyers do this so that these new terms can be incorporated into the transaction documents for all subsequent deals that they advise on.

Their contractual boundary pushing has been facilitated by a shift in which lawyer controls the drafting process. Since the mid-2000s, private equity lawyers have taken over control of the drafting of the transaction documents from the bank lawyers. According to private equity lawyer [#26], this reflects a change in thinking about who 'owns' the deal process overall:

> The banks are arranging the loan, but we're hiring the banks to arrange our deal into the market. So, we want to use our document that we're familiar with.

Bank lawyer [#41] said this shift in who holds the pen on the documents has given the private equity lawyer's a 'first drafter advantage' which is critical to the effectiveness of their strategies:

> Now you're presented with a document based on the sponsor's precedent and anything that you do to try and claw that back to a position where you feel your client is fully protected, it's you that's having to justify it.

According to private equity lawyer [#26]:

> Lawyers being who they are, if you let a lawyer draft the document, he digs his heels in, it's much harder to push a lawyer off a point if it's his own document, as

15 Michael Smets and others, '25 Years since "P2": Taking Stock and Charting the Future of Professional Firms' (2017) 4 Journal of Professions and Organization 91, 99.

16 Elisabeth de Fontenay, 'Law Firm Selection and the Value of Transactional Lawyering' (2015) 41 Journal of Corporation Law 393, 425–26.

> opposed to if it's just a lawyer sending comments on somebody else's documents. Its simple psychology.

In other words, once the private equity lawyer has inserted new provisions into the first draft of the documents for a new transaction, their control of the drafting for the entirety of the negotiation process enables them to vigorously defend these new provisions.

A one-size-fits-all logic determines the content of documents rather than the jurisdictional or even business context of the transaction.[17] In his study of English and German banking lawyers, Smets found the English lawyers applied concepts across jurisdictions without regard to jurisdictional concerns, 'transporting meaning across normative contexts'.[18] And Annalise Riles explored how the International Swap Dealers Association (ISDA) template is a form of regulatory governance for derivative contracts that crosses international borders whilst founded in assumptions rooted in English and New York law which often make little sense in a Japanese environment.[19] This phenomenon is also present in the leveraged finance practice area field. The difference is that as well as clumsy jurisdictional transplants, we see transplants between different industry sectors, for example, without much thought given to the precise business context of the transaction. Bank lawyer [#34] said private equity lawyers:

> take a 'one size fits all' approach to everything, which is, 'if we got this term through on our previous deal, then we want to apply it to a new deal'. And they're ignoring things like jurisdiction, industry, size of deal.

Private equity lawyer [#25] offered this example:

> You buy a particular business and the strategy is to break off two or three different parts and sell them because they're not part of the core business. And you negotiate in that specific deal the flexibility to do that with those particular divisions and strike a deal with the banks as to what they can do with the proceeds. The next deal comes along which doesn't have that strategy at all, but that flexibility is retained in there. And maybe it doesn't now say it's that division or that division

17 Kenneth Ayotte and Christina Scully, 'J. Crew, Nine West, and the Complexities of Financial Distress Forum Collection: Bankruptcy and Restructuring in Response to Exogenous Shocks' (2021) 131 Yale Law Journal Forum 363, 365.

18 Michael Smets, 'Institutional Work Taken Literally: How Logics Shift as Banking Lawyers "Get the Deal Done"' (2009 Academy of Management annual meeting, USA, 2009) 21 <http://publications.aston.ac.uk/id/eprint/18544/> accessed 20 May 2021.

19 Riles notes how the ISDA template required delivery of collateral within three days, eg, which was the practice is New York, but Japanese clearing systems could not transfer bonds this quickly. Riles (n 7) 59, 62.

or the other division, it now just says 'non-core assets'. And this business may not have any non-core assets.

In other words, the conditions and the considerations that apply in relation to target company *x* might be fundamentally different to target company *y* because they operate, for example, in different industry sectors, and/or different countries. But private equity lawyers have nevertheless become effectively agnostic as to the business and jurisdictional context of transactions.

Private equity lawyers have, thus, decontextualized debates with the bank lawyers over loan covenants from the specific conditions of each transaction. The draft documents tend to be presented by private equity lawyers to their bank lawyer counterparts as if they are what Stephen Choi and others describe as boilerplate— 'a uniform system of communication that is independent of any particular contractual context'.[20] A 'take it or leave it logic' can be detected in the private equity lawyers' strategies. Bank lawyer [#34] said 'there is this knee jerk reaction, to say 'no' to everything, without them thinking about it'. Private equity lawyers then frequently refuse to engage with the bank lawyers' comments; bank lawyer [#31] said they 'send out new drafts saying, "we've incorporated what we can in here now. Please confirm that it's agreed."' Kimberly Kirkland, in her study of litigators in corporate law firms in the United States, found that they often adopted these types of aggressive, as opposed to reasoned, approaches in their dealings with the lawyers acting for the other party to a dispute.[21] In contradistinction to Kirkland, this book shows how aggression is deployed strategically by one group of lawyers in a manifestation of their power over another.

The cleared-the-market logic described in the previous chapter is also important in this process, this time operating as a key component of the governing framework for private equity lawyer, as opposed to bank lawyer, sense-making. If a new term has cleared the market in the syndication of a previous deal, regardless of whether that prior deal's jurisdictional or business context is analogous to that of the current deal, both private equity lawyers and bank lawyers tend to give it a stamp of approval. Albeit loan and other transaction documents are now based on the private equity sponsor's—or its lawyer's—own precedent templates, as opposed to the LMA's standard forms, this dynamic has ensured that their terms have converged to a significant degree.

In the leveraged finance practice area, loan terms are hence carried across from transaction to transaction in a process of what Choi and others describe

[20] Stephen J Choi, Mitu Gulati, and Robert E Scott, 'The Black Hole Problem in Commercial Boilerplate' (2017) 67 Duke Law Journal 1, 4.

[21] Kimberly Kirkland, 'The Ethics of Constructing Truth, The Corporate Litigator's Approach', *Lawyers in Practice: Ethical Decision Making in Context* (University of Chicago Press 2012) 164, 166–67, 171. Kimberly Kirkland, 'Ethics in Large Law Firms: The Principle of Pragmatism' (2004) 35 University of Memphis Law Review 631, 712.

as 'repetition without reflection'.[22] Precedent documents are constantly updated and improved from the private equity sponsors' perspective and become the new starting point of negotiation on all subsequent deals. Contractual boundaries, and the allocation of risk between lenders and borrowers, constantly shift, albeit in only one direction, in favour of the private equity sponsor-backed borrowers. Documentary flexibilities 'won' on a deal by one private equity lawyer tend spread to other deals, so that terms which might have been conceded by the banks on a one-off basis for legitimate business reasons given the business or other context of a transaction become commonplace for all deals, regardless of its context. Improvements in terms achieved by one private equity lawyer or firm hence tend to stick, in that they are then adopted, and often expanded upon, by competitor firms. Private equity lawyers present their draft documents on each new transaction as compelling, as routine knowledge, as representative of a 'market standard position', which is implicitly widely accepted, and thus legitimate; by theorizing their everyday work in this way it becomes normalized and accepted by the actors in the field.[23] Private equity lawyer contractual boundary pushing has in this way become a structural practice of the leveraged finance practice area, an institutionalized mode of working.[24]

Whilst the contractual boundary-pushing strategy may—but will not always—align with a private equity lawyer's client's objectives, the strategy tends to be primarily motivated by their own self-interested, commercially pragmatic objectives.[25] Private equity lawyers and firms are engaged in intense competition with each other to be perceived as the best at 'moving the market', in documentary terms, further towards private equity sponsors. Lawrence Krieger argues that lawyers are often competitive in nature, and so inclined towards self-interest because they are 'prone to insecurity and an unhealthy need for status'.[26] Private equity lawyer [#36] said that two private equity-focused firms were 'engaged in a death match. Neither firm will give up a point that the other has won.' The firms build their profile and attract work by pursuing this strategy of improving terms on each transaction. The firms which are seen as the most successful at pushing aggressive terms for their private equity clients are considered by their competitors as the most prestigious due to their power to 'move the market' in loan terms in this way. They have, according to bank lawyer [#16], 'weaponized their position in the market'. Other firms copy their approach. Lawyers and firms tend to mimic the firm or firms they

22 Choi, Gulati, and Scott (n 20) 4.

23 Royston Greenwood, Roy Suddaby, and CR Hinings, 'Theorizing Change: The Role of Professional Associations in the Transformation of Institutionalized Fields' (2002) 45 The Academy of Management Journal 58, 75.

24 Smets (n 18); Greenwood, Suddaby, and Hinings (n 23) 75.

25 Moorhead and Cahill-O'Callaghan (n 6).

26 Lawrence S Krieger, 'Institutional Denial about the Dark Side of Law School, and Fresh Empirical Guidance for Constructively Breaking the Silence' (2002) 52 Journal of Legal Education 112. Cited in Moorhead and Cahill-O'Callaghan (n 6) 35.

perceive to be the most successful, and the most prestigious, in the field.[27] Paul DiMaggio and Walter Powell refer to this as 'mimetic isomorphism'.[28]

In the next section I explore a detailed example of this boundary-pushing activity.

5.3 Example: spurious 'add backs' in financial covenants

As I have already noted, the dramatic loosening in loan covenants did not stop with the move to covenant-lite. Since the mid-2000s there has been a further seismic shift in the balance in loan terms away from protecting banks and other lenders.[29] The contractual boundary-pushing strategies of private equity lawyers have played a key role in this evolution of loan terms. Private equity lawyers have advocated for a series of subsequent innovations to financial covenants, for example, including the spurious 'add backs' I consider in this section.[30]

Notwithstanding that covenant-lite loan structures have become the norm, financial covenants still offer a measure of protection for lenders since they must be met when borrowers seek to take certain important steps, for example when they wish to raise further debt, pay a dividend, or make an acquisition.[31] And a working capital facility will typically include a 'springing' covenant—meaning a financial covenant will be tested if the borrower seeks to draw the facility in excess of a minimum threshold, often set at 40% of the total facility limit, as borrowers tend to do when they are short of cash.[32] However, the range and complexity of the 'add backs' in the calculation of any financial covenants that remain has further diluted the extent to which financial covenants protect lenders in practice. The Financial Stability Board (FSB) found evidence that 'headline debt-to-EBITDA may be understated' in leveraged loan transactions, due to a multiplicity of add backs where a borrower can recognize certain 'synergies or operational improvements' which are particularly uncertain as to their scale, and whether they exist at all.[33] The FSB found that synergies and cost savings had often not been realized

[27] Paul J DiMaggio and Walter Powell W, 'The Iron Cage Revisited: Institutional Isomorphism and Collective Rationality', *The New Institutionalism in Organizational Analysis* (Chicago University Press 1991) 69.

[28] DiMaggio and Powell describe three types of isomorphic process: *coercive* (facilitated or coerced, by both formal and informal rules and regulations applicable to the organisation), *mimetic* and *normative*; these types are not always conceptually distinct, and in places may overlap and merge, ibid 68.

[29] 'Hot Leveraged Loan Market Puts Ebitda "Add-Backs" under Scrutiny' (n 1); 'When The Cycle Turns: The Continued Attack Of The EBITDA Add-Back' (n 1).

[30] 'Leveraged Loans Are Way Past "Cov-Lite"' *Financial Times* (16 November 2018) <https://www.ft.com/content/53014840-e0bf-374b-8d22-c9a9ea318a8d> accessed 16 February 2023; Paterson (n 10) 663–64.

[31] Donald Lowe and James Bell, 'COVID-19 and the Impact on Financial Covenants' [2020] Journal of International Banking and Financial Law 2.

[32] ibid.

[33] 'When The Cycle Turns: The Continued Attack Of The EBITDA Add-Back' (n 1); 'Vulnerabilities Associated with Leveraged Loans and Collateralised Loan Obligations' (Financial Stability Board, 19

two years after the loan had been entered into.[34] The International Organization of Securities Commissions (IOSCO) also recently reported that EBITDA add backs found in typical leveraged loan documents are 'uncertain, both in magnitude and timing, and may overstate EBITDA and thus understate debt-EBITDA leverage multiples'.[35] IOSCO warns about the risks associated with EBITDA add backs, pointing to research that shows them to be overly optimistic.[36] Lenders face potentially significant losses as a consequence.[37] IOSCO noted that leveraged borrowers can expect more challenging refinancing conditions with 'growing demand for refinancing from 2024 onwards due to significant maturity walls'; many weaker borrowers will be unable to secure refinancing and 'fall into financial distress and enter a restructuring of their debt'.[38]

Add backs are effectively an adjustment device which has the effect of artificially inflating the borrower group's profitability and hence its ability to pay interest to service the loan. In other words, a cost which once—under the traditional drafting of financial covenants—would have been deducted from income to reach the profit number is added back. These have been designed by private equity sponsors—with the help of their lawyers—to disguise real, often, underperformance, and to keep an ailing company out of default and away from the clutches of its creditors.[39]

Add backs tend to impact the determination of the borrower's EBITDA for any particular reference period. EBITDA is the concept typically used in financial covenants as a proxy for cash flow, a company's ability to service its debt. As it is not a concept found in accounting rules, it can be manipulated through contractually created adjustments.[40] EBITDA is already flawed as a proxy for profitability as it does not take into account a company's capital expenditure or working capital requirements.[41] The effect of the add backs is to further inflate this number by adding

December 2019) 9 <https://www.fsb.org/2019/12/vulnerabilities-associated-with-leveraged-loans-and-collateralised-loan-obligations/> accessed 2 July 2022. Cited in ibid 9.

[34] 'When The Cycle Turns: The Continued Attack Of The EBITDA Add-Back' (n 1); 'Vulnerabilities Associated with Leveraged Loans and Collateralised Loan Obligations' (n 33) 9. Cited in ibid 9.

[35] International Organisation of Securities Commissions, 'Leveraged Loans and CLOs, Good Practices for Consideration, Consultation Report CR05/2023' (September 2023) 12 <https://www.iosco.org/library/pubdocs/pdf/IOSCOPD746.pdf>.

[36] ibid 1; 'Leveraged Finance: Fifth Annual Study Of EBITDA Addbacks Finds Management Continues To Regularly Miss Projections' <https://www.spglobal.com/ratings/en/research/articles/230216-leveraged-finance-fifth-annual-study-of-ebitda-addbacks-finds-management-continues-to-regularly-miss-project-12ISCOS643170> accessed 7 February 2024.

[37] Trevor Clark, 'Accounting for COVID-19: Are Lawyers Helping Clients "Remould the Rules"?' (*Lawyer Watch*, 18 May 2020) <https://lawyerwatch.blog/2020/05/18/accounting-for-covid-19-are-lawyers-helping-clients-remould-the-rules/> accessed 25 May 2020.

[38] International Organisation of Securities Commissions (n 35) 13.

[39] 'Hot Leveraged Loan Market Puts Ebitda "Add-Backs" under Scrutiny' (n 1).

[40] John Gilligan and Mike Wright, *Private Equity Demystified: An Explanatory Guide* (Fourth Edition, Oxford University Press 2020) 145, 192–93.

[41] 'Hot Leveraged Loan Market Puts Ebitda "Add-Backs" under Scrutiny' (n 1).

back an amount equal to any exceptional and non-recurring costs which were first excluded from the base calculation of EBITDA.[42]

Common examples of such a cost are M&A fees, losses on the sale of an asset, or restructuring charges such as employee severance pay.[43] If these are genuinely one-off expenses then a case could be made that they should not be taken into account in assessing the borrower's longer-term ability to service debt. By adding them back, it can be argued that this brings EBITDA to a position which is more reflective of the usual, or steady state,performance of the borrower. However, in the relevant test period, it further distorts the picture of the borrower's capacity to service the loan.

John Gilligan and Mike Wright observe that there might be 'perfectly legitimate reasons to make the adjustment' but at the same time 'also temptations to massage the number to increase the amount of debt available to the business'.[44] The problem—the manipulation—is that now costs that might occur *in most years* are frequently added back.[45] And borrowers are now also typically able to add in amounts which boost their EBITDA—their profits—which are as yet unrealized and simply forecast; for example, anticipated synergies, and cost savings from an internal restructuring or an acquisition.[46]

I have noted already how leveraged buyouts are effectively a technique for transferring risk to lenders.[47] The risk with these spurious add backs is that there is a further transfer of risk to the lenders that should appropriately be borne by the private equity sponsor.[48] It results in a lack of transparency for lenders with the consequence that the debt might be over-sized; in other words, lenders may over-lend.[49] And it potentially means a financial covenant test that should have been failed—triggering an event of default and the lender rights that flow from it—is instead passed.

This was generally understood and acknowledged by my participants. For example, bank lawyer [#22] said that because of these addbacks, 'the financial covenants as a concept in these documents are pretty meaningless' as:

> even where businesses are in really dire financial problems, there is never a deterioration in EBITDA that gives the lenders an event of default and brings the sponsors to the table in any restructuring discussions.

42 Gilligan and Wright (n 40) 197.
43 'What Is a Nonrecurring Charge?' (*Investopedia*) <https://www.investopedia.com/terms/n/nonrecurringcharge.asp> accessed 15 March 2023.
44 Gilligan and Wright (n 40) 197.
45 ibid.
46 Lowe and Bell (n 31).
47 See Chapter 2.
48 Gilligan and Wright (n 40) 198.
49 ibid.

The problems associated with these types of artificial add-backs are compounded by the scope for subjectivity—who determines whether a cost is one off or not, for example—and the general lack of transparency for lenders in how EBITDA is calculated and reported. Lenders may not have the right to verify the calculations made by the sponsors, according to private equity lawyer [#37]:

> It's very tricky for banks to actually call out sponsors on it because they don't get to see the underlying calculations. We're never quite clear on how the debt incurrence is actually calculated.

That private equity lawyers are actively and enthusiastically advocating for spurious add backs and other adjustments to financial covenants is apparent from an article written by lawyers at a private equity-focussed law firm. It referred to 'well-advised' borrowers, 'over the past decade' having 'succeeded in remoulding the rules' for calculating EBITDA 'by introducing a range of subjective elements which make it easier to game the related financial covenants' and invites other private equity sponsors to do the same by explaining how to do it.[50] It is striking that private equity lawyers are publicly advocating that their clients 'remould the rules' and 'game' the covenants in this way. That private equity lawyers actively and enthusiastically advocated for these spurious add backs and other adjustments to financial covenants is also apparent from my data. Private equity lawyer [#37] said, for example: 'there is a lot of ambiguity around the way that the testing works in the documents and sponsor lawyers are pretty aggressive in their interpretation of things'. I consider the ethical implications of this type of lawyer activity in Chapter 6.

A spurious lawyer-led interpretation of typical financial covenants emerged during the COVID-19 pandemic. Several cash poor private equity-backed borrowers asserted in their discussions with lenders that for the purpose of covenant testing, the often-dramatic effects of the COVID-19 pandemic on their businesses should be ignored.[51] The aim was to ignore the effect of their reduced revenue due to government-imposed lockdowns, by adding back that lost revenue to inflate the EBITDA number they reported to their lenders. They were able to take advantage of both ambiguity in the language used in financial covenants, together with uncertainty in the meaning of the applicable accounting rules, the international financial reporting standards (IFRS).[52]

[50] Lowe and Bell (n 31); Clark (n 37).

[51] Lowe and Bell (n 31); Clark (n 37).

[52] 'IFRS - Home' <https://www.ifrs.org/> accessed 16 March 2023. Although companies are not required to report EBITDA under IFRS, these rules determine how component items are treated in the calculation of EBITDA. For example, IFRS changes in 2019 capitalized formerly off-balance sheet operating leases and resulted in rental expenses being instead deducted as depreciation and interest. This had the effect of increasing a company's EBITDA. 'IFRS 16 and Its Impact on EBITDA/Debt and Financial Covenants' (*Stevens & Bolton LLP*, 3 July 2018) <https://www.stevens-bolton.com/site/insights/articles/ifrs-16-and-its-impact-on-ebitdadebt-and-financial-covenants> accessed 16 March 2023.

Private equity lawyers asserted that the COVID-19 pandemic was an exceptional event and so was also an exceptional accounting event under IFRS. On this issue, IFRS is ambiguous. They argued that the pandemic, and the interruption to business revenues consequent upon it, should be treated like other exceptional items already expressly provided for in the loan covenants as exclusions, to be disregarded for the purposes of the covenants. This was notwithstanding it was not expressly referred to as an exceptional event, albeit the list of express exclusions might be stated to be 'non-exhaustive'.

EBITDA effectively became 'EBITDAC', so that, under this fiction—since revenues lost during the pandemic were never going to be recovered—the metric was now earnings before interest, tax, depreciation, amortisation and *coronavirus*.[53] The effect was that the borrower could replace the much reduced EBITDA revenue position for the period affected by the pandemic, with the much healthier EBITDA number for the corresponding reporting period in the previous year.[54] Market commentators generally agreed that this was a 'try on'.[55]

Having advocated for spurious interpretations of ambiguous financial covenant definitions in existing transactions during the COVID-19 pandemic, private equity lawyers then advocated for new drafting to be inserted in loan documents which embedded these spurious interpretations in the terms of new transactions. They insisted on the inclusion of 'EBITDAC'—now broadened out to cover pandemics and all similar 'shock' events—as an express term in new transactions.[56]

Private equity lawyers have been at the forefront of designing and advocating for these developments:[57] Private equity lawyer [#13] said:

> We're calling it a 'shock event' provision, which is similar to what came out when there was an Icelandic volcano. If there has been a shock event, then the borrower is allowed to test its covenants, rather than by reference to the last 12 months, you can look back to a different period, or you can use the base case as a proxy for what EBITDA would be, but for the shock event.

Whilst a case might be made by private equity lawyers that this is not unreasonable where there is a temporary dip in fortunes because of one-off 'shock events' like a pandemic, the real-world effects are potentially very serious for lenders. They lose their usual rights and entitlements that flow from a breach of financial covenant, in a scenario where the borrower's financial condition may have rapidly deteriorated.

[53] 'Pandemic Spawns New Reporting Term "Ebitdac" to Flatter Books' *Financial Times* (13 May 2020) <https://www.ft.com/content/5467518c-1b68-4712-9e74-e7cc949d8002> accessed 23 June 2022.

[54] See also Clark (n 37).

[55] 'Pandemic Spawns New Reporting Term "Ebitdac" to Flatter Books' (n 53).

[56] The Thyssenkrupp buyout in 2020 reportedly contained this term, 'Investors Rue Lack of Protections on €7.1bn Thyssenkrupp Debt' (n 2).

[57] See also Lowe and Bell (n 31); Clark (n 37).

In the past, they might have been expected to assert some measure of control and monitoring in this type of situation, to perhaps initiate discussions around potential debt restructuring measures with the private equity sponsor. Now, they must wait and see what happens and hope for the best. Lenders face potentially significant losses as a consequence.[58] Bank lawyer [#22] gave this example:

> I've got one deal at the moment where I act for the lender, and the business is in the leisure industry. It's extremely badly affected by the Coronavirus situation. This business recently put in a compliance certificate, and it has sailed through all of its financial covenants. But the company's going to run out of money in a couple of weeks.

The potential wider social effect of this private equity lawyer activity was neatly summarized by private equity lawyer [#11]:

> There's an awful lot of companies that quite frankly shouldn't exist. And they will be bumbling along for years.

5.4 Conclusion

The private equity lawyers' practice of relentless contractual boundary pushing has made a material contribution to the evolution of the terms of the financing documents typically seen in the leveraged finance sector. In shifting the terms of documents more squarely in their clients' favour, private equity lawyer action has had a profound effect on the allocation of risk between sponsors and arrangers, through a significant erosion of traditional protections for lenders. In effect, private equity lawyers have, in common with the bank lawyers, taken documentary terms beyond the point that the changes to field dynamics that began to emerge in the mid-2000s would have otherwise taken them to, symbolized by covenant-lite loans, through their discretionary and opportunistic behaviour. Private equity lawyers are here effectively 'making law', in that their actions have been a material contributing factor to the way in which leveraged finance contracts have developed.[59]

This private equity lawyer activity has likely led them to breach their ethical duties under the code of professional conduct to which they are subject, as I explore in the next chapter.

[58] Clark (n 37).
[59] Powell (n 4). Loughrey (n 4).

6
Private Equity Lawyers: Ethical Duties

6.1 Introduction

In this chapter, I explore what the case study means with respect to the observance by private equity lawyers of their ethical duties, the most applicable being, first, the duty to act in the best interests of each client and, second, the solicitor's duty to act with integrity. We see how the success of private equity lawyer strategies, such as contractual boundary pushing, depends on the coercive authority they wield over bank lawyers. An example of this private-equity-lawyer boundary-pushing activity is then explored—namely the imposition by private equity lawyers of new terms at the initial 'commercial grid' stage of the transaction—and its implications for the observance of their ethical duties are considered.

6.2 The duty to act in the best interests of each client

The duty to clients is rooted in the nature of a lawyer's relationship with their client, which is primarily contractual, but also involves elements of tort and the law of agency, implying fiduciary duties to the client.[1] It is also a specific duty in the Solicitors Regulation Authority's, SRA's, Standards and Regulations. In this section, I put the case that the strategies and practices of private equity lawyers which are revealed by my data may constitute breaches of Principle 7, which requires solicitors to act in the best interests of each client.[2]

Private equity lawyer [#18] saw their contractual boundary-pushing strategies I described in Chapter 5 in the following terms:

[1] Andrew Boon, *The Ethics and Conduct of Lawyers in England and Wales* (Bloomsbury Publishing 2014) 297–300; Jonathan Herring, *Legal Ethics* (OUP 2017) 120; 'SRA Code of Conduct for Solicitors, RELs and RFLs' (25 November 2019) <https://www.sra.org.uk/solicitors/standards-regulations/code-conduct-solicitors/> accessed 15 November 2020. The House of Lords has characterized the lawyer/client relationship as contractual, with the scope of the solicitor's duties determined by the express and implied term of the retainer, but where the lawyer also has fiduciary responsibilities to the client. *Hilton v Barker booth & Eastwood* [2005], 1 All ER 651, see paragraphs 28 and 29.

[2] 'SRA Principles' (25 November 2019) <https://www.sra.org.uk/solicitors/standards-regulations/principles/> accessed 6 July 2020.

> That's just part of being a good sponsor-side lawyer. Not just sitting on the precedent but trying to work so that all of your clients have the best terms you can achieve for them.

And private equity lawyer [#33] said they were simply responding to client demand:

> Our job, and what is wanted by more sponsors, is we're always seeking to optimise the terms.

These accounts suggest a misunderstanding by private equity lawyers of their professional duties. Private equity lawyers strategically seek to advance the interests of private equity sponsors *as a class*, rather than the interests of *each client* individually, as per their duty under SRA Principle 7.[3] To be considered competent pursuant to Rule 3. of the Code of Conduct, a solicitor is required to consider and take account of *each client's* particular 'attributes, needs and circumstances'.[4] In the SRA's Glossary, 'client' is defined as 'the *person* for whom you act and, where the context permits, includes prospective and former clients'.[5] No further guidance is given; but it seems unlikely this language permits solicitors to consider the interests of other clients over and above the client they have been mandated to act for on the particular matter. Most likely, the reference to 'prospective and former' is to ensure that individual clients benefit from certain duties that will apply before and after the period during which the solicitor is formally retained. For example, the duty to keep a client's information confidential does not cease when the individual matter is completed. In any event, solicitors also have very individual and particular duties to the client in contract, tort, and as fiduciaries.

This client-as-a-class logic is the framework through which private equity lawyers tended to make sense of, and give meaning to, their conduct in my interviews with them.[6] They drew on this narrative as a rhetorical strategy because it offered a convenient ethical justification for contractual boundary-pushing (or, pushing for aggressive terms that their client may not need) through a perceived—but misguided—interdependence of their own commercially pragmatic objectives (or, securing more lucrative sponsor-side work by being seen to be the most aggressive in pushing aggressive terms) with the interests of their private equity clients, but again, viewed as a client class and not individually.[7] As I have already noted, their

[3] ibid.

[4] 'SRA Code of Conduct for Solicitors, RELs and RFLs' (n 1).

[5] 'SRA Glossary' (11 March 2021) <https://www.sra.org.uk/solicitors/standards-regulations/glossary/> accessed 2 August 2023 (emphasis added).

[6] Patricia H Thornton, William Ocasio, and Michael Lounsbury, *The Institutional Logics Perspective: A New Approach to Culture, Structure, and Process* (OUP Oxford 2012) 149–50, 152.

[7] David Kershaw and Richard Moorhead, 'Consequential Responsibility for Client Wrongs: Lehman Brothers and the Regulation of the Legal Profession' (2013) 76 The Modern Law Review 26; Thornton, Ocasio, and Lounsbury (n 6) 8.

strategy is often disconnected from the requirements of individual clients, and indeed from the business and/or jurisdictional context of any given transaction. For example, bank lawyer [#44] explained to me how on one deal the private equity lawyer was pushing for the borrower to have the freedom to sell and lease back its valuable real estate assets:

> Given the whole value was within the real estate that this company owned, we were really struggling to get comfortable. And then when we were on an all-party call I said to the sponsor directly, 'do you plan on doing any sale and leasebacks?' And he goes, 'no, absolutely not. It's not part of the business model. We don't need it.'

There are further examples in my data of private equity lawyers pushing for broad flexibility in paying dividends, for example, where their client had a policy not to ask borrowers to pay them. Private equity lawyer [#25] said 'one of my clients, whilst it might have been given the flexibility, as an institution it very rarely takes dividends.'

Client autonomy is often the basis for much of the literature supporting the standard conception of the lawyer's role.[8] Some private equity lawyers sought to present themselves in my interviews with them as grounded in principles of client autonomy: that their stance enabled their clients to choose between the various options available to them. For example, private equity lawyer [#42] said:

> Our job is to give the clients options; we don't take the decisions for them.

They frequently do not actively seek to identify their individual client's objectives with respect to a transaction at its outset, however. Private equity lawyer [#13] said some clients 'leave you to get on with it. And they just check in with you.' Private equity lawyer [#12] suggested they were frequently negotiating not only legal but also 'commercial points, without even raising them with the sponsor.' Private equity lawyers rarely operate simply as neutral technocrats, advising their clients of their options without exercising a significant degree of discretion. As was noted in the previous chapter, how they exercise this discretion is driven just as much by intense competition with other private equity lawyers and the move-the-market logic than it is by a sense of loyalty to their clients. According to private equity lawyer [#35]:

[8] Tim Dare, 'Mere-Zeal, Hyper-Zeal and the Ethical Obligations of Lawyers' (2004) 7 Legal Ethics 24, 25. Christine Parker, 'A Critical Morality for Lawyers: Four Approaches to Lawyers' Ethics' [2004] Monash University Law Review 49, 52; Richard Moorhead and Rachel Cahill-O'Callaghan, 'False Friends? Testing Commercial Lawyers on the Claim That Zealous Advocacy Is Founded in Benevolence towards Clients Rather than Lawyers' Personal Interest' (2016) 19 Legal Ethics 30, 32.

> A good chunk of covenant loosening is driven by the law firms involved on the sponsor side, who like to be able to tell their sponsor clients that they've got the craziest terms that they can.

The implication is that pushing 'crazy' terms has become an end goal in itself. As Annalise Riles has observed, we should not assume that lawyers, as the users of legal tools, are completely in control of the outcome of their use; legal tools 'sometimes, mysteriously, overtake their users'.[9] The translation of US bond terms into European loan agreements by leveraged finance lawyers appears to have assumed a trajectory of its own, for example. Private equity lawyer [#32] said firms are:

> Pushing an agenda whereby the more private equity houses out there that are using our documents and pushing our points, the better it is for our brand.

This is a manifestation of the move-the-market logic, driven by intense competition between private equity lawyers and firms. Their strategies have become frequently disconnected from a determination by the lawyer of what their clients want or need. According to bank lawyer [#17] there is a 'fear' amongst private equity lawyers which leads to theirs adopting the practices of what are seen to be the most successful and prestigious private equity-focused law firms to 'defend their patch'. The result is that private equity lawyers and firms compete based on their perceived ability to drive the best terms for their clients, again, as a class, as opposed to individually. This drives them to seek to move the market in terms on each transaction. Bank lawyer [#27] said:

> We see [Firm A] will come up with something and then a month later it will be in [Firm B's] documents.

In-house lawyer [#17] described a 'league table' of private equity law firm prestige, 'around which they build a business strategy that is completely divorced from what their clients require commercially'. This is mostly prestige recognized within the narrow confines of this field. Private equity lawyers view as most prestigious those private equity lawyers who secure the role advising on the largest transactions for the leading global sponsors. Bank lawyers view those lawyers as the most prestigious given their capacity to hand out the designations that will lead to the most lucrative work for bank lawyers.

The strategy of contractual boundary pushing is sometimes communicated to clients as a pre-condition to their appointment. According to private equity lawyer [#33]:

[9] Annelise Riles, *Collateral Knowledge: Legal Reasoning in the Global Financial Markets* (University of Chicago Press 2011) 229.

> If a client simply wants us to base the terms on the template from a previous transaction, we often say to them, 'we're the wrong law firm for you'.

Where the scope of the retainer is made explicit in this way, the client has the option to choose another law firm to act for them. If the client accepts these terms and instructs this lawyer, then there is, to this extent, an alignment with their wishes. For a lawyer to specify their scope of work, in a way that so clearly is determined by reference to their commercial self-interests is unusual, however. Lawyers often provide a scope of work to protect themselves where they are retained on a capped fee arrangement, or to ensure they comply with legal and regulatory obligations, for example. That a private equity lawyer will not work with a client which is prepared to accept terms that are—at that moment—reflective of the market standard for leveraged loan terms emphasizes, both, how important this strategy of relentlessly pursuing improvements in terms is to this private equity lawyer, and how disconnected the strategy is from the interests of individual clients. The lawyer might claim that the contractual boundary-pushing strategy is in that client's best interests, but it is adopted not for this reason but because it is critical to their business model. It does not speak to the ethical duty that these lawyers have to act with independence, or their duty to act in *that client's* best interests.

Some private equity sponsors will be aware of and support their lawyers in pursuing contractual boundary-pushing activity. It might even be why they hired the lawyer or the firm in the first place. But this will not always be the case. And pushing for flexibility that the client does not need can have material negative effects for private equity sponsors as well as lenders. First, the private equity lawyers are here creating extra work for themselves, and for the bank lawyers, by pushing and perhaps defending new provisions that the client may not care about and may feel they do not need, lengthening the period of negotiation and potentially incurring additional legal fees and charging them to the client in the process.[10] There is also the risk that potential new lenders that might otherwise have bought the loan on syndication are dissuaded by the presence of the new and aggressive terms from doing so.[11] If terms are pushed so far that this endangers a successful syndication of the loan, investors can require an amendment of terms under the 'market flex' clause commonly included in the commitment documents.[12] This

[10] If they are paid on an hourly rate basis as opposed to a fixed fee arrangement.

[11] A leveraged loan is typically arranged by one or more investment banks, who then sell participations in the loan to a group of lenders, who may include banks but may also include non-banks such as CLOs, pension funds, insurance companies, and other institutional investors. The process of selling these participations is referred to as 'syndication' and the group of lenders who buy them tends to be called 'the syndicate'.

[12] The market flex clause allows the arrangers to require that amendments to be made to the transactions structure, price, and other terms so as to ensure a successful syndication. 'Richard Gray, Patrick Holmes, and Kevin Muzilla, 'Why Banks Should Look Again at Market Flex and MAC Clauses' (2003) 22 International Financial Law Review 18.

might have negative cost and reputational consequences for the private equity sponsor. Occasionally, private equity lawyers do push too far; on the €7.1bn debt financing in support of the leveraged buy-out of Thyssenkrupp's lifts business in 2020, the lawyers advising the private equity sponsors were reportedly forced to offer a long list of amendments to avoid a failed syndication of the debt.[13] The occasional climbdown by a private equity lawyer does not act as a brake on their contractual boundary activity, however. According to private equity lawyer [#43], they push for the best terms they can 'and then from there we go backwards during the syndication process if we need to.'

6.3 The duty to act with integrity

In this section, I put the case that the private equity lawyer practices and strategies that I have explored in this chapter will likely also conflict with their duties to act with integrity and not to take unfair advantage.

Under the Solicitors' Code of Conduct 1999, there was an express requirement that solicitors not behave offensively in their professional capacity.[14] Although this express duty does not appear in the current Code, private equity lawyers have a duty to act with integrity under Principle 5.[15] Integrity denotes a higher moral standard than honesty, requiring a 'moral soundness, rectitude and steady adherence to an ethical code'.[16]

The success of the private equity lawyers' relentless contractual boundary pushing is dependent upon the coercive authority over their bank lenders. A recurring theme in my interviews with bank lawyers were accounts of how they had experienced elevated levels of aggression, and emotion, directed at them by private equity lawyers during transactions.[17] For example, bank lawyer [#34] said that 'uncivilised behaviour'—including private equity lawyers routinely shouting at them—had become a normalized characteristic of their work. In my interviews with them, private equity lawyers sometimes openly admitted to bullying bank lawyers. According to private equity lawyer [#12]:

> it's fine to bully people, if you're working for the client, and that's the process, that's what you end up doing.

[13] Nikou Asgari and Robert Smith, 'Thyssenkrupp Backers Improve €7.6bn Debt Terms after Lenders Balk' *Financial Times* (30 June 2020) <https://www.ft.com/content/81864124-e50c-4670-92c1-756582bb664b> accessed 9 August 2021.

[14] Herring (n 1) 344.

[15] 'SRA Principles' (n 2).

[16] Lord Justice Rupert Jackson in *SRA v Wingate Evans* [2018] EWCA Civ 366 citing and approving previous authority, *Hoodless v Financial Services Authority* [2003] UKFSM FSM007.

[17] My data which points to a coercive identity adopted by private equity lawyers mostly comes from the accounts of bank lawyers but is also supported by several accounts from private equity lawyers.

Bank lawyer [#15]'s observation that 'sponsor's counsel can often be really, and quite arrogantly, aggressive, because it's their market' indicates the effect of the own-the-market logic that I have previously noted. The reference to 'it's their market' evidences a common understanding by the actors in this field that the private equity lawyers have assumed total ownership and management of the deal process.

Private equity lawyers further coerce the bank lawyers through their manipulation of the transaction process. A transaction's timetable tends to be set by the vendor of the business being sold, who will typically require a 'certain funds bid' from the sponsor by a specified date. But within this timetable, private equity lawyers control when, for example, the bank lawyers receive first drafts of the loan terms and set the deadline by which bank lawyers are required to respond with their comments. Bank lawyer [#35] said that the transaction process is designed by private equity lawyers to ensure bank lawyers constantly work under extreme time pressure: 'sponsor lawyers are definitely at the forefront of ensuring that.' Bank lawyer [#16] said that as a result, bank lawyers are frequently 'not sleeping for days'.

Private equity lawyers often require that a first draft of an issues list, summarizing the banks' comments on the transaction documents, is to be compiled by the bank lawyers and discussed with the banks in a very short timeframe, which according to bank lawyer [#34] can be as short as '24 hours to review the documents, and another 24 hours to go through them with the banks'. This is notwithstanding that, as private equity lawyer [#14] acknowledged, the commitment documents will include 'points of detail which are not immediately obvious to the untrained eye' and can run to hundreds, often thousands of pages. Bank lawyer [#34]—a senior associate—said:

> I just did a bid which had three bridge facilities in it, all with different terms, including delayed draw mechanics, it has a super senior RCF, an intercreditor agreement sat alongside, and obviously then you've got the commitment paper terms. So, it was three different base precedent documents, three different term sheets, all the commitment papers, etc. running into thousands of pages. And I called the partner and said at this point, I physically cannot do a proper review, given the deadline that they've given us.

Bank lawyer [#35] said: 'It is not uncommon for the papers to get dropped on you at 6pm on a Friday night and you spend your whole weekend reviewing them.'[18]

[18] There is a mounting body of literature that considers the effects of the large firm practice area context on lawyers' well-being; this is reviewed by Soon and others in their recent paper, Lucinda Soon, Almuth McDowall, and Kevin RH Teoh, 'Towards a Context-Specific Approach to Understanding Lawyers' Well-Being: A Synthesis Review and Future Research Agenda' (2023) Psychiatry, Psychology and Law 1.

Bank lawyer [#13] observed that 'it's not possible to advise the lenders of all the different permutations of these documents in a weekend'. The objective of the private equity lawyers in pursuing these tactics is clear, according to bank lawyer [#35]: 'Unquestionably people give more points away on the weekend, than they do during the week.'

Compounding the effect of this timetable manipulation, and the volume of documents to be reviewed, is that bank lawyers are now also required to act for multiple clients during this period, sometimes as many as ten or more. As previously noted, each bank competing for the arranging mandate on a syndicated deal used to be advised by a separate team, or 'tree', a partner supported by one or more associates of the same firm, with information barriers erected between the teams. However, now all the competing banks tend to be advised by a single partner/team at the same firm. This new practice is called a 'virtual tree', or 'trees in the head'. According to in-house lawyer [#17]:

> Our external lawyers often are acting on a pretty compromised basis. By that, I mean they have a lot of clients. They're a single team trying to navigate 10, 11, 12 clients; they don't get a lot of time with the documents.

6.4 The duty not to take unfair advantage

Solicitors are also under a duty not to take unfair advantage. Rule 1.1 of the SRA's Code of Conduct requires that solicitors do not abuse their position by taking 'unfair advantage' of their clients *or others*. Rule 1.4 requires that they not mislead their clients, the court, *or others*, either by act or omission (their own, or by being complicit in the acts or omissions of others). Also, the guidance notes to Principle 5, acting with integrity, state that the SRA may act against a firm or individual solicitor who has taken unfair advantage of a client *or a third party*.[19] The private equity lawyer strategies at the commercial grid phase of the transaction also raise questions as to their observance of both SRA Principle 5, acting with integrity, and also as to their compliance with the SRA's guidance on taking unfair advantage of a third party.[20]

A core component of the private equity lawyers' contractual boundary-pushing strategy—supported by their coercive authority—is to settle as many terms of the financing as possible in the initial stage of the transaction. This takes advantage of first, the competitive tension between banks which are, at this

[19] 'Acting with Integrity - Guidance' (25 November 2019) <https://www.sra.org.uk/solicitors/guidance/acting-with-integrity/> accessed 28 November 2020.

[20] 'SRA Principles' (n 2); 'Acting with Integrity' (23 July 2019) <https://www.sra.org.uk/solicitors/guidance/ethics-guidance/acting-with-integrity/> accessed 6 July 2020.

stage, still competing for the underwriting and arranging mandate, and second, that these banks do not yet have external legal counsel—the bank lawyers—advising them.

Typically, the lawyer and law firm designated to act for the banks is appointed after the banks competing for the arranging mandate have agreed to the material terms of the financing. Prior to this, the private equity sponsor usually undertakes a fishing expedition to see what terms might be available by inviting sometimes as many as thirty, or more, prospective arranging banks to review their proposed terms, with a view to narrowing the group of banks they will enter negotiations with to a smaller group willing to accept those terms. Private equity lawyer [#11] said:

> We put a grid together with our "ask", of the key commercial points and the key legal points, and put it in a grid, and then ask each bank to come back and populate that with their responses. And that is the precursor to a term sheet. So, the banks are competing against one another.

After this narrowing, the bank lawyer is designated to act for the smaller bank group who then compete for the mandate.

At the start of the process, the banks are sent a 'commercial grid' to review and comment on by the private equity sponsor or its lawyers. This label—commercial grid—often disguises its content and purpose. Historically, commercial grids were short and simply contained the private equity sponsor's proposed core economic terms, such as the amount of debt to be provided by the lenders, the amount of equity the sponsor will subscribe, the debt-pricing terms, and perhaps the financial covenants the sponsor proposed to include, and their levels. However, grids became longer and more complex when private equity lawyers began to assume control of the drafting of the commercial grid on behalf of their clients from the mid-2000s. Private equity lawyer [#32] emphasized the importance of their role in drafting the grid:

> Nowadays, the most sophisticated clients expect their law firms to draft the grid.

In-house lawyer [#17] said:

> These grids they send us are basically the whole deal, they're several pages long, they're all the terms, legal and commercial, and we're required to do that without counsel.

Private equity lawyers now tend to add terms covering legal and structuring matters, in addition to economic terms. Bank lawyer [#35] said:

> You will have things like security and guarantees in there, and that is definitely a legal point.

The grid may also contain complex financing options, as indicated by private equity lawyer [#23]:

> We often allow for a loan structure, bond structure, a credit funds/private credit structure. There's a whole menu of options.

This means the grid can be up to ten to fifteen pages, with the text written in very small font. These proposed terms are presented in the form of a Microsoft Excel spreadsheet, hence the term 'grid'. The format of the document is deliberately chosen, according to private equity lawyer [#26]:

> The reason it's in Excel is to kid banks that it's still basically commercial rather than a ton of legal stuff.

In the later stages of the transaction, the private equity lawyers are relatively free of constraints on their activities, but they still require a degree of cooperation from their bank lawyer counterparts to get the deal done, albeit bank lawyers tend to be accommodating due to the prevailing survival logic.[21] However, at the commercial grid stage, private equity lawyers have identified and taken advantage of an opportunity to settle terms, and effectively pre-bake them into the transaction documents, when they are entirely unopposed by external legal counsel for the banks.

The most significant legal term imposed by the private equity lawyers in the commercial grid is the incorporation by reference of the 'deal precedent'. Banks are required to agree in the commercial grid that the executed documents of a previous transaction, or the private equity sponsor's own house precedent documents, containing the full form legal terms, will be used as the basis for the transaction documents for the new transaction. Although they are given access to the documents comprising this deal precedent, it means that, according to private equity lawyer [#36], 'sometimes its 1,000 plus pages of precedents they've got to review'.

The effect is that the grid incorporates by reference the complex and lengthy full form terms of the credit, intercreditor, security and other finance documents. As private equity lawyer [#7] said:

> It certainly helps to take a lot of negotiation points off the table. The precedent might include some very important stuff around things like covenant definitions,

[21] Michael Smets, 'Institutional Work Taken Literally: How Logics Shift as Banking Lawyers "Get the Deal Done"' (2009 Academy of Management annual meeting, USA, 2009) 3 <http://publications.aston.ac.uk/id/eprint/18544/> accessed 20 May 2021.

> adjustments and other add backs that actually do have real value, including exceptions for incurring more debt.

The grid and the deal precedent are not legally binding, which means that the banks are not contractually bound by their terms until they are incorporated into the transaction documents, and these are executed at a later stage. The bank lawyers advise the banks on these documents should the bank proceed beyond the grid stage. But by then the terms of the grid—and the deal precedent—are already effectively settled, according to private equity lawyer [#35]:

> It is very unusual for banks to go back on the grid, because it's just not done in the market. That's the quickest way to get yourself kicked off a deal.

Bank lawyers—once appointed—will occasionally seek to retrospectively challenge terms in the draft transaction documents which featured in the grid and/or the deal precedent. In this event, the private equity lawyers tend to resist strongly and often aggressively. Private equity lawyer [#21] said:

> Where there is a grid which refers to a precedent our job is to say 'well I'm sorry, but that's in the precedent and that's what you agreed to'. That is a complete intellectual abdication, but that's how the market works.

Bank lawyer [#27] gave an example of this dynamic when they identified a significant issue in the documents that had been in the grid:

> I raise it and they say, 'Sorry, that's been agreed''. I say, 'Can we just discuss it?' I get: 'We don't want to discuss it anymore. We've told you it's agreed.'

With the survival logic forming an important part of the governing framework for their sense-making, bank lawyers theorize that challenging terms which have been carried across from the grid and/or the deal precedent may antagonize, and so jeopardize, the flow of further designation work from the private equity lawyers with whom they have established referral relationships. According to private equity lawyer [#19], 'bank lawyers have a certain institutional interest in not reopening those terms.'

A shared understanding hence exists between the private equity lawyers and the bank lawyers with whom they have established referral relationships that the grid and deal precedent terms have been, for all practical purposes, settled prior to their appointment. So, the practice of producing the grid, and the embedded deal precedent, is infused with a shared understanding by leveraged finance lawyers that its terms are to be considered settled, and not to be reopened by bank lawyers once they are appointed. This 'do not challenge the grid' logic results in a retrospective bank lawyer challenge being a relatively unusual occurrence in practice, as acknowledged here by bank lawyer [#31]:

> We get quite a lot of pushback if we try to reopen those settled grid points, and so we just have to accept that's an agreed set of terms.

Private equity lawyers are preparing commercial grids—which incorporate key legal as well as commercial terms, and, by reference, lengthy legal template documents—and sending them to banks at a time when those banks are competing with each other to win the mandate, and are not yet represented by external legal counsel. Some banks have in-house legal teams with lawyers who are specialists in leveraged finance, but many banks do not have that capability. According to bank lawyer [#12]:

> Sponsor lawyers try and agree a lot of terms before the banks have proper legal representation, in the hope that certain things don't get picked up ... by putting in some very complex terms and hoping that nobody notices and by using trickery.

Using the Microsoft Excel format for the commercial grid is an important component of this 'trickery', according to private equity lawyer [#26]:

> It makes it difficult to blackline, it makes it difficult for banks to follow and read. It gives the person creating it a real advantage.

In its warning notice on the use of Non-Disclosure Agreements (NDAs), the SRA made clear that the solicitor's duty to act in the best interest of the client does not override the solicitor's professional obligations to act with integrity, which with respect to NDAs includes not taking advantage of the other party to the NDA.[22] The duty not to take unfair advantage includes 'taking advantage of an opposing party's lack of legal knowledge' or where 'they have limited access to legal representation and advice', and/or 'applying undue pressure or using inappropriate aggressive or oppressive tactics in your dealings with the opposing party or their representative' which might include 'imposing oppressive and artificial time limits' or by 'discouraging them from taking legal advice'.[23]

These are all descriptions that might properly be applied to the practices of private equity lawyers at the initial commercial grid phase of the transaction. Ethical duties do not cease to apply where solicitors act for, and against, large business organizations, such as banks and private equity funds. The SRA's focus with respect

[22] 'Use of Non Disclosure Agreements (NDAs)—Warning Notice' (11 December 2020) <https://www.sra.org.uk/solicitors/guidance/non-disclosure-agreements-ndas/> accessed 20 April 2022.

[23] ibid.

to NDAs is where they are used to silence those vulnerable to sexual impropriety, for example, and large international banks are not vulnerable in the same way. But, as Emma Oakley and Steven Vaughan argue with respect to the client capture of corporate lawyers, vulnerability is not about absolute, but rather relative, power, and in the same way as corporate lawyers have shown themselves to be susceptible to powerful companies and financial institutions, so have banks shown themselves to be vulnerable to the power of private equity sponsors and their lawyers.[24]

Guidance can also be found in principles which seek to protect the interests of litigants in person. The SRA has made clear, in its 'Walking the Line' paper, that a solicitor's ethical duties under its Principles encompass a duty not to take unfair advantage of unrepresented third parties in litigation; here, the solicitor's duties to their own client need to be balanced against the interests of the court, the public interest, and the interests of others.[25] The solicitor's duty to maintain their independence from the client, and not simply act as the client's 'hired gun', is emphasized.[26] In *Al-Kandari v JR Brown & Co*,[27] Lord Bingham was of the view that a solicitor did not owe a duty to the other side. But—in contested civil litigation—Lord Bingham expressed the view that it may be that 'a solicitor for a limited purpose steps aside from his role as solicitor and agent of one party and assumes a different role, either independent of both parties or as agent of both'. This is not so much a duty to the other side but more a duty not to mislead the court, and not to make submissions which the lawyer knows to be untrue. Lord Neuberger has argued that 'self-respecting advocates' would 'have an understandable feeling of distaste' if they were to win a case simply because a point had not been pursued by the other party.[28]

Even though most of the commentary in the literature similarly relates to unrepresented litigants in person,[29] there is no compelling reason why these ethical principles should not apply equally to private equity lawyers in their dealings with the as yet unrepresented banks at the commercial grid phase of a transaction. Again, whilst the protection of often vulnerable litigants in person is rightly a higher priority in policy terms, this does not mean that we should not sanction lawyers exploiting vulnerability in corporate contexts; vulnerability is not absolute. As I have already noted, the banks here are susceptible to the market power of private equity sponsors and their lawyers.[30] In one sense, the case for extending the ethical

[24] Emma Oakley and Steven Vaughan, 'In Dependence: The Paradox of Professional Independence and Taking Seriously the Vulnerabilities of Lawyers in Large Corporate Law Firms' (2019) 46 Journal of Law and Society 83, 8, 12.

[25] 'Balancing Duties in Litigation' (27 November 2018) <https://www.sra.org.uk/risk/risk-resources/balancing-duties-litigation/> accessed 29 November 2020.

[26] ibid.

[27] [1988] QB 665.

[28] Lord Neuberger, 'The Lord Slynn Memorial Lecture 2016' para 31<https://supremecourt.uk/speeches/lord-neuberger-gives-the-lord-slynn-memorial-lecture-2016> (accessed 29 November 2020).

[29] See eg Herring (n 1) 350.

[30] Oakley and Vaughan (n 24) 8, 12.

principles cited in support of measures directed at the protection of litigants, in person, to the transactional context is even stronger, in that transactional lawyers are unconstrained by the rules and procedures of the court that may mitigate unethical behaviour in the litigation context.[31]

As already noted, there is also evidence in the data that private equity lawyers deliberately manipulate the transaction timetable to their advantage, leaving the release of the financing terms for review by bank lawyers to the latest possible moment. When the strategy of relentless contractual boundary pushing is coupled with this type of coercion, for example by denying the bank lawyers sufficient time to review the transaction documents, private equity lawyers are undermining the integrity of a process and taking unfair advantage of an inequality in resources. For example, private equity lawyer [#26] said:

> We are deliberately jamming the lenders, and the lenders' lawyers, with too much stuff too quickly, for them to properly review, comment and deal with, and let's be clear, we're doing that on purpose.

The SRA has been clear that failure to maintain high ethical standards leads to 'poor outcomes' and undermines the proper administration of justice, harms public trust in the legal profession, and ultimately undermines the rule of law.[32] Otherwise, there is little guidance provided by the SRA on what the duty to act with integrity means. My view, drawing on the legal ethics literature for a moment, is that taking advantage of the weakness of the opposing side's lawyer—even though we are considering here bank lawyers that act for large banking institutions and work in large international law firms—is difficult to justify on moral grounds, and so raises questions as to solicitor integrity. David Luban argues that notwithstanding lawyers may operate in an adversarial system, where each party advocates for their own client's position and attacks the position of their opponent, this does not provide them with an institutional excuse that allows them to distance themselves from the moral aspects of their role.[33] Luban is rightly dismissive of what he calls this 'adversary system excuse'.[34]

Alice Woolley and Bradley Wendel extend the idea that lawyers should not take advantage of unrepresented counterparties to situations where a lawyers' opposing counsel is simply ineffective, when that lawyer must 'take more responsibility for ensuring the merits of the case'.[35] William Simon argues that where a

[31] Kershaw and Moorhead (n 7) 26; Joan Loughrey, *Corporate Lawyers and Corporate Governance* (CUP 2011) 63.

[32] 'Risk Outlook 2018/2019' (17 July 2018) 27 <https://www.sra.org.uk/risk/outlook/risk-outlook-2018-2019/> accessed 23 November 2020.

[33] David Luban, *Lawyers and Justice: An Ethical Study* (Princeton University Press 1988), 123–24.

[34] David Luban, 'The Adversary System Excuse', *Lawyers: A Critical Reader* (The New Press 1997) 8.

[35] Alice Woolley and W Bradley Wendel, 'Legal Ethics and Moral Character' (2010) 23 Georgetown Journal of Legal Ethics 1065, 1077.

lawyer is aware that their counterpart has made a mistake in law, for example, they should 'rescue an opposing party from the unjust consequences of his own lawyer's error'.[36] As I have previously noted, the conditions of the leveraged finance practice area field feature a substantial imbalance in bargaining power; the banks' lawyers are inclined not to be adversarial in response to the private equity lawyers' activities, due to the prevailing influence of the survival and other field logics.[37] This means that since the mid-2000s the adversary system has effectively ceased to function in this field.[38] So a defence of the private equity lawyer's coercive strategies founded in an argument that the banks have an advocate putting their case robustly does not carry weight.[39]

Private equity lawyers might counter that their strategies promote the best interests of each client. The duty to act in the interests of each client is not, however, absolute. It must be balanced with other duties. The SRA has made clear that where a solicitor's various duties come into conflict, duties 'which safeguard the wider public interest' should 'take precedence over an individual client's interests'.[40] The SRA has stated that public interest duties are those which safeguard 'the rule of law, and public confidence in a trustworthy solicitors' profession and a safe and effective market for regulated legal services'.[41] Solicitors are instructed to inform their clients where their public interest duties outweigh their duty to them and to consider whether they are able to continue to act for them.[42] The SRA expects solicitors to decline instructions that would conflict with these duties.[43] These will include a solicitors' duty to maintain their independence from their client's interests.[44]

6.5 Conclusion

In summary, the private equity lawyer strategies and stances revealed by the case study are inconsistent with their duties to act in the best interests of each client, with integrity and to not to take unfair advantage of third parties, under the SRA's Standards and Regulations.

36 William H Simon, 'Role Differentiation and Lawyers' Ethics: A Critique of Some Academic Perspectives' (2010) 23 Georgetown Journal of Legal Ethics 987, 987.

37 Luban (n 33) 78.

38 Sujeet Indap, Barney Thompson, and James Fontanella-Khan, 'How a Private Equity Boom Fuelled the World's Biggest Law Firm' *Financial Times* (6 June 2019) <https://www.ft.com/content/13696928-86d5-11e9-a028-86cea8523dc2> accessed 7 June 2019.

39 Loughrey (n 31) 62.

40 'SRA Principles' (n 2).

41 ibid.

42 ibid; 'Use of Non Disclosure Agreements (NDAs)—Warning Notice' (n 22).

43 'Risk Outlook 2018/2019' (n 32) 29.

44 ibid 27.

In the next chapter, I explore how the activity of bank lawyers and private equity lawyers, taken together, has materially contributed to a collapse in documentary standards in the field. We see how this has had a dramatic impact on the contractual terms of complex, cross-border leverage finance transactions governing the allocation and pricing of risk by market participants.

7
The Corruption of Markets by Big Law

7.1 Introduction

We have seen in previous chapters the relationship between recurring situational factors of a major law firm practice area setting and the ethical decision-making of the lawyers who work in it.[1] This chapter explores how this decision-making can in turn have a dramatic impact on the conditions of financial markets, in this case the contractual terms of complex cross-border financial transactions governing the allocation and pricing of risk by market participants.

The data I collected reveal a general collapse in documentary standards in the leveraged finance sector. Leveraged loan documents have become ambiguous to the extent where several of my interviewees openly confessed to not fully understanding them. Key provisions are frequently virtually unintelligible. Documents often contain multiple defects and potential loopholes. This chapter explores the central role that lawyers have played in transforming loan terms in this way. Specifically, this chapter emphasizes the importance of analysing the provisions of typical transaction documents to obtaining a fuller understanding of how lawyer action and decision-making are linked to broader questions of lawyer integrity and competence. In this field, a leave-the-loopholes logic has emerged, for example, which means bank lawyers and private equity lawyers tend not to fix the problems with leveraged loan documents that they encounter.

This chapter is arranged as follows. It begins by describing what my data reveals about the extent of the uncertainty in the language of leveraged loan documents. Examples that frequently recurred in my interviews are described and analysed in detail. Next, the chapter explores what might be the potential causes of this uncertainty in loan documents. First, the macroeconomic phenomenon of loan and bond convergence is explored. Second, I explore the connected micro phenomenon—the role that lawyers have played. Next, I explore what the data revealed in this chapter means with respect to leveraged finance lawyers' ethical duties, the most applicable being first, the solicitor's duty to act with integrity, and second, the solicitor's duty of competence. The chapter then concludes.

[1] Richard Moorhead and others, 'Designing Ethics Indicators for Legal Services Provision' [2012] SSRN Electronic Journal 28, 42, 92 <http://www.ssrn.com/abstract=2159296> accessed 18 October 2018.

7.2 Pervasive uncertainty

In the restructuring of Intralot, a Greek gaming company, in 2022, the company's private equity sponsors relied on the controversial J. Crew 'trap door' procedure—imported from the United States—for the first time in Europe[2]. They were able to take advantage of ambiguous—but standard—language in its loan terms to transfer assets outside of the lenders' security net.[3] These assets were then offered as security for new loans ranking ahead of them.[4] This case highlights two material risks for lenders arising from the dramatic shift in the terms of leveraged loans. First, a loosening in loan covenants going well beyond covenant-lite,[5] so that protections for lenders have been significantly weakened, a phenomenon I explored in Chapter 2. Second, and the focus of this chapter, is that the Intralot case highlights the very real risk for lenders of uncertainty and defects in key terms.

Annalise Riles presents a picture of international derivatives transactions as a series of glitches resulting from lack of knowledge, 'genres of opacity', and a 'lack of understanding of the agency and expertise of others'.[6] Riles presents lawyer activity in the derivatives market as having a momentum all its own and 'not building anything in particular'.[7] Mitu Gulati and Robert. E Scott reviewed thousands of sovereign debt contracts and found that the lawyers in large international law firms mainly in New York who drafted and negotiated them often did not fully understand their terms.[8] In my interviews, several participants were similarly willing to admit to not always understanding the terms of leveraged finance documents.

[2] Jamie McDougall and others, 'Intralot's Drop-down Restructuring Games: Priming Pari Passu Noteholders, Circumventing Non-Consenters and Artificially Reducing Asset Values' [2022] The Journal of International Banking and Financial Law 5; Donald Lowe and James Bell, 'COVID-19 and the Impact on Financial Covenants' [2020] Journal of International Banking and Financial Law 2; 'KKR's Envision Deal Shows How Ugly Creditor Battles Are Getting - Bloomberg' <https://www.bloomberg.com/news/articles/2022-10-05/kkr-s-envision-deal-shows-how-ugly-creditor-battles-are-getting> accessed 14 October 2022.

[3] McDougall and others (n 2); Lowe and Bell (n 2); 'KKR's Envision Deal Shows How Ugly Creditor Battles Are Getting - Bloomberg' (n 2).

[4] McDougall and others (n 2); Lowe and Bell (n 2); 'KKR's Envision Deal Shows How Ugly Creditor Battles Are Getting - Bloomberg' (n 2).

[5] 'Leveraged Loans Are Way Past "Cov-Lite"' *Financial Times* (16 November 2018) https://www.ft.com/content/53014840-e0bf-374b-8d22-c9a9ea318a8d accessed 16 February 2023; Sarah Paterson, 'The Rise of Covenant-Lite Lending and Implications for the UK's Corporate Insolvency Law Toolbox' (2019) 39 Oxford Journal of Legal Studies 654, 663–64.

[6] Annelise Riles, *Collateral Knowledge: Legal Reasoning in the Global Financial Markets* (University of Chicago Press 2011) 64.

[7] Riles' account is not confined to lawyers but rather extends to those deploying 'technical legal knowledge' which encompasses a cast of experts—lawyers but also scholars and bureaucrats, for example. ibid.

[8] Mitu Gulati and Robert E Scott, *The Three and a Half Minute Transaction: Boilerplate and the Limits of Contract Design* (University of Chicago Press 2012).

Private equity lawyer [#21], for example, observed that 'the finance documents are long, opaque and extraordinarily difficult to navigate unless you are an expert.' And bank lawyer [#30] said 'most sophisticated finance lawyers find them really, really difficult to evaluate' and offered the following example where the private equity sponsor was proposing to make an acquisition:

> It's so fiendishly complicated to work out whether they could in fact do it. In a conventional loan agreement, I will look at the clauses headed up 'acquisitions' that will take me to a permission that says, 'permitted acquisition', and I can read that. But if I go to an incurrence-based covenant document, I won't find a section like that. It's buried in the 'permitted investments' bit, which in turn is buried in another covenant, which in turn goes to multiple other places in the document.

Private equity lawyer [#35] gave this example:

> You have five different clauses that say, "notwithstanding anything else in this document ... ", and sometimes they are contradictory to each other.

Participants frequently conceded that they struggled to understand what key provisions in typical leveraged loan documents meant and had reached the conclusion that the same is true for the other key stakeholders: private equity sponsors, the arranging banks, and the lenders.[9] Bank lawyer [#30], for example, said:

> The chances of most sponsors really getting their minds around them and understanding how they work is pretty limited.

In my interviews with them, it was apparent that the participants broadly shared an understanding that typically the documents are not only complex but also do not always make sense nor work very well. Although they were aware of several recurring glitches, they also shared an understanding that they did not need to fix any of these acknowledged problems. This phenomenon raises ethical questions as to lawyer competence, which I consider later in this chapter. Here, we see evidence of a further logic of the field: leveraged finance lawyers share a common understanding that leveraged finance documents do not need to have clear meaning. An uncertainty logic prevails.

Gulati and Scott showed how embedded flaws in financial contracts—their focus was on the *pari passu* clause in sovereign debt contracts—can remain 'harmless for long periods of time' until, for example, 'an adverse legal interpretation poses a systemic threat to the market'.[10] Similarly, uncertainty in leveraged finance

[9] See for example, McDougall and others (n 2).

[10] Stephen J Choi, Mitu Gulati, and Robert E Scott, 'The Black Hole Problem in Commercial Boilerplate' (2017) 67 Duke Law Journal 1, 13; Gulati and Scott (n 8).

documents may take some time to have an impact; should we have a sustained economic downturn it is likely that there will be multiple restructurings, formal insolvency proceedings, and related litigation involving disputes as to the meaning of loan terms. However, one high-profile example has already emerged, having featured in a series of restructurings, first in the United States and now in Europe.

The J. Crew trap door was frequently referred to by participants as an example of a loophole being exploited, in that an ambiguous term was relied on for a purpose for which it was not intended. Private equity lawyer [#20] said, of this tactic:

> You hear about things like that and you just think, well, that's obviously just frankly [ridiculous].

As Kenneth Ayotte and Christina Scully have noted, in the J. Crew case, the relevant clause in the loan agreement—Clause 7.02—was intended to permit J. Crew, a US company, to invest in its overseas subsidiaries to mitigate their tax liability, not to permit the transfer of the intellectual property assets of a value of $250mn out of the lenders' collateral pool so that the assets could be offered as collateral to a new group of lenders (this is the trap door).[11] Bank lawyer [#16] described this flexibility for sponsors to move valuable assets out from the collateral nets of the lenders and raise finance against it as 'just contrary to the underlying principles of leveraged lending'. This strategy was undertaken by J. Crew in consultation with both its investment banking and legal advisers.[12]

J. Crew is a US company, and the trap door has been utilized in a series of further restructurings of troubled US companies, including Neiman Marcus, Cirque du Soleil, Travelport, and PetSmart.[13] The trap door approach was relied upon in Europe for the first time in the restructuring of Intralot, a Greek gaming company, in 2022.[14] Albeit here the trap door was in the covenants of Intralot's high yield bonds, as opposed to a term loan, the principles remain the same.[15]

What these restructurings have in common is lender exposure to a distressed, cash-strapped borrower facing imminent insolvency, a provision of a debt contract which is unclear in its scope, and the opportunity for 'loophole lawyering' to avoid its commonly understood spirit and purpose. The common result was the transfer of assets of significant value from a 'restricted' group of subsidiaries (these are the companies whose assets and cash flows make up the lender's security pool) to an

11 Kenneth Ayotte and Christina Scully, 'J. Crew, Nine West, and the Complexities of Financial Distress Forum Collection: Bankruptcy and Restructuring in Response to Exogenous Shocks' (2021) 131 Yale Law Journal Forum 363, 366.

12 ibid.

13 ibid 372; McDougall and others (n 2).

14 McDougall and others (n 2).

15 ibid. Reorg, 'Intralot Plans to Implement Restructuring Through Out-of-Court Process With Scheme as Backup Option' <https://reorg.com/intralot-plans-to-implement-restructuring-through-out-of-court-process/> accessed 15 March 2023.

'unrestricted' group of subsidiaries which are not subject to the restrictive covenants (and are hence outside the lenders' security net) which then offered those assets as security for further debt provided by a new group of lenders (who as a result obtained first priority over those assets).[16]

Private equity lawyer [#11] was of the view that the J. Crew, Intralot, and other trap door cases are indicative of a broader problem with leveraged loan documents:

> J. Crew is very emotive among the lender community, but the reality is, with the deterioration in terms since 2014, you can do a lot of what the sponsors did on J. Crew just by using the explicit permissions in the credit agreement. You don't have to be that creative. You don't have to bend the provisions or bully people into doing things.

The prime example is the ambiguity in covenants restricting the ability of the borrower to raise further debt which was frequently raised by the participants in my interviews with them. Until the mid-2000s, the borrower's ability to incur further debt was highly restricted. Further debt was only permitted if the total amount did not exceed a relatively low monetary threshold, or 'basket'. To raise debt beyond the basket threshold, it was necessary to either obtain the consent of the lenders or refinance the loans entirely. Now the range of circumstances in which the borrower may incur further debt has significantly expanded.[17] Bank lawyer [#16] described this as 'a paradigm shift'. Loan documents now tend to feature multiple, and often complex, ambiguous, and even circular, debt permissions.[18]

Private equity lawyer [#23] said it was often impossible to determine with any certainty whether the borrower had the permission to raise further debt, and if so, by what amount, because the array of debt permissions often cross-referenced other provisions across the document, and amounts unused under one basket could be added to amounts available under another, so that:

> permissions go from A to Z, then aa to zz, then aaa to zzz. You've got 20, 30, 40 permissions, all of which can be allocated from one permission to another. When you actually track them through, it just leaves you scratching your head.

Another recurring, and related, example of an acknowledged defect in typical loan documents is linked to what a number of participants referred to as the

[16] McDougall and others (n 2).

[17] 'Investors Rue Lack of Protections on €7.1bn Thyssenkrupp Debt' *Financial Times* (26 June 2020) <https://www.ft.com/content/fae40c44-30af-4676-95ff-28feefa16890> accessed 23 June 2022. 'Vulnerabilities Associated with Leveraged Loans and Collateralised Loan Obligations' (Financial Stability Board, 19 December 2019) 8 <https://www.fsb.org/2019/12/vulnerabilities-associated-with-leveraged-loans-and-collateralised-loan-obligations/> accessed 2 July 2022.

[18] See eg, 'Investors Rue Lack of Protections on €7.1bn Thyssenkrupp Debt' (n 17).

'security-lite' approach, which has become the norm in Europe. I refer to this as the 'junior lender waiver and release glitch'.

In European leveraged buyouts, material target group companies now seldom grant security over all or substantially all their assets and cash flows. The collateral granted to lenders is typically limited to security over shares in the borrower and its holding company, some intercompany receivables, and some bank accounts at the borrower and holding company level. They are often not granted security over real estate, customer receivables, intellectual property, and bank accounts and other assets at the operating company level.

It is not just the limited asset coverage that represents a weakening in the lenders' security package. Even where security is taken, for example, over bank accounts or insurance policies, it may not be perfected. The obligation to obtain countersigned notices or acknowledgments from, say, banks and insurance companies is often a 'reasonable endeavours' as opposed to an absolute obligation, until an event of default has occurred.[19] This undermines the effect of the security because insolvency hardening periods only start to run during an acceleration scenario, and so it is likely that the security will not be recognized in the event of the borrower entering a formal insolvency process.[20]

Security-lite leaves the lenders reliant on a 'single point of enforcement': the charge over the shares in the borrower and/or its holding company. This gives the lenders, following an event of default, the power to take control of the borrower group, by enforcing share and receivables security at the top of the borrower group. They can transfer the shares in this 'topco', together with all the operating subsidiaries to a purchaser. The idea is that in a lender-led restructuring, a sale of topco shares will deliver everything that senior-secured lenders need. Hence, they do not need the ability to enforce security over the individual assets and cash flows of material group companies. But the effectiveness of the single point of enforcement is undermined by a defect in typical intercreditor agreements that was mostly widely acknowledged and understood by my participants: the junior-lender-waiver-and-release glitch.

The typical intercreditor agreement seen in transactions was, until the mid-2000s, based on the Loan Market Association (LMA)'s standard template.[21] It provided for the senior lenders to assume control of any junior security enforcement process, including the right to release security and waive all unsecured claims against the borrower upon an enforcement by the senior lenders of their share security at the holding company level.[22] This created the conditions for a 'debt free'

[19] 'Hardening Period' (*Practical Law*) <http://uk.practicallaw.thomsonreuters.com/9-500-8666?transitionType=Default&contextData=(sc.Default)> accessed 9 July 2022.

[20] ibid.

[21] Paterson (n 5) 668. 'Documents' <https://www.lma.eu.com/documents-guidelines/documents> accessed 5 July 2022.

[22] Paterson (n 5) 668.

sale of the borrower group by the senior lenders to a purchaser, the proceeds of which could be applied in repaying the senior loans. However, the LMA standard intercreditor is no longer the default template used in the large-cap leveraged buyout market. As previously noted, LMA templates have largely been superseded by the private equity sponsors' or their lawyers' standard precedents.

The result is that the junior lender release and/or waiver is frequently no longer included in intercreditor agreements in European transactions. A purchaser buying the shares in topco will typically expect group companies to be debt free and so this glitch will likely obstruct an enforcement sale by the lenders. Bank lawyer [#30] described how intercreditor agreements commonly include:

> protection against a junior creditor taking enforcement action in relation to its security, but no protection against the junior creditor taking unsecured action. So, a junior creditor could bring the pack of cards down by petitioning for liquidation of a particular entity within the group.

The consequence is a junior lender can file a liquidation petition against target group companies, and take other action as an unsecured creditor, since there is nothing in the intercreditor agreement to prevent them doing so. Lenders who think they are senior secured, and invest in and price the loan accordingly, are left without a robust, first ranking, security position. Lenders are, hence, vulnerable to risks associated with the compounding effect of multiple and ambiguous debt permissions and a defective security and intercreditor deal structure.

Material defects in European security and intercreditor frameworks such as these could result in significant losses for lenders. Private equity lawyer [#11] gave this warning:

> If you couple covenant-lite with security-lite, the lenders are not only more exposed to something going wrong, but when something does go wrong, they're more exposed. We need a downturn to really see how these documents are going to play out.

7.3 Loan and bond convergence

To some degree, ambiguity in loan terms arises from the growing complexity of leveraged buyout financings and an absence of disputes that are brought before courts for determining the meaning of ambiguous language, a phenomenon common to financial contracts more generally.[23] J-Crew's loan agreement was 101

[23] Choi, Gulati, and Scott (n 10) 8.

pages long, and included more than 87,000 words, for example.[24] The covenant prohibiting asset disposal was subject to twenty-one exceptions, contained thirty-two cross references to other clauses of the loan agreement and used forty-four defined terms.[25] Since the mid-2000s, typical capital structures of leveraged buy-outs have become highly sophisticated, often incorporating multiple layers of day one debt, and allowing for further layers of future debt to be raised and incorporated within the existing security and intercreditor framework without triggering the need for a full refinancing. The borrower may, pursuant to so-called 'accordion facilities', have the option, but without obligation on the part of the lenders, to add new facilities, without having to refinance the existing facilities and renegotiate new loan, security, and intercreditor agreements.[26] The loan, security, and intercreditor agreements for a single transaction have hence become voluminous, running to hundreds, sometimes thousands, of pages.

However, the field conditions which have led to pervasive ambiguity, loopholes, and defects in leveraged loan terms are mostly the consequence of a macroeconomic trend: loan and bond convergence. The term 'convergence' is in fact misleading; actually, what has occurred, according to one leading law firm, is a not a merger but a 'unidirectional shift' away from the LMA-style loan document terms towards the covenant-lite loan terms more familiar to high yield bond markets.[27] According to Sarah Paterson, loan and bond convergence is the effect of the emergence of the originate-to-distribute model, and the expansion of the investor base for the leveraged finance product to include Collateralised Loan Obligations (CLOs).[28]

Prior to the mid-2000s, arranging banks would both arrange and underwrite, or 'originate', the financing, but also typically 'hold' a significant proportion of the loan, and so retain an exposure to the credit risk of the borrower. This is the 'originate-to-hold' model. Because of the increased regulatory capital charges imposed on banks, and the entry into the market of a range of new, non-bank, investors after the global financial crisis, after arranging and underwriting (and perhaps even initially funding) the loan, arranging banks increasingly seek to 'distribute', or sell down, the loan through a syndication process.[29]

24 Ayotte and Scully (n 11) 363.

25 ibid.

26 John Gilligan and Mike Wright, *Private Equity Demystified: An Explanatory Guide* (4th edn, OUP 2020) 213.

27 The US style 'Term Loan B' document format follows a US high yield bond format, with New York law-governed incurrence covenants. 'High Yield Bonds and Leveraged Loans a Convergence of Terms | Ashurst' (25 April 2018) <https://www.ashurst.com/en/news-and-insights/insights/high-yield-bonds-and-leveraged-loans-a-convergence-of-terms/> accessed 23 June 2020.

28 Paterson (n 5) 663.

29 'Leveraged Loan Primer' (*S&P Global*, 2020) 36 <https://www.spglobal.com/marketintelligence/en/pages/toc-primer/lcd-primer> accessed 26 July 2022; 'The Capital Requirements Regulations 2013' <https://www.legislation.gov.uk/uksi/2013/3115/contents/made> accessed 16 July 2018.

Under this originate-to-distribute model, banks reduce, and often entirely eliminate, any ongoing credit exposure to the borrower of the loan, thus avoiding minimum regulatory capital charges.[30] This shift in business model can be seen as an extension of a trend that had begun much earlier; for example, Arthur Wilmarth charts the transition by the largest US banks from relationship banking to syndicated lending and securitization.[31] The loans are sold to commercial banks, who remain a significant lender constituency in European transactions, as well as CLOs and other institutional investors.[32] Even large private equity funds have set up private credit funds and become active lenders.[33] The originate-to-distribute model became firmly established as the dominant lending model in the European leveraged loan markets following the global financial crisis.

Parallel to banks switching to this new lending and underwriting model, there was an expansion of the investor base for the leveraged finance product to include CLOs.[34] CLOs invest in and then package up multiple leveraged loans for sale to investors that are less inclined than banks to closely monitor the performance of the borrower group, and to be interested in the workings and potential benefits of detailed contractual provisions.[35] Paterson, citing Kenneth Ayotte and Patrick Bolton, calls this 'reduced contract reading costs'. Banks have largely exited the market for leveraged loans in the United States.[36] In Europe, bank lenders have dramatically decreased their exposures to leveraged loans, albeit they remain the single largest class of investor.[37] The main effect of this change has been to largely replace one type of lender, banks, who were focused on maintaining a relationship with the borrower, and were willing to monitor its ongoing financial performance, with a range of other lender types, such as CLOs, that are mostly not so inclined.[38]

30 Banks may retain ongoing exposure under a revolving credit facility, but they will generally sell down all or a large proportion of the term loans to institutional and other non-bank lenders, who generally are unable, or do not wish to, provide revolving credit facilities. 'Vulnerabilities Associated with Leveraged Loans and Collateralised Loan Obligations' (n 17) 3–4; Charles-Henri Larreur, *Structured Finance: Leveraged Buy-Outs, Project Finance, Asset Finance and Securitization* (Wiley 2021) 44.

31 Arthur E Jr Wilmarth, 'The Transformation of the U.S. Financial Services Industry, 1975-2000: Competition, Consolidation, and Increased Risks' (2002) 2002 University of Illinois Law Review 215, 381–82. Cited in Elisabeth de Fontenay, 'Do the Securities Laws Matter - The Rise of the Leveraged Loan Market' (2013) 39 Journal of Corporation Law 725, 738, fn. 69.

32 Joe Rennison and Robert Smith, 'CLOs: Ground Zero for the next Stage of the Financial Crisis?' (13 May 2020) <https://www.ft.com/content/f10eaaac-0f4e-46bc-8f78-0754028da46a> accessed 22 July 2020. 'Leveraged Loan Primer' (n 29) 36; Larreur (n 30) 43.

33 'Private Equity Firms Are Cutting Out Banks and Funding LBOs Themselves' *Bloomberg.com* (11 August 2021) <https://www.bloomberg.com/news/articles/2021-08-11/blackstone-ares-are-turning-into-banks-for-lbo-financing> accessed 20 February 2023; Paterson (n 5) 663.

34 Paterson (n 5) 663.

35 Kenneth Ayotte and Patrick Bolton, 'Covenant Lite Lending, Liquidity and Standardization of Financial Contracts' in Kenneth Ayotte and Henry E Smith (eds), *Research Handbook on the Economics of Property Law* (Edward Elgar Publishing 2011) 174; Paterson (n 5) 662.

36 'Vulnerabilities Associated with Leveraged Loans and Collateralised Loan Obligations' (n 17). Gilligan and Wright (n 26) 20, 40, 46.

37 'Vulnerabilities Associated with Leveraged Loans and Collateralised Loan Obligations' (n 17). ibid.

38 Paterson (n 5) 662.

Elisabeth de Fontenay has argued that covenant-lite, for example, is thus explainable by understanding that institutional investors view loans as they do bonds, as 'passive investments that do not require extensive monitoring on their part'.[39]

These dynamics contributed to a convergence of US bond contractual terms with European leveraged loan contractual terms, as both investors/lenders and private equity sponsors became increasingly 'product agnostic'.[40] According to de Fontenay, 'that bonds and loans are now virtually interchangeable is nothing short of remarkable ... leveraged loans and high yield bonds currently feature strikingly similar pricing, non-price terms, participants and liquidity'.[41]

There are still two significant distinctions between bonds and loans: high yield bonds tend to be unsecured, although secured bond financings have become more common in recent years, and have a fixed rather than a floating rate of interest.[42] Otherwise, the once restrictive financial and other covenants in traditional, 'LMA style' leveraged loan documents have been diluted, becoming more flexible from the borrower's perspective through the inclusion of a series of terms typically seen in US high yield bond markets.[43] The highly restrictive covenants traditionally seen in leveraged loans, which required close monitoring by lenders, did not suit the new, non-bank, lender demographic.[44] This new investor base for leveraged loans brought with it a range of potential problems when faced with these traditional lender loan document forms: getting a majority of a widely dispersed group of CLO lenders to agree to a covenant amendment or waiver, which raised the possibility that an individual lender might cause 'hold out' problems, obstructing a potential restructuring of the company or its debt, for example.[45]

The convergence of the investor base for loans and bonds can be seen in the way in which senior facilities are now bifurcated into two tranches. Senior loans frequently now comprise a 'Term Loan A', the traditional amortizing term loan most suited to commercial bank lenders, and a non-amortizing loan, marketed to institutional investors, called a 'Term Loan B', which has regular interest payments and a 'bond-like' bullet repayment.[46] There will also typically be a committed revolving credit facility that can be drawn, paid back, and redrawn, usually provided by commercial banks.[47]

It was not inevitable, however, that this convergence of loan and bond terms—a macroeconomic trend—would lead to ambiguity, loopholes, and defects in the

39 de Fontenay (n 31) 729.
40 ibid 742.
41 ibid 727.
42 ibid 746.
43 Gilligan and Wright (n 26) 175; 'Documents' (n 21).
44 de Fontenay (n 31) 744.
45 ibid.
46 Paterson (n 5) 663.
47 'Leveraged Loan Primer' (n 29) 39; Larreur (n 30) 41; Gilligan and Wright (n 26) 198, 211.

language of loan documents. To understand why this happened, it is once again necessary to explore the role of leveraged finance lawyers.

7.4 Ambiguity as a lawyer strategy

As Joanna Gray has observed, financial markets are not 'somehow a given, a *fait accompli* designed and constituted by others within which lawyers simply advise and feed in a degree of legal ordering'.[48] Bank lawyer [#24] expressed a view of leveraged loan documents that was shared by several of the participants in this book:

> The concern is not only that these documents don't protect lenders in the way that they used to, but also, that they don't work very well. This is something that's being driven by sponsor firms.

Whilst loan and bond convergence might be explainable as a macro, as in market, trend, the physical merging of loan and bond terms in European leveraged loan documents was implemented principally by lawyers at its micro level. It is the way in which this was done that has materially contributed to the extensive uncertainty, loopholes, and defects in typical loan terms.

Gunther Teubner has highlighted how the transplant of legal rules from one jurisdiction to another can produce 'new divergences as their unintended consequences'.[49] In this field, contractual provisions, as opposed to legal rules, have been transplanted by lawyers from US bond documents into European leveraged loan documents, similarly without sufficient prior consideration given as to the range of potential unintended consequences.

The contractual transplant of US terms into European documents is responsible for the junior-lender-waiver-and-release glitch, for example. The US terms which have been included in European intercreditor agreements reflect the emergence of 'second lien' instruments in the US market.[50] These are effectively permitted 'second secured' lenders. In the United States, it was agreed that second lien lenders would not waive their enforcement rights as unsecured creditors since second lien debt is usually *pari passu* with the senior debt in terms of payment, albeit second ranking in terms of the proceeds of a security enforcement.[51] In the United States, this did not matter because at the first sign of financial distress

[48] Citing David Howarth's work, Joanna Gray, 'Lawyers and Systemic Risk in Finance: Could (and Should) the Legal Profession Contribute to Macroprudential Regulation?' (2016) 19 Legal Ethics 122, 134; David Howarth, *Law as Engineering: Thinking About What Lawyers Do* (Edward Elgar Publishing Ltd 2013) 129–30.

[49] Gunther Teubner, 'Legal Irritants: Good Faith in British Law or How Unifying Law Ends Up in New Divergencies' (1998) 61 The Modern Law Review 11.

[50] Larreur (n 30) 45.

[51] ibid.

the borrower group will typically file for protection under Chapter 11 of the US Bankruptcy Code and any such action is stayed by that proceeding.[52] Due to so called *ipso facto* and similar clauses in the Code, the junior lender cannot enforce its rights against the borrower during the currency of the Chapter 11 case.[53] The glitch in European intercreditor documents has arisen because in the United States—given Chapter 11 of the Code—there is no need to include junior lender waiver and release of unsecured claims language in a US intercreditor agreement.[54] Chapter 11 effectively replaces the need for it.

The physical process of merging loan and bond terms in documents was surprisingly crude. Provisions were clumsily transplanted by private equity lawyers into European leveraged loan documents from US bond documents. Private equity lawyer [#11] described how the bond covenants from a New York law governed high yield bond issue were 'literally just stapled to the back of the English law credit agreement so that the front end of the document is governed by English law, and the back end is governed by New York law'.

First, this creates uncertainty as to the applicable governing law according to which terms are to be interpreted. Bank lawyer [#16] said:

> There's a lack of clarity around conflicts of laws issues where you've got a New York law bond indenture, an English law intercreditor, an English law credit agreement, but with a New York law covenant appendix to it. And if you get a court judgement in one jurisdiction, it is unclear quite how it will work in the other.

Second, this approach has created uncertainty in the meaning of the language itself. Private equity lawyers were, according to private equity lawyer [#21], 'trying to sledgehammer US constructs into English loan agreements.' Bank lawyer [#38] gave the following example:

> You'll have a financial covenant in the main body of the document, with all the financial definitions that go along with that. And then you have separate financial definitions or provisions that apply to those financial definitions, in the high yield bond schedule. And the two don't always match up.

You may have, for example, a cap on the amount of cost savings and synergies that can be added back to EBITDA in the definitions found in the main body of the agreement, but this cap will not be included in the corresponding definition which appears in the schedule. These definitions are used in clauses throughout the

52 '11 USC Ch. 11: REORGANIZATION' <https://uscode.house.gov/view.xhtml?path=/prelim@title11/chapter11&edition=prelim> accessed 23 June 2022.
53 Paterson (n 5) 670.
54 '11 USC Ch. 11: REORGANIZATION' (n 52).

document and the schedule, but it is not clear which definition applies. Further, the clause of the agreement setting out the principles of construction does not make clear which is to take precedence. This duplication results in confusion as to how the cap applies, if it does at all.

Bank lawyer [#38] explained that just as much uncertainty can arise when US high yield bond covenants are integrated into the main body of loan agreements, as opposed to simply being appended in a schedule:

> On occasions people try to just incorporate all the bond covenants as they would in a normal loan. And it's been a bit of a disaster, it's made things even more confusing.

Private equity lawyer [#26] said they and other private equity lawyers were frequently 'importing high yield bond style covenants, with frankly impregnable sentences that run on for three pages'. This may be hyperbole, but the sentiment is supported in multiple accounts of other participants.

An important question is why would lawyers in Europe ever think that US drafting linked to a US insolvency protection regime would automatically work when blindly transplanted into a European context? Private equity lawyer [#23] said that just because there are plenty of examples of loans which have incorporated bond covenants and definitions:

> It doesn't mean anyone thought about it particularly well, it just comes from a long line of precedents, which has had all sorts of stuff folded into it.

Private equity lawyer [#35] also said:

> There's been a reluctance to take anything out of the document, just put more things into it. So, as you put more things into it, without thinking through how it all works, you can sometimes get documents that frankly don't hang together very well.

On this view, provisions were transplanted from US bond documents into European leveraged loan contracts without lawyers thinking too much about the implications. For example, private equity lawyer [#11] observed:

> Does it actually work? Has it actually been tested? And has this been analysed in the depth that is actually required? The answer is probably no.

In other words, it is possible that these loopholes and defects arose mostly by accident. Private equity lawyer [#21] said:

> Sponsor lawyers will often talk about how clever they are and how many clever little trap doors the documents have. The reality is a lot of the trap doors are, frankly, mistakes, which neither side knows are there.

There may be some more subtle and nuanced factors at play here too. Perhaps inertia has set in due to what Stephen Choi and others refer to as 'legacy costs'; to revisit a flawed provision of a contract could call in to question the meaning of similar clauses in previous executed contracts, and cast doubt on a lawyer's and/or firm's competence if they were involved in preparing and drafting them originally.[55] This conclusion is supported by Gulati and Scott's research; they found that lawyers advising on sovereign debt documents often did not fully understand them.[56] They tended to treat their own precedent documents as if they were a standard set of terms—a contract entirely made up of boilerplate almost—and the rote use of this precedent eroded the meaning of its terms over time.[57]

Clauses that are poorly constructed and understood can become what Choi and others have referred to as 'encrusted'.[58] They show how these types of aberrations in the meaning of contractual terms can persist for decades.[59] They are perpetuated in financial contracts over a period of years if borrowers or investors insist on having terms which reflect a market benchmark, even though the terms may not work, or if parties do not understand their effects.[60] In the leveraged finance practice area field, the draft documents are also presented by private equity lawyers to their bank lawyer counterparts as if they are boilerplate, not to be questioned or even thought about all that much.[61] Ambiguous terms and embedded defects in documents have hence been carried over from transaction to transaction.

However, on closer analysis of my data, it appears that the causes of persistent ambiguity are more nuanced than simple user error. Private equity lawyers, who, because they mostly control the drafting of the documents, were responsible for introducing the ambiguous provisions in the first place, now actively advocate for them to be maintained. They do this by applying intellectually spurious arguments.

The first such fallacious argument is where a private equity lawyer claims that loan and bond markets have fully converged, so that it is appropriate that European loans and US bonds should have the same terms. This is not the case. Private equity lawyer [#26] noted, for example, that: 'the provisions governing the tradability of bonds are much looser and more flexible than they are in the loan world.' Weaker covenants are more appropriate in bonds because if a bond investor

[55] Choi, Gulati, and Scott (n 10) 14.
[56] Gulati and Scott (n 8).
[57] ibid.
[58] Choi, Gulati, and Scott (n 10) 8.
[59] ibid 12.
[60] Choi, Gulati, and Scott (n 10).
[61] ibid 4.

does not like the bond terms it can typically trade out of them by selling them in a liquid bond market, especially as the bonds are typically listed on a recognized exchange. Loans, on the other hand, are relatively illiquid; the leveraged loan market is smaller and loans, unlike high yield bonds, are not publicly listed so that they will not always attract a willing buyer at an objectively determined price.[62] Loans are also commonly subject to restrictions on who lenders can sell to; usually governed by lists of approved and/or prohibited investors.[63] Often the prohibited list will include specialist distressed investors which are likely to be the investor class most willing to buy the loan if the borrower experiences financial difficulties, which is when lenders are most likely to want to sell. Private equity lawyer [#23] said there was hence no logical reason for banks to accept ambiguity in loan terms simply because it was a feature of bonds:

> The reason all the lacunas and holes were historically accepted in the bonds is because you can just sell out, right? But you can't with loans.

Bond investors also receive more information through disclosure requirements, for example. Loans and bonds hence remain different markets, albeit some of the boundaries between them have admittedly become blurred.

The second fallacious argument is where a private equity lawyer argues for increased flexibility for borrowers in important loan covenants such as those restricting further debt raising, on the basis that this is the position under US loans and/or bonds. This fails to consider that the United States has a uniform, and fundamentally different, security intercreditor and insolvency framework as compared to the multiple different frameworks found across Europe, as I have already noted. In-house lawyer [#17] gave an example of this flawed logic:

> Sponsor lawyers will say 'Oh, unsecured debt is not subject to an intercreditor in the US. So, you shouldn't have it here.' But the US has Chapter 11, which does the job of an intercreditor.

Bank lawyer [#30] said that senior lenders in the US were also able to offer flexibility over debt permissions because of the materially different security creation framework in the United States, where senior lenders:

> get security over everything, so there won't be any unencumbered assets of the group because everything will be first ranking secured in favour of the first lien lenders. So, they can take a more relaxed view of the borrower's ability to raise

62 Albeit loans may, like bonds, carry a credit rating.
63 Known as 'white lists' and 'black lists'.

other debt, because there are no unencumbered assets that could be pledged in favour of another lender.

In civil law jurisdictions in Europe, the granting of security to lenders can be a costly and time-consuming exercise. Separate instruments may need to be prepared and executed for different types of assets; and stamping, notarization, registration, and other formalities can take time and expense to implement.[64] And rules aimed at protecting a company's broader stakeholders can be complex and sensitive issues in leveraged finance transactions, making the granting of security either impossible or more challenging.[65] But security-lite structures, which as I have noted already have become the norm in Europe, have been imposed on lenders even in jurisdictions where it is relatively easy and inexpensive for a comprehensive security package to be granted. In England and Wales for example, not unlike the United States, a single deed can be used to create fixed and floating charges over all the property and assets of a company, for example.[66] In-house lawyer [#17] said that private equity lawyers nonetheless apply a 'one size fits all' logic, insisting on the security-lite package even in jurisdictions where it is relatively easy to grant comprehensive security:

> What sponsor lawyers started saying about two or three years ago was, 'well, you don't get that in Italy, and as you're happy to do deals there we are not giving it to you in the UK, or Ireland, or Germany'.

As I have previously noted, a one-size-fits-all logic tends to determine the content of documents rather than the business context of the transaction.[67] So why are the bank lawyers not challenging the private equity lawyers when they put forward these types of intellectually spurious arguments? Private equity lawyer [#23] said bank lawyers should be:

> rewriting big sections of the documents to make them clear, but there is zero appetite to do that'.

This lack of appetite of the bank lawyers is, once again, founded in the survival logic; notwithstanding the bank lawyers are largely familiar with these loopholes and defects they mostly waive them through if they have appeared in the terms of a

[64] For some examples, see 'Taking Security over Assets in Europe: Some Practical Considerations' <https://www.osborneclarke.com/insights/taking-security-assets-europe-practical-considerations> accessed 19 July 2022.

[65] ibid.

[66] 'Security in Finance Transactions' (*Pinsent Masons*, 30 August 2011) <https://www.pinsentmasons.com/out-law/guides/security-in-finance-transactions> accessed 14 July 2022.

[67] Ayotte and Scully (n 11) 365.

previous transaction. The bank lawyers are able to preserve their moral self-image by drawing on the cleared-the-market logic that I described in Chapter 3. Bank lawyers narrowly construe their role as simply checking whether terms have previously cleared the market—even if they are unintelligible or contain embedded defects and loopholes that have the potential to create significant additional risk for lenders.

7.5 Ethical implications (1): integrity (again)

In the previous chapter, I put the case that contractual boundary pushing by private equity lawyers likely conflicts with their duties to act with integrity under Principle 5 of the SRA's Principles.[68] Private equity lawyers are also potentially in breach of their duty to act with integrity by pursuing 'loophole lawyering' when making the most of the uncertainty and defects in leveraged loan documents that I have explored in this chapter. Yuval Feldman has observed that:

> Different types of people will react differently to legal ambiguity: for some people, ambiguity may reduce their ability to find legal loopholes, whereas for others it may allow various self-deception mechanisms associated with the concept of moral wiggle room.[69]

The ambiguity in loan terms that I have described has created plenty of scope for moral wiggle room in the leveraged finance practice area. Collectively these ambiguities create potential loopholes for private equity lawyers to take advantage of should they need or want to in the future.[70] Moorhead and others, in their study of in-house lawyers, found that attitudes to uncertainty were indicators of ethical inclination.[71]

EBITDA add backs and the subjectivity they generate, leave plenty of room for private equity lawyers to propose spurious interpretations, and create opportunities for the 'creative compliance' that Doreen McBarnet and Christopher Whelan have drawn attention to, where lawyers take advantage of ambiguous drafting, mistakes, loopholes, and grey areas.[72] Christine Parker and others have shown how

[68] 'SRA Principles' (25 November 2019) <https://www.sra.org.uk/solicitors/standards-regulations/principles/> accessed 6 July 2020.

[69] Yuval Feldman, *The Law of Good People* (CUP 2018) 150. On lawyers exploiting legal uncertainty, see also Doreen McBarnet and Christopher Whelan, 'The Elusive Spirit of the Law: Formalism and the Struggle for Legal Control' (1991) 54 The Modern Law Review 848; Joan Loughrey, 'Accountability and the Regulation of the Large Law Firm Lawyer' (2014) 77 The Modern Law Review 732.

[70] For a comprehensive treatment of the potential effects of embedded contractual uncertainty in finance documents, see Gulati and Scott (n 8).

[71] Richard Moorhead, Steven Vaughan, and Cristina Godinho, *In-House Lawyers' Ethics, Institutional Logics, Legal Risk and the Tournament of Influence* (Hart 2018).

[72] McBarnet and Whelan (n 69).

lawyers often lead this process, rather than being directed by their clients to engage in this practice.[73] Joan Loughrey has argued that creative compliance by lawyers was a major factor in the collapse of Enron, as well as being a significant contributor to the global financial crisis, where law was seen as a 'regulatory obstacle' to be structured around, rather than as a social good where the spirit, and not just the letter, of the rule should be observed.[74]

As we have seen, private equity lawyers introduced ambiguous provisions into documents—and now advocate for them to be maintained—applying intellectually spurious arguments. In particular, a series of fallacious arguments, based on false equivalents, have been deployed by private equity lawyers to frame their drafting, review, and negotiation of the terms of the loan documents. There is, then, a related question of whether private equity lawyers are adhering to their duty to act with integrity, and their wider public interest duties, when using coercive tactics and strategies, and advancing intellectually spurious arguments which are again enforced through coercion, in their dealings with bank lawyers.[75]

Moorhead and Hinchley found that corporate lawyers are prone to take advantage of uncertainty to advance the interests of their clients.[76] The outcome can be a weakening of a lawyer's sensitivity to the ethical aspects of a decision, with lawyers prone to putting their own interests ahead of the public interest.[77] Moorhead and Hinchley conclude that:

> All lawyers, be they in-housers or private practitioners, were very clear in seeing ethical problems not principally through the lens of professional principles, but through the social and economic lenses of business.[78]

Private equity lawyer [#23] said of private equity lawyers in general:[79]

> The more complexity, ambiguity, and errors they can insert into, or leave uncorrected, in the documents, and the more these flaws become embedded in market precedents over time, the better for their sponsor clients.

73 Christine E Parker, Robert E Rosen, and Vibeke Lehmann Nielsen, 'The Two Faces of Lawyers: Professional Ethics and Business Compliance with Regulation' 22 The Georgetown Journal of Legal Ethics 49.

74 Trevor Clark and others, 'Agency over Technocracy: How Lawyer Archetypes Infect Regulatory Approaches: The FCA Example' [2021] *24*(2), 91–110. Joan Loughrey, *Corporate Lawyers and Corporate Governance* (CUP 2011) 63, 71.

75 'SRA Principles' (n 68).

76 Richard Moorhead and Victoria Hinchley, 'Professional Minimalism? The Ethical Consciousness of Commercial Lawyers' (2015) 42 Journal of Law and Society 387, 399.

77 ibid 400–03.

78 ibid 411.

79 As already noted, it was not uncommon for participants to distance themselves from behaviour that they were willing to identify in others.

Private equity lawyers that draft loan documents are aware that where significant ambiguity and flaws are embedded in them this creates a range of opportunities for them to devise schemes and strategies to—in J. Crew style—utilize loopholes and defects if the borrower experiences financial distress in the future. They do this because they know that the bank lawyers are unlikely to challenge these ambiguities due to the survival and other field logics. In other words, when private equity lawyers are aware of an ambiguous clause, which has the potential to obscure its meaning, they have a choice: to try and clarify meaning where it is uncertain, or to allow it to subsist. The case study data suggest they tend to select the latter option. If they allow it to subsist, they may then have a further choice in the future, whether to seek to utilize that ambiguity, for their clients, and/or their own, advantage. Private equity lawyers are constantly faced with these types of choices.

It could be that their response—normally to do nothing—is unconscious, in that they do not necessarily think too much about it. As I have noted, Gulati and Scott have shown how ambiguous provisions can pass unnoticed and remain embedded in finance documents for decades.[80] However, my data supports an alternative conclusion: that these are purposeful errors. That ambiguity is also permitted to subsist, and utilized, by private equity lawyers as a deliberate strategy. The result is that drafting errors, and provisions which are circular, or contradict each other, are mostly left uncorrected and/or unclarified. Private equity lawyers frequently refuse to correct errors when bank lawyers identify and challenge them. Bank lawyer [#27] said:

> I can say, 'this makes no sense to me'. And they just come back saying 'we're not going to give any rationale for it, we're just going to say this is what's agreed'.

Private equity lawyer [#23] described their coercive response when bank lawyers seek to rectify errors or clarify language to remove or mitigate the effect of potential loopholes:

> If they try and reopen that, and say 'this bit doesn't particularly work, it's not well drafted, this bit is circular', absolutely those sorts of changes are not going to be well received.

Some private equity lawyers sought to distance themselves from this type of activity. For example, private equity lawyer [#4] said:

[80] Gulati and Scott (n 8).

> It's not a constructive or professional way of behaving. Are there places in the document that could be clearer? Yes, of course. Do you do something about it? Yes. If we find something that we think doesn't work, we try and fix it.

However, and even if this comment was a genuine reflection of behaviour, rather than simple moral distancing aimed at preserving a positive self-image, these lawyers were in the minority in my sample.

Private equity lawyer [#23] explained how leveraged finance loan documents have come to include a multiplicity of permissions that can be utilized by private equity lawyers. Even though the commercial meaning and purpose of the clause is clearly understood, a contrary interpretation may instead be proposed:

> To do stuff that perhaps wasn't in the spirit of the document, but is technically permitted, you can combine different permissions. So, for example, you will have a condition that says for every pound of equity you inject you can borrow two pounds of debt. It is effectively saying, if you're making an equity contribution, you'll be able to borrow a bit more because you've put in cash. Fair enough, right? So, if I put in £20 million, then I can borrow £40 million. There's then a separate permission, which is a distribution permission, which says, for every pound you put in, you can dividend a pound. So, the natural exploit is you say, right, well, I'll put in 10 million, I will borrow 20 million by reference to that ten under the definition. And then separately, I'll use the dividend permission to send that ten back up to the sponsor.

This 'natural exploit' tends to succeed because banks are unable to determine with certainty what the permitted level of debt that the borrower may incur, and so there is never a point at which over-indebtedness triggers an event of default.[81] According to private equity lawyer [#23], there might be '74 different debt definitions and these 36 different distribution permissions, and god knows what else, with multiple permutations of how it can be done'.

The strategy might be client-centred. Although, under the *contra proferentem* rule ambiguous language in a contract will be interpreted by a court against the party that proposed it, because these questions rarely if ever fall to be adjudicated in court, as a matter of practice, uncertainty in loan terms broadly favours the private equity sponsors.[82] It has the potential to shield an ailing company from default and possible enforcement action by its lenders: lenders need clarity of language

[81] Events of default are the prescribed circumstances in which lenders may demand early repayment of the loan.

[82] 'Contra Proferentem Rule' (*Practical Law*) <http://uk.practicallaw.thomsonreuters.com/4-383-2653?transitionType=Default&contextData=(sc.Default)&firstPage=true> accessed 27 July 2023.

to establish that an event of default has occurred before calling one, or risk severe legal and reputational ramifications.[83] Bank lawyer [#34] gave an example:

> We've seen this in the context of COVID. Many borrowers sought to draw down their RCF [revolving credit facility] in full, to maximise their liquidity. And we've had loads of inbound queries from lenders saying, 'have they met the conditions of drawdown?', because one of the conditions to drawdown is the absence of an event of default.'[84]

Where there is uncertainty in the drafting, banks are often left powerless to object to the sponsor taking a course of action, even if the spirit and original meaning of the provision was understood by all parties. Bank lawyer [#44] said:

> Ambiguity is sponsor friendly, because if it's a positive action, if there's ambiguity in debt incurrence or whatever, the company will just go ahead and do it and rely on the fact that where there's ambiguity, you're not going to challenge it.

These dynamics hand the power, and the discretion, to the private equity sponsors and their lawyers. This imbalance in power is what makes the taking advantage of these conditions unfair. As such, the private equity lawyers are not acting with integrity and so their stance is ethically problematic. Bank lawyer [#24] said:

> A sponsor, as borrower, is the one who always makes a determination as to whether or not it's in compliance with the documents. You're always reliant on the borrower to determine if something is permitted or not permitted.

Further, private equity lawyers might draft and insert new provisions that are ambiguous. According to private equity lawyer [#35], private equity lawyers were frequently 'drafting things so it's very hard to work out what the hell's going on.' As a result, covenants have long, rambling 'permitted' exceptions and near-unintelligible add backs, deductions, synergy calculations, and 'mulligans', the effect of which is to disguise real, often underperformance, by the borrower. Even fundamental events of default have been rendered virtually meaningless through multiple cure periods and rights, overly generous and overlapping *de minimis* thresholds, and extensive and contradictory carve-outs and exceptions.

There is evidence in my data that private equity lawyers actively take advantage of ambiguity. Private equity lawyer [#7] said:

[83] See eg, *Grupo Hotelero Urvasco SA v Carey Value Added SL & another* [2013] EWCH 1039 (Comm). Larreur (n 30) 41.

[84] See also Gilligan and Wright (n 26) 297.

> We've certainly been able to advise clients on things that we can exploit in documents.

Private equity lawyer [#11] said private equity lawyers had subjected the market to a 'barrage of abuse' by taking advantage of the ambiguity in loan terms.

7.6 Ethical implications (2): competence

Under Rule 3.2 of the SRA's Code of Conduct, a solicitor must ensure that the service they provide to a client is competent.[85] As I have noted, there has been a general collapse in documentary standards in the leveraged finance practice area. Leveraged finance lawyers have played a central role in transforming loan terms in this way and have largely ceased trying to fix problems. Private equity lawyer [#48] observed:

> It is an interesting debating point to what extent the point we have reached is a result of market forces or a failure of professional ethics. The answer is that it's a combination of those factors.

My participants, overall, considered themselves to be experts. In the interviews, they tended to present their expertise as being situated in their detailed knowledge of the terms of previous comparable transactions. For example, private equity lawyer [#28] said bank lawyers will often say to their clients 'well guys, you accepted it on *x* deal that we advised you on.' Bank lawyers see this as central to their role; bank lawyer [#18] presented this approach as the 'additional value you are adding to the deal; that additional colour is what sets one law firm apart from the other.'

Here bank lawyers can be seen drawing on the cleared-the-market logic as a self-justifying narrative, as if being familiar with the latest 'market position' on each of the detailed terms of the loan documents is the skill-set most highly prized by their bank clients. Bank lawyer [#44] said:

> Sometimes it's just a question of saying, look, it's cleared the market seven or eight times. And banks will sign off on that basis.

On this view, the expertise bank lawyers offer their bank clients no longer resides in their ability to identify, and suggest mitigants for, credit risks inherent in the deal structures and terms proposed by the private equity lawyers. Nor is the thing

[85] 'SRA Code of Conduct for Solicitors, RELs and RFLs' (25 November 2019) <https://www.sra.org.uk/solicitors/standards-regulations/code-conduct-solicitors/> accessed 15 November 2020.

of value prized by private equity sponsors the elegance and clarity of their lawyers' drafting, or their legal advice on technical legal issues. Private equity lawyer [#23] presented their strategy of constantly improving terms on each deal as an expression of their technical expertise: 'we feel that we're at the tip of the spear in terms of innovation and creativity.'

Does the case study raise questions then as to their competence? It is not as though the focus of the transactional lawyer's role has ever been primarily on the technical aspects of the law, of course. Through direct ethnographic observation of transactional lawyers in a Chicago law firm in the 1980s, and analysis of lawyers' time records, John Flood found that there was very little 'law' in the daily work of corporate lawyers: for example, process management took up the bulk of their time.[86] The work was also frequently highly commoditized: he found that associates were responsible for drafting documents, usually involving 'cutting and pasting an existing document'.[87] He observed plenty of negotiation and other interactions, but little legal writing and research. Their work hence covered 'areas of advising that are more fitted to business than law' and their main function was 'managing uncertainty and legal risk for their clients'.[88] Flood directly observed that in contractual negotiations, issues were 'traded' by either side, without evaluation of the legal significance of conceding traded points; this demonstrated for Flood that reaching consensus on the terms of the documents was an 'unfolding and contingent process' which contrasted with traditional conceptions of law as a 'principled discipline'.[89] This book adds further insights to Flood's findings by showing that corporate lawyers may not always view their role as managing uncertainty and legal risk for their clients.

Leveraged finance lawyer competence must also be assessed in the context of the highly commoditized leveraged finance deal process and the reliance on precedent-based documentation, as reflected in this observation by private equity lawyer [#35]:

> The idea that you go into a meeting room and fresh it out on the basis of first principles and negotiate with everyone in the room has kind of just gone.

The trend towards greater commoditization in the provision of legal services is emphasized by Richard Susskind, who argues that legal work is transitioning through five phases; the first two phases chart the shift from bespoke advice to

[86] John Flood, *What Do Lawyers Do?: An Ethnography of a Corporate Law Firm* (Quid Pro Books 2013) 28.
[87] ibid 91, 98–99.
[88] ibid 92.
[89] ibid 110.

commoditized advice which relies heavily on precedent documents, for example.[90] Susskind emphasizes the further transition to systemized/packaged/commoditized products which rely increasingly on technology-based services offering cheap but high-quality solutions to client problems.[91] Susskind's argument is essentially that large firms continue to promote their expertise in bespoke work whilst knowing that their ability to generate profit increasingly resides in their ability to commoditize their work.[92] William Henderson similarly argues that 'the artisan model of lawyering' is in decline; large law firms—because of expansion, globalization, lateral hiring and the general emphasis on driving higher and higher levels of profit per equity partner, have created a 'productivity imperative'.[93]

However, questions about leveraged-finance-lawyer competence remain. The non-leveraged finance lawyers in my sample certainly tended to have a low opinion of the technical skills of their colleagues. Bank lawyer [#9] said:

> They do not spend a lot of time thinking about legal issues when they're putting deals together. Some of them are very sharp, they are very clever people, but they don't seem to analyse issues.

Richard Moorhead and Victoria Hinchley observe that it is generally assumed that corporate lawyers are competent—and virtuous—and this is, for example, what supports their appointment on investigations and as reputational intermediaries in dealings with regulators.[94] There is some support for these types of claims in the literature. Robert Nelson, for example, stated that 'the practice of law in the large law firm is the highest form of legal craft' in that these firms deal with the most complex and constantly evolving legal issues.[95] And according to Eliot Freidson, a core trait of professionalism is the application of specialist knowledge and skill.[96] With one or two notable exceptions, the literature on corporate lawyers largely accepts such claims without significant scrutiny.

Notwithstanding large international law firms have increasingly adopted the logics and structures of large corporations,[97] James Faulconbridge and Daniel

[90] Richard E Susskind, *The End of Lawyers?: Rethinking the Nature of Legal Services / Richard Susskind.* (OUP 2008) 37. William D Henderson, 'From Big Law to Lean Law' (2014) 38 International Review of Law and Economics 5, 12.

[91] Susskind (n 90) 37. Henderson (n 90) 12.

[92] Susskind (n 90) 37. Henderson (n 90) 12.

[93] Henderson (n 90) 15.

[94] Moorhead and Hinchley (n 76) 391.

[95] Robert L Nelson, *Partners with Power: The Social Transformation of the Large Law Firm* (University of California Press 1988) 82.

[96] Eliot Freidson, *Professionalism, The Third Logic: On the Practice of Knowledge* (University of Chicago Press 2001) 217.

[97] JR Faulconbridge and D Muzio, 'The Financialization of Large Law Firms: Situated Discourses and Practices of Reorganization' (2009) 9 Journal of Economic Geography 641; Roy Suddaby and Daniel Muzio, 'Theoretical Perspectives on the Professions' 32 in Laura Empson and others, *The Oxford Handbook of Professional Service Firms* (OUP 2015) 8.

Muzio argue that technical expertise remains central to their professional identity.[98] On this view, specialist practice areas can be understood as groups of technical experts coming together to service elite clients, with individual partners leading and directing complex matters.[99] They found that financial targets were less important than peer pressure with respect to technical excellence.[100] They argue that the emergence of formal partner assessment, which now supplements informal peer pressure, and which assesses the quality as well as the profitability of a partner's work, is evidence that large law firms still prioritize a commitment to quality.[101] This book does not contest these claims with respect to large law firms overall, but rather suggests that their validity may be subject to significant variation across a firm's various practice areas.

We have some data that questions claims to non-corporate lawyer competence in England and Wales. Moorhead's empirical research on legal aid lawyers, for example, suggested that non-lawyers performing the same tasks were seen as more competent than lawyers.[102] Case failure statistics suggested there was substance to these perceptions.[103] To date there is limited, if any, equivalent data on corporate lawyers' claims to quality in England and Wales, however.

The idea of transactional corporate work being mostly commoditized and low on knowledge intensity was given empirical support by Gulati and Scott.[104] As with the sovereign debt contracts studied by Gulati and Scott, leveraged finance documents have become a 'black hole' into which complexity, ambiguity, and errors have become deeply entrenched.[105] A point of distinction with the work of Gulati and Scott is that in the leveraged finance practice area, confusion in meaning is not centred around a single clause, it permeates throughout the documents. Bank lawyer [#24] said:

> There are loads of problems with these documents. They are hundreds of pages long, and there are lots of loopholes. Some of which we know about, some of which would not be obvious to even a highly trained set of eyes.

What makes the case that leveraged finance lawyers are not competent even more compelling is that the existence of mistakes and errors in leveraged loans is quite blatant, even when compared to the sovereign debt documents studied by Gulati and Scott; it is mostly widely acknowledged, and its effects often understood, by

[98] James Faulconbridge and Daniel Muzio, 'Organizational Professionalism in Globalizing Law Firms' (2008) 22 Work, Employment and Society 7, 10.

[99] ibid 15–16.

[100] ibid.

[101] ibid 17.

[102] R Moorhead, 'Precarious Professionalism: Some Empirical and Behavioural Perspectives on Lawyers' (2014) 67 Current Legal Problems 447, 453–54.

[103] R Moorhead and others, *Quality and Cost: Final Report on the Contracting of Civil, Non-Family Advice and Assistance Pilot* (The Stationary Office 2001).

[104] Choi, Gulati, and Scott (n 10) 13; Gulati and Scott (n 8).

[105] Gulati and Scott (n 8).

the lawyers who practice in this field. This book shows how embedded uncertainty in complex commercial and financial contracts may not simply be unexpected and unplanned but can also be the consequence of lawyer strategies which are often quite openly and consciously pursued. The lawyers that practice in this field tend not to rectify the flaws in documents that they come across. The reason for this is the effects of the powerful market forces and events impacting this practice area, which have led to new logics which provide the framework for lawyer sense-making: for example, the survival logic that constrains the bank lawyers' willingness and ability to actively challenge private equity lawyer strategies, and the cleared-the-market logic which provides them with a convenient self-justification for this stance.

Large international law firms often claim that they are highly skilled in providing expertise in large cross-border transactional contexts, bringing customized solutions to bear in solving complex problems.[106] The case study sits uncomfortably with these types of claims. But this does not necessarily mean that leveraged finance lawyers are incompetent for the purposes of the SRA's Standards and Regulations. On the other hand, whilst accepting there has been a degree of commoditization in this field of practice, and possibly even a shift in the nature of the expertise that bank clients value in their lawyers, the blanket, one-size-fits-all and leave-the-loopholes logics and related practices found in the leveraged finance practice area raises important questions about the competence of leveraged finance lawyers.

The SRA's Code of Conduct is described as a 'framework for ethical and competent practice'.[107] To be considered competent, a solicitor must be able to 'draft documents which are legally effective' which includes 'using clear, accurate and succinct language'.[108] My data shows that both bank lawyers and private equity lawyers may not be adhering to this principle in their daily work.[109]

Emphasizing that solicitors owe duties to the court and to the wider public interest as well as to their clients, the SRA has made clear that 'solicitors are responsible for meeting high professional standards.'[110] The SRA has said that 'the public's confidence in the rule of law and the overall effectiveness of the legal system can also be negatively affected by poor standards of work and service'.[111] Uncertainty in leveraged finance documents have so eroded lender protections that this phenomena will likely impede the restructuring of distressed leveraged companies

[106] Marc Galanter, 'Mega-Law, An American Invention' (1982) 3 *Humanities* 16; Andrew Boon, *The Ethics and Conduct of Lawyers in England and Wales* (Bloomsbury Publishing 2014) 117.

[107] 'SRA Code of Conduct for Solicitors, RELs and RFLs' (n 85).

[108] ibid.

[109] In addition to risk of sanction for breach of their duties under professional codes of conduct, leveraged finance lawyers also face potential liability for breach of contract, breach of fiduciary duty and in negligence where they offer poor levels of service and competence to their clients, Jonathan Herring, *Legal Ethics* (OUP 2017) 240–48.

[110] 'Risk Outlook 2018/2019' (17 July 2018) 27 <https://www.sra.org.uk/risk/outlook/risk-outlook-2018-2019/> accessed 23 November 2020.

[111] 'Standards of Service' (16 November 2020) <https://www.sra.org.uk/sra/research-publications/risk-outlook-2020-21/standards-of-service/> accessed 18 March 2023.

and, as a result, potentially introduce unexpected social and economic costs.[112] This outcome has the potential to undermine the trust that clients place in large law firms, and I would argue, the wider public.

7.7 Conclusion

This chapter explored how the ethical decision-making of corporate lawyers can have a corrupting impact on the conditions of financial markets, in the form of the contractual terms of complex cross-border financial transactions governing the allocation and pricing of risk by that market's participants.

As experienced legal professionals, my participants might be considered to be experts in their field.[113] However, ambiguity and flaws have become embedded in leveraged loan documents because the lawyers involved in drafting and negotiating them either did not think about the effects of their drafting at all, or if they did, they did not necessarily care too much about its consequences. This chapter has shown how provisions have been transplanted into European leveraged loan documents from US bond documents, initially with insufficient thought being given by the lawyers involved as to their effects under European legal, insolvency, and security enforcement frameworks.

Documents are often littered with potential loopholes, which weaken the senior-secured position of the lenders. These developments should be considered in the context of dynamic forces and events affecting the leveraged finance practice area field, including the convergence of leveraged loan and bond markets and investors. Private equity lawyers have strategically utilized the opportunities afforded by this macro phenomena, however.[114] Discretionary private equity lawyer action at the micro level, enabled by these field conditions, has been a significant contributing and amplifying factor in this development. It appears that leveraged finance lawyers are as a result likely in breach of their ethical duties under the codes of professional conduct to which they are subject.

The next chapter considers the potential market and other causes of the leveraged finance lawyer action that I have explored so far.

[112] Choi, Gulati, and Scott (n 10) 15.

[113] The literature on interviewing lawyers, eg, often uses the term 'expert' as opposed to 'elite', to capture those with expertise (as compared to the average person) who may not also have power and privilege (eg, within the hierarchy of their organization), Vaughan, for example used 'elite', whereas, Korkea-aho and Leino preferred 'expert', Steven Vaughan, 'Elite and Elite-Lite Interviewing: Managing Our Industrial Legacy', in Alex Franklin and Paul Blyton (eds) *Researching Sustainability: A Guide to Social Science Methods, Practice and Engagement* (Routledge 2013) 107. Emilia Korkea-aho and Päivi Leino, 'Interviewing Lawyers: A Critical Self-Reflection on Expert Interviews as a Method of EU Research', European journal of legal studies, 2019, Vol. 11, SI, pp. 17-47 22, 31; William S Harvey, 'Strategies for Conducting Elite Interviews' (2011) 11 Qualitative Research 431, 5,7.

[114] For 'levels' analysis, see Paul J DiMaggio and Walter Powell W, 'Introduction', *The New Institutionalism in Organizational Analysis* (The University of Chicago Press 1991) 12.

8
The Corruption of Big Law by Markets

8.1 Introduction

This chapter explores the potential causes of the practice area logics that drive the dubious ethical conduct of corporate lawyers which is revealed by the case study.

When exploring motivations for lawyer action and ethical decision-making, the corporate lawyer literature tends to emphasize the importance of 'law firm logics' which emerged in response to Big Law's shift to financialized law firm governance which occurred in the 1980s and 1990s.[1] This is quite right but is also only part of the story. To fully understand what influences lawyer action it is necessary to also connect it to specific practice area logics, which are themselves the product of wider macroeconomic processes affecting the relevant practice area.[2] In other words, the search for contextual factors influencing corporate lawyer conduct should not be confined to law firm-wide pressures and incentives, such as those which flow from 'eat what you kill' remuneration models, for example. To identify and then evaluate the effect of the prevailing institutional logics that shape corporate lawyer action and decision-making, the range of a practice area's contextual conditions should be analysed, since these combine with law firm logics to create the pathways which facilitate individual lawyer action and ethical decision-making.[3] This chapter hence integrates an analysis of the effects of law firm logics with an analysis of the effects of macro-level forces and events affecting a practice area which can lead to a practice area developing a distinct set of internal practice area logics.[4]

In the leveraged finance practice area, the subject of the case study, a series of macroeconomic forces and events, including the global financial crisis, regulatory change directed at banks, a leveraged finance supply and demand disconnect, the blending of leveraged finance loan and bond markets, and a switch in bank lending and underwriting models in this market, have together shaped a distinct set of logics

[1] Janine Griffiths-Baker, *Serving Two Masters: Conflicts of Interest in the Modern Law Firm* (Hart Publishing 2002) 3–8.

[2] Patricia H Thornton, William Ocasio, and Michael Lounsbury, *The Institutional Logics Perspective: A New Approach to Culture, Structure, and Process* (OUP 2012) vii, 80–81.

[3] ibid 9.

[4] ibid vii, 80–81.

that shape the ethical decision-making of leveraged finance lawyers. The result is that leveraged finance lawyers think and act differently to lawyers in other practice areas—even when compared to their colleagues within their firm—because these logics comprise the framework within which they decide what is appropriate conduct in their daily work. Lawyers in other practice areas will sense-make within a different framework of logics which are specific to their own practice area.

The chapter is arranged as follows. I start by placing my findings in the context of the existing corporate lawyer literature, which emphasizes the motivation for lawyer action as most closely connected to the shift to financialized law firm governance. Next, I explore how powerful macro-forces and events must also be considered a contributing factor explaining corporate lawyer behaviour and ethical decision-making. In the leveraged finance practice area, macroeconomic dynamics led to private equity sponsors asserting their power over banks, which in turn translated into private equity lawyers asserting their power over bank lawyers. After this, I explore how discretionary lawyer action, taking advantage of the new logics of this field, has been a material factor shaping their practice area context.[5] In the final substantive section, I consider an example, the critical influence of a sub-group of private equity lawyers, who I refer to as the institutional entrepreneurs.[6] I show how real change to the conditions and logics of the leveraged finance practice area was effected by this sub-group of powerful private equity lawyers in particular, who drew on both the logics of their firm and the emergent logics of the markets in which they were operating.[7] The chapter then concludes.

8.2 Law firm logics: the logical starting point

The literature which seeks to explain the factors which influence corporate lawyer action and ethical decision-making rightly tends to emphasize the significant structural changes to large law firms that occurred in the 1980s and 1990s.[8] For example, incentives and pressures created under emergent 'eat what you kill' remuneration structures.[9] These types of firm-wide logics were raised only very occasionally in my interviews, however. For example, private equity lawyer [#7] referred to a:

[5] ibid v, vii; Paul J DiMaggio and Walter Powell W, 'Introduction', *The New Institutionalism in Organizational Analysis* (The University of Chicago Press 1991).

[6] Patricia H Thornton and William Ocasio, 'Institutional Logics and the Historical Contingency of Power in Organizations: Executive Succession in the Higher Education Publishing Industry, 1958-1990' (1999) 105 American Journal of Sociology 801, 99.

[7] Thornton, Ocasio, and Lounsbury (n 2) 177.

[8] See for example, Janine Griffiths-Baker (n 1) 3; Milton C Regan, *Eat What You Kill: The Fall of a Wall Street Lawyer* (University of Michigan Press 2004).

[9] Mitt Regan and Lisa H Rohrer, *BigLaw: Money and Meaning in the Modern Law Firm* (The University of Chicago Press 2020) 1, 77–95.

> pressure to perform business-wise, to succeed. Some of that's in-built, just human drive, and some of that comes from what the firm wants to see; you know a big deal is going to help move the needle of your financial quarter.

The significant structural changes to the legal profession and to large law firms in the 1980s and 1990s were relatively consistent across firms.[10] Mitt Regan and Lisa Rohrer, for example, interviewed partners of six firms in the US, and found that they 'face the same business pressures and respond to them in similar ways'.[11] For clarity, I have grouped these critical law firm logics under four headings.

Firstly, clients became less loyal to individual law firms in the 1980s and 1990s. Regan and Rohrer report that large corporate clients became more sensitive to the costs of external legal counsel, often insisting on discounts, fee estimates, and capped fee arrangements.[12] Corporate clients also built large and sophisticated teams of internal lawyers and took much of their legal work 'in-house'. In-house legal functions pressed for reduced external legal costs, loosening their long-standing ties with firms, and encouraging competition between firms.[13] Regan and Rohrer note that clients 'no longer nurture long term relationships with firms'.[14]

Regan and Rohrer argue that until the late twentieth century, large law firms largely operated in a 'seller's market'.[15] They describe how the financial crisis accelerated a shift to a buyer's market, as the 'pie' of corporate legal work reduced dramatically and competition intensified, and the commercial pressures on partners became elevated, as firms laid off significant numbers of partners who were considered unproductive, and increasingly moved to remuneration systems that rewarded productivity over seniority.[16]

Banks now routinely impose heavily discounted hourly rates, 'volume rebates', and other terms widely perceived by law firms as financially onerous, as the price for admission to their panels of preferred law firms.[17] In my interviews, banks were

10 Janine Griffiths-Baker (n 1) 3–8.

11 Regan and Rohrer (n 9) 9.

12 ibid 21. See also Marc Galanter and Thomas Palay, *Tournament of Lawyers: The Transformation of the Big Law Firm* (University of Chicago Press 1991); Marc Galanter and William D Henderson, 'The Elastic Tournament: The Second Transformation of the Big Law Firm' (Social Science Research Network 2008) SSRN Scholarly Paper ID 1104711 <https://papers.ssrn.com/abstract=1104711> accessed 6 December 2018; Regan (n 8).

13 Which Andrew Abbot refers to as 'intra-professional competition', Andrew Abbott, *System of Professions: An Essay on the Division of Expert Labor* (University of Chicago Press 1988); Roy Suddaby and Daniel Muzio, 'Theoretical Perspectives on the Professions' in Laura Empson and others, *The Oxford Handbook of Professional Service Firms* (OUP 2015) 38. Richard E Susskind, *The End of Lawyers?: Rethinking the Nature of Legal Services / Richard Susskind* (OUP 2008).

14 Regan and Rohrer (n 9) 21. See also Galanter and Palay (n 12); Galanter and Henderson (n 12); Regan (n 8).

15 Regan and Rohrer (n 9) 25.

16 See ibid 16–22.

17 ibid 21. See also Galanter and Palay (n 12); Galanter and Henderson (n 12); Regan (n 8).

often presented as having chosen to undermine, by effectively commoditizing, their relationships with the law firms they had previously enjoyed close and long-standing ties to.[18] For example, according to bank lawyer [#40]:

> Investment banks see lawyers as a service to be purchased. And the fact that the purchasing people at all the banks run the panel negotiations tells you what their view of lawyers is.

Here bank lawyers can be seen drawing on firm-level logics in making sense of their context. Banks were once seen as the ultimate client, that no lawyer or law firm could risk antagonizing; according to John Flood, writing in 2009, 'upset them and law firms can expect to see a significant part of their fee income evaporate'.[19] However, due to shifts in market dynamics, these assumptions must now be reassessed.

There has been a fundamental shift in how lawyers and law firms are viewed by their large corporate and bank clients, and the nature of the relationships that the law firms have with these clients' in-house legal teams, and vice versa. Robert Rosen, in arguing that 'We're All Consultants Now', observed that 'outside law firms become just one type of professional service firm'.[20] Claire Coe and Steven Vaughan, in their research into the independence of corporate lawyers in London-based firms, found that major corporate and financial institution clients imposed terms of engagement on firms, who were required to pitch for a position on the client's panel of firms.[21] Firms were 'under pressure to deliver "value for money" in an increasingly competitive environment'.[22] Large law firms are now effectively engaged in a procurement process, which meant they were 'losing distinctiveness as professionals' and becoming 'mere service providers'.[23] Rosen traces these developments to the 1980s, when 'inside counsel became "purchasing agents" for outside legal services. To minimize legal fees, among other reasons, only the legal department could authorize the employment of outside lawyers.'[24] This emergent 'service provider' logic appears to affect how bank lawyers in particular perceive their role,

[18] Claire Coe and Steven Vaughan, 'Independence, Representation and Risk: An Empirical Exploration of the Management of Client Relationships by Large Law Firms' (Social Science Research Network 2015) SSRN Scholarly Paper ID 2679005 <https://papers.ssrn.com/abstract=2679005> accessed 17 July 2018.

[19] John Flood, 'Ambiguous Allegiances in the Lawyer-Client Relationship: The Case of Bankers and Lawyers' <https://www.researchgate.net/publication/228135498_Ambiguous_Allegiances_in_the_Lawyer-Client_Relationship_The_Case_of_Bankers_and_Lawyers> accessed 9 June 2023 3.

[20] Robert Eli Rosen, 'We're All Consultants Now: How Changes in Client Organizational Strategies Influences Change in the Organization of Corporate Legal Services' (2002) 44 Arizona Law Review 637, 640.

[21] Coe and Vaughan (n 18) 1.

[22] ibid.

[23] ibid. See also Christopher J Whelan and Neta Ziv, 'Privatizing Professionalism: Client Control of Lawyers' Ethics Colloquium: Globalization and the Legal Profession' (2011) 80 Fordham Law Review 2577.

[24] Rosen (n 20) 668.

offering them a further convenient self-justification for interpreting their role as narrowly as possible to appear amenable to the private equity lawyers' objectives.

Bank lawyers also displayed a tendency to shift responsibility for their stance to their bank clients. For example, bank lawyer [#30] said:

> The arranging bank community only has itself to blame for a state of affairs where it's willing to accept this sort of arrangement.

This blame-the-client logic further helps them to give meaning to, and—in their mind—legitimize, their action.[25] Bank lawyers pointed out that banks had developed teams of in-house lawyers, often including specialists in leveraged finance, to mitigate the effects of any ethical challenges for their external counsel that might flow from the designation model. For example, bank lawyer [#22] said, 'ultimately, the banks are big enough boys, and they can, or should, look after themselves and stand up for their own interests'. These sorts of self-justifying narratives founded in a feeling that large bank clients need less protection, work in combination with others, for example, distorted notions of the expertise their clients want from them, allowing them to narrow the scope of their role without jeopardizing their moral self-image.

The survival logic works in harness with these client relationship logics. Regan and Rohrer argue that where corporate lawyers see themselves as mere service providers to their clients, for example, as opposed to trusted business advisors, this might negatively impact their motivation to provide a more rounded service, inviting lawyers to 'do the minimum'.[26] They argue that this stance gives lawyers 'perfectly acceptable rationales for embracing a narrow understanding of their responsibilities'.[27] Lawyers tend not to find the role of mere service provider rewarding or motivating.[28]

Responding to this dynamic, many large law firms have shifted their strategic focus away from large listed corporates and banks—their traditional client base—towards clients which are less procurement-led, and thus potentially more profitable, such as private equity sponsors.[29] They rely heavily on the help of external lawyers in both designing and administering leveraged buyout transactions on their behalf.[30] Private equity lawyers tend to establish close and longstanding relationships with individual private equity sponsors, often as a preferred firm, or

25 Thornton and Ocasio (n 6) 155, 159.

26 Regan and Rohrer (n 9) 209.

27 ibid 210.

28 ibid 203–11.

29 Sujeet Indap, Barney Thompson, and James Fontanella-Khan, 'How a Private Equity Boom Fuelled the World's Biggest Law Firm' *Financial Times* (6 June 2019) <https://www.ft.com/content/13696928-86d5-11e9-a028-86cea8523dc2> accessed 7 June 2019.

30 John Gilligan and Mike Wright, *Private Equity Demystified: An Explanatory Guide* (4th edn, OUP 2020) 9, 138.

as member of a small informal panel of firms. Private equity lawyer [#23] said 'It's often the case that we do 80% of a private equity fund's financing.'

Secondly, in the 1990s and early 2000s, firms grew significantly in size, with many becoming global business organizations.[31] Research by John Heinz and Edward Laumann, and also by Robert Nelson, emphasizes how, since the 1990s, large corporate law firms in the United States experienced accelerated growth and globalization,[32] and increasingly adopted corporate-style management strategies.[33]

In parallel, corporate law firms recruited professional managers in order to more tightly monitor and enforce partner productivity.[34] Joan Loughrey notes how 'corporate law firm career success typically depends on meeting commercial criteria such as achieving and excelling fee targets'.[35] Loughrey suggests corporate lawyers 'absorbed the corporate norms of their clients and their market environment', hiring management consultants 'who have encouraged law firms to become more like businesses' and hired 'non-lawyer managers' who influence strategy and culture.[36]

James Faulconbridge and Daniel Muzio, in their study of the largest firms in England, emphasize how this growth and globalization was accompanied by the 'financialisation' of large law firms and a new found 'obsession' with driving increased profit per equity partner (PEP) —the profits of the firm divided by the number of equity partners—in the period leading up to the global financial crisis.[37] They argue that large English law firms underwent an organizational transformation due to these 'financial logics' in the period between 1993 and 2008, with an emphasis on increasing PEP.[38]

Examples of steps taken by firms to increase PEP identified by Faulconbridge and Muzio include: increasing the firm's leverage ratio (the ratio of 'employed' fee earners to equity partners); increasing the number of salaried partners; de-equitizing 'underperforming' partners; focusing on practice areas seen as more profitable, such as capital markets and structured finance; focusing on profitable matters at the expense of client relationships; and the establishment of industry

[31] Janine Griffiths-Baker (n 1) 3–8.

[32] Carole Silver, 'Globalization and the U.S. Market in Legal Services - Shifting Identities' (1999) 31 Law and Policy in International Business 1093; JR Faulconbridge and D Muzio, 'The Financialization of Large Law Firms: Situated Discourses and Practices of Reorganization' (2009) 9 Journal of Economic Geography 641, 651.

[33] For example, see John P Heinz and Edward O Laumann, *Chicago Lawyers: The Social Structure of the Bar* (Russell Sage Foundation 1982); Robert L Nelson, *Partners with Power: The Social Transformation of the Large Law Firm* (University of California Press 1988); Gerard Hanlon, 'A Profession in Transition - Lawyers, the Market and Significant Others' (1997) 60 Modern Law Review 798; James Faulconbridge and Daniel Muzio, 'Organizational Professionalism in Globalizing Law Firms' (2008) 22 Work, Employment and Society 7; Whelan and Ziv (n 23).

[34] Laura Empson, *Managing the Modern Law Firm* (OUP 2007).

[35] Joan Loughrey, *Corporate Lawyers and Corporate Governance* (CUP 2011) 52.

[36] ibid 51–52.

[37] Faulconbridge and Muzio (n 32) 642, 659.

[38] ibid 649–55.

sector groups.[39] They connect these trends to the 'financialisaton' seen in listed companies, where there had been an emphasis on increasing shareholder value over the same period.[40] William Henderson also highlights this approach by law firm leaders in the United States, who became intent on maximizing current year revenues, with higher leverage (the ratio of associates to partners) and increased lateral hiring deployed as tools to grow PEP.[41] Firms also need to maintain high PEP to attract lateral hires—to do this they also tend to tightly manage performance by terminating those partners who do not match minimum income generation criteria.[42]

A related factor has been the rise of the legal press in the United Kingdom, which has transformed the common conception of law firm success, now defined primarily by reference to the, now mostly public, PEP metric.[43] A perception of which firms are the most successful is promoted and reinforced through the publication of financial performance data and league table rankings in the legal press and directories, giving the supposedly successful firms enhanced visibility. Previously, as Regan has noted, there was a 'scarcity of information about matters such as billing rates, firm profits, partnership agreements, partner compensation, associate salaries and even the identities of the firm's clients'.[44] A perception of which firms are the most successful is promoted and reinforced through the publication of financial performance data and league table rankings in the legal press and directories, giving the supposedly successful firms enhanced visibility.[45] Galanter and Henderson attribute this development to the explosion in lateral hiring; partners are now aware of which firms may offer them a path to higher remuneration.[46]

Thirdly, over this period there was also a shift in the way in which most large law firms tended to remunerate their partners. Loughrey notes that the UK firms which have followed many of the leading US firms in switching from lockstep to 'eat what you kill' models, which primarily reward a partner's ability to generate profitable work from clients, in other words, their 'rainmaking' abilities, likely experience a commensurate change in culture.[47] The lockstep system bases a partner's compensation solely or primarily on seniority—each year all partners progress in lockstep together up the scale. Regan and Rohrer note that this model is designed to encourage collaboration and foster 'a sense of collegiality and equality among

[39] ibid.
[40] ibid 643.
[41] William D Henderson, 'From Big Law to Lean Law' (2014) 38 International Review of Law and Economics 5, 10–11.
[42] ibid.
[43] Faulconbridge and Muzio (n 32) 648.
[44] Regan (n 8) 27.
[45] Faulconbridge and Muzio (n 32) 648.
[46] Galanter and Henderson (n 12) 1867.
[47] Loughrey (n 35) 51.

partners'.[48] Compensation systems in large law firms now increasingly reward partners who contribute most to the firm's PEP metric. Regan and Rohrer see this as evidence of a business logic: how a partner is rewarded has both material implications (they may have more or less money) and symbolic ones (what they are paid is seen as a reflection of their value to the firm; it is thus a system that 'allocates respect').[49] Larry Ribstein argued that individual performance-based remuneration models, as opposed to lockstep models based solely on seniority, incentivize partners to focus on developing their own reputations, as opposed to those of the firm.[50]

Fourthly, from the mid-1990s, law firm partners became more mobile—now there is frequent lateral movement of partners between large firms. Henderson explained that the attraction for law firm leaders of laterally hiring rainmaker partners is that they should, in theory at least, be able to generate sufficient income from clients to cover both the guaranteed take of that partner, the cost of associates and other staff the lateral either brings with them or needs to support their work, and the proportionate share of the office running costs, with a healthy surplus that contributes to—and boosts—the total profitability of the firm in which all partners benefit.[51]

Lateral hiring has become a principal growth strategy of the leading large firms in London. But this comes at a cost to the firm's culture—to attract lateral hire rainmaker partners, the firm needs to maintain high levels of profitability—measured in PEP; and, this again generates pressure to tightly manage partner performance, and terminate underperforming partners.[52] As John Flood has pointed out, firms are 'not averse to removing partners who do not generate sufficient work for the firm'.[53] In a chapter of their book entitled 'Pruning for Productivity', Regan and Rohrer note that 'since the 2008 economic downturn, law firms have become much more willing to lay off lawyers, including partners, whom they regard as unproductive'.[54]

Lateral moves by partners can impact their ethical decision-making because, as Henderson argues, the newly arrived partner may be focussed on 'adding value' to their new firm, and so may be more vulnerable to client capture and internal pressures to generate revenue.[55] Ribstein argued that excessive lateral hiring

48 Regan and Rohrer (n 9) 123. However, in my own experience lockstep also risks partners who feel they contribute more resenting those who they feel contribute less—this resentment may be felt most strongly of course by more junior lawyers.

49 ibid 121–22.

50 LE Ribstein, 'The Death of Big Law' [2010] Wisconsin Law Review 749, 755.

51 Henderson (n 41) 9.

52 ibid 10.

53 John Flood, *What Do Lawyers Do?: An Ethnography of a Corporate Law Firm* (Quid Pro Books 2013) 8.

54 Regan and Rohrer (n 9) 96.

55 Henderson (n 41) 5; Hugh Gunz, Sally Gunz, and Ronit Dinovitzer, 'Professional Ethics' [2015] The Oxford Handbook of Professional Service Firms 129.

'complicates a firm's ability to maintain a strong culture of trust and cooperation'.[56] Richard Moorhead and Victoria Hinchley found in their study of private practice and in-house lawyers that their respondents reported that 'cut-throat lateral-hiring' of partners diminished loyalty and concern for reputation.[57]

These four law firm business logics significantly influence the ethical decision-making of corporate lawyers. But while the firm's remuneration model, for example, may generate both pressures and incentives on a lawyer to maximize their revenue generation potential, this book reveals the strategies lawyers adopt to achieve these goals, and how the way in which they think and act are most closely connected to and conditioned by the conditions and logics of their practice area.[58] As Joan Huber notes, 'common sense and research makes all of us aware that everything interacts with everything else'.[59] Firm-wide logics, hence, work in combination with practice area logics to form the governing framework within which leveraged finance lawyers act and make decisions at the micro level of the field.[60] My approach is to also consider the effects of wider economic forces and events which impact a firm's practice areas unevenly and how these, when added to pressures and incentives emanating from the wider law firm environment, might motivate or constrain their individual action.[61]

8.3 Market forces and events shape also practice area logics

As well as the four business logics found within law firms considered in the previous section, my analysis considers the effects of macro-level forces and events in fashioning the specific conditions and logics of a practice area as a factor which can materially influence lawyer action and ethical decision-making. My data suggest that practice area logics are just as accessible to lawyers, if not more so, as are firm-wide logics. So, although the pressure a lawyer might feel to maximize their income generation, for example, is perhaps best explained by reference to firm-wide logics, how lawyers think about, and then act to execute, these sorts of objectives can be seen in how they respond to practice area-specific logics. In the leveraged finance practice area, for example, we have already seen how the survival logic combines with law firm logics to shape bank lawyer practices and ethical decision-making.

[56] Ribstein (n 50) 775; Henderson (n 41) 7.

[57] Richard Moorhead and Victoria Hinchley, 'Professional Minimalism? The Ethical Consciousness of Commercial Lawyers' (2015) 42 Journal of Law and Society 387, 403.

[58] Regan (n 8) 8.

[59] Joan Huber (ed), *Macro-Micro Linkages in Sociology* (1st edn, SAGE Publications, Inc 1991) 6; D Brent Smith, Benjamin Schneider, and Marcus W Dickson, 'Meso Organisational Behaviour: Comments on the Third Paradigm', *The SAGE Handbook of Organization Studies* (Second, SAGE Publications 2013) 149.

[60] Regan and Rohrer (n 9) 1, 77–95.

[61] Peter M Blau, *Inequality and Heterogeneity: A Primitive Theory of Social Structure* (Free Press 1977); Brent Smith, Schneider, and Dickson (n 59) 152.

To fully understand the causes of these types of practice area-specific logics, it is necessary to connect them to wider processes at both the macro and micro levels of the practice area, when viewed as an institutional field. As noted in the introduction to this book, the institutional logics perspective analyses the relative effects of micro and macro influences.[62] It concentrates on viewing institutional fields through a series of 'levels', individual (micro), organisational fields, institutional fields, (meso), and societies and economies (macro). It isolates macro-forces, or logics, and examines how these might exert influence at the micro level.

Applying this theoretical lens to the case study, we see how emergent macro-level field conditions since the mid-2000s have created the pathways for the leveraged finance lawyer action described in previous chapters. These conditions led to the ascendancy of private equity sponsors in their negotiations of loan terms with their banks, for example, and the narrowing of the scope, or more accurately, the emphasis, of the bank lawyer's role due to the banks' shift to an originate-to-distribute underwriting model.

The corporate lawyer literature tends to point to these types of macroeconomic factors only when they directly shape wider law firm logics. For example, Galanter and Henderson argue that changes in law firm business and partner remuneration models, and other trends such as the increased mobility of both partners and their clients, can be attributed to 'major structural changes in the market place' such as the globalization of corporate and financial institution clients.[63] Janine Griffiths-Baker, who found that large corporate law firms in London routinely ignored professional rules regarding conflicts of interest, attributed this finding to four principal causes, one of which was the 'globalisation of commerce'.[64] Gomez and Galanter also attribute 'unprecedented demand for high-end corporate legal services' to the growth in the scale and complexity of global trade.[65] This book similarly considers the wider influence of financial markets at the macro level but not simply as a driver of law firm logics. Financial market dynamics can also directly impact the structural conditions and logics of individual practice areas.[66] These market dynamics can impact the practices and logics of one practice area of a firm more than, or in different ways to, those of another. Or one or more practice areas may be impacted whilst others may not be affected by them at all.

In the case study, I have applied my familiarity—drawn from my time in practice as an international finance lawyer—with both financial markets and the international law firm environment to undertake a deep-dive exploration of a

62 Thornton, Ocasio, and Lounsbury (n 2) vii, 80–1.

63 Galanter and Henderson (n 12) 1906.

64 Janine Griffiths-Baker (n 1) preface.

65 Manuel A Gomez and Marc Galanter, 'The Many Lives of Big Law: Three Decades in the Evolution of Large Law Firms' in Richard L Abel, Hilary Sommerlad, Ole Hammerslev and Ulrike Schultz (eds), *Lawyers in 21st-Century Societies: Vol. 2: Comparisons and Theories* (Bloomsbury Publishing Plc 2022) 373.

66 Regan and Rohrer (n 9) 233.

corporate law firm practice area to explore the extent to which its connections to, and interactions with, the private equity and leveraged finance markets impacts the way lawyers view and carry out their roles in their everyday practice. A series of often connected macroeconomic events have transformed the logics of the leveraged finance practice area since the mid-2000s. Denise Rousseau and Robert House maintain that as well as focussing on individuals, groups, and organizations, researchers of institutional fields must also take into account events such as crises, since they tend to have transformative effects on the field's conditions.[67] Chief among the macro forces and events which have dramatically changed the conditions of the leveraged finance practice area field is the global financial crisis of 2007–09. As John Gilligan and Mike Wright have observed, the crisis 'rewrote the book' on leveraged finance debt markets, owing to the decade of 'sustained low interest rates and new debt market participants that resulted from it'.[68] The Financial Stability Board (FSB), an international body established in the wake of the global financial crisis to promote global financial stability, has also presented the global financial crisis as the pivot point, when market standard leveraged loan terms became significantly less protective for lenders and began offering significantly greater borrower flexibility.[69] Changes in the practices and logics of leveraged finance lawyers have also been significant and rapid in this period.[70]

The global financial crisis broke in the summer of 2007, sparking massive disruption in the leveraged loan market.[71] Leveraged lending levels collapsed, and large leveraged buyouts ceased for a time; banks' access to inter-bank and other wholesale funding dried up as confidence in their solvency plummeted, meaning they could no longer lend long term to support leveraged buyout transactions.[72] There was no new European leveraged buyout lending in the European large-cap market in 2008 and 2009, and it was not until Bain Capital and Advent bought WorldPay in 2010 that the market reopened.[73]

Following the financial crisis a wave of fresh regulation was directed at the banks that were seen to have caused the crisis, many of whom had experienced

[67] Denise M Rousseau and Robert J House, 'Meso Organizational Behavior: Avoiding Three Fundamental Biases' [1994] Journal of Organizational Behavior (1986-1998) 13; Brent Smith, Schneider, and Dickson (n 59) 160.

[68] Gilligan and Wright (n 30) preface.

[69] 'Vulnerabilities Associated with Leveraged Loans and Collateralised Loan Obligations' (Financial Stability Board, 19 December 2019) 7–8 <https://www.fsb.org/2019/12/vulnerabilities-associated-with-leveraged-loans-and-collateralised-loan-obligations/> accessed 2 July 2022.

[70] For the effect of macro events on micro level action, see DiMaggio and Powell (n 5) 11.There are similarities with Bourdieu's notion of *hysteresis*, where *habitus* becomes out of step with the field. Cheryl Hardy, 'Hysteresis', *Pierre Bourdieu: Key Concepts* (Routledge 2014) 126. Hardy describes hysteresis as a 'breakdown in the self-regulation (habitus) which was established to fit an individual to society'. ibid 129.

[71] For a discussion of the crisis more generally, see Rosa M Lastra and Geoffrey Wood, 'The Crisis of 2007–09: Nature, Causes, and Reactions' (2010) 13 Journal of International Economic Law 531.

[72] Gilligan and Wright (n 30) 178.

[73] 'RBS Agrees $3 Billion WorldPay Sale to Advent, Bain' *Reuters* (6 August 2010) <https://www.reuters.com/article/us-rbs-idUSTRE67516620100806> accessed 21 February 2023.

severe financial difficulties and required government support.[74] In particular, they were subjected to increased capital and liquidity requirements under 'Basle III', the revised post-crisis international regulatory framework for banks.[75] Banks must allocate capital to individual loans, and the amount of 'tier one' capital to be held against each loan increased significantly after the financial crisis. Since leveraged loans are generally sub-investment grade rated, or equivalent to sub-investment if not rated by a rating agency, they are highly risk-weighted assets for regulatory capital purposes, and therefore expensive for a bank to hold on its balance sheet; often the loan attracts a higher risk weighting than its nominal value.[76] So banks now typically sell them to non-bank investors which are not required to hold such capital.[77]

At the same time, institutional investors (the traditional investor base for bonds) such as insurance companies and pension funds, as well as hedge funds and Collateralised Loan Obligations (CLOs),[78] faced pressure under applicable regulatory regimes, including 'Solvency II', broadly, the international regulatory framework for non-bank financial institutions—to diversify into riskier, higher yielding investments, such as leveraged loans.[79] Quantitative easing by central banks following the financial crisis contributed to a sustained period of low interest rates.[80] This led to an appetite for leveraged finance loans, as an investment product, broadening beyond banks to encompass an array of new investors chasing for yield, at a time when their traditional investment products, such as government bonds, were yielding a return of close to zero. Investment banks found there was new and deep institutional investor demand for leveraged loans, and arranging and underwriting, then selling, leveraged loans became a highly lucrative business for them.

A dramatic change in the balance between leveraged loan supply and demand, also—together with regulation—created the conditions in which banks were incentivized to shift from their traditional originate-to-hold model to the new originate-to-distribute lending and underwriting model that I described in the previous

[74] 'Basle III', which has been implemented in the UK under 'The Capital Requirements Regulations 2013' <https://www.legislation.gov.uk/uksi/2013/3115/contents/made> accessed 16 July 2018; John Armour and others, *Principles of Financial Regulation* (OUP 2016) Ch.14.

[75] 'High Yield Bonds and Leveraged Loans a Convergence of Terms | Ashurst' (25 April 2018) 7 <https://www.ashurst.com/en/news-and-insights/insights/high-yield-bonds-and-leveraged-loans-a-convergence-of-terms/> accessed 23 June 2020; Gilligan and Wright (n 30) 25; 'Basel III: International Regulatory Framework for Banks' <https://www.bis.org/bcbs/basel3.htm> accessed 14 February 2023.

[76] Charles-Henri Larreur, *Structured Finance: Leveraged Buy-Outs, Project Finance, Asset Finance and Securitization* (Wiley 2021) 43–44; Gilligan and Wright (n 30) 26, 182.

[77] ibid.

[78] 'Vulnerabilities Associated with Leveraged Loans and Collateralised Loan Obligations' (n 69) 3–4.

[79] 'High Yield Bonds and Leveraged Loans a Convergence of Terms | Ashurst' (n 75) 7; Gilligan and Wright (n 30) 25; 'Solvency II' (23 January 2023) <https://www.bankofengland.co.uk/prudential-regulation/key-initiatives/solvency-ii> accessed 14 February 2023.

[80] Gilligan and Wright (n 30) 179.

chapter.[81] A global upsurge in the supply of cheap credit, far outstripping demand, resulted from the expansion of this investor base for leveraged loans beyond commercial and investment banks to a broad range of institutional investors, including CLOs.[82] A shortage of leveraged buyout deal opportunities led to a build-up of 'dry powder'—unspent capital in the hands of these potential lenders—and intense competition for arranging mandates among banks. The FSB reported in 2019 that looser covenants in leveraged loan documents were 'likely driven by high availability of funding' and the consequent 'competition for loan mandates by arrangers'.[83] These trends transformed the conditions and logics of the field in which leveraged finance lawyers work and resulted in the lawyer designation model and the survival logic which flows from it. Lawyer activity has hence been undertaken against the background of these market developments.[84]

These dynamics handed a significant bargaining power advantage to the private equity sponsors in their negotiations with the banks who arrange and underwrite leveraged loans.[85] The result was a 'buyer's market' where private equity sponsors could effectively dictate terms to their lenders.[86] Prior to this, banks were mostly dominant in the negotiation of loan terms; now the private equity sponsors held the balance of power in European leveraged buyouts.[87] Throughout what is often considered the first leveraged buyout boom (from the 1990s until the global financial crisis of 2007–09) the European leveraged buyout market was primarily a bank loan market, dominated in the United Kingdom by the leading deposit taking institutions such as NatWest, Barclays, HBOS, and Lloyds.[88] In this period, leveraged loan documents were generally considered to include the range of robust lender protections required to mitigate the credit risk presented by their private

[81] 'Leveraged Loan Primer' (*S&P Global*, 2020) 36 <https://www.spglobal.com/marketintelligence/en/pages/toc-primer/lcd-primer> accessed 26 July 2022; 'The Capital Requirements Regulations 2013' (n 74).

[82] CLOs are securities issued by a special purpose company, effectively a structured fund, which has acquired a portfolio of leveraged loans, typically arranged and underwritten by banks. The securities are secured, or collateralized, by this underlying portfolio of loans. 'Vulnerabilities Associated with Leveraged Loans and Collateralised Loan Obligations' (n 69) 3–4. 'Leveraged Loan Primer' (n 81) 36; Larreur (n 76) 43.The Powerful City Lawyer at The Center of a Private Equity Storm' *Bloomberg.com* (16 February 2023) <https://www.bloomberg.com/news/articles/2023-02-16/the-powerful-city-lawyer-at-the-center-of-a-private-equity-storm> accessed 16 February 2023.; Gilligan and Wright (n 30) 179.

[83] 'Vulnerabilities Associated with Leveraged Loans and Collateralised Loan Obligations' (n 69) 8; Gilligan and Wright (n 30) 209. Sarah Paterson, 'The Rise of Covenant-Lite Lending and Implications for the UK's Corporate Insolvency Law Toolbox' (2019) 39 Oxford Journal of Legal Studies 654, 664.

[84] See DiMaggio and Powell (n 5) 12–14.

[85] 'High Yield Bonds and Leveraged Loans a Convergence of Terms | Ashurst' (n 75). 'Vulnerabilities Associated with Leveraged Loans and Collateralised Loan Obligations' (n 69) 8; Gilligan and Wright (n 30) 209.

[86] 'A buyer's market refers to a situation in which changes to the underlying economic conditions that shape supply and demand mean that purchasers have an advantage over sellers in price negotiations.' 'Buyer's Market: Definition, Characteristics, Example' (*Investopedia*) <https://www.investopedia.com/terms/b/buyersmarket.asp> accessed 23 February 2023.

[87] Indap, Thompson, and Fontanella-Khan (n 29).

[88] Gilligan and Wright (n 30) 175.

equity-backed borrowers. According to Elisabeth de Fontenay, private equity sponsors tended to agree to restrictive loan agreement provisions since, at the time, there was little alternative.[89]

This meant that bank lawyers were themselves influential in the evolution of loan terms in this period, ensuring that loan terms broadly favoured lenders in this period. The Loan Market Association (LMA) coordinated efforts to standardize loan market documents from the late 1990s onwards;[90] although on the face of it this was largely seen as a bank-led initiative, I know from my own experience that the LMA's drafting committees were dominated by bank lawyers drawn from Magic Circle firms and that bank lawyers mostly controlled the drafting of the documents in leveraged buyout transactions. This 'bank friendly' position continued until the high yield bond market became established in Europe. Although high yield bonds started to emerge in European leveraged buyouts in the mid-2000s, they assumed greater prominence in the wake of the global financial crisis of 2007–09, given the expansion of the investor base for leveraged loans beyond banks to CLOs and other institutional investors; from this point, the market for leveraged finance loans ceased to be dominated by the banks.[91]

As a result of these dynamics, from the mid-2000s, the LMA finance document templates no longer tended to form the basis of the transaction documents seen in the large-cap market in Europe; a private equity sponsor's, or private equity law firm's loan, security and intercreditor document precedents became, and remain, the typical template starting point. And private equity lawyers now hold the pen, controlling the drafting process, and, as I have noted already, not always consistently with the business context of the transaction.[92]

At the same time, the precise scope of the bank lawyer's role became, in this evolutionary process, rather blurry. This is closely connected to the shift by the investment bank community to the originate-to-distribute model. Following this switch, the arranging banks and their lawyers still negotiated the terms of the transaction documents with the private equity sponsor and its lawyers. But since the arranging banks that originate these loans no longer hold the loan to maturity, they have a reduced incentive to ensure that loan terms appropriately protect the interests of lenders, as post-syndication of the loan they will, in the main, not be a lender themselves. This contributed to the emergence of the cleared-the-market logic that I described in Chapter 3. Bank lawyers now tend to focus their review of

[89] Elisabeth de Fontenay, 'Do the Securities Laws Matter - The Rise of the Leveraged Loan Market' (2013) 39 Journal of Corporation Law 725, 736.

[90] 'Documents' <https://www.lma.eu.com/documents-guidelines/documents> accessed 5 July 2022. The Loan Market Association claims to be the 'authoritative voice of the syndicated loan market' in Europe'.

[91] 'Vulnerabilities Associated with Leveraged Loans and Collateralised Loan Obligations' (n 69) 3–4.

[92] For an example of where this can lead, see Kenneth Ayotte and Christina Scully, 'J. Crew, Nine West, and the Complexities of Financial Distress Forum Collection: Bankruptcy and Restructuring in Response to Exogenous Shocks' (2021) 131 Yale Law Journal Forum 363, 365.

the documents on identifying, and advising the banks on, potential distribution risk issues only, as opposed to the broader category of credit risk and other issues of concern to the longer-term lenders of the loan. Hence, in practice, bank lawyers tend to interpret their role as primarily confined to simply ensuring that the terms proposed by private equity lawyers have previously 'cleared the market'.

Bank lawyer [#32] said that before the mid-2000s 'there had been a huge focus on the documents from the lender point of view, and on strong documents and on covenants, and being very, very careful with everything.' Consequently 'the documents were pretty pro-lender.' Under this new model, banks are no longer incentivized to achieve protective terms for lenders in the negotiation of terms. To the extent the arranging banks and their lawyers do have an interest in ensuring lenders' interests are protected, it is primarily directed at mitigating the risk of a failed syndication; weaker lender protections have the potential to obstruct an orderly sell down, or distribution, of participations in the loan.[93] This is commonly referred to as distribution risk. Not challenging terms which have previously cleared the market has hence emerged as a central logic of the field, drawn from field conditions at the macro level. It sits alongside the survival and owns-the-market logics in framing how lawyers act and make decisions.[94]

In my interviews, both bank lawyers and private equity lawyers tended to give meaning to their conduct through a market frame; they frequently pointed to the macroeconomic trends and forces I have described so far in this chapter as structural conditions of the field that conditioned their identity and the scope of their role. For example, bank lawyers attributed the evolutionary trends in loan documents to these emergent market conditions; in this way they sought to distance themselves and their own discretionary action from these developments. For example, bank lawyer [#27] said:

> Documentation is pretty borrower friendly in the large-cap leverage finance market. But there's a very simple reason for that. It's supply and demand.

The intense competition between arranging banks for the financing mandates on leveraged buyouts was also frequently drawn upon to explain documentary trends, for example.[95] Bank lawyer [#32] said:

[93] See eg the reports of the financing of Thyssenkrup in 2020, Nikou Asgari and Robert Smith, 'Thyssenkrupp Backers Improve €7.6bn Debt Terms after Lenders Balk' *Financial Times* (30 June 2020) <https://www.ft.com/content/81864124-e50c-4670-92c1-756582bb664b> accessed 9 August 2021.

[94] Roger Friedland and RogerR Alford, 'Bringing Society Back In: Symbols, Practices, and Institutional Contradictions', *The New Institutionalism in Organizational Analysis* (The University of Chicago Press 1991); Thornton, Ocasio, and Lounsbury (n 2) 44; DiMaggio and Powell (n 5).

[95] 'Vulnerabilities Associated with Leveraged Loans and Collateralised Loan Obligations' (n 69) 8; Gilligan and Wright (n 30) 209. Paterson (n 83) 664.

> It became tempting for underwriting banks to compete for sponsor work by offering softer terms, as they knew they could sell the deal down anyway.

The 'buyer's market' logic that resulted from the macroeconomic forces I have described became a central component of the governing framework for leveraged finance lawyer sense-making that has consequently both shaped, and allowed bank lawyers to self-justify, their subsequent action.[96] It has translated into the owns-the-market logic at the micro level of the field that I have previously described, which sees both bank lawyers and private equity lawyers sharing a common understanding that the private equity lawyers have assumed ownership and control of the transaction process. The participants—albeit fragmented according to their role acting for either arranging banks or private equity sponsors—not only shared a series of consistent views about the logics of their role and that of the other leveraged finance lawyers that they interact with in their work, but also some consistent ideas about the effects of these macro level, market-based logics on their work. This aligns with the findings of Moorhead and others in their study of in-house lawyers.[97] By identifying and understanding these practice area-specific logics and their effects, it is possible to determine what might influence an individual lawyer's framing of their choices and the meanings that they attach to their own behaviour and the behaviour of others.[98] I explore this further in the next section.

The private equity sponsor power over their bank lenders that I have described has translated into private equity lawyer power over bank lawyers.[99] As the most powerful actors in this field, private equity lawyers in particular have had a transformative effect on its practices and logics.[100] Their power is contingent on the once emergent, but now firmly established, power of their clients over banks and is evident in their transformative, and often deliberate and strategic, behaviour.[101] The series of macro forces and events buffeting the leveraged finance practice area field since the mid-2000s created the conditions under which private equity lawyers reviewed their options, and in most cases they have chosen to take advantage of them for their clients', and often their own, advantage. That they have made the most of these field conditions is evident in the move-the-market logic which drives their contractual boundary-pushing strategies, for example.[102] I use the

[96] Anthony Giddens, *The Constitution of Society: Outline of the Theory of Structuration* (University of California Press 1984).

[97] Richard Moorhead, Steven Vaughan, and Cristina Godinho, *In-House Lawyers' Ethics, Institutional Logics, Legal Risk and the Tournament of Influence* (Hart 2018) 208.

[98] Anthony Giddens, *Central Problems in Social Theory: Action, Structure, and Contradiction in Social Analysis* (University of California Press 1979); Thornton, Ocasio, and Lounsbury (n 2) 8.

[99] Thornton, Ocasio, and Lounsbury (n 2) 64.

[100] Roger Friedland and Roger R Alford, 'Bringing Society Back In: Symbols, Practices, and Institutional Contradictions', *The New Institutionalism in Organizational Analysis* (The University of Chicago Press 1991) 254. Nelson (n 33).

[101] Thornton, Ocasio, and Lounsbury (n 2) 169.

[102] ibid.

term 'entrepreneurial' to denote private equity lawyers taking advantage of their opportunities and reacting to pressures and incentives created by dramatic market forces and events to enact changes in practices and logics.[103] They do not, however, take financial risks in any material sense, which is usually implied by the use of the term entrepreneurial.[104] Instead, their capacity to act entrepreneurially is re-inforced by their coercive authority over bank lawyers, which they draw from their clients' power over the banks.

At the same time, a critical mechanism which might have been expected to constrain private equity lawyer opportunism—robust challenge from the bank lawyers—has been materially weakened.[105] Bank lawyer acquiescence can also be understood as an effect of emergent market conditions from the mid-2000s. That private equity sponsors and their lawyers were able to first impose designation on banks and bank lawyers, and then make the most of its effects, is a manifestation of their power. Its effects can be seen in the emergence of the survival logic which has shaped the collective identity of bank lawyers, allowing the private equity lawyers to pursue their commercially pragmatic objectives relatively unchecked. The survival logic has further consolidated and strengthened private equity lawyer power, facilitating their ability to further transform the structural conditions of the field through their coercive activity. The bank lawyers' limited power is closely connected to the survival logic; it has mostly led them to conclude that they should not provide robust challenge to the entrepreneurial and coercive activities of the private equity lawyers.

These types of micro- and macro-linkages play a critical role since they have combined with firm-level logics to create the conditions and logics of the practice area in which these lawyers work.[106]

[103] ibid 132. Cheryl Hardy, 'Hysteresis', *Pierre Bourdieu: Key Concepts* (Routledge 2014) 126.

[104] The Oxford English Dictionary definition is 'a person who sets up a business or businesses, taking on financial risks'. 'Entrepreneur, n.' <https://www.oed.com/view/Entry/62991> accessed 22 March 2023.

[105] Several other commonly found constraints on lawyer action that exist in other practice area fields are either missing or are weaker in this field. Formal constraints such as professional codes of conduct do not appear to restrain their coercive and entrepreneurial activity, for example. Client relationship logics at the level of the firm also do not appear to operate as a material constraint on private equity lawyer action. Traditionally, aggressive action by private equity lawyers might be expected to damage their firm's relationships with banks and jeopardize future bank mandates, for leveraged finance and lucrative work for lawyers in the firm's other practice areas. The most influential private equity firms have largely forsaken bank-side work, however. See Richard Moorhead and others, 'Designing Ethics Indicators for Legal Services Provision' [2012] SSRN Electronic Journal <http://www.ssrn.com/abstract=2159296> accessed 18 October 2018. Moorhead and Hinchley (n 57); Steven Vaughan and Emma Oakley, '"Gorilla Exceptions" and the Ethically Apathetic Corporate Lawyer' (2016) 19 Legal Ethics 50; Joan Loughrey, 'Accountability and the Regulation of the Large Law Firm Lawyer' (2014) 77 The Modern Law Review 732. For the effects of institutional constraints on micro-level action, see RL Jepperson, 'Institutions, Institutional Effects, and Institutionalism' 143–45, in DiMaggio and Powell (n 5). See also Thomas B. Lawrence and Roy Suddaby, 'Institutions and Institutional Work' in Stewart R Clegg, Cynthia Hardy, Thomas B Lawrence and Walter R Nord (eds), *The SAGE Handbook of Organization Studies* (SAGE 2006) 216.

[106] Brent Smith, Schneider, and Dickson (n 59) 153.

8.4 Embedded lawyer action

This book shines a light on the effects that a lawyers' own discretionary action may have on the structural conditions of their practice area. An exploration of the practice area context and environment in which lawyers work, their material structure, is critical to determining whether those conditions may have been permanently shaped, transformed even, by individual lawyer behaviour in responding to changed conditions.[107] These conditions, both established and emergent, create the pathways for the discretionary action of those lawyers, individually and collectively, that then further fashion the field's conditions and logics.

My data reveals the hierarchical position of lawyers in the leveraged finance practice area field, as well as the nature of their relationships with each other.[108] Lawyers are positioned depending on how much power they hold, with the bank lawyers holding a position subordinate to that of the private equity lawyers.[109] But this structural position is not entirely determinative of individual lawyer action.[110] The participants in my study hold both this objective position in the field, and have a subjective understanding of it; they are aware of and often choose to take advantage of the opportunities afforded by new field conditions and hierarchies and, in this way, the structure of the field has become embedded in them.[111] This subjective position-taking has profoundly influenced their understanding of the field and their role within it, and led them to develop the strategies I have outlined.[112]

Gulati and Scott trawled thousands of sovereign debt contracts and found a series of embedded flaws, which mostly evolved through lawyer's effectively looking away; in other words these flaws became embedded more by accident and neglect than by design.[113] My data reveals how lawyers also influence terms through their strategic behaviour, utilizing the emergent logics of their field.[114] The field's logics constitute the contextual framework within which private equity

[107] Thornton, Ocasio, and Lounsbury (n 2) v, vii; DiMaggio and Powell (n 5).

[108] They are also able to adopt stances which modify or change this position, Barbara Townley, 'Bourdieu and Organizational Theory: A Ghostly Apparition?', *The Oxford Handbook of Sociology, Social Theory, & Organization Studies* (OUP 2014) 41; Pierre Bourdieu, *Practical Reason: On the Theory of Action* (Stanford University Press 1998) 6.

[109] Or as Pierre Bourdieu would call it, 'capital', Townley (n 108) 45.

[110] Thornton, Ocasio, and Lounsbury (n 2) 45, 79.

[111] Pierre Bourdieu, *In Other Words: Essays Towards a Reflexive Sociology* (Stanford University Press 1990) 65. Townley (n 108) 46.

[112] Pierre Bourdieu, 'The Social Space and the Genesis of Groups' (1985) Social Science Information (Vol. 24, No. 2) 195, 734; Townley (n 108) 41.

[113] Mitu Gulati and Robert E Scott, *The Three and a Half Minute Transaction: Boilerplate and the Limits of Contract Design* (University of Chicago Press 2012).

[114] Michael Smets, 'Institutional Work Taken Literally: How Logics Shift as Banking Lawyers "Get the Deal Done"' (2009 Academy of Management annual meeting, USA, 2009) <http://publications.aston.ac.uk/id/eprint/18544/> accessed 20 May 2021.

lawyers make choices, for example; within this framework, they have largely chosen to pursue discretionary and opportunistic behaviour which has itself transformed the conditions of their practice area field, including a pendulum shift in the allocation of risk in loan covenants as between private equity-backed borrowers and their lenders.[115]

The global financial crisis is key to understanding what has happened. It precipitated a period of great disruption and change for the field, where strategic choice and deliberate action by lawyers took over from simply reproducing the existing practices and logics of this practice area.[116] Although they were already what Smets refers to as 'elite actors' in a 'mature field', private equity lawyers did not stand to gain from protecting the existing logics that existed in the early to mid-2000s, but rather from drawing on their new-found power to constantly challenge them.[117] The once emergent, and now prevailing, logics of the field have afforded them the opportunity to consider how they might act both entrepreneurially and coercively and effect institutional change.[118] The private equity lawyers are hence change agents who have disrupted the field by contesting existing logics through new strategies and practices which they have introduced.[119] Often they are executing a planned strategy and at other times experimenting with different practices as they seek to advance their self-interested goals.[120]

Where the conditions of a field of legal practice are relatively continuous, lawyer action is likely to be largely unconscious.[121] But changed field conditions since the mid-2000s have created the pathways for the often-conscious strategic action by private equity lawyers described in this book. Bank lawyers—as we saw in Chapter 3—have adapted their practices and logics in response. The changed conditions of the field due to the impact of powerful macroeconomic forces impacting the field have hence led the private equity lawyers to contest the prevailing logics of their field. Their context since the mid-2000s has been non-routine, meaning that individual lawyers have tended not to view the most readily accessible and available logics as applicable or relevant. Individual lawyers have hence deployed additional attention and processing, drawing on the new logics of the field, and this meant that deliberate and strategic activity by private equity lawyers became more likely to occur.[122]

115 Thornton, Ocasio, and Lounsbury (n 2) 53–54.

116 Loic JD Wacquant, 'Towards a Reflexive Sociology: A Workshop with Pierre Bourdieu' (1989) 7 Sociological Theory 26, 45; Claire Laurier Decoteau, 'The Reflexive Habitus: Critical Realist and Bourdieusian Social Action' (2016) 19 European Journal of Social Theory 303.

117 Smets (n 114) 5.

118 ibid.

119 ibid 3.

120 ibid 7.

121 Or 'taken for granted' as habits, scripts and schemas, using Di Maggio and Powell's terminology, DiMaggio and Powell (n 5); Thornton, Ocasio, and Lounsbury (n 2) 40–42, 84.

122 Thornton, Ocasio, and Lounsbury (n 2) 84.

8.5 Example: the institutional entrepreneurs

Bank lawyer [#13] observed:[123]

> There comes a point where these firms can't just keep employing people and paying them as much as they pay them unless they are able to deliver something really special.

The influence on the conditions of the field of a sub-group of actors who were not embedded in or committed to prevailing logics has been especially pronounced.[124] Real change was effected by a handful of powerful private equity lawyers; three or four names recurred most frequently in the interviews.[125] These powerful actors were often identified by name in my interviews; and were seen as transformative by introducing new ways of thinking and/or patterns of behaviour to the field.[126] For example, bank lawyer [#16] said: 'So, [name of private equity lawyer], his pitch is "I can get you more flexibility than was in the last deal".

Since they were often recruited on remuneration packages greater than were available to them at their former, mostly Magic Circle and other leading UK, firms, it is likely that this small group of lawyers felt the need to demonstrate added value. at their new, mostly US, firms. Bank lawyer [#32] said:

> When [identifies firm *x* by name] pays the big sum of money they're reputed to have paid [identifies lawyer *y* by name] to go to them, he does have to show some added value. He can't come in and carry-on doing deals on the same docs as before, otherwise, why are the clients going to think it worth paying the sort of huge fees on the deals that they do to justify those payments?

Here, we see a close connection between lawyer action and law firm logics, including the pressures and incentives that arise due to 'eat what you kill' remuneration models and enhanced levels of partner mobility. In other words, the lateral hiring of these partners brought with it a pressure on them to act entrepreneurially by delivering 'something special'. But the strategies they have adopted in response to these firm-level business logics are practice area-specific and intimately linked to practice area logics. Instead of moving to a US firm and carrying on doing deals on the same documentary terms, they adopted a deliberate strategy to be seen to be moving the market in loan terms ever further towards their private equity sponsor

[123] See eg James Fontanella-Khan, Sujeet Indap, and Barney Thompson, 'The Dawn of the Superstar Lawyer' *Financial Times* (9 April 2018) <https://www.ft.com/content/b9c96d04-376c-11e8-8eee-e06bde01c544> accessed 30 July 2018.

[124] Thornton and Ocasio (n 6) 99.

[125] Thornton, Ocasio, and Lounsbury (n 2) 177.

[126] Thornton and Ocasio (n 6) 97.

clients. That they were able to execute this strategy so successfully has been dependent largely on the survival logic and the consequential, mostly supine, stance of the bank lawyers.

This handful of entrepreneurial private equity lawyers have hence shown themselves to be less committed to the existing way of doing things.[127] They were not so embedded in or committed to the prevailing logics of the field at that time.[128] Instead they took advantage of emergent logics at the macro and meso levels of the field in the years following the global financial crisis to themselves exert a transformative influence on the field.

This group of private equity lawyers—practising in a small number of elite US firms—were viewed as the most prestigious by their private equity lawyer peers.[129] This prestige was linked to their success in winning mandates on the largest and most high-profile transactions. They have the closest relationships with the most powerful private equity sponsors, and consequently control a sizeable proportion of the designations that are the most attractive to bank lawyers. They hold what Thomas Lawrence and Roy Suddaby refer to as 'coercive authority', a dominance that has both effected and legitimated substantial change in the conditions of the field.[130] The coercive power they draw from their dominant clients has enabled them to wield significant influence over other lawyers in the field.[131] These private equity lawyers, in particular, have felt empowered to act coercively in the pursuit of their commercially pragmatic objectives by what Michael Smets has referred to as 'political dynamics'; in this case, the nature of their relationships with their powerful sponsor clients and the mostly acquiescent stance of the bank lawyers.[132]

Motivated by their own commercially pragmatic objectives, this sub-group of private equity lawyers has been engaged in a competition to be seen as the leading exponents of the strategy of moving the market in loan terms. Their strategy has now become institutionalized across the broader group of private equity lawyers.[133] The sub-group took the lead as institutional entrepreneurs in promoting changes in deal structures, processes, and documents, and this change then became diffused amongst the wider body of private equity lawyers through a process of mimetic isomorphism, where other lawyers and firms have mimicked the lawyers and firms they perceive to be the most successful, and the most prestigious,

[127] Thornton, Ocasio, and Lounsbury (n 2) 118.

[128] Thornton and Ocasio (n 6) 99.

[129] Or what is identified by Bourdieu as symbolic capital - what is *recognised* as valuable, Bourdieu (n 112) 725; Townley (n 108) 41. Further categories include *social* capital (broadly, resources in the form of networks of other agents with capital that an actor can call upon) and *cultural* capital (broadly, long-term tastes and dispositions acquired through early socialisation or through self-improvement).

[130] Thomas B. Lawrence and Suddaby (n 105).

[131] Royston Greenwood, Roy Suddaby, and CR Hinings, 'Theorizing Change: The Role of Professional Associations in the Transformation of Institutionalized Fields' (2002) 45 The Academy of Management Journal 58; Thomas B. Lawrence and Suddaby (n 105) 215. Smets (n 114) 23.

[132] Smets (n 114) 23.

[133] Thornton, Ocasio, and Lounsbury (n 2) 8.

in the field.[134] There has been what Patricia Thornton and William Ocasio refer to as a 'group mobilisation effect', with private equity lawyers coming to share a common understanding about the nature of their role.[135] This understanding is also shared, or at least is not actively contested, by the bank lawyers.

These institutional entrepreneurs hence led the change process, but for the changes they initially pioneered to be truly disruptive and transformative as institutional work it was critical that their contractual boundary-pushing practices were endorsed and supported more widely by the broader community of private equity lawyers.[136] The result has been a contagion of looser and uncertain deal terms across the market, which have become embedded in deal precedents drafted and then fiercely defended by private equity lawyers on subsequent transactions.

8.6 Conclusion

Dramatic change in the conditions and logics at the macro level of the leveraged finance practice area field provided the framework within which individual lawyers at its micro level made sense of their world, and it is this contextual framework which has shaped their ethical decision-making and the development of new strategies.[137] This embedded behaviour has been guided by their conscious determination of what best suits their commercial self-interests.[138] They have been able to pursue purposive action which has led to disruption in the conditions of the field, and the establishment of new patterns of working.[139] They held the power to manipulate the field's transaction structures, processes, and documents relatively freely and do so in order to pursue their own, as well as their clients', interests and take full advantage of the opportunities created by the emergent conditions of the field.[140]

134 Paul J DiMaggio and Walter Powell W, 'The Iron Cage Revisited: Institutional Isomorphism and Collective Rationality', *The New Institutionalism in Organizational Analysis* (CUP 1991) 68.

135 Thornton and Ocasio (n 6) 98.

136 Huseyin Leblebici and others, 'Institutional Change and the Transformation of Interorganizational Fields: An Organizational History of the U.S. Radio Broadcasting Industry' (1991) 36 Administrative Science Quarterly 333; Thomas B. Lawrence and Suddaby (n 105) 217.

137 Friedland and Alford (n 94); Thornton, Ocasio, and Lounsbury (n 2) 44.

138 Thornton, Ocasio, and Lounsbury (n 2) 79.

139 Thomas B. Lawrence and Suddaby (n 105) 216.

140 Paul Dimaggio, 'Interest and Agency in Institutional Theory' in LG Zucker (ed), *Institutional Patterns and Organisations: Culture and Environment* (Harper Business, 1988) 14; Thomas B. Lawrence and Suddaby (n 105) 215.

9
Conclusion

In this final chapter, I first summarize what I consider to be the implications of this book for large international law firms. Next, I offer some reflections on the important questions this book raises about the 'value add' that these firms often claim to offer clients, and ultimately also the extent to which clients can treat large international law firms as a trusted legal and business adviser. I then move on to consider what this book means for how regulators of the legal profession may better support lawyers in large international law firms in acting ethically. In the final section, I consider how the lawyer strategies and practices which are explored in this book may be contributing to the build-up of systemic risk in financial markets.

9.1 The implications for Big Law

This book contributes a series of empirically based insights into what drives the conduct and ethical decision-making of lawyers working in large international law firms These drivers are variable across the firm. Whilst lawyers in the different practice areas of a firm will be influenced by some common logics, a lawyer in one practice area may tend to think and act differently in their daily work to a lawyer in another practice area. This is because the range of logics that influence their behaviour will also include market-based logics which are unique to their practice area setting, in addition to what might be referred to as firm-wide logics, and it is all these logics taken together which comprise the framework within which these lawyers make ethical decisions. The case study reveals, for example, how the global financial crisis, the regulatory change directed at banks and the market supply and demand disconnect that followed it, and the switch by the bank community to an originate-to-distribute model, for example, are all macroeconomic dynamics which, when combined with law firm logics, created new logics in the leveraged finance practice areas of Big Law. These emergent logics created the pathways for strategic action by lawyers that, in turn, transformed the conditions of their practice area setting and the markets to which it is most closely connected.

Building on this finding, this book shows how recurring situational factors found in a Big Law practice-area which are themselves shaped to a considerable degree by market logics, can create an elevated risk of ethical misconduct by the lawyers who work in it.[1] To give one example which is developed in this book, it is well established in the literature that a corporate lawyer's susceptibility to their powerful clients and third parties creates challenges to their independence.[2] But this literature does not tend to consider whether this susceptibility might be stronger or weaker depending on which practice area a lawyer works in. To determine whether lawyers are more or less likely to come under ethical pressure due to bullying by their clients or third parties in the capital markets group or the competition group of a firm, for example, it is necessary to explore the distinct logics of each of those practice settings.

This book not only presents a detailed and comprehensive account of the types of pressures and challenges that corporate lawyers face in their daily work but also considers the implications of this data on their observance of the rules of professional conduct to which they are subject. The case study considers the extent to which a series of ethical duties in the Solicitors Regulation Authority's, SRA's, Standards and Regulations appear to have been breached by leveraged finance lawyer conduct.[3] Lawyer designation, for example, and the referral relationships that flow from it, put bank lawyers under immense ethical pressure, and likely lead them to breach the solicitors' duties to maintain their independence and to avoid own interest conflicts of interest. And the opportunistic practices and strategies that private equity lawyers have developed in response—including relentless contractual boundary pushing—likely also conflict with their duties as solicitors to act with integrity and not to take unfair advantage.

Understanding the practice area context in which corporate lawyers work in this way is critical when thinking about how individual lawyers might be better supported to, first, recognize ethical risks when they arise and, second, call upon their ethical duties under applicable codes of conduct when thinking about how to respond.[4] The type of empirical data offered in this book is, hence, critical to a proper assessment of the effectiveness or otherwise of professional codes of conduct in promoting the ethical conduct of lawyers in Big Law.[5]

[1] Richard Moorhead and others, 'Designing Ethics Indicators for Legal Services Provision' [2012] SSRN Electronic Journal 2159296, 28, 42, 92 <http://www.ssrn.com/abstract=2159296> accessed 18 October 2018.

[2] See for example, Ronit Dinovitzer, Hugh Gunz, and Sally Gunz, 'Unpacking Client Capture: Evidence from Corporate Law Firms' (2014) 1 Journal of Professions and Organization 99; Emma Oakley and Steven Vaughan, 'In Dependence: The Paradox of Professional Independence and Taking Seriously the Vulnerabilities of Lawyers in Large Corporate Law Firms' (2019) 46 Journal of Law and Society 83.

[3] 'SRA Principles' (25 November 2019) <https://www.sra.org.uk/solicitors/standards-regulations/principles/> accessed 6 July 2020; 'SRA Code of Conduct for Solicitors, RELs and RFLs' (25 November 2019) <https://www.sra.org.uk/solicitors/standards-regulations/code-conduct-solicitors/> accessed 15 November 2020; 'SRA Code of Conduct for Firms' (4 June 2023) <https://www.sra.org.uk/solicitors/standards-regulations/code-conduct-firms/> accessed 4 July 2023.

[4] Hugh Gunz, Sally Gunz, and Ronit Dinovitzer, 'Professional Ethics' [2015] The Oxford Handbook of Professional Service Firms 129.

[5] Janine Griffiths-Baker, *Serving Two Masters: Conflicts of Interest in the Modern Law Firm* (Hart Publishing 2002) 12.

This book also shows how this type of Big Law activity can have a dramatic impact on financial markets, in the form of the contractual terms of complex cross-border financial transactions which govern the allocation and pricing of risk by market participants. In the leveraged finance sector, for example, the subject of the case study, the loan documents have become overwhelmingly one sided, and the meaning of key provisions has become obscured by pervasive uncertainty in the language used, to the extent where market participants are unable to clearly evaluate, and hence accurately price, the risks that they face under them. The contractual boundary-pushing strategies of private equity lawyers have played a key role in this evolution of loan terms. This activity has contributed to a seismic shift in the balance in loan terms away from protecting banks and other lenders.[6] I explored how private equity lawyers have successfully advocated for multiple ambiguous and, mostly, spurious 'add backs' in financial covenants, for example.[7]

Whilst practice area logics comprise the framework for lawyer ethical decision-making, this book also showcases the importance of a lawyer's discretionary behaviour.[8] It thus explores how the conditions and logics of a Big Law practice area, and the markets to which it is connected, as fields of social activity, are also mediated by the action and discretion of the lawyers that practice in these fields.[9] As the case study shows, real change to the conditions and logics of a practice area can be effected when lawyers take advantage of the opportunities afforded by changes in the logics of law firms and markets, for example.[10]

Finally, this book also raises important questions about the 'value add' that Big Law often claims it offers to clients, and ultimately also the extent to which clients and the wider public can, and should, place their trust in Big Law. I consider these

[6] 'Hot Leveraged Loan Market Puts Ebitda "Add-Backs" under Scrutiny' *Financial Times* (10 February 2017) https://www.ft.com/content/ce5d0eee-eea0-11e6-930f-061b01e23655 accesed 15 February 2023; 'When The Cycle Turns: The Continued Attack Of The EBITDA Add-Back' <https://www.spglobal.com/ratings/en/research/articles/190919-when-the-cycle-turns-the-continued-attack-of-the-ebitda-add-back-11156255> accessed 2 July 2022.

[7] 'Leveraged Loans Are Way Past "Cov-Lite"' *Financial Times* (16 November 2018) https://www.ft.com/content/53014840-e0bf-374b-8d22-c9a9ea318a8d accessed 16 February 2023; Sarah Paterson, 'The Rise of Covenant-Lite Lending and Implications for the UK's Corporate Insolvency Law Toolbox' (2019) 39 Oxford Journal of Legal Studies 654, 663–64.

[8] The former are commonly referred to as realists, the latter as idealists or social constructionists, Frederick Erickson, 'A History of Qualitative Inquiry in Social and Educational Research', *The SAGE Handbook of Qualitative Research* (SAGE Publications 2018) 54. For a fuller typology of ontological approaches, see Yvonna S. Lincoln, Susan A. Lyneham, and Egon G. Guba, 'Paradigmatic Controversies, Contradictions, and Emerging Confluences, Revisited', *The SAGE Handbook of Qualitative Research* (Fifth, SAGE Publications 2018).

[9] In this sense my approach is consistent with a more contemporary view of the constructionist paradigm; a criticism of traditional or orthodox constructionism is, as James Holstein argues, that it simply focuses on 'stories' and how they are constructed, an approach he describes as 'empirically insubstantial', James A. Holstein, 'Advancing a Constructionist Analytics', *The SAGE Handbook of Qualitative Research* (SAGE Publications 2018); Norman K Denzin and Yvonna S Lincoln, *The SAGE Handbook of Qualitative Research* (SAGE Publications 2017) 402, 405.

[10] Patricia H Thornton, William Ocasio, and Michael Lounsbury, *The Institutional Logics Perspective: A New Approach to Culture, Structure, and Process* (OUP 2012) 177.

questions, and the implications for the legitimacy of these firms, in the sections that follow.

9.2 Can clients trust Big Law to add value

As Jeffrey Lipshaw has observed, the presence of business lawyers in financial and corporate transactions is not explained simply by their ability to 'add value' in strictly economic terms, through an anticipated contribution to an economic surplus.[11] Lawyers may be instructed out of habit, for example, or to provide reassurance in uncertain markets.[12] Even where a lawyer's involvement in a transaction does not add economic value, it can, as Lipshaw rightly argues, still be 'meaningful'.[13] Lawyers are often instructed for their prowess in managing highly complex, cross-border transactions, for example.[14] Even those companies and financial institutions with large in-house legal teams may instruct large law firms because whilst they have the necessary expertise they lack the necessary resources to handle these types of matters.[15] There is, nevertheless, a significant body of literature that considers the question of whether the involvement of Big Law adds economic value to corporate and financial transactions, regardless of a client's motivation for instructing them.

Perhaps most notable in this regard is Ronald Gilson, who considered the extent to which the involvement of business lawyers reduces transaction costs for the parties.[16] According to Gilson, lawyers add value as transaction costs engineers where the transaction is 'worth more, net of legal fees, as a result of the lawyer's participation'.[17] Gilson's argument is founded in capital asset pricing theory, which assumes a 'frictionless world' where there are no costs of transacting, where all parties to a transaction enjoy equal access to information, for example.[18] As Gilson correctly notes, this is not reflective of the real world.[19] Lawyers hence function as

[11] Jeffrey M Lipshaw, 'Beetles, Frogs, and Lawyers: The Scientific Demarcation Problem in the Gilson Theory of Value Creation' (2009) 46 Willamette Law Review 139, 143.
[12] ibid.
[13] ibid.
[14] ibid.
[15] LE Ribstein, 'The Death of Big Law' [2010] Wisconsin Law Review 749, 758, 760.
[16] Ronald J Gilson, 'Value Creation by Business Lawyers: Legal Skills and Asset Pricing' (1984) 94 The Yale Law Journal 239. Ronald Coase is widely considered to have first proposed the theory of transaction costs. Coase essentially argued that market transactions involve a series of costs, and that this cost of transacting is reduced when undertaken by firms. The most significant cost is, for Coase, determining the appropriate price, but will also include the costs of negotiating and agreeing the terms of a contract, for example. RH Coase, 'The Nature of the Firm' in Saul Estrin and Alan Marin (eds), *Essential Readings in Economics* (Macmillan Education UK 1995) 86.
[17] Gilson (n 16).
[18] ibid 253–54.
[19] ibid 255.

transaction cost engineers when they enable the parties to the transaction to act 'as if the assumptions on which capital asset pricing theory is based were accurate'.[20]

Gilson emphasized, in particular, how business lawyers enable the parties to a corporate acquisition transaction to resolve uncertainty.[21] For Gilson, a typical contract in which a seller agrees to sell the shares in a company to a purchaser addresses some of the frictionless assumptions that underpin capital asset pricing theory: that each party has equal access to information and that they have the same expectations, for example.[22] He posits as an example the 'earn out' clause, which addresses the potential for a mismatch to exist between future earnings expectations of the buyer and seller that affect the valuation—and hence the purchase price—of the company being acquired.[23] Gilson argues that lawyers resolved this uncertainty by dividing the price into an up-front, fixed payment and a deferred amount which is contingent on future revenues, such as the following year's sales.[24] Information shortfalls for the buyer are then further addressed through the inclusion of representations and warranties about the business given by the seller which mitigate the costs the buyer would incur in first acquiring and then verifying that information.[25] For Gilson, the earn out clause and the representations and warranties are a 'means of producing the information necessary to pricing the transaction at its lowest cost'.[26]

Gilson's article has inspired a significant body of literature in which scholars develop and refine his theory, often by offering up detailed and insightful examples of transaction types and contractual and other mechanisms where business lawyers, when seen through the lens of Gilson's theory, or variations of it, add value for all of the parties to a transaction.[27] Elisabeth de Fontenay, for example, presents the example of 'yank the bank' clauses that allow a borrower in leveraged loan agreements to remove and replace a lender in a lending syndicate that is blocking

[20] ibid.
[21] ibid 243.
[22] ibid 262.
[23] ibid 263.
[24] ibid 263–64.
[25] ibid 277, 280.
[26] ibid 279.
[27] See eg Rachel Landy, 'Exit Engineering' (31 January 2023) 3, footnote 4 <https://papers.ssrn.com/abstract=4413611> accessed 3 January 2024; Victor Fleischer, 'Regulatory Arbitrage' (2010) 89 Texas Law Review 227; George W Jr Dent, 'Business Lawyers as Enterprise Architects' (2008) 64 Business Lawyer (ABA) 279; Elisabeth de Fontenay, 'Law Firm Selection and the Value of Transactional Lawyering' (2015) 41 Journal of Corporation Law 393; Lisa Bernstein, 'The Silicon Valley Lawyer as Transaction Cost Engineer' (1995) 74 Oregon Law Review 239; Karl S Okamoto, 'Reputation and the Value of Lawyers' (1995) 74 Oregon Law Review 15; Manuel A Utset, 'Producing Information: Initial Public Offerings, Production Costs, and the Producing Lawyer Symposium on Business Lawyering and Value Creation for Clients' (1995) 74 Oregon Law Review 275; Nestor M Davidson, 'Values and Value Creation in Public-Private Transactions' (2008) 94 Iowa Law Review 937; Omari Scott Simmons and James D Dinnage, 'Innkeepers: A Unifying Theory of the In-House Counsel Role' (2011) 41 Seton Hall Law Review 77; Cathy Hwang, 'Value Creation by Transactional Associates Colloquium: Corporate Lawyers' (2019) 88 Fordham Law Review 1649; Steven L Schwarcz, 'Explaining the Value of Transactional Lawyering' (2006) 12 Stanford Journal of Law, Business & Finance 486.

a proposed amendment of the agreement's terms that is proposed by the borrower and which might also benefit the lender group as a whole.[28] And Annalise Riles shows how lawyers use collateral in over-the-counter derivatives transactions to reduce information costs—by insisting on collateral, one party does not need to investigate in any detail the financial circumstances of the other.[29] Riles describes collateral as a 'private legal technology' which has been developed, or at least refined, by lawyers to mitigate the temporal uncertainty of market risk.[30] Rachel Landy goes further, showing how lawyers that act for venture capital-backed startup companies are more than simply the 'one-off' transaction cost engineers envisaged by Gilson.[31] According to Landy, startup lawyers create value by providing value adding counsel at each stage of the company's lifecycle, readying these companies for their ultimate market exit in an IPO.[32]

My own data provides a measure of endorsement for aspects of Gilson's theory, as developed and refined in particular by De Fontenay, who depicts business lawyers adding value as aggregators of market information given their role as repeat players in corporate and finance transactions.[33] Especially, where terms are rapidly changing, lawyers are well placed to advise their clients of the current market position on terms so that this information can be factored into the client's pricing decision.[34] De Fontenay describes how leveraged finance lawyers develop digital databases with extensive 'side by side' comparisons of terms in other transactions, which reduce the billable hours spent by lawyers in advocating for new terms.[35] Consistent with De Fontenay's findings, lawyers in my study often reported to me that being familiar with the latest market position on each of the core terms of the loan documents was a skill set valued by their bank clients. Bank lawyer [#18], for example, presented this knowledge of the latest market position on terms as the 'additional value you are adding to the deal'.

There have been few outright challenges to Gilson's theory.[36] On the other hand, two empirical studies, without directly referencing Gilson, stand in contrast to the general picture he presented of lawyers greasing the wheels of international finance

[28] de Fontenay (n 27) 416.

[29] Although Riles does not reference Gilson, Annelise Riles, *Collateral Knowledge: Legal Reasoning in the Global Financial Markets* (University of Chicago Press 2011) 55.

[30] ibid 24.

[31] Landy (n 27) 2.

[32] ibid.

[33] de Fontenay (n 27) 402, 405, 424, 426.

[34] ibid 405, 424, 426.

[35] ibid 425–26.

[36] Perhaps the most direct challenge to Gilson's theory to date comes from Steven Schwarcz. Schwarcz concluded that his data from surveys of business lawyers and their clients only 'weakly supported' Gilson's theory. His data instead strongly supported a hypothesis that transactional lawyers add value by reducing regulatory costs. This outcome may be, as Schwarcz acknowledges, the result of self-reporting bias, with lawyers seeking to portray themselves as technical experts in the law, as opposed to simply risk managers or contractual draftspersons. Schwarcz (n 27) 498, 500. George Dent also draws attention to potential problems with the methodology used by Schwarcz. Dent (n 27) 295–95.

and commerce. Riles shows how international derivatives transactions contain embedded defects due to a pervasive lack of understanding of transactional documents and associated legal issues on the part of the lawyers and legal professionals who execute them.[37] Mitu Gulati and Robert E Scott reviewed thousands of sovereign debt contracts and found that the lawyers in large international law firms in New York who drafted and negotiated them tended not to fully understand their key terms.[38]

My case study findings similarly sit uncomfortably with Gilson's theory of lawyers as transaction costs engineers, and other economics-based theories, which advocate that Big Law adds value to financial and corporate transactions. According to Gilson, for business lawyers to act as transaction cost engineers, their involvement must be value accretive for all the parties to the transaction: '[I]f all a business lawyer offers is skill in distributive bargaining, the clients' joint decision would be to hire no lawyers at all.'[39] For example, if one client is represented by a good lawyer, and the other by a poor one, the value of the transaction is unlikely to increase overall: all that might be expected to happen is that one client receives a greater benefit than the other.[40] Gilson makes what he sees as a reasonable assumption that 'this disparity is unlikely to exist with any frequency'.[41] De Fontenay on the other hand, acknowledges that lawyers might not always add value to all parties and/or the transaction overall; but rather the effect of a lawyer's activities might be either 'value shifting'—improving the position of their client at the expense of the other party or parties—or 'value decreasing'—where it reduces the value of the transaction for all parties.[42] There is evidence of both of these outcomes in my data. As I have previously noted, leveraged loan terms have deteriorated in a way which negatively affects the value of the transaction to one of the parties, the lenders to a material degree. As I have shown, lawyer activity in the field of leveraged finance tends not to resolve, and frequently creates uncertainty in documentary terms and structures. This means these risks are, overall, not priced into the lending decision. Ultimately, the combined effect of lawyer activity in this field does not assist the transaction's parties to price the transaction at its lowest cost.[43]

The lenders' ability to protect themselves in the event of borrower financial distress has been materially diluted. For example, bank lawyers' failure to robustly push back against the ambiguous add backs to financial covenants advocated by private equity lawyers makes it possible for private equity-backed borrowers to raise an indeterminable amount of further debt in the future. At the same time

37 Riles (n 29) 64.
38 This phenomenon also raises ethical questions as to lawyer competence of course.
39 Gilson (n 16) 245.
40 ibid.
41 ibid 246.
42 de Fontenay (n 27) 421.
43 Gilson (n 16) 279.

there is a negative impact on the lenders' ability to monitor the borrower's financial position and act in the event of a breach of covenant/event of default, thereby reducing their ability to protect themselves through a lender-led restructuring of the borrower's indebtedness. And the types of defects in security structures and intercreditor agreements that I have noted mean senior lenders (who price their loans according to their senior status) may find themselves effectively subordinated to supposedly junior creditors. This is an example of value-shifting activity.

Whilst value-shifting activity by leveraged finance lawyers emerges very clearly from my data, due to the material dilution in lender protections caused by the pervasive uncertainty in loan terms, leveraged finance lawyer activity may sometimes be value destructive for private equity sponsors as well. De Fontenay offers an example of value decreasing lawyer activity: a lawyer who continually seeks to introduce new terms into documents where the benefit to their client of the inclusion of the term is outweighed by the cost of additional legal fees and the time spent in considering and negotiating that new term.[44] So why do private equity lawyers engage in contractual boundary pushing? It is reasonable to conclude that it is in part motivated not by the lawyer's desire to add value for their client but by their 'private incentives'. This might be, as de Fontenay has noted, 'the lure of increased billable hours'.[45] Or, as Yves Dezalay and Bryant Garth have argued, by lawyers pursuing career progression.[46] The two objectives are of course connected. Although there sometimes will and sometimes will not be alignment with their clients' interests and objectives, private equity lawyers' primary motivation for engaging in contractual boundary pushing is not to promote the interests of their clients. They do so in response to the pressures on them which are founded in financialized law firm governance.[47]

Leveraged finance lawyer activity can be seen as value decreasing where the parties are unable to properly identify, assess, allocate, and price the risks of the transaction due to pervasive uncertainty in loan terms. It appears that many lenders who invest in leveraged loans—the end buyers—do not have the appetite to evaluate and price the risk of the loans they invest in. The reasons for this are unclear. It may be because institutional investors are under pressure to seek higher yields, including under applicable regulatory regimes.[48] They may also consider leveraged

[44] de Fontenay (n 27) 422.

[45] ibid.

[46] Riles (n 29) 47; Yves Dezalay and Bryant G Garth, *Dealing in Virtue: International Commercial Arbitration and the Construction of a Transnational Legal Order* (University of Chicago Press 1996).

[47] William D Henderson, 'From Big Law to Lean Law' (2014) 38 International Review of Law and Economics 5, 15.

[48] 'High Yield Bonds and Leveraged Loans a Convergence of Terms | Ashurst' (25 April 2018) 7 <https://www.ashurst.com/en/news-and-insights/insights/high-yield-bonds-and-leveraged-loans-a-convergence-of-terms/> accessed 23 June 2020; John Gilligan and Mike Wright, *Private Equity Demystified: An Explanatory Guide* (4th edn, OUP 2020) 25; 'Solvency II' (23 January 2023) <https://www.bankofengland.co.uk/prudential-regulation/key-initiatives/solvency-ii> accessed 14 February 2023.

loans to be 'bond like', meaning that they are not overly concerned that they are investing in weakly covenanted and ambiguously worded debt instruments as they expect to be able to 'trade out' of them if needed, which assumes the existence of a liquid secondary market and does not take into account often extensive restrictions on who they can transfer to.[49] They may also consider that compromising on ambiguity may enhance their competitive position over more conservative investors. Or they may do so due to their own resource constraints, preferring not to dedicate reading time to the assessment of risk.[50] These factors appear to have led to an 'all loans must look the same' market logic from the end buyers of leveraged loans.

However, none of these factors detract from the conclusion that, due to the pervasive uncertainty in loan terms that I identified and explored in Chapter 7, those lenders who do wish to evaluate and price in the risk of the loans they invest in are unable to do so accurately. The participants in my interviews did not tend to dispute this conclusion. They frequently conceded that they struggled to understand what key provisions in typical leveraged loan documents meant and had reached the conclusion that the same is true for the other key transaction stakeholders: private equity sponsors, the arranging banks, and the end buyer lenders.[51] This finding of a lack of understanding by all parties to leveraged loans is also consistent with IOSCO's recent report which noted that 'issues have been identified with respect to the clarity of drafting' in leveraged loan documents and IOSCO has called for 'material covenants and associated terms contained in term sheets and loan documentation to be written in a clear, concise and effective manner that can be readily understood by the contracting parties'.[52]

This raises the question as to whether Big Law can be trusted as a legal and business advisor, which is critical to their business model and their legitimacy in the eyes of their clients. A significant number of law firm partners interviewed by Mitt Regan and Lisa Rohrer said that they aspired to be viewed by their clients as a 'trusted adviser'.[53] This required them to have a deep understanding of their client's business and strategy so that they could advise on both the spirit as well as the letter of the law, and in areas outside a strictly legal ambit.[54] Regan and Rohrer argue that

[49] Leveraged loans are also commonly subject to restrictions on who lenders can sell to; usually governed by lists of approved and/or prohibited investors, known as 'white lists' and 'black lists'.

[50] Kenneth Ayotte and Patrick Bolton, 'Covenant Lite Lending, Liquidity and Standardization of Financial Contracts' in Kenneth Ayotte and Henry E Smith, *Research Handbook on the Economics of Property Law* (Edward Elgar Publishing 2011) 174; Paterson (n 7) 662.

[51] See eg Jamie McDougall and others, 'Intralot's Drop-down Restructuring Games: Priming Pari Passu Noteholders, Circumventing Non-Consenters and Artificially Reducing Asset Values' [2022] The Journal of International Banking and Financial Law 5.

[52] International Organisation of Securities Commissions, 'Leveraged Loans and CLOs, Good Practices for Consideration, Consultation Report CR05/2023' (September 2023) 3, 11 <https://www.iosco.org/library/pubdocs/pdf/IOSCOPD746.pdf>.

[53] Mitt Regan and Lisa H Rohrer, *BigLaw: Money and Meaning in the Modern Law Firm* (The University of Chicago Press 2020) 203–11.

[54] ibid.

a trusted advisor may not simply lay out the risks for the clients, but may advise against proceeding in a way which is legal but unwise'.[55] The type of lawyer activity explored in the case study has the potential to undermine the trust that clients and the public place in the reputational capital of Big Law.

This book contributes an in-depth empirical evaluation of claims by large international law firms to be purveyors of cutting-edge technical expertise and high-quality service. With one or two notable exceptions, the literature on corporate lawyers has to date largely accepted these claims without close scrutiny.[56] This literature largely accepts that Big Law adds value by offering quality assurance to, and acting as reputational intermediaries for, their clients.[57] According to Erwin Smigel, writing about New York lawyers in the 1950s, large law firms were so successful because clients were prepared to pay a premium for expert advice.[58] Nelson argued that the high fees of these firms depend on specialist knowledge and skill being accepted as a given by clients, as a form of quality assurance.[59] Otherwise, clients will seek lower cost advice or build in-house capacity.[60] Partners in Big Law, hence, need to convince clients of their unique competence, to avoid clients doing the work internally, or giving the work to other 'lesser' firms.[61]

The organizational literature on professional services firms similarly asserts that the 'knowledge intensity' of large law firms is central to their success.[62] The partnership form is portrayed as encouraging partners to enforce quality through 'clan control'.[63] Emmanuel Lazega, in his study of collegial networks in a New England corporate law firm, found that traditional theories of collegiality within a knowledge intensive organization with a flat hierarchical structure, such as a law firm partnership, were too simplistic; there were in fact complex, 'multiple and informal relationships' between members, an informal pattern of ties, which facilitated efficient cooperation between them.[64] Quality, he argued, is key in a knowledge-based business, and is primarily controlled through interpersonal relationships, manifested mostly in lawyers seeking the views and advice of their peers.[65] Except where there was a client complaint, partners did not generally peer review each other's

[55] ibid 209.

[56] For example, Mitu Gulati and Robert E Scott, *The Three and a Half Minute Transaction: Boilerplate and the Limits of Contract Design* (University of Chicago Press 2012); Stephen J Choi, Mitu Gulati, and Robert E Scott, 'The Black Hole Problem in Commercial Boilerplate' (2017) 67 Duke Law Journal 1.

[57] See eg Robert L Nelson, *Partners with Power: The Social Transformation of the Large Law Firm* (University of California Press 1988) 3; Ribstein (n 15) 758, 760.

[58] Erwin O Smigel, *The Wall Street Lawyer* (The Free Press of Glencoe 1964) 343.

[59] Nelson (n 57) 3.

[60] ibid.

[61] ibid 9–10.

[62] Michael Smets and others, '25 Years since "P2": Taking Stock and Charting the Future of Professional Firms' (2017) 4 Journal of Professions and Organization 91, 94–95.

[63] ibid 95.

[64] Emmanuel Lazega, *The Collegial Phenomenon: The Social Mechanisms of Cooperation Among Peers in a Corporate Law Partnership* (OUP 2001).

[65] ibid 37.

work (other than formal legal opinions).[66] Good work was, however, praised, and there was criticism of, and gossip relating to, poor quality work. Collegial networks hence operated as a form of quality control, as a 'social process' involving knowledge sharing and informal peer review.[67] The firm encouraged members to seek 'second opinions' from their colleagues, principally from those partners with the 'authority to know'.[68]

This central claim to technical expertise and excellence has largely remained a key element of the business model of large international law firms. For example, Linklaters', then managing partner, Tony Angel implemented a strategy in the early 2000s to put 'clear blue water' between the firm and its main rivals by pursuing a strategy of 'premium work for premium clients'.[69] Gerard Hanlon argues that both the firm and an individual's ability to attract new work, particularly in developing often lucrative new areas of practice, depends on clients placing their trust in their reputational capital.[70] Hanlon cites the example of Marty Lipton of Watchell, Lipton, Rose and Katz who is credited with developing the market for hostile takeovers in the United States, and inspiring the 'poison pill' defence.[71] Marc Galanter and Henderson argue that high levels of reputational capital further act as 'glue', serving to keep partners, as well as their clients, at the firm.[72]

Due to information asymmetry, clients are generally poorly placed to assess the actual quality of the service they receive.[73] Larry Ribstein describes legal services as a 'credence' good, the quality of which clients must take on trust.[74] Corporate clients—even those with large in-house legal teams—instruct large law firms where they lack the necessary technical expertise and/or resources to handle large, complex cross-border matters.[75] Large law firms hence invest heavily in the reputation of their firm as a trusted advisor, as a signal of their quality.[76] On this basis, large firms are able to charge a premium to clients. Ribstein argued that corporate clients purchase the reputational capital of Big Law, and/or rely on the quality assurance that they offer.[77] Joan Loughrey argues that their role:

[66] ibid 153, 155–56.
[67] ibid 150.
[68] ibid 151.
[69] 'Linklaters (A): Seeking Clear Blue Water' (*Harvard Law School The Case Studies*) <http://casestudies.law.harvard.edu/linklaters-a-seeking-clear-blue-water/> accessed 10 June 2023.
[70] Gerard Hanlon, 'Institutional Forms and Organizational Structures: Homology, Trust and Reputational Capital in Professional Service Firms' (2004) 11 Organization 186, 203.
[71] Hanlon (n 70). See also William H Starbuck, 'Keeping a Butterfly and an Elephant in a House of Cards: The Elements of Exceptional Success' (1993) <https://papers.ssrn.com/abstract=2708152> accessed 8 June 2023.
[72] Marc Galanter and William D Henderson, 'The Elastic Tournament: The Second Transformation of the Big Law Firm' (Social Science Research Network 2008) SSRN Scholarly Paper ID 1104711 1866 <https://papers.ssrn.com/abstract=1104711> accessed 6 December 2018.
[73] Smets and others (n 62) 94–95.
[74] Larry E Ribstein, 'Ethical Rules, Agency Costs, and Law Firm Structure' (1998) 84 Virginia Law Review 1707, 1712–13.
[75] Ribstein (n 15) 758, 760.
[76] Smets and others (n 62) 94–95.
[77] Galanter and Henderson (n 72) 1866.

facilitates market exchanges and reduces the cost of capital to clients, since third parties are more willing to deal with parties when reputational intermediaries – who are independent repeat players in the market and have more to lose and less to gain if the client's statements are false – have staked their own reputation on the statements being accurate.'[78]

For John Flood, reputational capital is what draws the clients of large law firms to them; as actors in the business and financial worlds, these large companies claim that they can be trusted by their counterparties, regulators, and others that they interact with, because they have an elite law firm advising them, which serves to sanctify their relationships.[79] Mitt Regan similarly points out that a lawyer who has relationships with other parties involved in a transaction 'may serve as a reputational intermediary who makes negotiations go more smoothly because the other parties know and trust him.'[80] Moorhead and Hinchley found that lawyers act as reputational intermediaries in another way; if they advise their clients that something is permitted, under a regulatory rule for example, their clients then feel exempted from making any judgement themselves, simply reporting to regulators that their lawyers told them the proposed action was permitted.[81] According to Ronald Gilson and Robert Mnookin, because large law firms act as a quality assurance mechanism for clients in this way it is critical that they maintain high standards, closely monitoring the work of their lawyers; otherwise, they risk materially diminishing their reputational capital.[82] Where they do not, the risk is that their core business model is undermined.

Ribstein's prediction of the death of Big Law is contested, but the case study data offers a degree of empirical support to his central thesis.[83] Ribstein argued that the future success of Big Law was under threat due to changes in law firm logics which had broken down the informal quality policing processes of the type identified by Nelson and Lazega.[84] In particular, Ribstein argued that individual performance-based remuneration models, as opposed to lockstep models based solely on seniority, incentivized partners to focus on developing their own reputations as

[78] Joan Loughrey, *Corporate Lawyers and Corporate Governance* (CUP 2011) 77.

[79] John Flood, 'Lawyers as Sanctifiers: The Role of Elite Law Firms in International Business Transactions Symposium: Globalization of the Legal Profession' (2007) 14 Indiana Journal of Global Legal Studies 35, 38.

[80] Milton C Regan, *Eat What You Kill: The Fall of a Wall Street Lawyer* (University of Michigan Press 2004) 316.

[81] Richard Moorhead and Victoria Hinchley, 'Professional Minimalism? The Ethical Consciousness of Commercial Lawyers' (2015) 42 Journal of Law and Society 387, 399–400.

[82] Ronald J Gilson and Robert H Mnookin, 'Sharing among the Human Capitalists: An Economic Inquiry into the Corporate Law Firm and How Partners Split Profits' (1984) 37 Stanford Law Review 313. Nelson (n 57) 63.

[83] Ribstein (n 15); Henderson (n 47). For a contrary view, see Eli Wald, 'Smart Growth: The Large Law Firm in the Twenty-First Century Colloquium: Globalization and the Legal Profession' (2011) 80 Fordham Law Review 2867.

[84] Nelson (n 57); Lazega (n 64).

opposed to those of the firm.[85] On top of this, Ribstein argued that excessive lateral hiring 'complicates a firm's ability to maintain a strong culture of trust and cooperation'.[86]

The risk for Big Law is that individual partners are now incentivized to build their own reputations and not those of the firm, and to develop practices—particularly building a portable client base—that make them attractive to the next firm they might plan to move to. Ribstein argued that the future success of Big Law was under threat precisely because the principal product they sell to clients—what he called reputational bonding—had been diluted by their accelerated growth, increased focus on profit generation, global expansion, and significant lateral hiring.[87] Henderson, building on Ribstein's argument, asserts that large law firms are now largely trading on their 'legacy reputations'.[88] Galanter and Henderson—in their influential 'elastic tournament' paper—argue that in adopting an 'eat what you kill' culture where profit is prioritized over professional values, large firms have ceased to be trusted counsel and become more of a hired gun.[89]

We should not get carried away of course. Big Law is not down and out by any stretch of the imagination. As Bruce MacEwan has argued, the adage that 'nobody ever got fired for hiring' —here you can insert the name of most elite law firms—still applies, but the risk for Big Law is apparent, that their legacy reputations are under threat.[90] Henderson concludes that 'most large law firms seem to be managed for the short-term benefit of individual rainmaking partners', meaning that the firms' reputational capital is dwindling by the day.[91] As a result, Henderson posits that they will be ill-prepared to protect themselves against economic trends and technological innovation which may challenge their very survival in the longer term.[92]

To date there has been little empirical basis for Ribstein's claims in the data we have. A question that has not been empirically explored, for example, is whether there might be pockets of large law firms where claims to technical expertise and high-quality service are consistently weaker than in others, and how this variability might be connected to the conditions and logics of that practice area field.

85 Ribstein (n 15) 755.

86 ibid 775; Henderson (n 47) 7.

87 Ribstein (n 15) 753; Henderson (n 47) 6.

88 Henderson (n 47) 15.

89 Galanter and Henderson (n 72) 1898; Russell G Pearce and Eli Wald, 'The Relational Infrastructure of Law Firm Culture and Regulation: The Exaggerated Death of Big Law' (Social Science Research Network 2013) SSRN Scholarly Paper ID 2627733 117 <https://papers.ssrn.com/abstract=2627733> accessed 5 December 2018.

90 Bruce MacEwen, 'Nobody Ever Got Fired for Hiring Skadden | Adam Smith, Esq.' (*Adam Smith Esq.*) <https://adamsmithesq.com/2004/04/nobody_ever_got/> accessed 11 June 2023. Cited in Henderson (n 47) 15.See also, Bruce MacEwen, *Growth Is Dead: Now What?: Law Firms on the Brink / Bruce MacEwen; Foreword by Peter J. Kalis.* (Adam Smith, Esq 2013).

91 Henderson (n 47) 16.

92 Pearce and Wald (n 89) 110.

My findings emphasize the risk that the practices of lawyers in the leveraged finance practice area field have the potential to severely taint Big Law's reputation and brand for high quality and superior competence. My data, hence, raises questions over the capacity of leading US, Magic Circle, and other large international law firms to continue to offer quality assurance to their clients and thus justify the trust that corporate clients place in them and the premium fees Big Law is able to charge them as a result.

9.3 Big Law, ethics, and the need for meaningful regulation

In pockets of elite international law firms, such as leveraged finance, where ethical pressures are so widely acknowledged and understood, an important question is why so few lawyers put their ethical duties ahead of their commercial self-interest in any meaningful way. First, it is well established that solicitors in large law firms tend to have a poor understanding of their professional duties.[93] Richard Moorhead and Victoria Hinchley found that 'professional ethics exert minimal, superficial influence over a more self-interested, commercially-driven pragmatism.'[94] And Emma Oakley and Steven Vaugan show how lawyers in large firms are mostly ethically apathetic.[95]

My participants tended not to refer to specific ethical principles, such as independence, or integrity, when describing ethical tensions in their everyday work, which I interpret as evidence of this general detachment from professional regulation. It was noteworthy, for example, that many of my participants appeared unaware that the Law Society had ceased to be the regulator and supervisor of solicitors in England and Wales, even though it handed over its duties in this regard to the SRA upon the passing into law of the Legal services Act (LSA) in 2007.[96] Bank lawyer [#29] was not atypical when remarking:

> Some sponsor counsel are, quite frankly, rude and unprofessional, and I'm sure I could take them to the Law Society and get them struck off for a breach of professional duties and ethics.

Second, there is support in the legal ethics literature for a degree of scepticism as to whether lawyers—particularly those who work in large international law

[93] David B Wilkins, 'Some Realism about Legal Realism for Lawyers: Assessing the Role of Context in Legal Ethics' in Leslie C Levin and Lynn M Mather (eds), *Lawyers in Practice: Ethical Decision Making in Context* (University of Chicago Press 2012) 31–32. Moorhead and Hinchley (n 81).

[94] Moorhead and Hinchley (n 81).

[95] Steven Vaughan and Emma Oakley, '"Gorilla Exceptions" and the Ethically Apathetic Corporate Lawyer' (2016) 19 Legal Ethics 50.

[96] Although an independent body, the SRA remains an arm of the Law Society.

firms—can compartmentalize financial incentives, on the one hand, and their ethical duties to their client and to act with independence on the other. According to Ted Schneyer, it is necessary to consider 'the common financial, psychological and organisational pressures of law practice' when considering how lawyers act when faced with an ethical choice.[97] Paul Thagard shows that this is supported by evidence from neuroscience; those in positions of responsibility:

> have no way of knowing whether their decisions emanate from the biases they have acquired from personal interests instead of good reasoning that takes their responsibilities into account. People ... naturally lack a mental mechanism to detect such divergences.[98]

Hugh Gunz and others have observed that it is 'naive to assume that professionals are able to maintain a level of autonomy that places them above the temptations of the commercial world', especially as large corporate law firms are 'deeply embedded in and an integral part of that world.'[99] Alice Woolley and Bradley Wendel's research supports a conclusion that how lawyers act and make decisions most closely correlates to the conditions of their field of practice.[100] The mere existence of these conditions may even, according to Leslie Levin, 'blind lawyers to the fact that they are faced with an ethical decision in the first place'.[101]

The case study shows how the survival logic plays a central role in the ethical reasoning of bank lawyers, for example. When blended with the effects of the law firm logics that I have described in previous chapters, it acts as a constraint on the ability of bank lawyers to oppose the private equity lawyers in the negotiation of the loan terms which the latter propose.[102] The result, according to bank lawyer [#22], is that:

> the average lender counsel in the leveraged finance market will care far more about what the sponsor and their lawyers and advisors will think than what the lender thinks.

[97] Ted Schneyer, 'Moral Philosophy's Standard Misconception of Legal Ethics' (1984) 1984 Wisconsin Law Review 1529, 1543. Cited in Vaughan and Oakley (n 95) 55.

[98] Paul Thagard, 'The Moral Psychology of Conflicts of Interest: Insights from Affective Neuroscience' (2007) 24 Journal of Applied Philosophy 367, 373–74; Jonathan Herring, *Legal Ethics* (OUP 2017) 183.

[99] Gunz, Gunz, and Dinovitzer (n 4) 128.

[100] Alice Woolley and W Bradley Wendel, 'Legal Ethics and Moral Character' (2010) 23 Georgetown Journal of Legal Ethics 1065, 1071.

[101] Leslie C Levin, 'Bad Apples, Bad Lawyers or Bad Decisionmaking: Lessons from Psychology and from Lawyers in the Dock Book Review Essay' (2009) 22 Georgetown Journal of Legal Ethics 1549, 1561.

[102] Thornton, Ocasio, and Lounsbury (n 10) 145.

This poor grasp of ethical duties and an inability to compartmentalize does not automatically mean, however, that a failure to act in the best interest of clients, and with independence, will always be the consequence. Some bank lawyers will draw on reserves of moral courage, but they will tend to be in a minority; as Woolley and Wendel observe, to commit to ethicality, to the exclusion of the range of firm and practice area incentives and pressures that they face, an individual lawyer will frequently have to operate as something of a maverick: exuding a significant degree of self-confidence, immune to private equity lawyer coercion, for example; ignoring the financial incentives on offer; and given the risk of being boycotted for future designated work, be prepared to be somewhat reckless as to their own career prospects.[103]

The survival logic can be seen as weakening any inclination that might have otherwise existed for bank lawyers to consider the ethical dimensions of their day-to-day practice.[104] They discount this applying a blame-the-client mindset. They are offered a financial incentive to favour the private equity lawyer that designated them over the group of banks which they formally act for. It is reasonable to conclude that even where a bank lawyer is fully cognisant of their ethical duties, a bank lawyer's ability in any instance to objectively delineate between what is in the best interests of their own clients from those of the private equity sponsors and their lawyers has been severely compromised. This is due to their economic reliance on their referral relationships with private equity lawyers. Where a bank lawyer's primary focus is on these types of schemes which are designed to generate profit for themselves and their firm, so that their judgement is substantially influenced by this imperative, meaning that where the interests of their client become secondary, their independence can be considered to have been compromised.[105]

We have also seen how private equity lawyers are engaging in purposeful errors. A case could be made that this is an affront to legal certainty, a central pillar of the rule of law. The rule of law is, as Brian Tamanhaha has noted, an 'elusive concept;' perhaps even, as Tom Bingham has observed, open to 'ideologically abuse and general overuse'.[106] There is, however, a sense that in creating, allowing to subsist, and then taking advantage of legal uncertainty, the private equity lawyers do not have fidelity to the law itself. Bingham argues that the independence of lawyers is

[103] Woolley and Wendel (n 100) 1081, 1097.

[104] Maryam Kouchaki and others, 'Seeing Green: Mere Exposure to Money Triggers a Business Decision Frame and Unethical Outcomes' (2013) 121 Organizational Behavior and Human Decision Processes 53; Moorhead and Hinchley (n 81) 402–03.

[105] See *SRA v Brian Laurence Miller and David Joel Gore*, SDT Case No. 10619-2010, 3 October 2011, para 178. Cited in Claire Coe and Steven Vaughan, 'Independence, Representation and Risk: An Empirical Exploration of the Management of Client Relationships by Large Law Firms' (Social Science Research Network 2015) SSRN Scholarly Paper ID 2679005 47 <https://papers.ssrn.com/abstract=2679005> accessed 17 July 2018.

[106] Brian Z Tamanaha, *On the Rule of Law: History, Politics, Theory* (CUP 2004) 3; Tom Bingham, *The Rule of Law* (Penguin Books 2010) 5.

no less important to the rule of law than the independence of judges.[107] The independence of lawyers in the transactional setting is equally key to the rule of law, in that lawyers who are not independent may not promote, and may even obstruct for their own ends, just transaction processes, which, as William Simon has argued, are the surest route to the achievement by both parties to the transaction of a just outcome.[108]

In addition to reviewing leveraged finance lawyer compliance with the SRA's specific principles and rules, as I did in earlier chapters, there is a threshold issue that must first be considered. To be considered competent, the SRA requires that a solicitor must be able to apply the ethical concepts which govern their role and behaviour as a lawyer, recognize ethical issues when they arise, exercise effective judgement in addressing them, and identify the relevant principles and rules of professional conduct and follow them.[109] Solicitors must also be able to resist pressure to condone, ignore, or commit unethical behaviour.[110] It is likely then, that a solicitor who is found to be in breach of a specific ethical rule or principle is also in breach of this more general competence requirement. A 'serious breach' of the Code can result in the SRA taking enforcement action against an individual solicitor. A failure or breach 'may be serious either in isolation or because it comprises a persistent or concerning pattern of behaviour'.[111]

All of this has the potential to undermine client, and indeed public, trust in Big Law. Should this happen, it will have a contagion effect, tainting the reputation of solicitors and the wider legal profession more generally. Julian Webb and Donald Nicolson emphasize how trust in individual lawyers has been superseded by trust in the legal profession as an institution.[112] When lawyers do not adhere to codes of professional conduct, this has the potential to undermine public trust in the profession.[113] This happened with accountants following the collapse of Enron in 2002, for example.[114] But it is not just these types of large and very public scandals that threaten trust in lawyers; the 'drip, drip' of ethical lapses, can, as Hugh Gunz and others have observed, 'feed a popular cynicism' about the value and purpose of lawyers.[115] Reflecting this concern, the SRA's Principle 2 requires that solicitors act in a way which upholds public trust in the solicitors' profession.[116]

[107] Ensuring fearless representation for those unable to represent themselves 'however unpopular or distasteful their case may be,' Bingham (n 106) 92–93.

[108] William H Simon, 'Ethical Discretion in Lawyering' (1987) 101 Harvard Law Review 1083.

[109] 'Statement of Solicitor Competence' (9 August 2022) <https://www.sra.org.uk/solicitors/resources/continuing-competence/cpd/competence-statement/> accessed 10 March 2023.

[110] ibid.

[111] 'SRA Code of Conduct for Solicitors, RELs and RFLs' (n 3).

[112] Julian Webb and Donald Nicolson, 'Institutionalising Trust: Ethics and the Responsive Regulation of the Legal Profession' (1999) 2 Legal Ethics 148; Herring (n 98) 62–63.

[113] Gunz, Gunz, and Dinovitzer (n 4) 123.

[114] ibid 129.

[115] ibid.

[116] 'SRA Principles' (n 3).

The SRA is responsible for 'upholding public confidence in the provision of legal services'.[117]

Although there is the danger that this book might deepen popular cynicism surrounding the ethics of lawyers, and accepting that real change in lawyer behaviour depends on regulators of the legal profession deciding to engage with this type of empirical material and with these types of ethical concerns, there is a pressing need for empirical accounts like this book which shed light on the extent to which corporate lawyers comply with ethical codes of professional conduct.

Many of the ethical rules and principles in the SRA's Standards and Regulations are rather vague and abstract, however, which, when added to resource constraints, impacts enforcement.[118] This might be because, as Richard Moorhead has argued, professional codes of conduct in England and Wales were mostly written to address litigation issues, as opposed to transactional commercial practice.[119] On the whole, the Standards and Regulations do not tend to address the specific types of ethical challenges Big Law lawyers are likely to face in practice. This makes it difficult to reach clear conclusions on the interpretation of these duties to determine if they have been adhered to in any given situation.[120]

As I have already noted, solicitors in large law firms tend to have a poor understanding of their professional duties.[121] For example, Claire Coe and Steven Vaughan found that their interviewees' understanding of the concept of independence was generally poor.[122] This could be because corporate lawyers may be prone to believe (wrongly) that public interest duties do not apply to them, given they act for corporate clients and not individuals.[123] Another, and likely more material, factor is, as Vaughan and Emma Oakley have noted, that the professional rules for solicitors in England and Wales tend to be written in relatively vague terms, so that 'they cease having a deontological character—as duties—and start to take on the character of 'virtues'.[124]

The SRA, in the introduction to its Principles, makes clear that they 'comprise the fundamental tenets of ethical behaviour that we expect all those that we regulate to uphold'.[125] The Principles are, however, very broad in scope; they adopt language drawn from moral duties, and have been left relatively undefined.[126] In

[117] 'SRA Enforcement Strategy' (21 January 2022) <https://www.sra.org.uk/sra/corporate-strategy/sra-enforcement-strategy/> accessed 4 July 2023.

[118] 'SRA Standards and Regulations' (25 November 2019) <https://www.sra.org.uk/solicitors/standards-regulations/> accessed 21 June 2022.

[119] R Moorhead, 'Precarious Professionalism: Some Empirical and Behavioural Perspectives on Lawyers' (2014) 67 Current Legal Problems 447, 26.

[120] Herring (n 98) 88.

[121] Wilkins (n 93) 31–32. Moorhead and Hinchley (n 81).

[122] And there was a lack of training of junior lawyers on ethics, Coe and Vaughan (n 105) 2, 8, 52, 62, 63.

[123] Wilkins (n 93) 31–32. Moorhead and Hinchley (n 81).

[124] Vaughan and Oakley (n 95) 56.

[125] 'SRA Principles' (n 3).

[126] Vaughan and Oakley (n 95) 56.

other words, as Vaughan and Oakley argue, since they are not written as 'rules to be obeyed' they are mostly not understood as such by solicitors, and so will not tend to form a material component of a solicitor's governing frame of reference when they make ethical decisions in their day-to-day work.[127] The SRA's principles even have the potential to conflict with each other; for example, the duty to the client versus the rule of law and the administration of justice.[128] Further, the boundaries between them are indistinct, so that they tend to overlap, with little clarity provided as to which principle or rule applies in any given situation. Whilst the SRA's Code of Conduct contains some fairly specific rules, for example, as to the duties to keep client information confidential, and to avoid conflicts of interest, it mostly deliberately omits detailed guidance on them.[129] A further complicating factor is that solicitors have fiduciary duties which exist at common law and which overlap with their ethical duties under the SRA's Standards and Regulations.[130] As a consequence, the risk is that the SRA's Standards and Regulations fail to achieve their principal purpose of mitigating the risk of lawyers in Big Law avoiding their professional ethical duties.[131] The risk is that the light touch, minimalistic approach of the Standards and Regulations does not support Big Law lawyers in acting ethically; Oakley and Vaughan, for example, describe the concept of the independent lawyer as a 'convenient myth' designed to justify such light touch regulatory approaches.[132]

The effect is that, as Joan Loughrey has argued, 'the regulatory framework . . . fails to hold transactional lawyers to account for the significant regulatory risks that they present.'[133] Oakley and Vaughan refer to a 'regulatory framework that leaves the internal workings of large corporate law firms singularly unscrutinised.'[134] This problem is not confined to England and Wales. Ian Kirkpatrick and Mirko Noordegraaf point to research which suggests that large law firms are 'increasingly immune to the normative and coercive influence of their respective professional associations'.[135] This is likely because Big Law is largely seen by regulators as relatively low risk, given they tend to have relatively sophisticated internal compliance

[127] ibid.
[128] ibid.
[129] Herring (n 98) 88.
[130] Gunz, Gunz, and Dinovitzer (n 4) 120. ibid 129.
[131] Yuval Feldman, *The Law of Good People* (CUP 2018) xi–xii, 11–12, 193, 197.
[132] Oakley and Vaughan (n 2) 84.
[133] Joan Loughrey, 'Accountability and the Regulation of the Large Law Firm Lawyer' (2014) 77 The Modern Law Review 732, 743.
[134] Oakley and Vaughan (n 2).
[135] Ian Kirkpatrick and Mirko Noordegraaf, 'Organizations and Occupations: Towards Hybrid Professionalism in Professional Service Firms?' in Laura Empson and others, *The Oxford Handbook of Professional Service Firms* (OUP 2015) 99; James Faulconbridge and Daniel Muzio, 'Organizational Professionalism in Globalizing Law Firms' (2008) 22 Work, Employment and Society 7; Royston Greenwood and Roy Suddaby, 'Institutional Entrepreneurship In Mature Fields: The Big Five Accounting Firms' (2006) 49 Academy of Management Journal 27.

teams and procedures.[136] As Loughrey has argued, these firms tend to generally regulate themselves, with the SRA in this jurisdiction largely confining its role to ensuring they have robust compliance systems in place; this 'risk based' enforcement has led to a lack of scrutiny of, and an inability to assess the level of risks presented by, the lawyers working in these large law firms.[137] This book will hence inform debates around appropriate regulatory approaches in the market for corporate legal services. The SRA might consider making its formal rules of ethics less ambiguous for example, to ensure they achieve their principal purpose of mitigating the risk of lawyers avoiding their professional ethical duties.[138]

Vaughan and Oakley argue that 'taking seriously the occupational and relational stresses and strains of corporate lawyering as vulnerabilities can help sensitise us to the situational and systematic hazards of contemporary legal practice.'[139] It is important that regulators of the legal profession take seriously the influence that not only powerful clients, but also third parties, acting as quasi-clients, exert over corporate lawyers. In the leveraged finance area, the SRA could, as a starting point, consider issuing guidance, or a warning notice, to clarify its expectations of leveraged finance lawyers, and reminding them of their ethical duties, as it did with non-disclosure agreements.[140] The SRA should also consider issuing specific rules, or guidance, as to the particular ethical 'smoking guns' revealed by my data, which elevate the risk of leveraged finance lawyers acting unethically.[141] It might consider, for example, prohibiting the practices of lawyer designation and trees in the head, which are prominent examples of such smoking guns in this field. It might also consider issuing guidance making clear that it is the duty of solicitors to clearly disclose in writing to clients before commencing work on a transaction the existence of any lawyer-to-lawyer referral relationships that relate to the matter in hand.

A counter argument to this type of regulatory intervention might be that it addresses a symptom, rather than the underlying cause. It would not address the disparity in bargaining power between banks and private equity sponsors, for example, and it is possible banks may in any event still gravitate towards lawyers and law firms that have strong links with private equity lawyers and law firms in the hope of better positioning themselves for mandates.[142] However, as Simon Salzedo

136 Lord Hunt, 'The Hunt Review of the Regulation of Legal Services' (The Law Society 2009) 6 <https://www.lsc.qld.gov.au/__data/assets/pdf_file/0016/260035/The-Hunt-Review-of-the-Regulation-of-Legal-Services-NZ-Dec-2009.pdf>; Loughrey (n 78) 296.

137 Loughrey (n 78) 297; Julie Rose O'Sullivan, 'Professional Discipline for Law Firms - A Response to Professor Schneyer's Proposal' (2002) 16 Georgetown Journal of Legal Ethics 1, 85–86.

138 Feldman (n 131) xi–xii, 11–12, 193, 197.

139 Oakley and Vaughan (n 2).

140 'Use of Non-Disclosure Agreements (NDAs)—Warning Notice' (11 December 2020) <https://www.sra.org.uk/solicitors/guidance/non-disclosure-agreements-ndas/> accessed 20 April 2022.

141 Feldman (n 131) x–xi.

142 Simon Salzedo and Tom Wood, 'Improper Leverage? Own Interest Conflicts and the Designation Model in Leveraged Finance Transactions' (2023) 4 Journal of International Banking and Financial Law 209, 211.

KC and Tom Wood rightly note, this is beside the point; the whole purpose of the SRA's conflict of interest rules is to prevent the risk of conflicts arising.[143] This observation can be extended to the entirety of the SRA's rules of ethics; their purpose is to support lawyers in acting ethically, and to protect the clients of solicitors from the range of harms that might flow from ethical misconduct. To continue to permit designation, and related practices such as virtual trees, trees in the head, is to consciously green light the creation and maintenance of conditions which we know lead to not only the risk of, but actual, conflicts of interest, not to mention severely compromised independence, low levels of integrity, breaches of confidentiality, and questionable levels of competence. If lawyers and law firms were both fully cognisant of their ethical duties, and willing to prioritize them above financial, prestige and other incentives, such a prohibition would not be necessary. Lawyers and law firms would voluntarily withdraw from markets where they were placed in such ethically challenging situations. However, the data I have collected shows that this does not happen in practice. These challenges have been facing leveraged finance lawyers for long enough that we know that major law firms will not police themselves to a solution. Regulatory intervention is hence called for.

This is not to say that financial services regulation does not also have a role to play here. The shift to the originate-to-distribute model means that the arranging banks that originate leveraged loans tend not to hold the loan to maturity, so they have a reduced incentive to ensure that loan terms appropriately protect the interests of lenders. Financial services regulators confronted this issue with respect to another financial market, securitization, in the aftermath of the global financial crisis. Their solution was to require arrangers of securitizations to continue to have 'skin in the game' by retaining 5 per cent of the net economic risk of the transaction until maturity.[144] An equivalent regulatory intervention in the leveraged finance market would help to align the interests of arrangers more closely with lenders, and resolve the lack of clarity and all round confusion as to the precise scope of the bank lawyers' role.

We should be realistic about the prospects of these kinds of regulatory action taking place, however. Some of the ethical issues flagged in the case study have, after all, been on the SRA's radar since at least 2015 when Coe and Vaughan issued their report.[145] Further, as I noted in Chapter 4, the SRA may have even actively facilitated the continuation of an ethically dubious practice that emerged in the period since that report, by issuing guidance in response to large law firm lobbying which effectively gave an official stamp of approval to 'virtual trees, trees in the head'. As Loughrey has observed, it may take a scandal affecting the legal

143 ibid.

144 For more detail, see Alexander Collins and Nick Shiren, 'Risk Retention in EU and UK Securitisations' [2021] LexisPSL Banking & Finance <https://www.cadwalader.com/uploads/media/SA-0321-038_Co-branded_Practice_Note_PDF_Risk_retention_PN.pdf>.

145 Coe and Vaughan (n 105).

profession in the United Kingdom of Enron-style proportions to support the 'business case for ethics' before legal services and financial market regulators and policy makers open a debate on the appropriate regulation and supervision of Big Law.[146]

9.4 The intersection between corporate lawyers and systemic risk

Annalise Riles has observed that 'markets are not abstract machines to be reduced to a few equations or theorems, but messy contexts, full of contradictory forces and elements, actors, languages, institutions, ways of living and knowing.'[147] Lawyers, their motivations, and their ways of doing things are not peripheral but rather central to how markets operate.[148] Joanna Gray has highlighted the role of lawyers in the structuring and documentation of financial instruments that significantly contributed to the financial crisis, under which:

> banks and other lenders could pass on the credit risks of the very considerable amount of lending (not all of it of the highest quality) that they had been engaging in prior to 2008.[149]

Gray has also observed that:

> throughout the construction of post-crisis blame narratives, while bankers were being stripped of knighthoods and publicly shamed and regulators quietly moved on, there was a resounding silence around lawyers.[150]

Gray argues that lawyers played a central role in the structuring and documentation of financial instruments that significantly contributed to the financial crisis.[151]

[146] Loughrey (n 78) 309.
[147] Riles (n 29) 61.
[148] ibid.
[149] Joanna Gray, 'Lawyers and Systemic Risk in Finance: Could (and Should) the Legal Profession Contribute to Macroprudential Regulation?' (2016) 19 Legal Ethics 122, 124.
[150] ibid 127–28. Although the role of lawyers has attracted some scrutiny from scholars, see for example, Steven L Schwarcz, 'Keynote Address: The Role of Lawyers in the Global Financial Crisis' (Social Science Research Network 2010) SSRN Scholarly Paper ID 1532794 <https://papers.ssrn.com/abstract=1532794> accessed 13 May 2019; Shaun Barnes, Kathleen G Cully, and Steven L Schwarcz, 'In-House Counsel's Role in the Structuring of Mortgage-Backed Securities' (2012) 2012 Wisconsin Law Review 521; Donald Langevoort, 'Getting (Too) Comfortable: In-House Lawyers, Enterprise Risk and the Financial Crisis' [2011] Georgetown Law Faculty Working Papers 154 <http://scholarship.law.georgetown.edu/fwps_papers/154>.
[151] Joanna Gray, 'Lawyers and Systemic Risk in Finance: Could (and Should) the Legal Profession Contribute to Macroprudential Regulation?' (2016) 19 Legal Ethics 122; Steven L Schwarcz, 'Keynote Address: The Role of Lawyers in the Global Financial Crisis' (Social Science Research Network 2010) SSRN Scholarly Paper ID 1532794 <https://papers.ssrn.com/abstract=1532794> accessed 13 May 2019.

Joan Loughrey argues that it is likely that they did not report the risks associated with these structured finance transactions to financial regulators as they mostly saw their role as simply executing their client's instructions.[152] The risk is that the type of lawyer behaviour revealed by my data leads to outcomes which may have these types of wider, societal effects.

There is extensive literature on the question of whether lawyers should act as gatekeepers, with a role to play in helping to deliver financial stability, a public good.[153] And whether they should be enrolled by financial regulators in ensuring the achievement of these goals.[154] Gray argues that lawyers should assist financial regulators 'to detect, minimise and prevent systemic risk erupting again in the financial sector'.[155] Further, David Kershaw and Richard Moorhead have argued that lawyers should in certain circumstances be subject to consequential responsibility for wrongs committed by their clients.[156]

This book shows how lawyers have again been active in shaping the conditions of financial markets, in this case leveraged finance, alongside private equity sponsors, banks, and other leading participants in this market. In my interviews, participants occasionally reflected on the wider consequences of leveraged finance lawyer action. For example, bank lawyer [#26] said, of private equity lawyers, 'they're doing a job for their clients, but it is morally suspect as it introduces risk to the wider financial markets'. And bank lawyer [#27] said: 'these innovations in the documents, both intentional and unintentional, will definitely have an impact in the next downturn.'

A shift in the terms of leveraged loan documents has been noted with alarm, both in the media[157] and by central banks and international financial regulatory and supervisory bodies. I have already highlighted warnings by the former Governor of the Bank of England as to what he considered to be a new threat to global financial stability; an acceleration in the global volume of leveraged debt with weak lender protections.[158] Weaker covenants and uncertainty in leveraged

[152] Loughrey (n 133) 743, 746.

[153] See eg John C Coffee, *Gatekeepers: The Role of the Professions in Corporate Governance: The Professions and Corporate Governance* (OUP 2006); David Chaikin, 'Corporate Lawyers and the Challenge of the Professional Gatekeeper Paradigm' [2013] The 5th International Conference on Financial Criminology (ICFC) 2013 "Global Trends in Financial Crimes in the New Economies" 9; Sung Hui Kim, 'Lawyer Exceptionalism in the Gatekeeping Wars' (2010) 63 SMU Law Review 65; Loughrey (n 78) Ch.7.

[154] Julia Black, 'Mapping the Contours of Contemporary Financial Services Regulation' (2002) 2 Journal of Corporate Law Studies 253.Cited by Gray (n 149) 129.

[155] Gray (n 149) 122.

[156] David Kershaw and Richard Moorhead, 'Consequential Responsibility for Client Wrongs: Lehman Brothers and the Regulation of the Legal Profession' (2013) 76 The Modern Law Review 26.

[157] See eg 'Leveraged Loans Are Way Past "Cov-Lite"' (n 7). Cited in Paterson (n 7) 655.

[158] Philip Aldrick, 'Leveraged Loans at Pre-Crisis Levels — and I'm Worried, Says Carney' (The Times, 17 Janaury 2019) <https://www.thetimes.co.uk/article/leveraged-loans-at-pre-crisis-levels-and-i-m-worried-says-carney-r3s9qt59r> accessed 2 July 2022.

finance documents have so eroded lender protections that this phenomena will likely impede the restructuring of distressed leveraged companies and, as a result, potentially introduce unexpected social and economic costs.[159] This will especially be the case unless all parties have fully understood—and priced in—the effects of these weaknesses. The Financial Stability Board, an international body established in the wake of the global financial crisis to promote global financial stability, concluded however, that this is not in fact the case.[160] And some participants also endorsed this view. For example, bank lawyer [#34] observed:

> I think the reality is lenders don't know what they're buying into. And does it worry me? Yeah, it does.

Yet European leveraged loans, as an asset class, continue to be actively promoted to potential lenders as an attractive investment.[161] As of December 2018 the total amount of global leveraged loans was estimated at anywhere between US$1.4 trillion and US$3.2 trillion.[162] By 2022, the European leveraged loan market alone was estimated to have grown to €270 billion.[163] Concern has been expressed about the scale and precariousness of the leveraged loan sector, generated both by a boom in the number of leveraged buyouts and increasing leverage levels in recent years. Between 2010 and 2019, the average leveraged buyout leverage ratio (the ratio of the borrower's debt (minus cash) to its annual earnings before interest payments, tax and two accounting items, depreciation and amortization) increased from an average of four times to over six times, placing severe strain on borrowers' ability to service their interest payments.[164] This has led to speculation that a collapse in this market, given its scale, could have serious systemic consequences and even trigger another global financial crisis.[165]

Whether there is a direct connection between leverage finance lawyer conduct and a build-up of global systemic risk, and whether leveraged finance lawyers owe

159 Choi, Gulati, and Scott (n 56) 15.

160 'Vulnerabilities Associated with Leveraged Loans and Collateralised Loan Obligations' (19 December 2019) <https://www.fsb.org/2019/12/vulnerabilities-associated-with-leveraged-loans-and-collateralised-loan-obligations/> accessed 2 July 2022.

161 Ares, 'European Leveraged Loans: An Allocation That's Here to Stay' (2022) <https://www.aresmgmt.com/sites/default/files/2022-06/TCE-00171_Euro-Loans-White-Paper-vF.pdf>.

162 Although the precise definition of leveraged lending (of which lending to fund leveraged buyouts is a sub-set) is contested, 'Vulnerabilities Associated with Leveraged Loans and Collateralised Loan Obligations' (n 160).

163 'Leveraged Loan Primer' (S&P Global 2020) 4 <https://www.spglobal.com/marketintelligence/en/pages/toc-primer/lcd-primer> accessed 26 July 2022.

164 'Leveraged Loans: Baked In' *Financial Times* (6 June 2019) <https://www.ft.com/content/d204f5e8-8877-11e9-97ea-05ac2431f453> accessed 9 June 2019.

165 Caroline Binham, 'BoE Warns Over Growth of Risky Corporate Loans' *Financial Times* (17 October 2018) <https://www.ft.com/content/1cac7c12-d1e7-11e8-a9f2-7574db66bcd5> accessed 18 October 2018; Robin Wigglesworth, 'Leveraged Loan Boom Is Storing up Nasty Problems' *Financial Times* (24 August 2018) <https://www.ft.com/content/ffeda26e-a70b-11e8-926a-7342fe5e173f> accessed 3 October 2018.

duties to the lenders as third parties who ultimately bear these risks but who they do not technically act for, would each be fertile areas for further research. On the other hand, it is not unreasonable to speculate that leverage finance lawyers' contribution to the documentary trends that I explore in this book may bear some relationship to wider concerns that have been expressed around global systemic risks associated with the leveraged finance sector.

Regulatory interventions have so far mostly centred on limiting the concentration of leveraged loans in the banking sector.[166] Given that lenders may include not only banks but also institutional investors such as pension funds, and insurance companies, lending directly or indirectly via Collateralised Loan Obligations,[167] these interventions are likely to have limited effect in mitigating the potential substantial build-up of systemic risk in the global financial system.[168] The recent downturn in market conditions due to higher interest rates and general economic uncertainty, and the increasing likelihood of borrower default, may now lead to greater scrutiny by financial and legal services market regulators of the role played by the lawyers, on both sides of the sponsor/lender divide, in this sector.[169] There are signs that this scrutiny may have started. The International Organization of Securities Commissions commenced a review of potential conduct risks—including as may be presented by the lawyer designation model—in the European leveraged finance market, for example.[170]

[166] Paterson (n 7) 665. Eg, European Central Bank, 'Leveraged Transactions, - Supervisory Expectations Regarding the Design and Functioning of Risk Appetite Frameworks and High Levels of Risk Taking' (2022) <https://www.bankingsupervision.europa.eu/press/letterstobanks/shared/pdf/2022/ssm.2022_letter_on_leveraged_transactions.en.pdf>. 'Vulnerabilities Associated with Leveraged Loans and Collateralised Loan Obligations' (n 160). Gilligan and Wright (n 48) 20, 40, 46.

[167] Joe Rennison and Robert Smith, 'CLOs: Ground Zero for the next Stage of the Financial Crisis?' (13 May 2020) <https://www.ft.com/content/f10eaaac-0f4e-46bc-8f78-0754028da46a> accessed 22 July 2020.

[168] Unless one takes the view that the collapse of even a significant number of these types of institutional lender would not pose systemic risks to the financial system. Paterson (n 7) 665.

[169] Mayra Rodriguez Valladares, 'Probability Of Default Is Rising For High Yield Bonds And Leveraged Loans' (*Forbes*, 26 September 2022) <https://www.forbes.com/sites/mayrarodriguezvalladares/2022/09/26/probability-of-default-is-rising-for-high-yield-bonds-and-leveraged-loans/> accessed 27 October 2022.

[170] 'Regulators Turn Attention to Designated Counsel in Leveraged Finance Deals' (*Law.com International*, 9 February 2023) <https://www.law.com/international-edition/2023/02/09/financial-regulators-turn-attention-to-designated-counsel-in-leveraged-finance-deals/> accessed 28 March 2023. I am cited in this article.

APPENDIX 1

Research Methods and Design

Introduction

This appendix describes and interrogates the qualitative methodology I chose to collect the empirical data on which the case study relies. I begin with a critical analysis of my research methods and design, including how I selected and sourced participants. I describe how I addressed potential concerns around my own positionality and insider status. I then offer a critical assessment of the rigour of my approach before concluding with some critical reflection as to the ethical aspects of my research.

The interviews

I found that I was mostly treated as an 'insider' in my interviews with leveraged finance lawyers.[1] My insider status was nuanced, rather than absolute, however. For example, I am a former finance practitioner in a large UK law firm, so I may be more inclined to see as justifiable behaviours which are ethically problematic, by lawyers in this type of firm. Further, as a former, mostly bank-side, partner of a UK firm, I am conscious that I might be more prone to condemn the practices of the borrower-side private equity lawyers who, overall, practice in US law firms. I constantly reflected on each of these identities when evaluating my data.[2]

To pursue my research objectives, I undertook forty-seven semi-structured interviews, the majority with partners and senior associates of international law firms based in London who were specialists in leveraged finance.[3] I conducted these interviews in two phases: ten pilot interviews were held between June and September 2019, and the remainder of the interviews occurred between April and August 2020.

The qualitative interview, as a method to study lawyers working in large corporate law firms, is the most frequently adopted in the corporate lawyer literature.[4] The semi-structured

[1] David Silverman, *Doing Qualitative Research* (SAGE 2017) 381. It is key to a constructionist grounded theory approach that a researcher reflects on the effect of researcher positionality, Kathy Charmaz, Robert Thornberg, and Elaine Keane, 'Evolving Grounded Theory and Social Justice Inquiry', *The SAGE Handbook of Qualitative Research* (Fifth, Sage Publications 2018) 421–22.

[2] On the multiple identities assumed by qualitative researchers in the research process, see Yvonna S. Lincoln, Susan A. Lyneham, and Egon G. Guba, 'Paradigmatic Controversies, Contradictions, and Emerging Confluences, Revisited', *The SAGE Handbook of Qualitative Research* (Fifth, SAGE Publications 2018) 143.

[3] Two participants were in-house lawyers at leading investment banks.

[4] Richard Moorhead and others, 'Designing Ethics Indicators for Legal Services Provision' [2012] SSRN Electronic Journal 2159296, 28 <http://www.ssrn.com/abstract=2159296> accessed 18 October 2018. The following are examples of empirical studies of corporate lawyers which primarily adopted a qualitative interview method: Erwin O Smigel, *The Wall Street Lawyer* (The Free Press of Glencoe 1964); Robert L Nelson, *Partners with Power: The Social Transformation of the Large Law Firm* (University of California Press 1988) 31–32; Emmanuel Lazega, *The Collegial Phenomenon: The*

interview is also probably the most widespread method adopted in social science research more broadly.[5] Though I appreciate and acknowledge that it is, relative to other potential methods, a convenient and efficient path to fulfilling research objectives,[6] I chose the semi-structured interview method as my primary aim was to obtain detailed descriptions of the participants' daily working lives.[7]

As I have already noted, practice area-based distinctions are seldom identified in empirical research on the ethics of corporate lawyers. One reason for this could be the methodology used by the researcher. For example, Mitt Regan and Lisa Rohrer posed questions such as 'have you ever been asked by a client to do anything which made you feel uncomfortable?' and 'have you ever seen colleagues behave in ways that you regarded as ethically problematic?'[8] This is an accessible means to generate a broad picture of the ethical inclination of corporate lawyers. The researcher does not require a deep understanding of what corporate lawyers do on a day-to-day basis—which is often obscured by the complexity and jargon of financial markets, for example—to undertake this type of research. But the risk with this approach is that the data obtained does not account for the specific conditions and logics of a lawyer's practice area that might influence their ethical decision-making.

Further, adopting this type of approach to questioning means valuable findings depend on participants first being able to clearly identify a phenomenon that they have experienced as actually or potentially unethical. If they do, valuable data may be revealed. For example, participants in Claire Coe and Steven Vaughan's study, when asked for their views on corporate lawyer independence, reported that bank lawyers in leveraged finance transactions had relationships with private equity sponsors which they felt might serve to constrain the bank lawyers' professional autonomy.[9] In later but connected work, Emma Oakley and Vaughan also pointed to this phenomenon as evidence of how 'novel, potentially hazardous, ethically dubious practices may become routinised and unremarkable aspects of

Social Mechanisms of Cooperation Among Peers in a Corporate Law Partnership (OUP 2001); Janine Griffiths-Baker, *Serving Two Masters: Conflicts of Interest in the Modern Law Firm* (Hart Publishing 2002); Kimberly Kirkland, 'Ethics in Large Law Firms: The Principle of Pragmatism' (2004) 35 University of Memphis Law Review 631; James Faulconbridge and Daniel Muzio, 'Organizational Professionalism in Globalizing Law Firms' (2008) 22 Work, Employment and Society 7; Eli Wald, 'Smart Growth: The Large Law Firm in the Twenty-First Century Colloquium: Globalization and the Legal Profession' (2011) 80 Fordham Law Review 2867; Richard Moorhead and Victoria Hinchley, 'Professional Minimalism? The Ethical Consciousness of Commercial Lawyers' (2015) 42 Journal of Law and Society 387; Claire Coe and Steven Vaughan, 'Independence, Representation and Risk: An Empirical Exploration of the Management of Client Relationships by Large Law Firms' (Social Science Research Network 2015) SSRN Scholarly Paper ID 2679005 <https://papers.ssrn.com/abstract=2679005> accessed 17 July 2018; Steven Vaughan and Emma Oakley, '"Gorilla Exceptions" and the Ethically Apathetic Corporate Lawyer' (2016) 19 Legal Ethics 50; Swethaa S Ballakrishnen, '"She Gets the Job Done": Entrenched Gender Meanings and New Returns to Essentialism in India's Elite Professional Firms' (2017) 4 Journal of Professions and Organization 324; Sundeep Aulakh and Joan Loughrey, 'Regulating Law Firms from the Inside: The Role of Compliance Officers for Legal Practice in England and Wales' (2018) 45 Journal of Law and Society 254; Robert G Lee and Steven Vaughan, 'The Contaminated Land Regime in England and Wales and the Corporatisation of Environmental Lawyers' (2010) 17 International Journal of the Legal Profession 35; Mitt Regan and Lisa H Rohrer, *BigLaw: Money and Meaning in the Modern Law Firm* (The University of Chicago Press 2020).

[5] Svend Brinkmann, 'The Interview' in Norman K Denzin and S Yvonna , Lincoln (eds), *Sage Handbook of Qualitative Research* (2018) 579.

[6] ibid 589.

[7] ibid 580.

[8] Regan and Rohrer (n 4) 14.

[9] ibid 59

occupational life.'[10] Coe and Vaughan were not given any examples, however, and so were unable to consider what it was about the conditions and logics of the leveraged finance practice area that had given rise to this phenomenon, nor explore its broader effects.[11]

My approach was to also ask open questions but with the purpose of obtaining descriptions and perceptions of the participants' day-to-day practice.[12] I asked them about the types of clients they worked for and the work they did for them. I asked them to describe their relationship with their clients. I asked them to tell me about any market practices or conventions, including in relation to transaction processes or documents, that impacted the work they did for their clients. I asked them to tell me about any pressures they faced, and how these might affect the work they did for their clients. I asked for concrete examples drawn from their transactional experience, many of which I have included in this book, since these tend to be more reliable accounts of real experiences than generalized accounts.[13]

As a former international finance practitioner myself, the extensive jargon and complex concepts common to this field of practice tended not to become a barrier to understanding.[14] I was able to establish common ground with my participants as I mostly understood their vocabularies.[15] The interviewees did not, on the whole, need to explain the basic elements of deal structures and processes, or common provisions included in leveraged finance transaction documents; this meant they could focus their answers on the nuances and complexities of those structures, processes, and provisions that I was less familiar with. For example, bank lawyer [#6], in recounting an example of how—in their view—most bank lawyers were not properly advising their lender clients on the risks inherent in poorly drafted leveraged loan documents, gave an account of the effects of this phenomenon on the operation of the net leverage covenant in a distressed scenario, without first pausing to explain its role and purpose in the documentation. It was assumed that I knew this already. This meant we moved more quickly to the consideration of richer data items.

In contrast, previous researchers of corporate lawyers have mostly had to build up their knowledge during the research process, and develop their interview questions as they proceed, making comparison of responses and the identification of themes difficult. In the initial period at least, the danger is that the interviewer will lack credibility and authority in the eyes of the interviewee, with the interviewee being, as a result, less willing to be open and informative about their experiences.[16] Erwin Smigel adapted his approach as he went along, for example, switching from structured interviews to a more semi-structured approach, and using vignettes.[17] He notes that initially there was a reluctance to talk to him, but this became less of a problem the more interviews he conducted as he was able to display knowledge garnered from previous interviews, helping with credibility and making interviewees more forthcoming.[18] John Heinz and Edward Laumann found themselves having to constantly

[10] Emma Oakley and Steven Vaughan, 'In Dependence: The Paradox of Professional Independence and Taking Seriously the Vulnerabilities of Lawyers in Large Corporate Law Firms' (2019) 46 Journal of Law and Society 83, 24.

[11] ibid 59

[12] Brinkmann (n 5) 580.

[13] ibid 587.

[14] Patricia H Thornton and William Ocasio, 'Institutional Logics and the Historical Contingency of Power in Organizations: Executive Succession in the Higher Education Publishing Industry, 1958-1990' (1999) 105 American Journal of Sociology 801, 159.

[15] ibid.

[16] Smigel, for example, acknowledges this, Smigel (n 4) pp.17–21.

[17] ibid 23.

[18] Vaughan calls this 'elite-lite' interviewing, Steven Vaughan, 'Elite and Elite-Lite Interviewing: Managing Our Industrial Legacy', *Researching Sustainability: A Guide to Social Science Methods, Practice and Engagement* (Routledge 2013) 113.

discuss their research with practitioners, and attend conferences, to obtain an ethnographic perspective against which to contextualize their data.[19] Of course, my ability to talk confidently about the nuances and complexities of leveraged finance also increased as I conducted further interviews, but my background as a practitioner certainly enabled me to hit the ground running and increase the quality of the data collected in the early interviews.

I was alert to the danger that the interviewees might distort responses to fit their own perceptions of their elite status, as opposed to reflecting their own perceptions or experiences.[20] A particular danger with semi-structured interviews is that data might be limited by response and social desirability bias, a particular concern when interviewing experts and elites, especially when asking them to report on their own behaviour.[21] Robert Rosen has observed that:

> self-reports of elite actors, like lawyers, are especially suspect, for often they are speeches to an audience (other than the interviewer). If lawyers are not always selling themselves, at least some always speak for the record to promote their interests.[22]

To mitigate potential social desirability bias, I avoided questions that directly asked participants to disclose instances of ethical misconduct, their own, or of others they interacted with.[23] Instead, my questions explored their everyday experiences in practice, and as it transpired, these accounts frequently disclosed examples of potential ethical misconduct, and situational factors and potential indicators of such misconduct.[24]

I nevertheless encountered numerous instances of what appeared to be social desirability bias. For example, participants frequently gave examples of unethical conduct by other lawyers who they identified by name (sometimes the other lawyers they named were also participants in my study); on the other hand, it was relatively rare for a participant to offer examples of unethical conduct they themselves had engaged in (including those participants who had been specifically identified as engaging in such conduct by other participants).[25] Where particular lawyer dispositions, practices, and strategies were frequently reported as having been observed in others, and when viewed together with the size and spread of the sample, I have concluded that that phenomenon does indeed exist.

As I have already noted, before commencing my research I had some pre-conceived ideas about what might be going on in the leveraged finance practice-area field.[26] Drawing on my own experience in practice is consistent with a contemporary, or constructionist, form of grounded theory, which supports the researcher bringing relevant existing knowledge to

[19] Simon Halliday and Patrick Schmidt, *Conducting Law and Society Research: Reflections on Methods and Practices* (CUP 2009) 65.

[20] Vaughan (n 18) 110–11; Emilia Korkea-aho and Päivi Leino, 'Interviewing Lawyers: A Critical Self-Reflection on Expert Interviews as a Method of EU Research', European journal of legal studies, 2019, Vol. 11, SI, pp. 17-47 31, 35. Silverman (n 1) 25.

[21] Vaughan (n 18) 110. Moorhead and others (n 4) 28; Korkea-aho and Leino (n 20) 32; William S Harvey, 'Strategies for Conducting Elite Interviews' (2011) 11 Qualitative Research 431.

[22] Robert Eli Rosen, 'We're All Consultants Now: How Changes in Client Organizational Strategies Influences Change in the Organization of Corporate Legal Services' (2002) 44 Arizona Law Review 637, 638.

[23] For example, Moorhead and Hinchley sought to mitigate the potential for social desirability bias by telling participants that they were not being assessed on their ethicality, but rather on their ethical reasoning, Moorhead and Hinchley (n 4) 394. See also Vaughan and Oakley (n 4) 57; Aulakh and Loughrey (n 4) 259.

[24] Silverman (n 1) 290.

[25] ibid 289; Korkea-aho and Leino (n 20) 38.

[26] Silverman (n 1); Charmaz, Thornberg, and Keane (n 1) 431.

bear on the research process, provided that any assumptions and biases are both acknowledged and subjected to critical reflection.[27] For example, I had a hunch that bank lawyers might be adopting a stance in negotiations more accommodating to the private equity lawyers than might have been the case but for the lawyer designation model. My data, as it transpires, largely support this preconceived idea. On the other hand, prior to commencing the interviews I had no real appreciation of the material role that private equity lawyers have played in contributing to the bank lawyers' stance through their coercive activities. I have therefore been able to add nuance and further context to the analysis of the stance commonly adopted by bank lawyers in their dealings with private equity lawyers.

A qualitative interview is, as Svend Brinkmann has noted, 'a social construction of communicative processes'; a somewhat artificial environment that may of itself, particularly in this case through my own positionality as the interviewer, influence the data collected.[28] Given the profile and characteristics of the participants in this book, the interviewer and the interview context exerted less influence on my data than if they were, say, members of a vulnerable social group.[29] On the other hand, the participants' status as experts presented potential challenges not found with other types of participant. Smigel experienced difficulties in accessing and interviewing the participants in his study, finding them to be 'high-priced, in the main conservative, busy attorneys, and many of them had little faith or interest in sociology'.[30] My experience as a former practitioner helped overcome some of these challenges, mitigating, for example, potential credibility, control, power, and information asymmetry issues.

My impression was that my insider status was, overall, viewed positively by the participants. I was seen as a more credible participant to a conversation about the complex world of international finance.[31] In the interview context, my insider status encouraged participants to share their experiences openly and frankly.[32] The main benefit was to create a more intimate relationship between myself and the interviewees, which I consider helped facilitate

[27] As originally developed by Glaser and Strauss, grounded theory was a reaction against the then dominant positivist paradigm of quantitative research in the social sciences; they made the case for qualitative studies to also be seen as rigorous and capable of generating theory, as opposed to being mere descriptive accounts of social phenomena, lacking in any theoretical analysis. A debate has, however, ensued as to the precise characteristics of grounded theory. 'Orthodox' grounded theory encourages the researcher to develop the themes and codes which emerge from the data without any preconceptions. However, Charmaz and others offer a contemporary perspective, arguing for a constructionist form of grounded theory which demands not that the researcher deny the existence of preconceived ideas, but rather acknowledge them, whilst otherwise approaching data analysis with an open mind and remaining 'theoretically agnostic'. For Charmaz and others, grounded theory 'involves reasoning about experience for making theoretical conjectures—inferences—and then checking them through further experience—empirical data.' So, whilst 'orthodox' grounded theory proposes that the literature review should be undertaken after, or towards the end of, data collection to eliminate the influence of preconceived ideas drawn from that literature, a contemporary constructionist perspective instead argues that research should be informed by a literature review undertaken at the outset, otherwise the researcher may fail to ask the appropriate questions, for example. Silverman (n 1) 140; Charmaz, Thornberg, and Keane (n 1) 431; Barney G Glaser and Anselm L Strauss, *The Discovery of Grounded Theory: Strategies for Qualitative Research* (Routledge 2017).. Charmaz, Thornberg, and Keane (n 1) 431. ibid 419; Yvonna S. Lincoln, Susan A. Lyneham, and Egon G. Guba (n 2) 143.

[28] Brinkmann (n 5) 578.

[29] Vaughan (n 18) 107. Korkea-aho and Leino (n 20) 22; Harvey (n 21) 5,7.

[30] He hadn't encountered the same difficulties when interviewing 'small town lawyers'. Heinz and Laumman grappled with understanding how lawyers think, Smigel (n 4) 17–19. Halliday and Schmidt (n 19) 65.

[31] Vaughan (n 18) 110.

[32] Korkea-aho and Leino (n 20) 33, 37; Harvey (n 21) 6; Vaughan (n 18) 106.

data discovery, with the participants mostly appearing relaxed and comfortable.[33] I was also able to probe and challenge their responses, constantly verifying the participants' accounts against my own experience from practice, as well as the accounts of other participants in my study, rather than having to assume they were always 'right', or honest, or comprehensive.[34]

Research design

In this section, I explain my approach to, and the design of, the interview process.

Ten pilot interviews were conducted during the months of June to September 2019. My purpose with the pilot interviews was to use them to form a clearer idea of the phenomena I wished to research, the types of lawyer I wished to interview, and to refine the questions I wanted to ask.[35] To assemble my sample, I followed a 'snowballing' approach, an approach to sampling that involves asking invited participants who fit the research criteria to then recommend or refer other potential participants.[36] Overall, I identified a series of initial themes to take forward as the focus of the full interviews. For example, several of the participants in the pilot phase wished to talk about designation and its effects.

A further thirty-seven interviews were undertaken between April and August 2020. This time I thought more carefully about how best to structure my sample selection; my sample population (including both participant inclusion and exclusion criteria); my sample size; and my sample sourcing.[37] Since my research objective was to study how the practice-area environment influences the conduct and ethical-decision-making of leveraged finance lawyers,[38] they make up a significant proportion of my sample (37 out of 47, around 79 per cent). The remainder are lawyers practising in the mainstream corporate and the mainstream banking practices, most of whom were interviewed in the pilot phase.[39] By broadening the sample to include some non-leveraged finance lawyers I was able to triangulate some different perspectives which I consider has served to enrich my findings.[40]

The sample also included two senior in-house lawyers who were specialist leveraged finance lawyers employed by investment banks. The data I obtained from the two in-house lawyers was especially valuable. In Chapter 3, I draw heavily on my interview with in-house

[33] Brinkmann refers to this as a 'romantic paradigm'. Brinkmann refers to an approach that seeks to mine data 'like nuggets buried in the ground' as 'Neopositivist', and an approach seeks to facilitate the 'giving birth' of the inner thoughts of the interviewee as 'Romantic', Brinkmann (n 5) 586. I do not see any contradiction in adopting a pragmatic approach which combines interview paradigms; as Brinkmann notes, these paradigms are 'prototypical, and there are no sharp boundaries between them.' ibid 586–87.

[34] Brinkmann (n 5) 591. Silverman (n 1) 430.

[35] Korkea-aho and Leino (n 20) 34; Yujin Kim, 'The Pilot Study in Qualitative Inquiry: Identifying Issues and Learning Lessons for Culturally Competent Research' (2011) 10 Qualitative Social Work: Research and Practice 190.

[36] C Parker, S Scott, and A Geddes, 'Snowball Sampling' [2019] SAGE Research Methods Foundations <http://methods.sagepub.com/foundations/snowball-sampling> accessed 29 March 2023.

[37] I adopted the 'four point' approach to sampling proposed by Robinson, Oliver C Robinson, 'Sampling in Interview-Based Qualitative Research: A Theoretical and Practical Guide' (2014) 11 Qualitative Research in Psychology 25.

[38] Silverman (n 1) 135.

[39] For a COLP's responsibilities, see 'Responsibilities of COLPs and COFAs - Guidance' (25 November 2019) <https://www.sra.org.uk/solicitors/guidance/responsibilities-of-colps-and-cofas/> accessed 25 March 2023.

[40] Flick calls this 'data triangulation', Uwe Flick, 'Triangulation', *The SAGE Handbook of Qualitative Research* (Fifth, SAGE Publications 2018) 446.

Role of lawyer	Number
Bank lawyers	20
Private equity lawyers	17
Mainstream banking lawyers	4
Mainstream M&A lawyers	3
Bank in-house lawyers	2
Compliance officer for legal practice	1
Total	47

Figure A1.1 The sample.

lawyer [#17] for example, as this participant's accounts of the subtleties of the dispositions and strategies that bank lawyers have developed in response to the survival logic, including their use of anodyne language when giving advice to their clients, are, I have concluded, especially insightful.

The precise makeup of the sample is shown in Figure A1.1.

As I was interested in exploring phenomena across a practice-area field in which many firms participate, I interviewed lawyers from a range of firms which practice in this field.[41] Since both UK and US firms are active in the leveraged finance practice-area field,[42] I further stratified my sample by firm geographic heritage, but not otherwise as between different types of corporate law firm.[43] A roughly equal proportion of lawyers from UK and US heritage firms were included in the sample.[44]

Researchers have often sourced corporate lawyer participants by initially contacting the senior partner, managing partner, head of department, or compliance officer of a firm, with a request for them to nominate potential participants in the study.[45] One drawback with this approach is that firm and practice-area leaders may refuse to nominate lawyers, or refuse

[41] A number of studies which have explored the social or organizational structure of law firms, or explored 'what lawyers do', focussed their study on one or a handful of firms, for example, Nelson (n 4); Lazega (n 4); John Flood, *What Do Lawyers Do?: An Ethnography of a Corporate Law Firm* (Quid Pro Books 2013); Wald (n 4) 2875.

[42] See James Fontanella-Khan, Sujeet Indap, and Barney Thompson, 'The Dawn of the Superstar Lawyer' *Financial Times* (9 April 2018) <https://www.ft.com/content/b9c96d04-376c-11e8-8eee-e06bde01c544> accessed 30 July 2018; Sujeet Indap, Barney Thompson, and James Fontanella-Khan, 'How a Private Equity Boom Fuelled the World's Biggest Law Firm' *Financial Times* (6 June 2019) <https://www.ft.com/content/13696928-86d5-11e9-a028-86cea8523dc2> accessed 7 June 2019. Paul Hodkinson 'Why Buyout Firms Are Becoming More Attractive Clients than Banks' (*LegalWeek. 6 February 2019*) <https://www.law.com/legal-week/2019/02/06/why-buyout-firms-are-becoming-more-attractive-clients-than-banks/> accessed 7 February 2019.

[43] Vaughan and Coe also stratified their sample by reference to UK and US firm heritage, Coe and Vaughan (n 4) 86. Nelson stratified his firms according to 'traditional' and bureaucratic' and 'general' and 'specialised'. These distinctions are no longer relevant in the legal profession in England and Wales. Nelson (n 4) 29; Laura Empson, *Leading Professionals Power, Politics, and Prima Donnas* (OUP 2018).

[44] It is worth noting that firm heritage does not always correspond to jurisdiction of qualification; many US-qualified lawyers work at UK firms and many lawyers qualified in England and Wales work at US firms, for example.

[45] For example, this approach was adopted in two previous studies of corporate lawyers in London; Coe and Vaughan (n 4); Vaughan and Oakley (n 4) 58.

permission for lawyers in their firm who wish to participate.[46] I hence chose to source my participants by approaching individual lawyers directly.

I initially adopted a randomized strategy. My sample was mostly drawn from partners and senior associates/counsel[47] at eighteen leading firms named in the top four tiers of *Legal 500*'s London list of leading firms for acquisition finance in London, as it existed in March 2020.[48] I was able to supplement the initial list with further partners, and also to identify associates (the *Legal 500* listings only identify partners)[49] by reviewing the websites of the leading firms named in *Legal 500* in each of the target practice areas.[50]

These firms are among the most active in large scale international leveraged finance transactions.[51] All 18 firms are large international firms. Of these, 7 are UK firms (including 4 of the 5 'Magic Circle' firms');[52] the remainder (11 firms) are the London offices of leading US firms. The split of participants between UK and US firms is shown in Figure A1.2 below.

I generated two Excel lists, one for partners, and one for associates. I was able to populate the lists with the names and email addresses of 101 partners and 81 senior associates respectively. Each list was randomized to produce a list of partners and associates in random order using an online random sequence generator.[53] I sent email invitations to participants in batches of ten at two weekly interviews.

The sample population in much of the empirical research on corporate lawyers is limited to law firm partners.[54] My sample included senior associates and counsel, to provide a counterpoint to the perspectives of partners, to triangulate different perspectives. My intention was to enrich my findings given their different hierarchical standpoint.[55] Associates may have alternative perspectives due to the different requirements of their role; for example, they are generally under less pressure than are partners to generate revenue, and so may be less inclined to justify behaviours designed to meet this objective which on the face of it appear to them inappropriate.[56] My response rate amongst senior associates I contacted pursuant to the random sampling approach was poor, however; the vast majority did not

46 Emily Carroll and Steven Vaughan, 'Matter Mills and London-Lite Offices: Exploring Forms of the Onshoring of Legal Services in an Age of Globalisation' (2019) Legal Ethics 22(1):1-25 1, 10.

47 For the purposes of this book, a senior associate is a solicitor qualified in England and Wales with four years post-qualification experience, or its equivalent in the case of associates qualified in Australia, New Zealand, and South Africa. I included Counsel in the list of associates as opposed to the partner list as they generally share more common attributes with associates than partners; they do not participate in profits, for example.

48 Legal500.com/c/london/finance/acquisition-finance/, March 2020, accessed 30 March 2020.

49 The same is true of the *Chambers* lists.

50 Ronit Dinovitzer, Hugh Gunz, and Sally Gunz, 'Unpacking Client Capture: Evidence from Corporate Law Firms' (2014) 1 Journal of Professions and Organization 99, 103.

51 All the firms in the first three tiers are included, plus three firms from tier 4.

52 The fifth Magic Circle firm, though ranked in the fourth tier, had no lawyers listed in Legal 500's leading lawyers list, and I was only able to identify one partner from the firm's biography in Legal 500, the firm's website, and from LinkedIn.

53 https://www.random.org/sequences/ (accessed 15 April 2020).

54 See for example, Smigel (n 4); Faulconbridge and Muzio (n 4); Moorhead and Hinchley (n 4) 394; Richard Moorhead and Rachel Cahill-O'Callaghan, 'False Friends? Testing Commercial Lawyers on the Claim That Zealous Advocacy Is Founded in Benevolence towards Clients Rather than Lawyers' Personal Interest' (2016) 19 Legal Ethics 30, 42. An exception is Dinovitzer et al in their study of client capture in Canadian firms, where as well as interviewing associates, they divided the partners they interviewed into 'junior to mid-level', 'senior to mid-level' and 'senior' categories, Dinovitzer, Gunz, and Gunz (n 50) 103. See also Vaughan and Oakley, where the participants ranged from newly qualified solicitors to senior partners Vaughan and Oakley (n 4).

55 Uwe Flick (n 40) 446, 454.

56 Regan and Rohrer (n 4) 59.

Firm type	Number
US	26
UK	19
Bank in-house lawyers	2
Total	47

Figure A1.2 The split of participants from UK and US firms.

Seniority of lawyer	Number
Partner	37
Senior Associate	8
IHL, Senior	2
Total	47

Figure A1.3 The split of partners and associates.

respond to my email, even negatively. The handful that did respond indicated that they would need partner approval to participate in the study. So, I modified my approach by asking partner interviewees in my later interviews to recommend an associate colleague. This snowballing approach was helpful in increasing the number of associates in the sample, albeit associates still make up a relatively small proportion of the total.

The final split of partners and associates across the sample is shown in Figure A1.3.

To ensure a sufficiently sized sample, I ultimately invited all 182 lawyers on the list, and then further supplemented the sample with some snowballing. This means I did not achieve pure randomization, and neither did I achieve an equal and/or proportionate coverage of the various sub-groups.[57] I decided to prioritize ensuring that I achieved a sample of sufficient size.[58]

Although I did not have a target sample size in mind,[59] most of the previous empirical studies of corporate lawyers adopting qualitative in-depth interviews as the primary method feature a sample of anything from 20 to 60 participants.[60] So, I applied this range as

[57] Silverman (n 1) 266.

[58] ibid 265, 274.

[59] Brinkmann criticizes the drift in qualitative research toward an 'audit culture' which emphasis 'calculability', seeing it as inherent to quantitative but not qualitative research, Brinkmann (n 5) 591.

[60] For example, Lee and Vaughan had 14 participants, Moorhead and Hinchley had 21 (11 private practice, 9 in-house), Kirkland had 22, Faulconbridge and Muzio had 25, Wald had 30, Dinovitzer and others had 50, Vaughan and Oakley had 57, Vaughan and Coe had 58 (53 private practice, 5 in-house), although Ballakrishan was something of an outlier with 139. Lee and Vaughan (n 4); Moorhead and Hinchley (n 4); Kirkland (n 4); Faulconbridge and Muzio (n 4); Wald (n 4); Dinovitzer, Gunz and Gunz (n 50); Vaughan and Oakley (n 4); Coe and Vaughan (n 4); Ballakrishnen (n 4).

a rough guide to an appropriate target sample size. I ceased interviews and commenced analysis when I considered that my data had reached theoretical saturation, when no new data was emerging, which happened to be after 47 interviews had been conducted.[61] The size of the sample means I have been able to collect subjective but consistent data from multiple participants, which verifies and supports that data collectively.[62] Inevitably, the personal accounts of the participants are snapshots of their individual experiences, but taken collectively they build a coherent picture of how the participants as a whole tended to make sense of their everyday work in the setting of their practice area.[63] My principal objective was to obtain subjective data from multiple participants so that I could verify and support that data collectively and identify where the accounts of participants suggested a substantial consensus.[64]

My pilot interviews were undertaken in the period prior to the COVID-19 pandemic and so I conducted them 'in person', generally in a meeting room at the offices of the relevant participant's firm in London.[65] My subsequent interviews were undertaken remotely; at this time the United Kingdom was subject to government-imposed national lockdowns owing to the pandemic. Initially, I was sceptical about the interviews being conducted over the telephone/online: I was concerned this might jeopardize the quality of data collected by limiting the potential to establish rapport, resulting in less detailed responses being offered, and reducing the potential for quality data, and might also impede recording and proper transcription.[66] However, even without the non-verbal communication and cues of the in-person setting, I found participants were mostly relaxed and willing to share information about their experiences.[67] Also, away from their offices, on 'neutral' ground—usually they were calling me from their homes during the 'work from home' conditions that prevailed though most of 2020—the participants perhaps felt more comfortable to talk openly, increasing the potential for high-quality data to be collected.[68]

The meetings were scheduled to last for one hour and most were concluded within this time; a handful lasted for around ninety minutes. I recorded and fully transcribed the interviews, so that I would be able to assess the verbatim text of what the participants said, without necessarily adding my own interpretations.[69] The audio recordings and verbatim transcripts—including my questions in full—allowed me to continually reassess my data and allowed my analysis to develop.[70]

In the later stages of this project, in October 2022, I published an opinion piece highlighting some of the initial findings arising from my interview data in a widely read

[61] Alan Bryman, *Social Research Methods* (5th edn, OUP 2016) 412; Silverman (n 1) 269. Benjamin Saunders and others, 'Saturation in Qualitative Research: Exploring Its Conceptualization and Operationalization' (2018) 52 Quality & Quantity 1893.

[62] Janice Morse, 'Reframing Rigour in Qualitative Inquiry', *The SAGE Handbook of Qualitative Research* (Fifth, SAGE Publications 2018) 798; Yvonna S. Lincoln, Susan A. Lyneham and Egon G. Guba (n 2) 117.

[63] Silverman (n 1) 47; Norman K Denzin and Yvonna S Lincoln, *The SAGE Handbook of Qualitative Research* (SAGE Publications 2018) 20.

[64] Janice Morse (n 62) 798; Yvonna S. Lincoln, Susan A. Lyneham, and Egon G. Guba (n 2) 117.

[65] Brinkmann (n 5) 595.

[66] Harvey (n 21) 9; Korkea-aho and Leino (n 20) 44.

[67] This was reflective of an acknowledged bias against telephone interviews. There is a lack of evidence that telephone interviews generate lower quality data. Gina Novick, 'Is There a Bias against Telephone Interviews in Qualitative Research?' (2008) 31 Research in Nursing & Health 391.

[68] Brinkmann cautions researchers to reflect on the influence of the interview context, such as home versus office, Brinkmann (n 5) 595.

[69] Silverman (n 1) 397, 477.

[70] ibid 34, 293.

practitioner-focussed journal, *The Lawyer*.[71] This provoked some further valuable feedback from practitioners. For example, a former Magic Circle partner, who had since moved to a major private equity-focussed US firm, sent me a long and detailed written account of their own experiences by email, and kindly made themselves available for a follow-up meeting. The opinion piece also led to invitations to engage with debt market participants and legal and financial regulators at finance industry and legal services industry conferences, workshops, and meetings. For example, I joined a panel at the European Leveraged Finance Association's annual conference in November 2022. The consequence of this engagement was that I was able to supplement the data I collected in my interviews and to further contextualize and consider its impact in a 'real world' setting.

Rigour and reliability

The European leveraged loan market is mostly private, which means that leveraged loan documents are not publicly available.[72] I have consequently been unable to review actual leveraged finance transaction documents. The result is that what I say about documentary trends, for example, is primarily based on what the participants told me about transaction documents in the interviews, supplemented by my review of relevant academic research in this field (which is relatively limited), information gleaned from press commentary, articles written by law firms, and my own knowledge and experience drawn from my experience in legal practice. Therefore, what I present may in places oversimplify what are very complex provisions, or even in places misunderstand or misdescribe their technical aspects.

Having said this, a number of elements of my research approach and design serve to bolster the rigour and quality of my study.[73] For example, I have verified my data, and identified patterns emerging, across multiple participants from various firms, thus ensuring that my findings are not open to the criticism that they may be idiosyncratic or anecdotal.[74] I collected many similar examples of phenomena to enhance the quality of my data and the overall rigour of my analysis at the conceptual level.[75] I have only made claims that a

[71] Trevor Clark, 'Ethically Dysfunctional: The Problem with Designation in Leveraged Finance' (*The Lawyer*, 18 October 2022) <https://www.thelawyer.com/ethically-dysfunctional-the-problem-with-designation-in-leveraged-finance/> accessed 18 October 2022.

[72] In contrast to the sovereign debt documents studied by Mitu Gulati and Robert. E. Scott, Mitu Gulati and Robert E Scott, *The Three and a Half Minute Transaction: Boilerplate and the Limits of Contract Design* (University of Chicago Press 2012). Short form loan documents, often referred to as 'fundable papers', seen in public to private (P2P) transactions in the UK, where the private equity sponsor bids for a public traded company via a tender offer, are available to view on the website of the UK Takeover Panel, for example. These documents commit the lenders to provide financing for a short period only, and the facilities in them are often never drawn, it is financing put in place merely to satisfy the 'certain funds' requirements of the UK Takeover Code at the time a public bid is announced. These documents typically include a skeletal covenant package. This short-term financing is typically replaced by long-term financing prior to completion of the acquisition if the bid is successful. 'Financing an Offer for a Public Company: The Certain Funds Requirement' (*Practical Law*) <http://uk.practicallaw.thomsonreuters.com, accessed 12 July 2022; 'Principles of Takeover Regulation' (*Practical Law*) <http://uk.practicallaw.thomsonreuters.com, accessed 12 October 2021.

[73] Although there is disagreement as to the criteria to be applied in assessing the rigour and quality of qualitative research, or indeed whether it is appropriate to apply criteria at all, Martyn Hammersley, 'The Issue of Quality in Qualitative Research' (2007) 30 International Journal of Research & Method in Education 287, 288. On rigour in qualitative research, see Janice Morse (n 62).

[74] Silverman (n 1) 264, 278; Janice Morse (n 62) 812.

[75] Janice Morse (n 62) 809, 812.

phenomenon in this practice area setting is typical where multiple participants have attested to its presence and after having carefully considered counterexamples and deviant cases.[76]

My research design also incorporates a degree of triangulation which has enabled me to present a fuller, in-depth picture. I have done this by constantly assessing the data collected in the semi-structured interviews against my own personal experience, whilst at the same time reflecting on my assumptions and biases; contrasting the experiences of private equity and bank lawyers in my sample;[77] seeking academic and practitioner feedback by writing in practitioner journals[78] about, and speaking at academic and business conferences on, my initial findings; triangulating different perspectives in order to enrich my findings; for example, by contrasting the perspectives and standpoint of lawyers in UK firms with those of lawyers in US firms, and by contrasting the views of partners with those of associates, from their different hierarchical standpoints, and against the 'client' perspective of two in-house lawyers.[79] Comparing my data from these different sources and standpoints enhanced the results, allowing data from one source to inform results from the other source, and to highlight any contradictions in my data.[80]

Other elements of my research design that have enhanced the rigour and quality of my findings include: my approach to sampling, especially the sample size, and the way in which I selected and approached participants, my choice of the semi-structured interview method and the use of an interview schedule, the recording and verbatim transcription of interviews, pursuing saturation of data, the inclusion of quotations to illustrate my findings, and continual reflexivity as to my own assumptions, biases, positionality and influence in the interview setting.[81]

Ethical considerations

A significant concern with respect to the ethics of qualitative research is around the potential for a dynamic of power and oppression to exist between interviewer and interviewee.[82] Although I initiated each interview and set its initial parameters, I have concluded the potential for power asymmetry to distort my data is limited, given the expert status of the participants, and the nature of the questions I put to them.[83] The interviewees, as experienced professionals, were skilled at techniques of counter control, such as evasion, or topic-shifting, for example.[84] I also only interviewed solicitors with four or more years of

[76] Jennie Popay, Anne Rogers, and Gareth Williams, 'Rationale and Standards for the Systematic Review of Qualitative Literature in Health Services Research' (1998) 8 Qualitative Health Research 341, 341, 348.

[77] Flick calls this 'data triangulation': "the combination of different data sources that are examined at different times, places and persons." Uwe Flick (n 40) 446.

[78] Trevor Clark, 'The Pendulum Swing in Leveraged Finance Loan Terms: The Role of Designation' (2023) 38 Journal of International Banking Law and Regulation 45.

[79] Uwe Flick (n 40) 454.

[80] ibid 448.

[81] For an example of a checklist, A Tong, P Sainsbury, and J Craig, 'Consolidated Criteria for Reporting Qualitative Research (COREQ): A 32-Item Checklist for Interviews and Focus Groups' (2007) 19 International Journal for Quality in Health Care 349.

[82] Denzin and Lincoln (n 3) 32–33; Gaile S. Canella and Yvonna S Lincoln, *The SAGE Handbook of Qualitative Research* (SAGE Publications 2018) 83–85.

[83] For a discussion of the potential effects of asymmetrical power dynamics in interviews, see Brinkmann (n 5) 587–90.

[84] ibid 589.

post-qualification experience, to further mitigate the risks flowing from power asymmetry between myself and the interviewees.

I am aware of the potential negative professional and reputational implications of my findings for individual lawyers and firms should it be possible to identify them from the interview extracts I include in this book. All the interviews were based on informed consent. The participants received an initial e-mail from me before the interview commenced which, among other things, detailed the voluntary nature of the process, including their right to withdraw at any time. They were also informed of how data protection and confidentiality requirements would be met. I asked at the beginning of every interview for their consent to the recording of interviews, and this was always given. The confidential and non-attributable nature of the interview was made clear to all participants in an e-mail sent to them ahead of the interview and reiterated orally by me at the start of each interview. I have been careful to ensure that it is not possible to identify any of the participants or their firms from the extracted quotes that I have included.

Glossary of Terms

Arranging and underwriting banks: the banks which negotiate the terms of the loan documents with the private equity sponsor and then sell the loans to lenders in a syndication process.

Bank lawyers: in this book this term is used to denote the lawyers who advise the arranging and underwriting banks on the financing aspects of leveraged buyouts.

Borrower: the borrower of the loan, which in an LBO, is typically a specially incorporated vehicle (SPV) which is 'sponsored'—as in the equity share capital of that SPV is owned, directly or indirectly—by a private equity sponsor.

Cleared the market: a contractual term included in loan documents is considered to have *cleared the market* if it did not obstruct a successful syndication of the leveraged loans in a previous transaction—and so the presumption is it can be safely included in the terms of a new loan transaction without risk of obstructing its syndication.

CLO, see also *Collateralised loan obligations*: securities issued by a special purpose company, effectively a structured fund, which has acquired a portfolio of leveraged loans, typically arranged and underwritten by banks. The securities are secured, or collateralised, by this underlying portfolio of loans.

Collateralised loan obligations, see CLO

Commercial grid: a summary of proposed economic and increasingly legal terms which is issued to potential arranging and underwriting banks by the private equity sponsor, or its lawyers, at the initial stage of a transaction. Usually in *Excel* format (hence 'grid').

Commitment documents: the package of documents sent to the group of potential arranging banks who are retained following the commercial grid phase; this can extend to hundreds or even thousands of pages, as it includes terms sheets for all facilities, commitment letters, and often full form documents.

Convergence: a process whereby the investor base for leveraged loans and high yield bonds converged, also used to denote a convergence in loan and bond terms.

Covenant-lite (Cov-lite) loans: These are loans with limited financial covenants and which are tested on an 'incurrence' basis. This means the financial metric in the covenant is only tested upon the borrower choosing to take a given action, for example, when *incurring* further debt, paying a dividend, making an acquisition, or other specified event, as opposed to at regular intervals, as with more traditional 'maintenance' covenants (where the covenant is tested on an ongoing basis, or at regular intervals, such that compliance with the covenant must be *maintained*).

Credit risk: broadly, the risk that the borrower may fail to repay the loan due to a deterioration in its financial position.

Designation, see also *Lawyer Designation*: where the lawyer and firm appointed to advise the banks in a leveraged buyout is chosen (that is, *designated*), and that lawyer's fees are paid for, by the private equity sponsor, which had at the time my interviews for this book were undertaken become the norm in large-scale leveraged finance transactions in Europe.

Direct lender: usually a private credit fund that both originates and then 'takes and holds' a loan to maturity.

Distribution risk: broadly, a risk that may obstruct a successful syndication of the loan, which may include credit risks.

EBITDA: earnings before interest, tax, depreciation, and amortization. Used as a proxy for cash flow, a company's ability to service its debt.

Events of default: the prescribed circumstances set out in a loan agreement in which lenders may demand early repayment of the loan; these will include, for example, failure to pay, insolvency, and breach of financial covenant.

FSB, see also *The Financial Stability Board*: an international body established in the wake of the global financial crisis to promote global financial stability.

High yield bonds: publicly traded debt instruments with a higher rate of interest than 'investment grade' bonds (those rated as low risk by a recognized credit rating agency), and that, in an LBO, often do not share in the transaction's security package.

Investment grade: an investment grade is awarded by a credit rating agency and indicates a low risk of default. To be considered investment grade, the debt of a company must be rated at BBB-/Baa3 or higher by Standard and Poor's or Moody's. Anything below this is considered non-investment grade.

Lawyer Designation, see *Designation*

LBO, see also *Leveraged buyout*: an acquisition of a company where a significant portion of the purchase price is financed by debt, together with a relatively small amount of equity. This allows the acquirer to take over a company mostly using borrowed money, which is typically secured/collateralised by the target company's assets. The cash flow of the target company is relied on to service the debt. LBOs are often used by private equity firms, who acquire companies with the intention of improving their performance and eventually selling them for a profit. Using a significant proportion of debt (leverage) to buy the target company increases the returns for the private equity fund purchaser on their equity investment.

Lender: the provider of the loan, and the bearer of credit risk. Includes the arranging and underwriting banks as original lenders, as well as lenders who subsequently invest in the loan when it is syndicated by the arranging and underwriting banks, and lenders which buy the loan in the secondary market. In LBOs, the lenders may include banks but will also include CLOs and other institutional investors.

Leverage: borrowings.

Leveraged buyout, see *LBO*.

Leveraged finance lawyers: the lawyers within a large corporate law firm who advise the arranging and underwriting banks on the one hand, and the private equity sponsors on the other, on the financing aspects of leveraged buyouts.

LMA, see also *The Loan Market Association*: a body established to represent the corporate loan markets in Europe, and which has sought to standardize loan documents used across corporate and leveraged loan markets.

M&A: mergers and acquisitions (broadly, the buying and selling of companies).

Magic Circle: a name adopted in the UK legal press in the 1990s to denote a group of five London-based law firms that are often considered to be the leading UK firms in the areas of corporate, banking and finance law, comprising, Allen & Overy, Clifford Chance, Freshfields Bruckhaus Deringer, Linklaters, and Slaughter & May.

Mainstream banking lawyers: in this book, this term is used to denote those lawyers in corporate law firms that advise banks as lenders of loans, or, as the case may be, companies as borrowers of loans, that do not finance a leveraged buyout (i.e. investment grade lending).

Mainstream corporate lawyers: in this book, this term is used to denote lawyers that advise companies, as opposed to private equity funds, on, for example, their mergers and acquisitions activity.

Market Flex (or simply 'flex'): a clause in the commitment documents which allows the arranging and underwriting banks to require that amendments be made to the transaction structure, price, and other terms so as to ensure a successful syndication.

Originate to distribute: a financing model adopted by the bank community since the mid-2000s whereby the senior debt facilities used to acquire the target are arranged and underwritten ('originated') and then syndicated/sold ('distributed') to the lenders.

PEP, see *Profit per Equity Partner*

Private credit, private credit fund: private credit typically denotes funding by a lender which is not a bank, and which is typically provided by a private credit fund. Whilst a private equity fund obtains an ownership stake in the company, a private credit fund typically lends money to a company without obtaining an ownership stake in it.

Private equity fund: tends to be legally organised as a limited partnership. The general partner of the fund is usually a corporate entity. The investors (typically comprising banks, insurance companies, sovereign wealth funds, high net-worth individuals, and other sophisticated investors) invest as limited partners in the limited partnership.

Private equity lawyers: in this book, this term is used to denote the lawyers who advise the private equity sponsors on the financing aspects of leveraged buyouts.

Private equity sponsor: a private equity fund which invests in, or 'sponsors', a borrower in a leveraged buyout.

Profit per Equity Partner: broadly, the distributable annual profits of a law firm divided by the number of equity partners of the firm, a financial metric used to measure the financial performance of law firms.

RCF, see *Revolving Credit Facility.*

Revolving facility (also working capital facility, or 'RCF'): a type of loan facility typically provided by a commercial bank which the target group will usually require for working capital purposes, which can be constantly drawn and repaid. To be contrasted with a Term loan.

Security-lite: an approach which has emerged in Europe since the mid-2000s whereby lenders are only granted a limited security package, usually over holding company shares and intercompany loans, as opposed to comprehensive security over all of the assets and cash flows of the target group.

SRA, see also *The Solicitors Regulation Authority*: the regulator of solicitors in England & Wales.

Syndication: a leveraged loan is typically arranged by one or more investment banks, who then sell participations in the loan to a group of lenders, who may include banks but may also include non-banks such as CLOs, pension funds, insurance companies, and other institutional investors. The process of selling these participations is referred to as 'syndication' and the group of lenders who buy them tends to be called 'the syndicate'. In larger leveraged loans, the syndicate can comprise tens and even hundreds of lenders. Syndication spreads the risk—lenders are only at risk as to their portion of the loan. Each participation is a separate loan but the lenders agree to a common set of loan terms governed by a single loan agreement.

Target company/group: the company or group of companies acquired or to be acquired in a leveraged buyout.

Term loan: a type of loan where a fixed amount of money is borrowed and repaid in regular instalments over a set period (the term). To be contrasted with a revolving loan, where the borrower can borrow and repay multiple times within the same credit limit. In LBOs, the senior loans frequently comprise a 'Term Loan A', the traditional amortizing term loan most suited to commercial bank lenders, and a non-amortizing loan, marketed to institutional investors, called a 'Term Loan B', which has a 'bond-like' bullet repayment.

The Financial Stability Board, see *FSB.*

The Loan Market Association, see *LMA.*

The Solicitors Regulation Authority, see *SRA.*

Bibliography

Abbotsbury LN of, 'Lord Upjohn Lecture 2012: Reforming Legal Education' (2013) 47 The Law Teacher 4

Abbott A, *System of Professions: An Essay on the Division of Expert Labor* (University of Chicago Press 1988)

Abel RL, Sommerlad H, Hammerslev O, and Schultz U, *Lawyers in 21st-Century Societies: Vol. 2: Comparisons and Theories* (Bloomsbury Publishing Plc 2022)

Access Group, The 'Solicitor Referral Arrangements: How to Maintain Independence and Compliance' (29 April 2022) <https://www.theaccessgroup.com/en-gb/blog/lgl-solicitor-referral-arrangements/> accessed 27 February 2023

A&O Shearman 'A&O Shearman Merger Successfully Completed' <https://www.aoshearman.com/news/ao-shearman-merger-successfully-completed> accessed 27 December 2024

Archer MS, 'Morphogenesis versus Structuration: On Combining Structure and Action' (1982) 33 The British Journal of Sociology 455

Ares, 'European Leveraged Loans: An Allocation That's Here to Stay' (Ares Management 2022) <https://www.aresmgmt.com/sites/default/files/2022-06/TCE-00171_Euro-Loans-White-Paper-vF.pdf>

Armour J and others, *Principles of Financial Regulation* (OUP 2016)

Ashurst 'High Yield Bonds and Leveraged Loans a Convergence of Terms' (25 April 2018) <https://www.ashurst.com/en/news-and-insights/insights/high-yield-bonds-and-leveraged-loans-a-convergence-of-terms/> accessed 23 June 2020

Asgari N and Smith R, 'Thyssenkrupp Backers Improve €7.6bn Debt Terms after Lenders Balk' *Financial Times* (30 June 2020) <https://www.ft.com/content/81864124-e50c-4670-92c1-756582bb664b> accessed 9 August 2021

Aulakh S and Loughrey J, 'Regulating Law Firms from the Inside: The Role of Compliance Officers for Legal Practice in England and Wales' (2018) 45 Journal of Law and Society 254

Ayotte K and Scully C, 'J. Crew, Nine West, and the Complexities of Financial Distress Forum Collection: Bankruptcy and Restructuring in Response to Exogenous Shocks' (2021) 131 Yale Law Journal Forum 363

Ayotte K and Smith HE, *Research Handbook on the Economics of Property Law* (Edward Elgar Publishing 2011)

Ballakrishnen SS, '"She Gets the Job Done": Entrenched Gender Meanings and New Returns to Essentialism in India's Elite Professional Firms' (2017) 4 Journal of Professions and Organization 324

Bank for International Settlements, 'Basel III: International Regulatory Framework for Banks' (2010) <https://www.bis.org/bcbs/basel3.htm> accessed 14 February 2023

Barnes S, Cully KG, and Schwarcz SL, 'In-House Counsel's Role in the Structuring of Mortgage-Backed Securities' (2012) 2012 Wisconsin Law Review 521

Berlin M, Nini G, and Yu EG, 'Concentration of Control Rights in Leveraged Loan Syndicates' (2020) 137 Journal of Financial Economics 249

Bernstein L, 'The Silicon Valley Lawyer as Transaction Cost Engineer' (1995) 74 Oregon Law Review 239

Bhaskar R, *A Realist Theory of Science* (2nd edn, Routledge 1977)

Billett MT and others, 'Bank Skin in the Game and Loan Contract Design: Evidence from Covenant-Lite Loans' (2016) 51 Journal of Financial and Quantitative Analysis 839

Bingham T, *The Rule of Law* (Penguin Books 2010)

Binham C, 'BoE Warns over Growth of Risky Corporate Loans' *Financial Times* (17 October 2018) <https://www.ft.com/content/1cac7c12-d1e7-11e8-a9f2-7574db66bcd5> accessed 18 October 2018

Black J, 'Mapping the Contours of Contemporary Financial Services Regulation' (2002) 2 Journal of Corporate Law bbStudies 253

Blau PM, *Inequality and Heterogeneity: A Primitive Theory of Social Structure* (Free Press 1977)

Bloomberg.com, 'KKR's Envision Deal Shows How Ugly Creditor Battles Are Getting ' <https://www.bloomberg.com/news/articles/2022-10-05/kkr-s-envision-deal-shows-how-ugly-creditor-battles-are-getting> accessed 14 October 2022

—'Private Equity Firms Are Cutting Out Banks and Funding LBOs Themselves' (11 August 2021) <https://www.bloomberg.com/news/articles/2021-08-11/blackstone-ares-are-turning-into-banks-for-lbo-financing> accessed 20 February 2023

—, 'Private Lenders Lawyer Up as Unease Grows Over Appointed Counsel' (5 July 2022) <https://www.bloomberg.com/news/articles/2022-07-05/private-lenders-lawyer-up-as-unease-grows-over-appointed-counsel> accessed 21 September 2022

—, 'The Powerful City Lawyer at The Center of a Private Equity Storm' (16 February 2023) <https://www.bloomberg.com/news/articles/2023-02-16/the-powerful-city-lawyer-at-the-center-of-a-private-equity-storm> accessed 16 February 2023

Blumberg AS, 'The Practice of Law as Confidence Game - Organizational Cooptation of a Profession' (1966) 1 Law & Society Review 15

Boon A, *The Ethics and Conduct of Lawyers in England and Wales* (Bloomsbury Publishing 2014)

Bourdieu P, 'The Social Space and the Genesis of Groups' (1985) 24(2) Social Science Information 195

—, *Practical Reason: On the Theory of Action* (Stanford University Press 1998)

—, *The Social Structures of the Economy* (Polity 2005)

Brent Smith D, Schneider B, and Dickson MW, 'Meso Organisational Behaviour: Comments on the Third Paradigm', *The SAGE Handbook of Organization Studies* (Second, SAGE Publications 2013)

Brinkmann S, 'The Interview' in Denzin NK and Lincoln YS (eds), *Sage Handbook of Qualitative Research* (Sage Publications 2018)

Bryman A, *Social Research Methods* (5th edn, OUP 2016)

'BVCA Private Equity and Venture Capital Map', British Private Equity & Venture Capital Association <http://www.privateequitymap.co.uk/> accessed 12 June 2019

Cane P and Kritzer H, *The Oxford Handbook of Empirical Legal Research* (OUP 2010)

Canella GS and Lincoln YS, *The SAGE Handbook of Qualitative Research* (SAGE Publications 2018)

Carroll E and Vaughan S, 'Matter Mills and London-Lite Offices: Exploring Forms of the Onshoring of Legal Services in an Age of Globalisation' (2019) 22(1) Legal Ethics 1–25

Cassidy J, 'The Coronavirus Is Exposing Wall Street's Reckless Gamble on Bad Debt' [2020] *The New Yorker* <https://www.newyorker.com/business/currency/the-coronavirus-is-exposing-wall-streets-reckless-gamble-on-bad-debt> accessed 2 July 2022

Cetina KK, Schatzki TR and Savigny E von, *The Practice Turn in Contemporary Theory* (Routledge 2005)

Chaikin D, 'Corporate Lawyers and the Challenge of the Professional Gatekeeper Paradigm' [2013] The 5th International Conference on Financial Criminology (ICFC) 2013 'Global Trends in Financial Crimes in the New Economies' 9

Chapter 11, US Bankruptcy Code https://www.govinfo.gov/content/pkg/USCODE-2011-title11/html/USCODE-2011-title11.htm (accessed 5 January 2025)

Charmaz K, Thornberg R, and Keane E, 'Evolving Grounded Theory and Social Justice Inquiry', *The SAGE Handbook of Qualitative Research* (Fifth edn, Sage Publications 2018)

Chavkin DF, 'Why Doesn't Anyone Care about Confidentiality - (And, What Message Does That Send to New Lawyers)' (2012) 25 Georgetown Journal of Legal Ethics 239

Choi SJ, Gulati M, and Scott RE, 'The Black Hole Problem in Commercial Boilerplate' (2017) 67 Duke Law Journal 1

City of London Law Society, 'Response of the CLLS Professional Rules and Regulation Committee to the SRA's Consultation "A Question of Trust"' (29 January 2016)

Clarfelt H and Livsey A, 'Defaults on Leveraged Loans Soar to Highest Rate in 4 Years' *Financial Times* (24 December 2024) <https://www.ft.com/content/e6ba508c-4612-4b4a-9a6b-ecde6fc91c12> accessed 27 December 2024

Clark T, 'Accounting for COVID-19: Are Lawyers Helping Clients "Remould the Rules"?' (*Lawyer Watch*, 18 May 2020) <https://lawyerwatch.blog/2020/05/18/accounting-for-covid-19-are-lawyers-helping-clients-remould-the-rules/> accessed 25 May 2020

——, 'Ethically Dysfunctional: The Problem with Designation in Leveraged Finance' (*The Lawyer*, 18 October 2022) <https://www.thelawyer.com/ethically-dysfunctional-the-problem-with-designation-in-leveraged-finance/> accessed 18 October 2022

——, 'The Pendulum Swing in Leveraged Finance Loan Terms: The Role of Designation' (2023) 38 Journal of International Banking Law and Regulation 45

Clark, T, Moorhead, R, Vaughan, S, & Brener, A (2021) 'Agency over technocracy: how lawyer archetypes infect regulatory approaches: the FCA example' *Legal Ethics*, *24*(2), 91–110. https://doi.org/10.1080/1460728x.2022.2059742

Clegg SR, Hardy C, Lawrence TB, and Nord WR, *The SAGE Handbook of Organization Studies* (SAGE 2006)

Coase RH, 'The Nature of the Firm' in Saul Estrin and Alan Marin (eds), *Essential Readings in Economics* (Macmillan Education UK 1995)

Coe C and Vaughan S, 'Independence, Representation and Risk: An Empirical Exploration of the Management of Client Relationships by Large Law Firms' (Social Science Research Network 2015) SSRN Scholarly Paper ID 2679005 <https://papers.ssrn.com/abstract=2679005> accessed 17 July 2018

Coffee JC, *Gatekeepers: The Role of the Professions in Corporate Governance: The Professions and Corporate Governance* (OUP 2006)

Collins A and Shiren N, 'Risk Retention in EU and UK Securitisations' [2021] LexisPSL Banking & Finance <https://www.cadwalader.com/uploads/media/SA-0321-038_Co-branded_Practice_Note_PDF_Risk_retention_PN.pdf>

Corporate Finance Institute, 'Leveraged Finance - How Leverage Is Used to Increase Equity Returns' <https://corporatefinanceinstitute.com/resources/knowledge/finance/what-is-leveraged-finance/> accessed 12 June 2019

Daicoff SS, *Lawyer, Know Thyself: A Psychological Analysis of Personality Strengths and Weaknesses* (American Psychological Association 2004)

Danermark B and others, *Explaining Society: An Introduction to Critical Realism in the Social Sciences* (Routledge 2005)

Dare T, 'Mere-Zeal, Hyper-Zeal and the Ethical Obligations of Lawyers' (2004) 7 Legal Ethics 24

Davidson NM, 'Values and Value Creation in Public-Private Transactions' (2008) 94 Iowa Law Review 937

de Fontenay E, 'Do the Securities Laws Matter - The Rise of the Leveraged Loan Market' (2013) 39 Journal of Corporation Law 725

——, 'Law Firm Selection and the Value of Transactional Lawyering' (2015) 41 Journal of Corporation Law 393

Decoteau CL, 'The Reflexive Habitus: Critical Realist and Bourdieusian Social Action' (2016) 19 European Journal of Social Theory 303

Dent GW Jr, 'Business Lawyers as Enterprise Architects' (2008) 64 Business Lawyer (ABA) 279

Denzin NK, 'Review of Explaining Society: Critical Realism in the Social Sciences' (2004) 33 Contemporary Sociology 249

Denzin NK and Lincoln YS, *The SAGE Handbook of Qualitative Research* (SAGE Publications 2018)

Dezalay Y and Garth BG, *Dealing in Virtue: International Commercial Arbitration and the Construction of a Transnational Legal Order* (University of Chicago Press 1996)

DiMaggio P, 'Interest and Agency in Institutional Theory' in LG Zucker (ed) Institutional Patterns and Organisations: Culture and Environment (Harper Business 1988)

DiMaggio PJ and Powell WW, 'Introduction', *The New Institutionalism in Organizational Analysis* (The University of Chicago Press 1991)
——, 'The Iron Cage Revisited: Institutional Isomorphism and Collective Rationality', *The New Institutionalism in Organizational Analysis* (CUP 1991)
Dinovitzer R, Gunz H, and Gunz S, 'Unpacking Client Capture: Evidence from Corporate Law Firms' (2014) 1 Journal of Professions and Organization 99
Empson L, *Managing the Modern Law Firm* (OUP 2007)
——, *The Oxford Handbook of Professional Service Firms* (OUP 2015)
——, *Leading Professionals Power, Politics, and Prima Donnas* (OUP 2018)
Erickson F, 'A History of Qualitative Inquiry in Social and Educational Research', *The SAGE Handbook of Qualitative Research* (SAGE Publications 2018)
European Central Bank, 'Leveraged Transactions, - Supervisory Expectations Regarding the Design and Functioning of Risk Appetite Frameworks and High Levels of Risk Taking' (2022) <https://www.bankingsupervision.europa.eu/press/letterstobanks/shared/pdf/2022/ssm.2022_letter_on_leveraged_transactions.en.pdf>
Faulconbridge J and Muzio D, 'Organizational Professionalism in Globalizing Law Firms' (2008) 22 Work, Employment and Society 7
——, 'The Financialization of Large Law Firms: Situated Discourses and Practices of Reorganization' (2009) 9 Journal of Economic Geography 641
Feldman Y, *The Law of Good People* (CUP 2018)
Field HM, 'Offshoring Tax Ethics: The Panama Papers, Seeking Refuge from Tax, and Tax Lawyer Referrals The Sanford E. Sarasohn Conference on Critical Issues in Comparative and International Taxation II: Taxation and Migration' (2017) 62 Saint Louis University Law Journal 35
Financial Stability Board, 'Vulnerabilities Associated with Leveraged Loans and Collateralised Loan Obligations' (19 December 2019) <https://www.fsb.org/2019/12/vulnerabilities-associated-with-leveraged-loans-and-collateralised-loan-obligations/> accessed 2 July 2022
Financial Times, 'KKR Presents Mouth-Watering Boots Debt' (6 July 2007)
——, 'Hot Leveraged Loan Market Puts Ebitda "Add-Backs" under Scrutiny' (10 February 2017)
——, 'Leveraged Loans Are Way Past "Cov-Lite"' (16 November 2018)
——, 'Leveraged Loans: Baked In' (6 June 2019)
——, 'Investors Rue Lack of Protections on €7.1bn Thyssenkrupp Debt' (26 June 2020)
——, 'Pandemic Spawns New Reporting Term "Ebitdac" to Flatter Books' (13 May 2020)
——, 'Linklaters Becomes Latest Law Firm to Phase out "Lockstep" Pay Model' (15 December 2021)
——, 'Blame Private Equity for the End of London Lawyers' Lockstep' (5 January 2022)
——, 'Reviled Tax Break for Private Equity Proves Hard to Kill Off' (30 July 2022)
——, 'UK's "Magic Circle" Law Firms Struggle to Grow in US amid Sinking Pound' (11 October 2022)
Fleetwood S, 'Bhaskar and Critical Realism', *The Oxford Handbook of Sociology, Social Theory, & Organization Studies* (OUP 2014)
Fleischer V, 'Regulatory Arbitrage' (2010) 89 Texas Law Review 227
Flick, U 'Triangulation', *The SAGE Handbook of Qualitative Research* (Fifth edn, SAGE Publications 2018)
Flood J, 'Anatomy of Lawyering: An Ethnography of a Corporate Law Firm' (ProQuest Dissertations Publishing 1987) <http://search.proquest.com/docview/303616292/?pq-origsite=primo> accessed 18 October 2018
——, 'Lawyers as Sanctifiers: The Role of Elite Law Firms in International Business Transactions Symposium: Globalization of the Legal Profession' (2007) 14 Indiana Journal of Global Legal Studies 35
——, 'Ambiguous Allegiances in the Lawyer-Client Relationship: The Case of Bankers and Lawyers' https://www.researchgate.net/publication/228135498_Ambiguous_Allegiances_in_the_Lawyer-Client_Relationship_The_Case_of_Bankers_and_Lawyers accessed 9 june 2023

——, 'Transnational Lawyering: Clients, Ethics and Regulation', in Leslie C Levin and Lynn Mather (eds), *Lawyers in Practice, Ethical Decision Making in Context* (The University of Chicago Press 2012)

——, *What Do Lawyers Do?: An Ethnography of a Corporate Law Firm* (Quid Pro Books 2013)

Fontanella-Khan J, Indap S, and Thompson B, 'The Dawn of the Superstar Lawyer' *Financial Times* (9 April 2018) <https://www.ft.com/content/b9c96d04-376c-11e8-8eee-e06bde01c544> accessed 30 July 2018

——, 'How a Private Equity Boom Fuelled the World's Biggest Law Firm' *Financial Times* (6 June 2019) <https://www.ft.com/content/13696928-86d5-11e9-a028-86cea8523dc2> accessed 9 August 2021

Francis A, 'Legal Ethics, the Marketplace and the Fragmentation of Legal Professionalism' (2005) 12(2) International Journal of the Legal Profession 173

Franklin J, 'Cov-Lite Leaves Borrowers Happy and Lenders Gloomy' [2019] International Financial Law Review <https://www.proquest.com/docview/2286662340/abstract/C5A29494C3504C9BPQ/1> accessed 2 July 2022

Freidson E, *Professionalism, The Third Logic: On the Practice of Knowledge* (University of Chicago Press 2001)

Friedland R and Alford R, 'Bringing Society Back In: Symbols, Practices, and Institutional Contradictions', *The New Institutionalism in Organizational Analysis* (The University of Chicago Press 1991)

Galanter M, 'Mega-Law, An American Invention' (1982) 3 *Humanities* 16

Galanter M and Henderson WD, 'The Elastic Tournament: The Second Transformation of the Big Law Firm' (Social Science Research Network 2008) SSRN Scholarly Paper ID 1104711 <https://papers.ssrn.com/abstract=1104711> accessed 6 December 2018

Galanter M and Palay T, *Tournament of Lawyers: The Transformation of the Big Law Firm* (University of Chicago Press 1991)

Giddens A, *Central Problems in Social Theory: Action, Structure, and Contradiction in Social Analysis* (University of California Press 1979)

——, *The Constitution of Society: Outline of the Theory of Structuration* (University of California Press 1984)

Gilligan J and Wright M, *Private Equity Demystified: An Explanatory Guide* (4th edn, OUP 2020)

Gilson RJ, 'Value Creation by Business Lawyers: Legal Skills and Asset Pricing' (1984) 94 The Yale Law Journal 239

Gilson RJ and Mnookin RH, 'Sharing among the Human Capitalists: An Economic Inquiry into the Corporate Law Firm and How Partners Split Profits' (1984) 37 Stanford Law Review 313

Glaser BG and Strauss A, 'The discovery of grounded theory : strategies for qualitative research' (2017) Routledge.*Global Legal Post, The*, 'Goldman Sachs Leveraged Finance Group Loses Enthusiasm for Linklaters' (4 August 2014) <http://m.globallegalpost.com/global-view/goldman-sachs-leveraged-finance-group-loses-enthusiasm-for-linklaters-43888593/> accessed 12 October 2019

Gomez MA and Galantar M, 'The Many Lives of Big Law: Three Decades in the Evolution of Large Law Firms' in Richard L Abel and others, *Lawyers in 21st-Century Societies: Vol. 2: Comparisons and Theories* (Bloomsbury Publishing Plc 2022).

Gray J, 'Lawyers and Systemic Risk in Finance: Could (and Should) the Legal Profession Contribute to Macroprudential Regulation?' (2016) 19 Legal Ethics 122

Gray R, Holmes P, and Muzilla K, 'Why Banks Should Look Again at Market Flex and MAC Clauses' (2003) 22 International Financial Law Review 18

Greenwood R and Hinings CR, 'Radical Organizational Change', *The SAGE Handbook of Organisation Studies* (Second, SAGE Publications 2013)

Greenwood R and Suddaby R, 'Institutional Entrepreneurship In Mature Fields: The Big Five Accounting Firms' (2006) 49 Academy of Management Journal 27

Greenwood R, Suddaby R, and Hinings CR, 'Theorizing Change: The Role of Professional Associations in the Transformation of Institutionalized Fields' (2002) 45 The Academy of Management Journal 58

Griffiths-Baker J, *Serving Two Masters: Conflicts of Interest in the Modern Law Firm* (Hart 2002)
Gulati M and Scott RE, *The Three and a Half Minute Transaction: Boilerplate and the Limits of Contract Design* (University of Chicago Press 2012)
Gunz H, Gunz S, and Dinovitzer R, 'Professional Ethics' [2015] The Oxford Handbook of Professional Service Firms 113–34
Halliday S and Schmidt P, *Conducting Law and Society Research: Reflections on Methods and Practices* (CUP 2009)
Hammersley M, 'The Issue of Quality in Qualitative Research' (2007) 30 International Journal of Research & Method in Education 287
Hanlon G, 'A Profession in Transition - Lawyers, the Market and Significant Others' (1997) 60 Modern Law Review 798
——, 'Institutional Forms and Organizational Structures: Homology, Trust and Reputational Capital in Professional Service Firms' (2004) 11 Organization 186
Hardy C, 'Hysteresis', *Pierre Bourdieu: Key Concepts* (Routledge 2014)
Harvard Law School, 'Linklaters (A): Seeking Clear Blue Water' <http://casestudies.law.harvard.edu/linklaters-a-seeking-clear-blue-water/> accessed 10 June 2023
Harvey WS, 'Strategies for Conducting Elite Interviews' (2011) 11 Qualitative Research 431
Heinz JP and Laumann EO, *Chicago Lawyers: The Social Structure of the Bar* (Russell Sage Foundation 1982)
Henderson WD, 'From Big Law to Lean Law' (2014) 38 International Review of Law and Economics 5
Herring J, *Legal Ethics* (OUP 2017)
Higgins A, 'Referral Fees - The Business of Access to Justice' (2012) 32 Legal Studies 109
Holstein JA, 'Advancing a Constructionist Analytics', *The SAGE Handbook of Qualitative Research* (SAGE Publications 2018)
'House of Commons - Treasury - Tenth Report' <https://publications.parliament.uk/pa/cm200607/cmselect/cmtreasy/567/56702.htm> accessed 18 July 2022
Howarth D, *Law as Engineering: Thinking About What Lawyers Do* (Edward Elgar Publishing Ltd 2013)
Huber J (ed), *Macro-Micro Linkages in Sociology* (1st edition, SAGE Publications, Inc 1991)
Hwang C, 'Value Creation by Transactional Associates Colloquium: Corporate Lawyers' (2019) 88 Fordham Law Review 1649
International Organisation of Securities Commissions, 'About IOSCO' <https://www.iosco.org/v2/about/?subsection=about_iosco> accessed 19 December 2024
——'Leveraged Loans and CLOs, Good Practices for Consideration, Consultation Report CR05/2023' (September 2023) <https://www.iosco.org/library/pubdocs/pdf/IOSCOPD746.pdf>
International Reporting Standards, 'IFRS - Home' <https://www.ifrs.org/> accessed 16 March 2023
Investopedia 'Buyer's Market: Definition, Characteristics, Example' <https://www.investopedia.com/terms/b/buyersmarket.asp> accessed 23 February 2023
——, 'IOU: What It Is, How It Works, and Examples' <https://www.investopedia.com/terms/i/iou.asp> accessed 12 March 2023
——, 'What Is a Nonrecurring Charge?' <https://www.investopedia.com/terms/n/nonrecurringcharge.asp> accessed 15 March 2023
Jensen MC and Meckling WH, 'Theory of the Firm: Managerial Behavior, Agency Costs and Ownership Structure' (1976) 3 Journal of Financial Economics 305
Jepperson RL, 'Institutions, Institutional Effects, and Institutionalism'in DiMaggio PJ and Powell W, *The New Institutionalism in Organizational Analysis* (The University of Chicago Press 1991)
Keen T, 'Referral Fees and Fee Sharing – Where Are We Now?' (*Birmingham Law Society. One Profession. One Region. One Voice*, 1 June 2021) <https://birminghamlawsociety.co.uk/referral-fees-and-fee-sharing-where-are-we-now/> accessed 27 February 2023
Kershaw D and Moorhead R, 'Consequential Responsibility for Client Wrongs: Lehman Brothers and the Regulation of the Legal Profession' (2013) 76 The Modern Law Review 26

Kim SH, 'Lawyer Exceptionalism in the Gatekeeping Wars' (2010) 63 SMU Law Review 65

Kim Y, 'The Pilot Study in Qualitative Inquiry: Identifying Issues and Learning Lessons for Culturally Competent Research' (2011) 10 Qualitative Social Work: Research and Practice 190

Kirkland K, 'Ethics in Large Law Firms: The Principle of Pragmatism' (2004) 35 University of Memphis Law Review 631

——, 'The Ethics of Constructing Truth, The Corporate Litigator's Approach', *Lawyers in Practice: Ethical Decision Making in Context* (University of Chicago Press 2012)

Kirkpatrick I and Noordegraaf M, 'Organizations and Occupations: Towards Hybrid Professionalism in Professional Service Firms?' in Laura Empson and others, *The Oxford Handbook of Professional Service Firms* (OUP 2015) 92–112

KKR, 'KKR Today' (2 June 2014) <https://www.kkr.com/kkr-today> accessed 26 June 2023

Korkea-aho E and Leino P, 'Interviewing Lawyers: A Critical Self-Reflection on Expert Interviews as a Method of EU Research' (2019) 11(SI) European Journal of Legal Studies, 17

Kouchaki M and others, 'Seeing Green: Mere Exposure to Money Triggers a Business Decision Frame and Unethical Outcomes' (2013) 121 Organizational Behavior and Human Decision Processes 53

Krieger LS, 'Institutional Denial about the Dark Side of Law School, and Fresh Empirical Guidance for Constructively Breaking the Silence' (2002) 52 Journal of Legal Education 112

Landy R, 'Exit Engineering' (31 January 2023) SSRN Scholarly Paper ID 4413611 <https://papers.ssrn.com/abstract=4413611> accessed 3 January 2024

Langevoort D, 'The Organizational Psychology of Hyper-Competition: Corporate Irresponsibility and the Lessons of Enron' (2002) 70 George Washington Law Review 968

——, 'Getting (Too) Comfortable: In-House Lawyers, Enterprise Risk and the Financial Crisis' [2011] Georgetown Law Faculty Working Paper 154 <http://scholarship.law.georgetown.edu/fwps_papers/154>

Larreur C-H, *Structured Finance: Leveraged Buy-Outs, Project Finance, Asset Finance and Securitization* (Wiley 2021)

Lastra RM and Wood G, 'The Crisis of 2007–09: Nature, Causes, and Reactions' (2010) 13 Journal of International Economic Law 531

Law Gazette, 'Solicitors' Referral Code 1998 -- Review of the Introduction and Referral Code' <https://www.lawgazette.co.uk/news/solicitors-referral-code-1998-review-of-the-introduction-and-referral-code-/20839.article> accessed 27 February 2023

Lawrence T and Suddaby R, *Institutions and Institutional Work* (SAGE 2006)

Law Society, The, Solicitors' Code of Conduct 2007 (2009)

——, 'Conflict of Interests Practice Note' (2023) <https://www.lawsociety.org.uk/topics/client-care/archive/conflict-of-interests-july-2023> accessed 19 December 2024

——, 'Professional Ethics' <https://www.lawsociety.org.uk/topics/ethics/> accessed 21 December 2024

Lawyer, The 'Lenders Aren't Happy - and Lawyers Are in the Ethical Firing Line' (6 October 2022) <https://www.thelawyer.com/lenders-arent-happy-and-lawyers-are-in-the-ethical-firing-line/> accessed 6 October 2022

Lazega E, *The Collegial Phenomenon: The Social Mechanisms of Cooperation Among Peers in a Corporate Law Partnership* (OUP 2001)

Leblebici H and others, 'Institutional Change and the Transformation of Interorganizational Fields: An Organizational History of the U.S. Radio Broadcasting Industry' (1991) 36 Administrative Science Quarterly 333

Lee RG and Vaughan S, 'The Contaminated Land Regime in England and Wales and the Corporatisation of Environmental Lawyers' (2010) 17 International Journal of the Legal Profession 35

'Legal Aid, Sentencing and Punishment of Offenders Act 2012' <https://www.legislation.gov.uk/ukpga/2012/10/section/56/enacted> accessed 27 February 2023

Legal Business, 'Global London: The Big Long – Inside Sidley's Daring Attempt to Relaunch as a Private Equity Leader' (8 April 2019)

Legal Week, 'Why Buyout Firms Are Becoming More Attractive Clients than Banks' (2019)

——, 'Kirkland Secures $56M in Fees for Toys "R" Us Bankruptcy' (2019)
——, 'Regulators Turn Attention to Designated Counsel in Leveraged Finance Deals' (2023)
Levin LC, 'Bad Apples, Bad Lawyers or Bad Decisionmaking: Lessons from Psychology and from Lawyers in the Dock Book Review Essay' (2009) 22 Georgetown Journal of Legal Ethics 1549
Levin LC and Mather LM, *Lawyers in Practice: Ethical Decision Making in Context* (The University of Chicago Press 2012)
Lewin K, 'Behavior and Development as a Function of the Total Situation', *Manual of Child Psychology* (John Wiley & Sons, Inc 1946)
Lincoln YS, Lyneham SA, and Guba EG, 'Paradigmatic Controversies, Contradictions, and Emerging Confluences, Revisited', *The SAGE Handbook of Qualitative Research* (Fifth edn, SAGE Publications 2018)
Lipshaw JM, 'Beetles, Frogs, and Lawyers: The Scientific Demarcation Problem in the Gilson Theory of Value Creation' (2009) 46 Willamette Law Review 139
Loan Market Association, 'Documents' <https://www.lma.eu.com/documents-guidelines/documents> accessed 5 July 2022
Lord Hunt, 'The Hunt Review of the Regulation of Legal Services' (*The Law Society* 2009) <https://www.lsc.qld.gov.au/__data/assets/pdf_file/0016/260035/The-Hunt-Review-of-the-Regulation-of-Legal-Services-NZ-Dec-2009.pdf>
Loughrey J, *Corporate Lawyers and Corporate Governance* (CUP 2011)
——, 'Accountability and the Regulation of the Large Law Firm Lawyer' (2014) 77 The Modern Law Review 732
Lowe D and Bell J, 'COVID-19 and the Impact on Financial Covenants' [2020] Journal of International Banking and Financial Law 2
Luban D, *Lawyers and Justice: An Ethical Study* (Princeton University Press 1988)
——, 'The Adversary System Excuse', *Lawyers: A Critical Reader* (The New Press 1997)
MacEwen B, *Growth Is Dead: Now What?: Law Firms on the Brink / Bruce MacEwen; Foreword by Peter J. Kalis* (2013, Adam Smith, Esq.)
——, 'Nobody Ever Got Fired for Hiring Skadden" (21 April 2004, Adam Smith Esq.) <https://adamsmithesq.com/2004/04/nobody_ever_got/> accessed 11 June 2023
Maton K, 'Habitus', *Pierre Bourdieu: Key Concepts* (Second, Routledge 2014)
Matsumoto D, 'Culture, Context, and Behavior' (2007) 75 Journal of Personality 1285
McBarnet D and Whelan C, 'The Elusive Spirit of the Law: Formalism and the Struggle for Legal Control' (1991) 54 The Modern Law Review 848
McDougall J and others, 'Intralot's Drop-down Restructuring Games: Priming Pari Passu Noteholders, Circumventing Non-Consenters and Artificially Reducing Asset Values' [2022] The Journal of International Banking and Financial Law 5
McVea H, '"Heard It through the Grapevine": Chinese Walls and Former Client Confidentiality in Law Firms' (2000) 59 The Cambridge Law Journal 370
Moore MT, 'Private Equity Buyouts and Corporate Governance: Contrasting the "80s and 00s"' (2007, REFGOV Working Paper Series: REFGOV-CG-17) <https://sites.uclouvain.be/cpdr-refgov/publications/Working%20Papers/Corporate%20Governance%20-%20CG_(10.08.2007_19h08)_WP-CG-17.pdf>
Moorhead R, *Quality and Cost: Final Report on the Contracting of Civil, Non-Family Advice and Assistance Pilot* (The Stationary Office 2001)
——, 'Precarious Professionalism: Some Empirical and Behavioural Perspectives on Lawyers' (2014) 67 Current Legal Problems 447
——, 'Should Clifford Chance's Corruption Initiative Be Taken Seriously?' (*Lawyer Watch*, 20 December 2018) <https://lawyerwatch.blog/2018/12/20/should-clifford-chances-corruption-initiative-be-taken-seriously/> accessed 20 December 2018
Moorhead R and others, 'Designing Ethics Indicators for Legal Services Provision' [2012] SSRN Scholarly Paper ID 2159296<http://www.ssrn.com/abstract=2159296> accessed 18 October 2018

Moorhead R and Cahill-O'Callaghan R, 'False Friends? Testing Commercial Lawyers on the Claim That Zealous Advocacy Is Founded in Benevolence towards Clients Rather than Lawyers' Personal Interest' (2016) 19 Legal Ethics 30

Moorhead R and Hinchley V, 'Professional Minimalism? The Ethical Consciousness of Commercial Lawyers' (2015) 42 Journal of Law and Society 387

Moorhead R, Vaughan S, and Godinho C, *In-House Lawyers' Ethics, Institutional Logics, Legal Risk and the Tournament of Influence* (Hart 2018)

Morse J, 'Reframing Rigour in Qualitative Inquiry', *The SAGE Handbook of Qualitative Research* (Fifth edn, SAGE Publications 2018)

Mowday RT and Sutton RI, 'Organizational Behavior: Linking Individuals and Groups to Organizational Contexts' (1993) 44 Annual Review of Psychology 195

Neale MA and others, 'A Decision Perspective on Organizations: Social Cognition, Behavioural Decision Theory and the Psychological Links to Micro-and Macro-Organizational Behaviour', *The Sage Handbook of Organisation Studies* (Second, SAGE Publications 2013)

Nelson RL, *Partners with Power: The Social Transformation of the Large Law Firm* (University of California Press 1988)

Neuberger, Lord, 'The Lord Slynn Memorial Lecture 2016' para 31<https://supremecourt.uk/speeches/lord-neuberger-gives-the-lord-slynn-memorial-lecture-2016> accessed 29 November 2020

Newman A, 'Linklaters Falls out of Favour with Goldman's City Leveraged Finance Team' (*LegalWeek*, 2014) <https://www.law.com/legal-week/2014/08/04/linklaters-falls-out-of-favour-with-goldmans-city-leveraged-finance-team/> accessed 12 October 2019

Nicolson D and Webb JS, *Professional Legal Ethics: Critical Interrogations* (OUP 1999)

Novick G, 'Is There a Bias against Telephone Interviews in Qualitative Research?' (2008) 31 Research in Nursing & Health 391

Oakley E and Vaughan S, 'In Dependence: The Paradox of Professional Independence and Taking Seriously the Vulnerabilities of Lawyers in Large Corporate Law Firms' (2019) 46 Journal of Law and Society 83

Okamoto KS, 'Reputation and the Value of Lawyers' (1995) 74 Oregon Law Review 15

Olatawura O, 'The Theatre of Dreams - Manchester United FC, Globalization, and International Sports Law' (2005) 16 Marquette Sports Law Review 287

Oliver C, 'Strategic Responses to Institutional Processes' (1991) 16 Academy of Management Review 145

Oxford English Dictionary, 'Entrepreneur, n.' <https://www.oed.com/view/Entry/62991> accessed 22 March 2023

Orlikowski WJ, 'Improvising Organizational Transformation Over Time: A Situated Change Perspective' (1996) 7 Information Systems Research 63

Osborne Clarke, 'Taking Security over Assets in Europe: Some Practical Considerations' (2019) <https://www.osborneclarke.com/insights/taking-security-assets-europe-practical-considerations> accessed 19 July 2022

O'Sullivan JR, 'Professional Discipline for Law Firms - A Response to Professor Schneyer's Proposal' (2002) 16 Georgetown Journal of Legal Ethics 1

Parker C, 'A Critical Morality for Lawyers: Four Approaches to Lawyers' Ethics' [2004] Monash University Law Review 49

Parker C and Evans A, *Inside Lawyers' Ethics* (CUP 2018)

Parker C, Scott S, and Geddes A, 'Snowball Sampling' [2019] SAGE Research Methods Foundations <http://methods.sagepub.com/foundations/snowball-sampling> accessed 29 March 2023

Parker CE, Rosen RE, and Nielsen VL, 'The Two Faces of Lawyers: Professional Ethics and Business Compliance with Regulation' 22 The Georgetwon Journal of Legal Ethics 49

Paterson S, 'The Rise of Covenant-Lite Lending and Implications for the UK's Corporate Insolvency Law Toolbox' (2019) 39 Oxford Journal of Legal Studies 654

Patterson S and Zakrzewski R, *McKnight, Paterson, & Zakrzewski on the Law of International Finance* (Second, OUP 2017)

Pearce RG and Wald E, 'The Relational Infrastructure of Law Firm Culture and Regulation: The Exaggerated Death of Big Law' (Social Science Research Network 2013) SSRN Scholarly Paper ID 2627733 <https://papers.ssrn.com/abstract=2627733> accessed 5 December 2018

Perlman AM, 'A Behavioral Theory of Legal Ethics' (2015) 90 Indiana Law Journal 1639

. Pinsent Masons, 'Security in Finance Transactions' (30 August 2011) <https://www.pinsentmasons.com/out-law/guides/security-in-finance-transactions> accessed 14 July 2022

Pistor K, *The Code of Capital: How the Law Creates Wealth and Inequality* (University Press 2019)

Pitchbook, 'Number of Active PE Firms up 143% since 2000: A Global Breakdown' <https://pitchbook.com/news/articles/number-of-active-pe-firms-up-143-since-2000-a-global-breakdown> accessed 12 June 2019

Popay J, Rogers A, and Williams G, 'Rationale and Standards for the Systematic Review of Qualitative Literature in Health Services Research' (1998) 8 Qualitative Health Research 341

Powell MJ, 'Professional Innovation: Corporate Lawyers and Private Lawmaking' (1993) 18 Law and Social Inquiry 423

Practical Law 'Contra Proferentem Rule' <http://uk.practicallaw.thomsonreuters.com/4-383-2653?transitionType=Default&contextData=(sc.Default)&firstPage=true> accessed 27 July 2023——, 'Financing an Offer for a Public Company: The Certain Funds Requirement' <http://uk.practicallaw.thomsonreuters.com/5-370-3957?transitionType=Default&contextData=(sc.Default)&firstPage=true> accessed 12 July 2022

——, 'Hardening Period' <http://uk.practicallaw.thomsonreuters.com/9-500-8666?transitionType=Default&contextData=(sc.Default)> accessed 9 July 2022

——, 'Market Flex' <http://uk.practicallaw.thomsonreuters.com/8-386-0578?transitionType=Default&contextData=(sc.Default)&firstPage=true> accessed 22 July 2021

——, 'Principles of Takeover Regulation' <http://uk.practicallaw.thomsonreuters.com/Document/I535A4670EFF511E68E2DE26F6B06B139/View/FullText.html?originationContext=document&transitionType=DocumentItem&ppcid=56a76aafccbd428dbf04836be755b0a1&contextData=(sc.Default)&comp=wluk> accessed 12 October 2021

Regan MC and Rohrer LH, *BigLaw: Money and Meaning in the Modern Law Firm* (The University of Chicago Press 2020)

Regan MC, *Eat What You Kill: The Fall of a Wall Street Lawyer* (University of Michigan Press 2004)

Rennison J and Smith R, 'CLOs: Ground Zero for the Next Stage of the Financial Crisis?' (13 May 2020) <https://www.ft.com/content/f10eaaac-0f4e-46bc-8f78-0754028da46a> accessed 22 July 2020

Reorg, 'Intralot Plans to Implement Restructuring Through Out-of-Court Process With Scheme as Backup Option' <https://reorg.com/intralot-plans-to-implement-restructuring-through-out-of-court-process/> accessed 15 March 2023

Reuters, 'RBS Agrees $3 Billion WorldPay Sale to Advent, Bain' (6 August 2010) <https://www.reuters.com/article/us-rbs-idUSTRE67516620100806> accessed 21 February 2023

——, 'RLPC-Boots LBO Loans Test Covenant-Lite Model' (30 March 2007) <https://www.reuters.com/article/alliance-boots-takeover-loan-idUKL3048613020070330> accessed 20 February 2023

Ribstein LE, 'Ethical Rules, Agency Costs, and Law Firm Structure' (1998) 84 Virginia Law Review 1707

——, 'The Death of Big Law' [2010] Wisconsin Law Review 749

Riles A, *Collateral Knowledge: Legal Reasoning in the Global Financial Markets* (University of Chicago Press 2011)

Robbennolt JK, 'Behavioral Ethics Meets Legal Ethics' (2015) 11 Annual Review of Law and Social Science 75

Robinson OC, 'Sampling in Interview-Based Qualitative Research: A Theoretical and Practical Guide' (2014) 11 Qualitative Research in Psychology 25

Rosen RE, 'We're All Consultants Now: How Changes in Client Organizational Strategies Influences Change in the Organization of Corporate Legal Services' (2002) 44 Arizona Law Review 637

Rostain T and Regan MC (eds), *Confidence Games: Lawyers, Accountants, and the Tax Shelter Industry* (MIT Press 2014)

Rousseau DM and House RJ, 'Meso Organizational Behavior: Avoiding Three Fundamental Biases' [1994] Journal of Organizational Behavior (1986–1998) 13

Salzedo S and Wood T, 'Improper Leverage? Own Interest Conflicts and the Designation Model in Leveraged Finance Transactions' (2023) 4 Journal of International Banking and Financial Law 209

Saunders B and others, 'Saturation in Qualitative Research: Exploring Its Conceptualization and Operationalization' (2018) 52 Quality & Quantity 1893

Schneyer T, 'Moral Philosophy's Standard Misconception of Legal Ethics' (1984) 1984 Wisconsin Law Review 1529

Schwarcz SL, 'Explaining the Value of Transactional Lawyering' (2006) 12 Stanford Journal of Law, Business & Finance 486

——, 'Keynote Address: The Role of Lawyers in the Global Financial Crisis' (Social Science Research Network 2010) SSRN Scholarly Paper ID 1532794 <https://papers.ssrn.com/abstract=1532794> accessed 13 May 2019

Scott W Richard, *Institutions and Organizations* (2nd edn, Sage 2001)

Seo M-G and Creed WED, 'Institutional Contradictions, Praxis, and Institutional Change: A Dialectical Perspective' (2002) 27 The Academy of Management Review 222

Silver C, 'Globalization and the U.S. Market in Legal Services - Shifting Identities' (1999) 31 Law and Policy in International Business 1093

Silverman D, *Doing Qualitative Research* (SAGE 2017)

Simmons OS and Dinnage JD, 'Innkeepers: A Unifying Theory of the In-House Counsel Role' (2011) 41 Seton Hall Law Review 77

Simon WH, 'Ethical Discretion in Lawyering' (1987) 101 Harvard Law Review 1083

——, 'Role Differentiation and Lawyers' Ethics: A Critique of Some Academic Perspectives' (2010) 23 Georgetown Journal of Legal Ethics 987

Smets M, 'Institutional Work Taken Literally: How Logics Shift as Banking Lawyers "Get the Deal Done"' (2009 Academy of Management annual meeting, USA, 2009) <http://publications.aston.ac.uk/id/eprint/18544/> accessed 20 May 2021

——, '25 Years since "P2": Taking Stock and Charting the Future of Professional Firms' (2017) 4 Journal of Professions and Organization 91

Smigel EO, *The Wall Street Lawyer* (The Free Press of Glencoe 1964)

Smith C and Rennison J, 'Debt Machine: Are Risks Piling up in Leveraged Loans?' *Financial Times* (21 January 2019) <https://www.ft.com/content/64c9665e-1814-11e9-9e64-d150b3105d21> accessed 21 January 2019

Solicitors Regulation Authority, The, 'Risk Outlook 2018/2019' (17 July 2018) <https://www.sra.org.uk/risk/outlook/risk-outlook-2018-2019/> accessed 23 November 2020

——, 'Balancing Duties in Litigation' (27 November 2018) <https://www.sra.org.uk/risk/risk-resources/balancing-duties-litigation/> accessed 29 November 2020

——,'Acting with Integrity—Guidance' (25 November 2019) <https://www.sra.org.uk/solicitors/guidance/acting-with-integrity/> accessed 28 November 2020

——,'Lack of Independence - Case Studies' (25 November 2019) <https://www.sra.org.uk/solicitors/guidance/lack-independence/> accessed 23 November 2020

——, 'Referral Fees LASPO and SRA Principles—Warning Notice' (25 November 2019) <https://www.sra.org.uk/solicitors/guidance/referral-fees-laspo-sra-principles/> accessed 27 February 2023

——, 'Responsibilities of COLPs and COFAs—Guidance' (25 November 2019) <https://www.sra.org.uk/solicitors/guidance/responsibilities-of-colps-and-cofas/> accessed 25 March 2023

——, 'SRA Code of Conduct for Solicitors, RELs and RFLs' (25 November 2019) <https://www.sra.org.uk/solicitors/standards-regulations/code-conduct-solicitors/> accessed 15 November 2020

——, 'The Prohibition of Referral Fees in LASPO 56 60—Guidance' (25 November 2019) <https://www.sra.org.uk/solicitors/guidance/prohibition-of-referral-fees-in-laspo-56-60/> accessed 27 February 2023

——,'SRA Principles' (25 November 2019) <https://www.sra.org.uk/solicitors/standards-regulations/principles/> accessed 6 July 2020

——,'SRA Standards and Regulations' (25 November 2019) <https://www.sra.org.uk/solicitors/standards-regulations/> accessed 21 June 2022

——,'Conflicts of Interest—Guidance' (3 February 2020) <https://www.sra.org.uk/solicitors/guidance/conflicts-interest/> accessed 27 October 2020

——, 'Investment Schemes—Warning Notice' (17 August 2020) <https://www.sra.org.uk/solicitors/guidance/investment-schemes-including-conveyancing/> accessed 2 March 2023

——, 'Standards of Service' (16 November 2020) <https://www.sra.org.uk/sra/research-publications/risk-outlook-2020-21/standards-of-service/> accessed 18 March 2023

——, 'Use of Non-Disclosure Agreements (NDAs) - Warning Notice' (11 December 2020) <https://www.sra.org.uk/solicitors/guidance/non-disclosure-agreements-ndas/> accessed 20 April 2022

——, 'SRA Glossary' (11 March 2021) <https://www.sra.org.uk/solicitors/standards-regulations/glossary/> accessed 2 August 2023

——, 'Confidentiality of Client Information—Guidance' (30 June 2022) <https://www.sra.org.uk/solicitors/guidance/confidentiality-client-information/> accessed 24 March 2023

——, 'SRA Enforcement Strategy' (21 January 2022) <https://www.sra.org.uk/sra/corporate-strategy/sra-enforcement-strategy/> accessed 4 July 2023

——, 'Statement of Solicitor Competence' (9 August 2022) <https://www.sra.org.uk/solicitors/resources/continuing-competence/cpd/competence-statement/> accessed 10 March 2023

——, 'SRA Code of Conduct for Firms' (4 June 2023) <https://www.sra.org.uk/solicitors/standards-regulations/code-conduct-firms/> accessed 4 July 2023

'Solvency II' (23 January 2023) <https://www.bankofengland.co.uk/prudential-regulation/key-initiatives/solvency-ii> accessed 14 February 2023

Soon L, McDowall A, and Teoh KRH, 'Towards a Context-Specific Approach to Understanding Lawyers' Well-Being: A Synthesis Review and Future Research Agenda' [2023] Psychiatry, Psychology and Law 1

S&P Global, 'Leveraged Finance: Lenders Blinded By Cov-Lite? Highlighting Data On Loan Covenants And Ultimate Recovery Rates' (2018) <https://www.spglobal.com/ratings/en/research/articles/180412-leveraged-finance-lenders-blinded-by-cov-lite-highlighting-data-on-loan-covenants-and-ultimate-recovery-rates-10493116> accessed 2 July 2022

——, 'Leveraged Loan Primer' (*2020*) <https://www.spglobal.com/marketintelligence/en/pages/toc-primer/lcd-primer> accessed 26 July 2022

——, 'When The Cycle Turns: The Continued Attack Of The EBITDA Add-Back' <https://www.spglobal.com/ratings/en/research/articles/190919-when-the-cycle-turns-the-continued-attack-of-the-ebitda-add-back-11156255> accessed 2 July 2022

——, 'Leveraged Finance: Fifth Annual Study Of EBITDA Addbacks Finds Management Continues To Regularly Miss Projections' (2023) <https://www.spglobal.com/ratings/en/research/articles/230216-leveraged-finance-fifth-annual-study-of-ebitda-addbacks-finds-management-continues-to-regularly-miss-project-12643170> accessed 7 February 2024

Squires SE and Squires S, *Inside Arthur Andersen: Shifting Values, Unexpected Consequences* (FT Press 2003)

Starbuck WH, 'Keeping a Butterfly and an Elephant in a House of Cards: The Elements of Exceptional Success' (1993) SSRN Scholarly Paper ID 2709152 <https://papers.ssrn.com/abstract=2708152> accessed 8 June 2023

Stevens & Bolton LLP 'IFRS 16 and Its Impact on EBITDA/Debt and Financial Covenants' (3 July 2018) <https://www.stevens-bolton.com/site/insights/articles/ifrs-16-and-its-impact-on-ebitdadebt-and-financial-covenants> accessed 16 March 2023

Suddaby R and Muzio D, 'Theoretical Perspectives on the Professions' in Laura Empson and others, *The Oxford Handbook of Professional Service Firms* (OUP 2015)

Susskind RE, *The End of Lawyers?: Rethinking the Nature of Legal Services / Richard Susskind* (OUP 2008)
Tamanaha BZ, *On the Rule of Law: History, Politics, Theory* (CUP 2004)
Teubner G, 'Legal Irritants: Good Faith in British Law or How Unifying Law Ends Up in New Divergencies' (1998) 61 The Modern Law Review 11
Thagard P, 'The Moral Psychology of Conflicts of Interest: Insights from Affective Neuroscience' (2007) 24 Journal of Applied Philosophy 367
'The Capital Requirements Regulations 2013' <https://www.legislation.gov.uk/uksi/2013/3115/contents/made> accessed 16 July 2018
Thomson P, 'Field', *Pierre Bourdieu: Key Concepts* (Second, Routledge 2014)
Thornton PH and Ocasio W, 'Institutional Logics and the Historical Contingency of Power in Organizations: Executive Succession in the Higher Education Publishing Industry, 1958-1990' (1999) 105 American Journal of Sociology 801
Thornton PH, Ocasio W, and Lounsbury M, *The Institutional Logics Perspective: A New Approach to Culture, Structure, and Process* (OUP 2012)
Times, The, 'Leveraged Loans at Pre-Crisis Levels—and I'm Worried, Says Carney' (The Times, 17 Janaury 2019) <https://www.thetimes.co.uk/article/leveraged-loans-at-pre-crisis-levels-and-i-m-worried-says-carney-r3s9qt59r> accessed 2 July 2022
Todd P, *Textbook on Trusts* (4th edn, Blackstone Press 1999)
Tong A, Sainsbury P, and Craig J, 'Consolidated Criteria for Reporting Qualitative Research (COREQ): A 32-Item Checklist for Interviews and Focus Groups' (2007) 19 International Journal for Quality in Health Care 349
Torys LLP, 'The J.Crew "Trap Door" and Its Implications for the Future of Leveraged Finance' (2019) <https://www.torys.com/Our%20Latest%20Thinking/Publications//2019/05/the-j-crew-trap-door-and-its-implications-for-the-future-of-leveraged-finance/> accessed 23 June 2022
Townley B, 'Bourdieu and Organizational Theory: A Ghostly Apparition?', *The Oxford Handbook of Sociology, Social Theory, & Organization Studies* (OUP 2014)
Utset MA, 'Producing Information: Initial Public Offerings, Production Costs, and the Producing Lawyer Symposium on Business Lawyering and Value Creation for Clients' (1995) 74 Oregon Law Review 275
Valladares MR, 'Probability of Default Is Rising For High Yield Bonds And Leveraged Loans' (2022, *Forbes*) <https://www.forbes.com/sites/mayrarodriguezvalladares/2022/09/26/probability-of-default-is-rising-for-high-yield-bonds-and-leveraged-loans/> accessed 27 October 2022
Vaughan S, 'Elite and Elite-Lite Interviewing: Managing Our Industrial Legacy', in Franklin A and Blyton P (eds) *Researching Sustainability: A Guide to Social Science Methods, Practice and Engagement* (Routledge 2013)
Vaughan S and Oakley E, '"Gorilla Exceptions" and the Ethically Apathetic Corporate Lawyer' (2016) 19 Legal Ethics 50
Wacquant LJD, 'Towards a Reflexive Sociology: A Workshop with Pierre Bourdieu' (1989) 7 Sociological Theory 26
——, 'On the Tracks of Symbolic Power: Prefatory Notes to Bourdieu's `State Nobility'' (1993) 10 Theory, Culture & Society 1
Wald E, 'Smart Growth: The Large Law Firm in the Twenty-First Century Colloquium: Globalization and the Legal Profession' (2011) 80 Fordham Law Review 2867
Webb J and Nicolson D, 'Institutionalising Trust: Ethics and the Responsive Regulation of the Legal Profession' (1999) 2 Legal Ethics 148
Whelan CJ and Ziv N, 'Privatizing Professionalism: Client Control of Lawyers' Ethics Colloquium: Globalization and the Legal Profession' (2011) 80 Fordham Law Review 2577
Wigglesworth R, 'Leveraged Loan Boom Is Storing up Nasty Problems' *Financial Times* (24 August 2018) <https://www.ft.com/content/ffeda26e-a70b-11e8-926a-7342fe5e173f> accessed 3 October 2018

Wilkins DB, 'Team of Rivals? Toward a New Model of the Corporate Attorney/Client Relationship' (2009) 62 Current Legal Problems 478

——, 'Some Realism about Legal Realism for Lawyers: Assessing the Role of Context in Legal Ethics' in Leslie C Levin and Lynn M Mather (eds), *Lawyers in Practice: Ethical Decision Making in Context* (University of Chicago Press 2012)

Wilmarth AEJ, 'The Transformation of the U.S. Financial Services Industry, 1975-2000: Competition, Consolidation, and Increased Risks' (2002) 2002 University of Illinois Law Review 215

Woolley A and Wendel WB, 'Legal Ethics and Moral Character' (2010) 23 Georgetown Journal of Legal Ethics 1065

Yago G, *Junk Bonds: How High Yield Securities Restructured Corporate America* (Illustrated edition, OUP 1990)

Index

For the benefit of digital users, indexed terms that span two pages (e.g., 52–53) may, on occasion, appear on only one of those pages.